T0250840

Lecture Notes in Computer Science 640

Edited by G. Goos and J. Hartmanis

Advisory Board: W. Brauer D. Gries J. Stoer

C. Sledge (Ed.)

Software Engineering Education

SEI Conference 1992
San Diego, California, USA, October 5-7, 1992
Proceedings

Springer-Verlag

Berlin Heidelberg New York
London Paris Tokyo
Hong Kong Barcelona
Budapest

Series Editors

Gerhard Goos
Universität Karlsruhe
Postfach 69 80
Vincenz-Priessnitz-Straße 1
W-7500 Karlsruhe, FRG

Juris Hartmanis
Department of Computer Science
Cornell University
5149 Upson Hall
Ithaca, NY 14853, USA

Volume Editor

Carol Sledge
Software Engineering Institute, Carnegie Mellon University
Pittsburgh, PA 15213-3890, USA

Carnegie Mellon University
Software Engineering Institute

CR Subject Classification (1991): D.2, K.3.2

ISBN 3-540-55963-9 Springer-Verlag Berlin Heidelberg New York
ISBN 0-387-55963-9 Springer-Verlag New York Berlin Heidelberg

Typesetting: Camera ready by author/editor
45/3140-543210 - Printed on acid-free paper

Preface

The Sixth SEI Conference on Software Engineering Education was held in San Diego, California, on October 5 to 7, 1992. This annual conference is sponsored by the Products Program of the Software Engineering Institute, a federally funded research and development center of the U.S. Department of Defense. For the last two years, it has also been held in conjunction with the Association for Computing Machinery and the IEEE Computer Society. The conference is a forum for discussion of software engineering education and training among members of the academic, industry, and government communities. This year's conference theme was "putting the 'engineering' into software engineering." You will find papers in this proceedings that reflect this theme, addressing various aspects of applying the principles and methods of traditional engineering disciplines to software engineering.

The 24 papers, 5 panels, and 1 tutorial were selected for the conference by a program committee consisting of the following:

Maribeth B. Carpenter, *Software Engineering Institute*
Neal S. Coulter, *Florida Atlantic University*
Gary Ford, *Software Engineering Institute*
Chris Gustafson, *Lockheed*
Norman E. Gibbs, *Software Engineering Institute*
Nancy R. Mead, *Software Engineering Institute*
Keith R. Pierce, *University of Minnesota, Duluth*
Anneliese von Mayrhauser, *Colorado State University*

In addition to the above people, the following were referees:

Mark A. Ardis, Jim Babcock, F. Terry Baker, Marilyn Bates, Daniel L. Berry, James Bieman, A. Winsor Brown, Frank Calliss, Bradley D. Carter, Lynn Carter, Charles Collins, Jed Coxon, Joseph F. Delgado, Jorge Diaz-Herrera, Erin Dixon, Robert Doherty, Merlin Dorfman, Frank A. Etlinger, Eduardo Fernandez, Frank Friedman, David Garlan, Harvey K. Hallman, Robert L. Hedges, Daniel Hocking, Theresa Homisak, James Hooper, Nick Kamenoff, Elliot Koffman, Robert Korfhage, Herb Krasner, Patricia K. Lawlis, David Lefkovitz, Michael J. Lutz, Barbara Meyers, John Miklos, Loretta Moore, J. Fernando Naveda, Kurt Olender, Mike Overstreet, Cherri Pancake, Bernard Rackmales, Dennis Ray, Jerry Sandvos,

Raj Tewari, Richard Thayer, Frances L. Van Scoy, Judy Vernick, Bryant York, John Werth, Laurie Werth.

This year marks the establishment of an Industry-University Initiative for Software Engineering Education. The program committee has formed this initiative as a catalyst for bringing together university educators and nearby industry and government organizations. We encourage industry and government to sponsor a faculty member's participation in the CSEE, with the hope of stimulating further collaboration and interest in understanding one another's needs. At the time these proceedings went to press, we had early commitments from Bell Northern Research and from Motorola, Inc., Radio Products Group. We gratefully acknowledge the support of these organizations and look forward to the expansion of this initiative in the next few months and its continuation at CSEE '93 and beyond.

As is usual with an undertaking of this size and scope, nothing would have been accomplished without an excellent support staff. The level of success is due to the efforts of Mary Ellen Rizzo, more than anyone else, for her tireless work in handling administrative matters, including tracking papers, referees, and final manuscripts. Mary Rose Serafini and Bernadette Chorle kept the budget and provided continuity. The expert advice and support of Helen Joyce, Wendy Rossi, and others in the Events group made it possible for this conference to run so smoothly. My sincere thanks to them, the program committee, the reviewers, and all who have contributed to the conference.

Pittsburgh, Pennsylvania
June 1992

Carol A. Sledge
Conference Chair, CSEE '92

Contents

Keynote Address

Toward a Discipline for Software Engineering
Speaker: Watts S. Humphrey,
Software Engineering Institute

Is Software Engineering?
Speaker: Anthony Hall,
Praxis Systems plc

Toward a Discipline for Software Engineering

Keynote Address
Sixth SEI Conference on
Software Engineering Education

Watts S. Humphrey
Software Engineering Institute
Carnegie Mellon University
Pittsburgh, PA 15213

Abstract. The rapid pace of software technology places increasing demands on human talent and ability. While improved tools and methods will certainly help, it is also clear they are not sufficient. The challenge for software engineering education is thus to instill the basic disciplines software professionals will need to meet the enormous demands to face them in the future.

In many fields, competent work is not possible until the professionals know and practice basic disciplines. It is not a question of creativity versus discipline; creative work is simply not possible without discipline. When software engineers finish their formal schooling, they should know and understand their own capabilities. They should see what works best for them and what they can learn from the variations in their own performance. They should incorporate these lessons in explicit personal practices and share these practices with their peers, subordinates, and superiors. They should promulgate their successes, seek guidance on their weaknesses, and learn to build on the experience of others.

To accelerate the development of our field, we need a framework to help our graduates understand and grow themselves. This framework should establish an ethic of personal bests; of practicing, building, and combining these bests to produce consistently superior performance; and of business environment. Many measures can be applied to software engineering performance. The challenge is to learn among individuals, and how these measures can be supported so they are practical to use, to track, and to analyze. Without such measures, we cannot even understand our own performance, let alone improve it.

Is Software Engineering?

Anthony Hall

Praxis Systems plc

Engineering is the use of science to solve practical problems. It is important because when we want any significant new artefact, we expect engineers to provide it. Usually, we expect engineers to succeed; furthermore, we understand why they do: even if we don't understand the details of their discipline we expect them to know what principles are relevant and to be able to use these principles to predict the behaviour of their artefacts before they are built. We believe that there *are* principles behind every branch of engineering, and we expect the community to enforce standards of professionalism so that those principles are adequately applied.

Education and training for engineers is well · established. The necessary scientific and mathematical principles are known, and there is a large body of experience in their application. Engineers are equipped with knowledge, with a coherent framework for organising that knowledge and with the means to fill in the details that they do not carry in their heads through standard handbooks. Above all, perhaps, engineers acquire a professional attitude: they expect to work according to rigorous standards, to check everything they do before they do it, to calculate whether their designs are correct or not, to be open to scrutiny in the same way that scientists are open; in short, they expect to get things right.

Software engineering has existed in name and as an aspiration since 1968. I am trying to be a software engineer, and my company is trying to be a software engineering company. Some universities are trying to teach software engineering. Some customers are trying to ensure that their suppliers are software engineers.

We cannot yet claim to have succeeded. We have certainly made a lot of progress, but we have still not acquired the basic characteristics of engineers. Graduates coming into the field have not received an engineering education, and our mode of working is more that of craftsmen than engineers. The fundamental reason for this is that we do not have an adequate scientific basis for what we do.

It is true that there is some science of computation known. But this is as if chemical engineers had atomic theory, and some understanding of simple molecules, but no thermodynamics, no theories of bulk matter, and no concept of unit processes.

The science we are looking for, therefore, is not a theory of small computations: it is the computing analogy of thermodynamics and fluid mechanics. The fact is that there *is* such a science developing: it is fairly new, it has many gaps and it is still frightening to many people. But it can be used, it can be taught and it does offer real benefits. It is, of course, the application of mathematics to the specification, design and verification of software.

Why do I call this a science, in contrast with the methods that are currently popular? It is not, except in a trivial sense, a body of knowledge. But it is a scientific *method* in that a specification, if it is mathematically expressed, is a theory about the software. Like a scientific theory, it has two very powerful properties:

1. It has predictive power: the behavior of the software can be defined before it is actually produced.

2. It can be tested: we can tell when a mathematical specification is wrong, for example by showing that it has some undesirable consequence; furthermore, a subsequent development step can be verified against the specification.

In contrast, popular design methods like object-oriented development are at present no more than the rules of thumb used by a craftsman. Some of them may be very good rules of thumb (I suspect that object-oriented design, for example, *is* a very good one), but they do not have the predictive power or verifiability of a mathematical specification. You cannot tell, by looking at an object structure diagram, how the system will behave; more importantly there is no objective way of telling whether the object structure is in any sense correct or not.

My claim is, therefore, that to make software into an engineering discipline we must make sure that the methods we use are scientific, so that they give predictable and verifiable results. Why do we not yet do this? I think there are two reasons:

1. The necessary theory simply does not yet exist for all aspects of development.

2. Many software practitioners do not have the necessary knowledge to use the methods that do exist; more importantly, they do not believe that such methods are useful.

These are not problems that can be solved by education alone: academic researchers must continue to develop the relevant science; practitioners must change their expectations and attitudes from those of craftsmen to those of engineers; and educators must instil both the necessary knowledge and a rigorous engineering approach.

There are plenty of rigorous methods already known and used in software development. Some kinds of software development - for example compiler writing - may indeed have achieved the status of engineering because the underlying theory is so well understood. Some rigorous methods are overtly mathematical; others, such as finite state machines, are often presented in diagrammatic form but do have a mathematical foundation. Others, such as prototyping, are not mathematical at all but share the property of predictability: you can find certain kinds of errors using a prototype as surely as you can find other kinds of errors using a mathematical specification.

However, there is a lot still to be done. Although we have good notations for *specification*, we do not have nearly such powerful methods for *design*. We have no formal basis for decomposition, for example. Our notations for dealing with concurrency are far from tractable, and modelling time-dependent behavior is still difficult. We also need to understand more about the domains of applicability of the methods which do exist, and how different methods fit together.

Software practitioners have a role to play in developing the science, most obviously by encouraging research in areas which are relevant to their concerns. For this to be effective we have to find ways of reconciling the different but complementary interests and timescales of academic research and industrial practice. More immediately, though, the role of the practitioner must be to use what science is already available: partly because only by use will it be tested and refined, but mainly because even though our current methods are not complete they do lead to better, more predictable, development.

Finally, how does all this affect education? I should like to make three proposals.

First, we should recognize that software engineering is the application of all applicable science to the development of software, within an understood and controlled process. Software engineering is not a small subsection of the computer science course; rather, computer science is part of the necessary background for a software engineer.

Second, we should rigorously distinguish what is scientific from what is merely believed to be good craftsmanship; methods that have a scientific basis should be preferred wherever they exist. The crucial question that students should ask about any method they are taught is "why does it work?".

Third, we must change people's attitudes. A typical computing project has as its motto 'try this and see if it works'. If we are to teach real engineers, we should tell them to 'measure this against its predicted behaviour and make sure it is within specification'.

When we do that we will have a generation of software developers who know what to do, know why they are doing it, and expect, with good reason, that what they do will be successful.

Session 1:

Software Engineering Education in the 1990s
Moderator: Norm E. Gibbs, Software Engineering Institute

Software Engineering Education in the 1990s—The Way Forward
Douglas D. Grant, Swinburne University of Technology

Experience with a Course on Architectures for Software Systems
David Garlan, Mary Shaw, Chris Okasaki, Curtis M. Scott, Carnegie Mellon University and Roy F. Swonger, Digital Equipment Corporation

On Teaching the Rational Design Process
Terry Shepard, Royal Military College of Canada and Dan Hoffman, University of Victoria

Software Engineering Education in the 1990s - The Way Forward

Douglas D Grant

Department of Computer Science
Swinburne University of Technology
Hawthorn, Victoria, Australia 3122

Abstract. This paper discusses the future of Software Engineering education in Australia in the 1990s from the perspective of the current debate on the separation of Computer Science and Software Engineering as academic disciplines. It supports the prevailing view that maintaining the unity of Computer Science and Software Engineering is of critical importance.

1.   Introduction

This paper attempts to contribute to the contemporary debate on the possible separation of Computer Science (hereafter abbreviated CS) and Software Engineering (hereafter abbreviated SE) [7]. It is written from an Australian perspective, but most of the pertinent details transcend locale.

Two influential documents on the development of undergraduate education in SE are the report of Ford [6], prepared for the SEI, and the report prepared by a joint working party of the British Computer Society and the (British) Institution of Electrical Engineers [3]. Both these reports encourage the development of undergraduate SE degrees. The report of Ford pragmatically concludes that the most likely route to development of an SE degree is via evolution from a CS degree. The British report is perhaps more forthright in its recommendation that engineering-accredited SE degrees be developed, and that the relevant engineering professional society should recognise SE as an engineering discipline with requirements comparable with those of other engineering disciplines. (Ford argues that a similar development in the USA would be more difficult, given current professional accreditation requirements.)

Perhaps as a result of the impetus of these reports, there has emerged recently the suggestion that the development of SE degrees might be accompanied by a split of the discipline of SE from that of CS, with a resultant split in typical university department structures. Gibbs [7] has written perhaps the most effective paper in this debate. He recognises the separateness of SE as a discipline, and emphasises the urgency of resolving the future evolution of both SE and CS. Gibbs would prefer the disciplines to remain united, but suggests that the danger of separation is high. He does not, however, advocate that we should abandon the trend to undergraduate SE degrees, but rather indicates that it may be possible for the academic computing community to adapt so that SE and CS may evolve together.

Other distinguished computer scientists, Wulf [16] and Shaw [14], for example, have taken an opposing view, although they desire reforms in computing education of a similar nature.

They see the development of SE degrees as diverting attention away from the necessary reforms (in a SE direction) that must be accomplished in typical CS degrees.

The international debate on the future development of various aspects of computing education is particularly well-timed from an Australian perspective. In Australia all but one of the universities is (federal) government funded. The Federal Government Department of Employment, Education and Training (DEET) in 1991 commissioned a 'discipline review' of computing degree and diploma courses [4]. Such reviews of disciplines have become common recently, and form a major component of the accountability of universities to their funding masters.

A major recommendation of this review was the need for courses to take more seriously the preparation of graduates for professional practice. (This is precisely the concern of [3], [6], [7], [14] and [16], even though the authors of these documents come to different conclusions about mechanisms for realisation.) The review essentially fails to recognise SE as a distinct computing discipline. This may be attributed to the fairly small group of academics and practitioners in Australia who promote SE as a discipline, the importance placed by government on the opinion of that section of industry that equates 'computing' with 'information systems', the failure of the engineers to recognise SE as a discipline distinct from the more general Computer Systems Engineering, and to the strength of the Computer Science establishment. This shortcoming notwithstanding, those promoting SE education can take heart from the general thrust of the conclusions of the review.

The occasion of the review has been seen as a good catalyst for self-analysis of the CS discipline, which in Australia as in the USA has been roundly criticised for failing to produce the sorts of graduates demanded by industry. One of the members of the DEET review panel, a leading CS academic, has committed to print his vision of academic CS in Australia in the 1990s [10]. He proclaims the need to be more accountable to the future employers of graduates in curriculum design, and indicates the need to guard against what he perceives as threats to the discipline. In these threats he lists that of encroachment from engineering in the guise of SE, and suggests that CS departments need to defend their intellectual claim to SE. In this he echoes the sentiments of some North American authors [16], [14].

Although the debate in the USA over the potential for a split between the disciplines of CS and SE has not (yet) carried over to Australia, Lister's paper clearly foreshadows the danger of this occurring. There is not yet an established tradition in Australia of graduate (far less undergraduate) programs specifically in SE. However in recent years there have been proposals [2] and implementations [13], [8] of degrees either in SE or in CS with a substantial SE content. As such programs are initiated in greater numbers, and perhaps encounter some of the developmental difficulties experienced in the USA, it is to be expected that the danger for a disciplinary split will intensify.

Within this framework, how should educators with a sympathy for SE proceed if we desire to strengthen the SE profession in Australia?

This paper is written from the following perspective :

> we need to be graduating many more 'software engineers' than 'computer scientists' [15]

- there is a coherence between CS and SE which demands a structural unity of the disciplines [7]

- whilst the balance between CS and SE in undergraduate education might need to shift, there is a need to maintain vigorous research in CS as well as in SE

- accreditation and certification issues are important for a mature profession, and must be considered as we make critical choices [6]

- there are constraints placed upon educational developments by funding authorities, which force an unfortunate degree of pragmatism upon decision makers.

It is pertinent to place this paper within my own professional framework : I am head of a relatively large Computer Science Department in an Applied Science Faculty in a small technologically-oriented university, which also has a large Engineering Faculty which offers a Computer Systems Engineering major.

My department offers a CS degree which has a strong SE orientation [8]. The engineering emphasis, however, does not pervade the whole degree. Most of the computing content of the Computer Systems Engineering degree offered by the Engineering Faculty is contained in the CS degree, where it is generally treated with more depth. The CS degree has considerably more practical work, with an emphasis on team projects which are of considerably larger scale than the individual programming projects of the CSE degree. The latter degree has a more substantial hardware emphasis. Students on the CSE degree enjoy a considerable volume of engineering education, both generic and in other engineering disciplines (primarily, but not exclusively, electrical and electronic engineering).

I shall argue later that for SE to flourish as an academic discipline in synergy with CS, it is important for academic computer scientists to accept the importance of an engineering emphasis, and to bear this in mind in the learning environment they create for their students. This has clear implications for my department, as it requests an openness to change.

As department head, I face the challenge of positioning my department as the university develops in the 1990s. Assuming that the department determines that SE should be a major focus, and has the opportunity to choose its future organisational locus, should we seek to become an engineering department, offering an engineering degree, or should we remain an applied science department, offering a CS degree with a strong engineering flavour ? Are there other, better directions for us to take?

This paper, therefore, is a result of practical reflection on the very real choices facing an actual CS department.

2. Demand for Computing Graduates

What sort of computing graduates should our universities be producing, and in what proportions? This is one of the fundamental questions raised by the discipline review [4].

Employers of computing graduates in Australia would collectively suggest that historically we have produced too many CS graduates with a tendency to value theory over practice, individual work over teamwork and a technological rather than human perspective on real world problems. This judgement is now widely accepted internationally, not only within the SE community [5], [15], but also more and more within the CS community [4], [10], [16]. There are different plausible (and not so plausible) responses to this situation [16], [14], [11] which fall short of (and indeed oppose) the development of undergraduate SE degrees.

A starting point for those concerned with dictating policy is that there is substantial demand for graduates who

.   *have a good understanding of CS fundamentals*
.   *understand the implications of engineering a product*
.   *have experience in team work*
.   *understand human and organisational perspectives on systems development.*

This demand can be fulfilled by developing SE degrees and / or CS degrees with a strong SE emphasis. The debate that remains addresses the issue of whether the latter of these approaches is adequate, or whether we really need full SE degrees. As mentioned in the introduction, from the hypothesis that the close relationship of the computing disciplines must be maintained, strong opinions on both sides of this debate have been offered.

An issue that must be confronted as a prelude to this debate is that of the distinction between engineering and applied science. If practical systems development is all to be classified as 'engineering', then perhaps accredited engineering degrees are required, and the alternative not defensible from a professional perspective. If, on the other hand, one may apply a scientific discipline to problem solving without being an engineer, then perhaps the 'CS with SE emphasis' is feasible.

The engineering profession in Australia frequently bemoans the fact that the ratio of engineers to scientists in the country is far too low (particularly in comparison to other countries such as Germany and Japan). In common opinion, Australia is a country which produces many good ideas (the scientists are outstanding!) but too few industrial developments of these ideas (because there are not enough engineers !) To redress this we should increase the relative proportion of engineering graduates to science graduates.

This is an attractive, but essentially specious argument. Most science graduates do not discover new things. Applied Science graduates in particular tend to gain employment in areas where they are just as concerned with product and process development as engineers, albeit on a smaller scale. Employers are generally pleased with the attributes of applied science graduates.

The issues discussed in the last three paragraphs tend to draw emotionally and politically charged points of view. A simplistic, but at least partially valid distinction between engineering and applied science is that the scale of problems requiring full engineering discipline is larger. In recognising that the problems encountered in industry are of all shapes and sizes, it is then appropriate to accept that we should aim to graduate students from both engineering and applied science degrees.

In the context of determining the desired mix of different kinds of computing graduates, it is important to assess the employment destination of graduates, both now and in projection. In fact, most computing graduates in Australia do not find employment on large-scale software development projects. (Particularly in non-MIS areas, usually engineering graduates are hired for the large scale projects. However their *Software Engineering* skills are often limited.) The employment-oriented skills demanded by employers are generally oriented to *small* team oriented development.

From this perspective, it is entirely plausible that an appropriate curriculum can be developed which falls short of a full engineering program. The development of CS degrees including a strong SE flavour would meet such a need.

A fair general conclusion is that we need to develop computing curricula which emphasise application based on theoretical foundations. The extent to which SE and 'Applied CS' should contribute is a matter for employment demand and government policy to influence. There is room for both kinds of program.

3.   The Coherence of CS and SE

In presenting three possible views of the relationship between the content of 'computing' and the content of SE, Gibbs [7] implicitly defends the view that the contents overlap in a significant way.

Building on Gibbs' model, one might view the coherence between CS and SE as suggested in Figure 1 below. This indicates the overlap of CS and SE, with SE founded on the strong science base. Each 'sub-discipline' such as Computer Graphics or Artificial Intelligence has its fundamental science foundation, but one should not ignore the engineering discipline required to build real systems with Graphics or AI content.

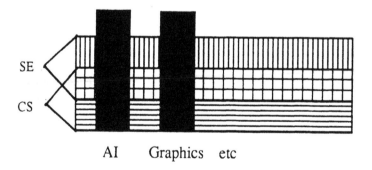

Figure 1 : A View of the Relationship between CS and SE

This view of the relationship between CS and SE, with CS providing a firm foundation and with areas like Graphics and AI sustained by science and engineering practice, implies the necessity for coherent future development of avoiding a CS and SE split. It places SE as a 'horizontal' discipline, like the science on which it is founded, promoting a unified approach to applications development which transcends detail.

The ability for SE and CS to develop synergistically in the future is significantly dependent on recognition of their strong interdependence and the fact that this will be sustained by avoiding academic divorce of the disciplines. (Note that it is an *interdependence*. Many scientific discoveries are made through the development of engineering processes, and even of engineered products!)

Localising this argument, if the degree offered by my department is to be consistent with the model of Figure 1, then those who teach Graphics and AI (for example) need to imbue their teaching with a balance of both a CS and SE philosophy. Issues of specification and program correctness, for example, need to be embraced. In general, our students (and it is important to emphasise that this is true of our students, but need not be true of CS students of all universities) study Graphics and AI because they may at some stage develop systems for others to use which require Graphics or AI components. They should engineer such systems, and so need to understand the implications of SE methodology in the context of the specialist areas.

4.   Research Issues

It is important to recognise that the development of the discipline of SE is highly dependent on the continuing advancement of CS. There must be no diminution of the CS research effort. On the other hand, growth is needed in SE research. In Australia there is a trend to greater industry / academia collaboration in research, and clearly a field like SE has the potential for such collaboration to yield fruitful, applicable research. Wulf [16] and Shaw [14] emphasise most strongly the need for expansion of SE not to hinder the development of CS.

One of the reasons for the resistance to SE from the CS 'establishment' is the perception that a change of balance in undergraduate computing education might have ramifications for the balance of university research programs in computing. The continuation of support for many current CS research projects might seem to be threatened by a growth of SE.

Such threats are probably real, but also probably justified. As with all sections of the academic community, the CS research community must come to terms with the need for greater accountability to industrial and government sponsors. Strong links with SE research are likely to assist CS research promote credibility in this regard. Accordingly, it is important to develop sensible research *strategies* which emphasise the mutual dependence of CS and SE.

5.   Accreditation and Certification

The seminal paper by Ford [6] discusses SE accreditation and certification issues in detail, but is directed at the USA scene. However most of the points made by Ford are relevant in Australia.

In Australia, CS degrees are accredited by the computing professional body, the Australian Computer Society (ACS). The ACS does not have the status enjoyed by, for example, the engineering professional body (IEAust). However in recent years there has been a growth in professionalism in computing in Australia, as evidenced, for example, by the ACS 'Practising Computing Professional' (PCP) scheme [12]. Curriculum impositions by the ACS have been directed by ACM and IEEE curriculum documents. As yet there has been no response to 'Curriculum 91' [1].

Engineering degrees have to be accredited by IEAust, who impose some quite strict requirements which are less concerned with fine detail than overall philosophy. Recently IEAust has recognised the new accreditation category of 'Engineering Technologist' for degrees which, though less than full engineering degrees, still have a strong engineering science thrust. A CS degree with a SE thrust may be acceptable for accreditation under this category.

Accreditation interacts with certification. Thus to be a PCP one has to be at least an associate member of the ACS, and the simplest route to becoming a member of the ACS is to receive a degree which is accredited by the ACS, followed by a prescribed minimum amount of professional experience. One maintains PCP status by undertaking a minimum amount of continuing education on a yearly basis. At least one major data modelling consultancy in Melbourne insists on all its employees maintaining PCP status, and such practices, although in their infancy, are expected to proliferate. To become a Chartered Professional Engineer (CPE) one has to graduate with an engineering degree accredited by IEAust, followed by a prescribed minimum amount of professional experience. (CPE status can be gained by graduating with an applied science degree, for example, followed by substantially more relevant engineering experience.) There is a continuing education requirement for the maintenance of CPE status.

Frequently there are advertised computing positions which require appointees to be accredited engineers. (An example is a recently advertised lectureship in Computer Systems Engineering in my university, whose duties are likely to be very similar to those of many of the staff in my department who are not engineers.) There might be expected to be growth in this practice as the demands of developing safety-critical software increase.

As in the USA, many Australian employers of what might be termed 'software engineers' have preferred to employ engineers, who (they believe) can be taught easily to apply their engineering approach to the development of large software systems. This is not (yet) because they require engineering certification as a result of legislation, but rather because they believe that it is the optimal hiring policy. As Gibbs suggests [7], this can be dangerous, although maybe less so than employing traditional CS graduates. The philosophy is so ingrained in a number of employers, however, that it might be rather hard to convince them to employ a good graduate of a CS program which has a strong SE emphasis.

The legislative position of CPE status is becoming more significant, primarily through moves in some states of Australia to limit the liability in certain circumstances of engineers with CPE status. Accordingly one can expect a growth in the number of positions requiring appointees to have CPE status. This may well in time affect the hiring strategies of a greater number of organisations developing software, particularly safety-critical software.

As a consequence of this practice there are clearly some advantages in the development of engineering-accredited SE programs. This is perhaps more possible in Australia than Ford [6] suggests for the USA. It is certainly viable to view SE as a subset of Computer Systems Engineering, and therefore to use the latter as the basis for SE accreditation. This is currently being pursued by La Trobe University in Melbourne [13].

The arguments of Sections 3 and 4 regarding the synergy of the disciplines of CS and SE, taken in conjunction with the conclusions of this section, imply that a university department wishing to offer a fully accredited SE degree ought to be positioned organisationally to permit this to happen. In Australia, several CS departments have moved to the Engineering Faculty in recent years to improve the interaction of their discipline with Electrical and Electronic Engineering. Others straddle Science and Engineering faculties. There is no single solution to the organisational location problem. What is important is that any impediments to the offering of an accredited SE degree be removed.

6. Differences between SE degrees and CS Degrees with a SE Orientation

Is the curriculum experienced by the graduate who undertakes a CS degree with a SE emphasis adequate from an engineering perspective?

In Australia, the following are the major criteria that need to be satisfied by an accredited engineering program [9]:

- the course must extend over four full-time years of study

- generally the course must be offered in a multi-disciplinary engineering school

- the course must contain

  - substantial content in mathematics, physical and other basic sciences
  - engineering science material, not concentrated entirely in one field
  - engineering synthesis or design and related communication skills
  - engineering applications material, including project work, particular to a branch of engineering
  - basic principles of management associated with the practice of engineering
  - professional responsibility, social effects and ethical aspects of engineering practice
  - not less than twelve weeks of practical experience relevant to engineering obtained outside the teaching establishment

Clearly three year applied science degrees fall well short, in general, of these requirements. Four year applied science degrees are offered - either honours degrees, where students take additional advanced courses and generally write a minor research thesis, or cooperative education degrees, where students spend 12 months undertaking paid work in industry. The extensions provided by these do not bridge the gap to the engineering requirements.

Gibbs [7] has argued against the need for the SE curriculum to "take the ABET accredited engineering core of 'beam-bending' and 'sand-pounding'". However he staunchly defends the need for computing students to study engineering methods, processes and paradigms. The issue, then, is whether a study of these *within a single disciplinary setting* is adequate. Clearly IEAust think this is not enough to make an engineer, but in general the Software Engineering discipline leaders think it is enough to begin to make a Software Engineer. (Of course, no undergraduate education makes anything! All it can do is lay foundations. From this perspective, continuing education is perhaps more important from an accreditation and certification perspective than a degree.)

The additional year of an engineering program permits considerable breadth of engineering experience denied the student in the typical applied science program. As a consequence the engineering graduate often has a broader view of the context of the discipline than the applied science graduate, and is often able to contribute professionally at a higher level in the first year of employment. For graduates proceeding to participation on large scale projects, the full undergraduate engineering experience is probably desirable.

In Section 2 I argued that the demand pattern for computing graduates is such that not all need to have a full engineering education. The three year applied science degree with an SE flavour is highly appropriate as an option within the full range of computing degrees.

7. Funding Issues

Engineering degrees cost more than CS degrees. Or rather, in Australia, the government gives universities more money to support engineering students than computer science students! The interpretation placed by my university on the model used to fund it results (roughly) in a ratio of 2.2 / 1.6 in favour of an engineering student. Further, an engineering degree is four years long, as opposed to three years for a CS degree. This results in accounting which attributes the cost of producing an engineering graduate as being approximately 80% higher than the cost of producing a CS graduate.

The recent discipline review [4] has unequivocally stated that the base funding for CS needs to equal that of engineering. Even if government and / or universities were to respond to this in their funding models, there would remain the 4 year / 3 year differential. Therefore it is most unlikely that government will respond to an initiative to replace routinely three year applied science degrees with four year engineering degrees.

From this perspective, it appears that to further the cause of SE, it is essential to move forward on two fronts, recognising (as Shaw and Wulf have done [14], [16]) that the development of SE principles within the confines of a CS degree is valid, and also that there is a role for engineering-accredited SE degrees (as concluded by the British report [3]).

8. Conclusion

Industry needs software engineers, applying their processes to all kinds of computer systems development. Consequently we must graduate software engineers.

We need to recognise, however, that not all systems are large, and that the discipline needed to build large systems is not needed in its entirety for small systems development. Conversely, however, we must also recognise that the development of small systems also requires processes of an engineering nature.

The majority of our computing graduates require much of the knowledge and many of the skills which encompass the discipline of SE. Accordingly most of our computing degree courses should have a practical orientation. Some of these courses should be full SE programs, offered as engineering programs under the requirements of engineering accreditation. The others should embrace, within an applied CS framework, the central tenets of SE.

The best organisational mechanism for the development of SE as a discipline is through a department which unites CS and SE, situated appropriately in a university's structure to permit the offering of an accredited engineering degree.

Regardless of degree structure, the structural unity of CS and SE should be maintained, in order that the engineering is effectively grounded in science and that together the computing disciplines might enjoy the synergy of common purpose. This is particularly true in terms of government lobbying. It is of central importance for the future of SE that CS is not disadvantaged as a discipline because of a perceived detachment from the reality of SE.

To maintain the unity it is vital to view the sub-areas of CS as having engineering relevance; one must engineer AI systems, and one must engineer graphics systems. It is essential to develop an ethos which encourages research scientists to teach engineering principles.

Finally, and most importantly, the advance of SE must not be accompanied by a retreat of CS. The disciplines should together combine to advance the state of computing practice.

9. Acknowledgments

Thanks are due to Simon Harriss and Ross Smith for assisting me to bring coherence to this paper.

10. References

[1]   ACM / IEEE-CS Joint Curriculum Task Force, *Computing Curricula 1991*, Feb. 1991.

[2]   Bailes, P.A. and Salzman, E.J., "A Proposal for a Bachelor's Degree Program in Software Engineering", *SEI Software Engineering Education Conference 1989*, Springer Verlag Lecture Notes in Computer Science Vol. 376, (Gibbs, N.E. (ed)), 90 - 108.

[3]   British Computer Society and Institution of Electrical Engineers, *A Report on Undergraduate Curricula for Software Engineering*, June 1989.

[4]   *Discipline Review of Computer Studies and Information Sciences Education*, AGPS, Canberra, 1992.

[5]   Ford, G.A.. and Gibbs, N.E., "A Master of Software Engineering Curriculum", *IEEE Computer*, Vol. 22, No. 9(September 1989), 59 - 71.

[6]   Ford, G., *1990 SEI Report on Undergraduate Software Engineering Education*, Tech Report MU/SEI-90-TR-3, Software Engineering Institute, Carnegie-Mellon University, Pittsburgh, 1990.

[7]   Gibbs, N.E., "Software Engineering and Computer Science: the Impending Split?", *Education and Computing*, Vol. 7(1991), 111 - 117.

[8]   Grant, D.D. and Smith, R., "Undergraduate Software Engineering - An Innovative Degree at Swinburne", *Australian Software Engineering Conference 1991*, (Bailes P. A. (ed))149 - 162.

[9]   Institution of Engineers, Australia, *Accreditation Policies and Procedures Relating to Professional Engineering Undergraduate Courses*, December 1991.

[10] Lister, A., "Clouds and Silver Linings", *Proceedings of the 15th Australian Computer Science Conference*, World Scientific, Singapore, 1992.

[11] Parnas, D.L., "Education for Computing Professionals", *IEEE Computer*, Vol. 23, No. 1(January 1990), 17 - 22.

[12] "PCP - Practising Computer Professionals", *Victorian Bulletin, Australian Computer Society*, December 1990, 10 - 11.

[13] Reed, K. and Dillon, T.S., "An Undergraduate Software Engineering Major Embedded in a Computer Systems Engineering Degree", *SEI Software Engineering Education Conference 1990*, Springer Verlag Lecture Notes in Computer Science Vol. 423, (Deimel, L.E. (ed)), 49 - 66.

[14] Shaw, M., "We Can Improve the Way We Teach CS Students", *Computing Research News*, Vol. 4, No. 1(1992), 2 - 3 (letter to the editor).

[15] Tully, C., "A Failure of Management Nerve and Vision", *13th International Conference on Software Engineering*, IEEE Computer Society Press, May 1991, 154 - 155. (Note : Tully's point was emphasised more in his panel presentation than in his position paper.)

[16] Wulf, W.A., "SE Programs Won't Solve our Problems", *Computing Research News* Vol. 3, No. 5(1991), 2.

Experience with a Course on Architectures for Software Systems

David Garlan[1], Mary Shaw[1], Chris Okasaki[1],
Curtis M. Scott[1], and Roy F. Swonger[2]

[1] School of Computer Science
Carnegie Mellon University
Pittsburgh, PA 14213 ***

[2] Digital Equipment Corporation
Nashua, NH 03062

Abstract. As software systems grow in size and complexity their design problem extends beyond algorithms and data structures to issues of system design. This area receives little or no treatment in existing computer science curricula. Although courses about specific systems are usually available, there is no systematic treatment of the organizations used to assemble components into systems. These issues – the *software architecture* level of software design – are the subject of a new course that we taught for the first time in Spring 1992. This paper describes the motivation for the course, the content and structure of the current version, and our plans for improving the next version.

1 Overview

The software component of the typical undergraduate curriculum emphasizes algorithms and data structures. Although courses on compilers, operating systems, or databases are usually offered, there is no systematic treatment of the organization of modules into systems, or of the concepts and techniques at an architectural level of software design. Thus, system issues are seriously underrepresented in current undergraduate programs. Further, students now face a large gap between lower-level courses, in which they learn programming techniques, and upper-level project courses, in which they are expected to design more significant systems. Without knowing the alternatives and criteria that distinguish good architectural choices, the already-challenging task of defining an appropriate architecture becomes formidable.

We have developed a course that will help to bridge this gap: *Architectures for Software Systems*. Specifically, the course:

*** Development of this course was funded in part by the Department of Defense Advanced Research Project Agency under grant MDA972-92-J-1002. It was also funded in part by the Carnegie Mellon University School of Computer Science and Software Engineering Institute (which is sponsored by the U.S. Department of Defense). The views and conclusions contained in this document are those of the authors and should not be interpreted as representing the official policies, either expressed or implied, of the U.S. Government, the Department of Defense, or Carnegie Mellon University.

- teaches how to understand and evaluate designs of existing software systems from an architectural perspective,
- provides the intellectual building blocks for designing new systems in principled ways using well-understood architectural paradigms,
- shows how formal notations and models can be used to characterize and reason about a system design, and
- presents concrete examples of actual system architectures that can serve as models for new designs.

This course adds innovative material to existing curricula on the subject of software architectures. It also helps define the field of software architecture by organizing and regularizing the concepts and by enabling the education of software designers in those concepts.

2 Background and Rationale

As the size and complexity of software systems increases, the design problem goes beyond the algorithms and data structures of the computation: designing and specifying the overall system structure emerges as a new kind of problem. Structural issues include gross organization and global control structure; protocols for communication, synchronization, and data access; assignment of functionality to design elements; composition of design elements; scaling and performance; and selection among design alternatives.

This is the *software architecture* level of design. There is a considerable body of work on this topic, including module interconnection languages, templates and frameworks for systems that serve the needs of specific domains, and formal models of component integration mechanisms. However, there is not currently a consistent terminology to characterize the common elements of these fields. Instead, many architectural structures are described in terms of idiomatic patterns that have emerged informally over time. For example, typical descriptions of software architectures include statements such as:

- "Camelot is based on the client-server model and uses remote procedure calls both locally and remotely to provide communication among applications and servers." [S+87].
- "Abstraction layering and system decomposition provide the appearance of system uniformity to clients, yet allow Helix to accommodate a diversity of autonomous devices. The architecture encourages a client-server model for the structuring of applications." [FO85]
- "We have chosen a distributed, object-oriented approach to managing information." [Lin87]
- "The easiest way to make the canonical sequential compiler into a concurrent compiler is to pipeline the execution of the compiler phases over a number of processors. ...A more effective way [is to] split the source code into many segments, which are concurrently processed through the various phases of compilation [by multiple compiler processes] before a final, merging pass recombines the object code into a single program." [S+88]

Other software architectures are carefully documented and often widely disseminated. Examples include the International Standard Organization's Open Systems Interconnection Reference Model (a layered network architecture) [Pau85], the NIST CASEE Reference Model (a generic software engineering environment architecture) [Ear90], and the X Window System (a windowed user interface architecture) [SG86].

It is increasingly clear that effective software engineering requires facility in architectural software design. First, it is important to be able to recognize common paradigms so that high-level relationships among systems can be understood and so that new systems can be built as variations on old systems. Second, detailed understanding of software architectures allows the engineer to make principled choices among design alternatives. Third, an architectural system description is often essential to the analysis and description of the high-level properties of a complex system. Fourth, fluency in the use of formal notations for describing architectural paradigms allows the software engineer to communicate new systems designs to others.

Regrettably, software architectures receive little or no systematic treatment in most existing software engineering curricula, either undergraduate or graduate. At best, students are exposed to one or two specific application architectures (such as for a compiler or for parts of an operating system) and may hear about a few other architectural paradigms, but no serious attempt is made to develop comprehensive skills for understanding existing architectures and developing new ones. This results in a serious gap in current curricula: students are expected to learn how to design complex systems without the requisite intellectual tools for doing so effectively.

We have developed a course to bridge this gap. This course brings together the emerging models for software architectures and the best of current practice. It examines how to approach systems from an architectural point of view. Other curriculum proposals have touched on this subject, but to our knowledge this is the first implementation of a full course in the area.

3 Philosophy and Course Overview

3.1 Objectives

We designed a course for senior undergraduates and students in a professional master's program for software engineering. By the end of this course, students should be able to:

- Recognize major architectural styles in existing software systems.
- Describe an architecture accurately.
- Generate reasonable architectural alternatives for a problem and choose among them.
- Construct a medium-sized software system that satisfies an architectural specification.
- Use existing definitions and development tools to expedite such tasks.
- Understand the formal definition of a number of architectures and be able to reason precisely about the properties of those architectures.
- Understand how to use domain knowledge to specialize an architecture for a particular family of applications.

3.2 Approach

We believe that important skills for designing complex systems can be provided by a course that examines systems from an architectural point of view. Specifically, our course considers commonly-used software system structures, techniques for designing and implementing these structures, models and formal notations for characterizing and reasoning about architectures, tools for generating specific instances of an architecture, and case studies of actual system architectures. It teaches the skills and background students need to evaluate the underlying architecture of existing systems and to design new systems in principled ways using well-founded architectural paradigms.

Since this is an entirely new course rather than a modification of an existing course, the major challenge in its development was to define and delimit its intellectual content. While the ability to recognize and use software architectures is essential for the practicing software engineer, there is to date no codified body of knowledge that deals specifically with this subject. Rather, relevant material is scattered over published case studies, standards reports, formal models, informal system documentation, and anecdotal experience. We have collected many of these sources, distilled them into a corpus of presentable knowledge, and discovered ways to make that knowledge directly usable by university students and the software engineering community at large.

Our approach focuses on developing four specific, related topic areas:

Classification: In order to use software architectures, it is first necessary to be able to recognize an architectural style and to describe a system in terms of its architecture. The tools required to describe and categorize common architectural models include notations for defining architectures and a taxonomy of existing models. In addition to introducing the student to these tools, this topic addresses the problem of architectural selection to solve a given software engineering problem. It covers both high-level architectural idioms (e.g., pipeline architectures) and specific reference models (e.g., the OSI layered model).

Analysis: Effective use of a software architecture depends on the ability to understand and reason about its properties (such as functional behavior, performance, developmental flexibility, evolvability, and real-time behavior). Such analysis can be applied to many kinds of architectural description, but it is particularly effective in the context of formal descriptions, where the power of mathematics can be exploited. This topic therefore covers techniques for analyzing an architecture. It introduces students to formal and informal methods and illustrates the ways in which formal analysis can be used to evaluate and select among architectural alternatives [Fi87] [GD90].

Tools: Certain architectures have evolved to the point where there is system support for defining applications using them and for executing those applications once they are built. Examples include Unix support for single-stream pipeline architectures, compilers for module interconnection languages (such as Ada package specifications), and IDL (Interface Description Language) readers and writers for shared data. Facility with such tools is a valuable skill for using the supported architectures in the context of current technology. Moreover, existing tools provide good illustrations of the kinds of automated support that we can expect to become pervasive as the field becomes more fully developed and populated with useful architectures.

Domain-Specific Architectures: Specific knowledge about an application domain can improve the power of the notations and tools for constructing systems in that domain. The same holds true for architectures, and there is active research and industrial development in the area of domain-specific software architectures [DSS90]. The course looks at a number of these to understand how domain knowledge can be exploited in designing an architecture tailored to a specific application family.

We rely heavily on case studies in each of these topic areas. These are used to motivate the importance and scope of architectural approaches, illustrate what has been done so far, and give students models for creating architectural descriptions of their own. In addition to examining existing case studies, students are expected to carry out a significant case study of their own. By doing this they practice applying the techniques of architectural description and analysis and contribute to the field by adding to the body of carefully documented architectural descriptions.

4   Course Description

In this section, we give an overview of each topic covered in the course. This information is summarized in Figure 1. Each row of the figure contains the lecture number, the major topic and subtopic covered in the lecture (as described below), the reading which the student is to have completed prior to attending the lecture, and the homework assignment (if any) to be discussed or turned in on that date. The assignments are numbered A1 through A4, with the course project due at the end of the semester. These are discussed in sections 4.3 through 4.5.

Introduction (2 lectures)

- *Orientation.* What is the architectural level of software design, and how does it differ from intra-module programming? Overview of the course.
- *What is a Software Architecture?* Constructing systems from modules. Some familiar kinds of architectures. Some common kinds of modules. [Sha90b, DK76, PW91]

Architectural Idioms (5 lectures)

- *Objects.* Information hiding, abstract data types, and objects. Organizing systems by encapsulating design decisions, or "keeping secrets." [PCW85, Boo86, WBJ90]
- *Pipes & Events.* Two architectural idioms: pipes and event systems. Pipes support a dataflow model. Event systems support loosely-coupled components interacting via event broadcast. [Par72, GKN88]
- *Multi-process Systems.* Organizing systems as collections of independent computations that run cooperatively on one or many processors. [And91]

Lecture	Topic	Subtopic	Reading	Assignment
1	Introduction	Orientation		
2		What is a SW Arch?	[Sha90b, DK76, PW91]	
3	Architectural	Objects	[PCW85, Boo86, WBJ90]	
4	Idioms	Pipes & Events	[Par72, GKN88]	
5		Multi-process Systems	[And91]	
6		Blackboards	[Nii86a, Nii86b]	
7		Heterogeneous Design	[Sha90a, Sha91]	A1 discuss
8	MILs	Classical MILS	[PDN86, LS79]	
9		Unix Pipes	[Bac86]	A1 due
10		SML & Ada	[H$^+$88, I$^+$83]	
11		Augmentations	[Per87, Gro91]	A2 discuss
12	Formal Models	Intro to Z	[Spi89b, Sha85]	
13		Industrial Experience	[GD90, HK91]	A2 due
14		Executable Specs	[Zav91]	
15		Event Systems	[GN91]	A3 discuss
16		Pipes and Filters	[AG92]	
17	Domain-Specific	Data Processing	[Fis91, RC86]	A3 due
18	Architectures	Distd, Heterogeneous	[BWW88, D$^+$91]	
19		Real-Time	[SG90, Sta88]	
20		Robotics	[HR90, SST86]	
21		Communication	[Tan81]	A4 discuss
22	Tools & Envts	Hints on Syst Design	[Lam84]	
23		Design Guidance	[Lan90]	A4 due
24		Arch. Transformers	[Bis87, BAP87]	
25		System Generators	[LS86, Joh86, BO91]	
26		Envt. Generators	[HGN91]	Proj due
27	Student Project			
28	Presentations			
29				

Fig. 1. Summary of Course Topics

- *Blackboards.* Sharing complex knowledge about a problem; making progress when you can't tell in advance what order to impose on the subproblems. [Nii86a, Nii86b]
- *Heterogeneous Design.* Designers don't have to limit themselves to a single architectural idiom. Examples of systems that use several idioms at various places in the system. [Sha90a, Sha91]

Module Interconnection Languages (4 lectures)

- *Classical MILS.* Historically, the earliest large systems were developed in procedural languages. The most common of the MILs reflect this in their emphasis on importing and exporting names of procedures, variables, and a few other constructs. [PDN86, LS79]
- *Unix Pipes.* The Unix paradigm connects independent processes by data flow.

The organization of the processes and the style and tools for connection are substantially different. [Bac86]

- *Module Interconnection in Standard ML and Ada.* An important property of modern module interconnection languages is the ability to parameterize modules. This is represented by generics in Ada and functors in SML. [H$^+$88, I$^+$83]
- *Augmentations to Module Interfaces.* Future prospects for module interconnection. How to augment a module's interface so that it conveys more than signatures. [Per87, Gro91]

Formal Models of Software Architecture (5 lectures)

- *Introduction to Z.* Basic notation of the Z Specification Language. The schema calculus. [Spi89b, Sha85]
- *Industrial Experience with Formal Models.* Use of formal models to understand, document, and analyze system architectures in two major industrial case studies. [GD90, HK91]
- *Paisley.* Executable specification language that supports some elementary performance analysis. [Zav91]
- *Event Systems.* Formal model of event systems. Specialization of abstract formal models to describe specific systems. [GN91]
- *Pipes and Filters.* Abstract model of pipes and filters. Use of formalism to explain what a software architecture is and to analyze its properties. [AG92]

Domain-Specific Architectures (5 lectures)

- *Data Processing.* Architectures for management information systems. [Fis91, RC86]
- *Distributed, Heterogeneous Computing.* Applied pipe and filter architectures. Architectures to support flexible processor allocation and reconfiguration. [BWW88, D$^+$91]
- *Real-Time System Architectures.* Real-time schedulers: rate-monotonic scheduling, cyclic executives, and others. Conditions under which a particular real-time architecture can be applied. [SG90, Sta88]
- *Architectures for Mobile Robotics.* Software organization of reactor-effector systems that operate in an uncertain environment. The CMU task control architecture. [HR90, SST86]
- *Layered Architectures for Communication.* Network protocols based on layered model of communication abstractions. Special emphasis on ISO Open System Interconnection (OSI) standard. [Tan81]

Tools, Environments, and Automated Design Guidance (5 lectures)

- *Hints on System Design.* Sage guidance and rules of thumb about designing good systems. [Lam84]
- *Automated Design Guidance.* The selection of a software architecture should depend on the requirements of the application. This example of a system shows how to make the structural design of a user interface explicitly dependent on the functional requirements. [Lan90]

- *Architecture Transformers.* Semi-automatic conversion of the uniprocessor version of a system to a multiprocesor version; not fully general, but works under clearly stated conditions. [Bis87, BAP87]
- *System Generators.* Automatic production of certain classes of systems from their specifications. [LS86, Joh86, BO91]
- *Environment Generators.* Automatic production of environments from descriptions of the tasks to be performed. [HGN91]

5 Assignments

5.1 Purpose

The purpose of the assignments, as in any course, is to help students master the material. Assignments serve the additional purpose of demonstrating the students' mastery of the material, thereby establishing a basis for evaluation.

Students begin by examining and understanding existing work in the area. Then they apply what they've seen and heard, first by trying to emulate it and then by performing analysis. Three kinds of assignments lead students through these activities.

First, the course is organized around written papers and lectures that present and interpret this material. We believe that the lectures are most useful if they provide interpretation, explanation, and additional elaboration of material students have already read and thought about. In addition to assigning readings, we provide guidance about the important points to read for and questions to help students focus on the most significant points in the reading.

Second, four two-week assignments ask students to apply the lecture material. Three of these assignments require students to develop small software systems in specific architectural styles. The fourth is a formal analysis task, which allows the students to work with a specific architectural formalism.

Third, students examine existing software systems to determine their architectures. We identified several systems of about 20 modules. For the final project of the course, each student team analyzed the actual system structure of one of these and interpreted the designer's architectural intentions.

We organized the students into teams of two (with one team of three because an odd number of students enrolled). This encouraged students to enhance their understanding through discussions with another student, reduced the amount of overhead required of any one student to get to the meat of a problem, and allowed us to partially compensate for differences in programming language and other related experience. The course included both undergraduate students and students in the Master of Software Engineering program; to the extent possible we paired undergraduates with graduates so that their experience would complement each other.

Since students often tend to spend most of their attention and energy on the components of a course that contribute to the final grade, we used the allocation of credit as a device to focus them on the most important activities. To this end, we included four factors in the grading basis. Here is the description of these factors as stated in the initial course handout:

- *Readings: (25%)* Each lecture will be accompanied by one or more readings, which we expect you to read *before* you come to class. To help you focus your thoughts on the main points of the reading we will assign a question to be answered for each of the reading assignments. Each question should be addressed in less than a page, due at the beginning of the class for which it is assigned. Each of these will be evaluated on a simple ok/not-ok basis and will count for about 1% of your grade.
- *Homework Assignments: (40%)* There will be four homework assignments. Each will count 10% of your grade. The first three will be system-building exercises. Their purpose is to give you some experience using architectures to design and implement real systems. You will work in groups of two (assigned by us) to carry out each assignment. To help clarify your designs we will hold a brief, un-graded design review for each assignment during class a week before it is due. Groups will take turns presenting their preliminary designs and getting feedback from the class and instructors. The fourth assignment will give you some practice using formal models of software architectures.
- *Project: (25%)* There will be a course project, designed to give you some experience with the architecture of a substantial software system. You will analyze an existing software system from an architectural point of view, document your analysis, and present the results to the rest of the class. Your grade will depend both on the quality of your analysis and also on the presentation of that analysis.
- *Instructors' judgement: (10%)*

5.2 Readings

No textbook exists for this course. Background material for the course consisted of readings, primarily from professional journals, selected to complement the lectures and discussions. The objective was for every student to read each paper before the corresponding class lecture.

To ensure this, a short homework assignment was set for each class. Each homework consisted of a few questions to be answered about the readings. These assignments were due at the beginning of the corresponding lecture and discussion. Though the single grade attached to a particular assignment would not significantly affect the course grade, the cumulative effect of these individual grades resulted in significant weight being placed on the readings.

A beneficial side effect of this policy was that it obviated the need for examinations. The incremental learning process was monitored and reinforced by the assignments, so there was no need for a final exam to measure student progress. As a result, end-of-semester energy could be productively directed to the course project.

Each reading was accompanied by hints which identified points to look for in each paper and gave advice on parts to ignore. These hints helped students to focus on the important concepts in each paper, and were particularly important because of the wide variety of notations and languages introduced in the readings.

Here are some examples of the hints we gave:

- In these readings you will be exposed to many different languages. You should not try to learn the specific syntax of each language, nor should you memorize

the specific features of each language. Rather, you should try to get a feel for the design space of module interconnection languages—what it is possible to represent and what it is desirable to represent.
- First and foremost, read to understand the blackboard model and the kinds of problems for which it is appropriate. Study Hearsay and HASP to see how the model is realized in two rather different settings. Look at the other examples to see the range of variability available within the basic framework.

The questions for each assignment also played an important role in focusing the intellectual energies of the students. The questions were structured to have the students understand the concepts involved, rather than simply read to complete the homework. Since the reading and homework combined were intended to take only a couple of hours, the questions dealt with major points and did not require deep thought or analysis.

Here are some examples of the questions we asked:

- What are the essential differences between the architectural style advocated by Parnas and that advocated by Garlan, Kaiser, and Notkin?
- What abstract data type does a pipe implement? What common implementation of that abstract data type is used to implement pipes?
- What is the problem addressed by sharing specifications in SML? Why doesn't this come up with Ada generics?
- What are the major abstractions of an interconnection model? How are these specialized in the unit and syntactic models?

5.3 Architectural Development Tasks

Believing that one must constructively engage a style to understand it, we assigned programming tasks in three different architectural idioms. For each task, we supplied an implementation in the required idiom that used several components from an available collection. The assignment required students to extend the implementation *in the same style* by reconnecting parts, using other components, or minimally changing components. The choice of this format was driven by two guiding principles:

- The attention of the students should be focused at the architectural level rather than at the algorithms-and-data-structures level. (Students should already know how to do the latter.)
- It is unreasonable to expect the accurate use of an unfamiliar idiom without providing illustrative sample code employing that idiom.

A pleasant side-effect of this choice of format was that problems more closely resembled software maintenance/reuse than building a system from scratch. In addition, we were faced with a considerable diversity of programming language background among the students. It's easier to work in an unfamiliar language if you have a working starting point.

To encourage cooperation and to balance unfamiliarity with particular programming languages and systems, students worked in pairs on the programming tasks. However, each task had a set of questions to be answered individually.

A major objective of this course is for students to leave with an understanding of the essential features of a given problem that make a particular architectural choice appropriate or inappropriate. To do this, we assigned variations of a single core problem for all three tasks, differing primarily in the features related to the choice of idiom. By assigning the same basic problem for each architectural idiom, we avoided the risk of students associating problem class X with architectural idiom Y, instead promoting understanding of the features of each problem that should lead the designer to choose that idiom. By varying the features related to the architectural choice, we also discouraged students from leaving each solution in the same basic architectural idiom, adding only the superficial trappings of the second idiom. For example, by changing the requirements on the system, we ensured that an event-driven solution would not merely be a pipes & filters solution "dressed up" to look like an event-driven system.

Because the problems involved not only the production of a working system but also the analysis of an architectural style, we held design reviews halfway through each assignment. These reviews were presented by the students in the class, with each team making one presentation sometime during the semester. The reviews were not graded; they thereby provided a means for the class to engage in discussions about the architectural style and for the instructors to guide the student solutions (both those being presented and those of the students watching the presentation) by asking pointed questions. These presentations were performed during class time, and their schedule is presented in Figure 1.

The core task chosen was the KWIC indexing problem[Par72, GKN88]. In this problem, a set of lines (sequences of words) is extended to include all circular shifts of each line, and the resulting extended set is alphabetized. This core problem was varied in each architectural idiom as follows:

Object-Oriented: This variation was *interactive*: a user enters lines one at a time, interspersed with requests for the KWIC index. Students were supplied with a system which generated the KWIC index without the circular shifts (i.e., a line alphabetizer) and asked to include the shifts. In addition, students were asked to omit lines which began with a "trivial" word (e.g., *and* or *the*).

Pipes & Filters: In this variation, students were asked to generate a batch version which generated KWIC indices of login and user names (as generated by the *finger* command). Students carried out two tasks. In one task, students used the Unix shell to connect "modules" such as the common Unix commands *finger*, *sort*, and *uniq*. A second task required them to connect the same modules in a pipe organization too complex to describe in the shell, so that they had to use raw pipes from within C. As before, they began with solutions which alphabetized lines but did not generate circular shifts.

Event-driven (implicit invocation): This variation extended the problem for the object-oriented architecture with a *delete* command. Students were required to reuse existing modules, augmenting them with event bindings to establish how they communicated.

5.4 Formal Modelling

To develop skill in understanding and manipulating formal models we assigned a task that required students to extend an existing formal model of a software architecture.

As with the architectural development tasks the formal modelling task builds on an existing base—in this case the formal model developed by Garlan and Notkin of event systems [GN91]. In this work the authors showed how a simple model of systems based on event broadcast could be specialized for a number of common systems, including Smalltalk MVC, Gandalf programming environments, the Field programming environment, and APPL/A.

The students were asked to perform similar specializations for two different architectures: spreadsheets and blackboard systems. In addition, they were asked to provide a commentary that answered the following questions:

1. What important aspects of the modelled architectures are (intentionally) left out of the model?
2. For the blackboard system, would it be possible to model some notion of "non-interference"?
3. For the spreadsheet system, is the *Circular* property defined in the events paper a useful concept? Why or why not?
4. Based on the formal models, briefly compare each of the two new systems with the other ones that were formally modelled. For example, you might explain which of the other systems are they most similar to.

5.5 Analysis and Interpretation of a System

In addition to the assignments described above, students also examined and described the architecture of a non-trivial system. About midway through the semester we asked each group of students to select a system from a list of candidates that we supplied. Alternatively, students could volunteer a system of their own, provided it met the criteria outlined below.

The students' task was to complete an architectural analysis of the chosen system by the end of the semester. This analysis was required to include the following components:

1. **Parts catalog:** A list of the modules in the system, making the interfaces explicit, together with an explanation of what each one does.
2. **Interconnections catalog:** A list of the connections between modules together with a descriptions of each.
3. **Architectural description:** A description of the system's architecture, using the vocabulary developed in the course.
4. **Critique:** An evaluation of how well the architectural documentation for the system matches the actual implementation.
5. **Revision:** Suggestions for ways that the system architecture could have been improved.

In addition to a written analysis students were expected to present their analysis to the class. We allotted three days at the end of the semester for this. The grade on the project was determined both by the written analysis and the presentation.

In selecting candidate systems we attempted to find systems that are tractable but challenging. Specifically, we applied the following criteria for selection:

- **Size:** Ten to twenty modules containing between 2,000 and 10,000 lines of code.
- **Documentation:** It should have enough system documentation that students do not need to start from raw code to do their analysis.
- **Resident guru:** There should be someone in the local environment who knows the system and can answer questions about its design and implementation.

6   Evaluation

6.1   Lessons from the Initial Offering

The first offering of the course ran during the spring semester of the 1991-1992 academic year at Carnegie Mellon University. Four undergraduate students and seven Master of Software Engineering students took the course. There were also half a dozen regular auditors. The lessons we have learned as a result of that offering are based upon the students' progress in learning the course material and on evaluation of the course by the students themselves.

Content. It is clear that a sufficiently large body of knowledge exists to support a course in software architecture. When we designed this version we were unable to include all the topics of interest, and we made some hard decisions among alternative materials for the topics we did include.

The specific topics of the course had varying success. The section on architectural idioms was particularly valuable. While the section on MILs was important to have included in the course, we now feel we spent too much time on that topic. Two lectures would have been more appropriate than the four that we scheduled. The formal methods segment worked out well, but for students with no exposure to Z, it required considerably more effort than the other sections. (Almost all of the master's level students had already had a course in formal methods.) The lectures on domain-specific software architectures were of mixed value, since these lectures were predominantly given by invited speakers. The section on tools and environments was reasonably successful, but suffered from the fact that there is relatively little material directly applicable to software architectures.

Many of the readings were quite good; others should be replaced. The best of the readings included Nii's survey of Blackboard Systems [Nii86a, Nii86b], Andrews' survey of distributed architectures [And91], Shaw's overview of architectural styles [Sha90a], Parnas' classic "Criteria" [Par72] and A7 papers [PCW85], the Perry Inscape paper [Per87], a paper on implicit invocation by Garlan, Kaiser, and Notkin [GKN88], Lampson's hints on system design [Lam84], and Lane's paper on the concept of the design space [Lan90]. The course syllabus would have been much better if we had been able to find good readings about Unix pipes, management information system architectures, the ISO Open Systems Interconnection model, and architectural tools. We would also like to find readings about object-oriented systems that deal specifically with architectural issues, rather than programming issues.

The assignments that involved construction and analysis of systems were generally quite valuable, as they gave students practice in applying the principles of the course. However, we felt that we could have chosen tasks that would have both challenged the students more than we did, and at the same time focused on some of the more important issues of architectural design.

Chosing good practical problems is one of the most difficult (and important) parts of developing such a course. Part of the problem centers around finding systems that are of the right size and complexity. On the one hand, it is important to find systems that are large enough to represent nontrivial architectures. On the other hand, there is a limit to the size of system students that can handle, particularly given the fact that we wanted students to have experience with several architectures.

Our approach to the problem was to give students a working system and a collection of parts that they could reuse and modify in adapting the system to the task assigned. Overall this was a good approach, although it takes a lot of preparation to make it successful. We attempted to use Booch components [Boo87] for the first and third assignments, and the standard Unix tools for the second assignment. However, many of the software needed in the solutions to the problems could not be found in these standard collections. As a result a majority of the code in the starting frameworks was developed by us from scratch. For example we used only one Booch component package (a total of 200 lines), but wrote 1400 lines of Ada and 300 lines of C for the frameworks provided to the students.

Another aspect of the problem of chosing good assignments is to find problems that exploit the target architecture but do not have a single solution. Our assignments were not sufficiently rich to accomplish this. Moreover, time constraints prevented us from making more parts available than were absolutely required for the assignments, so the students did not face the challenge of selecting an architectural solution from a rich parts kit.

One issue involving the assignments was the use of multiple programming languages. We wanted to avoid giving the impression that there is a one-to-one mapping between programming languages and architectures. However, our parts kit (the Booch components) was in Ada, and our version of the Ada compiler did not provide a library for manipulating Unix pipes. This led us to use Ada for the first and third assignments, and C for the second.

Format. The division of the course into the major topics had some advantages, but overall was viewed as needing revision. The course lectures touch each of the architectural idioms three times: to introduce the idiom, to examine a suitable module connection language or tool, and to introduce a formal model and analysis technique useful within the idiom. In addition, some idioms reappear in domain-specific examples. In retrospect, a course organization that factors the course along the lines of architectural idioms seems more appropriate.

We were pleased to teach from selected readings. The readings allowed students to hear the ideas in the voices of their creators. Moreover, we believe the state of of knowledge in software architectures is not advanced enough to provide a single canonical picture of the various architectures. Further, we were able to order the topics appropriately to meet our ideas of how the topics should be presented, and to flexibly schedule the guest lecturers.

The chief disadvantages of using readings as source material are that notations and terminology vary from paper to paper, and that the architectural significance of a paper may not be well articulated. It is also a nuisance to deal with copyright considerations (though many of the papers carry blanket permissions for educational use).

Assigning questions on the class readings was a good idea. It served both to focus students' attention and to encourage them to do the reading in advance. This worked well enough that we could plan lectures that elaborated and interpreted the material rather than repeating it.

The task formats worked well in terms of the amount of time allotted and overall structure of the assignments. However, one challenge lay in the diversity of language experience among the students. In particular, Ada was familiar to some students, but new to others. While this course was not intended to be a "programming course," we found it necessary to provide a brief Ada help session for students without Ada experience. This session's effectiveness was limited because it was held outside normal class hours and was not directly graded. Ideally in an architectures course, however, all students should know the programming languages to be used for the assignments prior to entering the class.

Using groups to accomplish the assignments had generally positive results. By mixing graduate and undergraduate students on each team, the teams formed a balanced collection of strengths which enabled them to grasp the essentials of the programming assignments quickly. Also, having a team environment allowed the students to discuss the architectural issues among themselves in a more structured format than might otherwise have been available. We believe this would have been even more effective if a more challenging set of problems were presented.

Comments From Students. We distributed two course evaluations to students, one midway through the course and one at the end. Overall student responses were quite positive. Typical comments were: "I've noticed that I'm viewing problems in other classes from a different perspective," and "I now finally understand what we were doing when we built that system in the way we did."

At a more detailed level the students felt that the study of architectural idioms was most important, and that it provided a foundation for a body of knowledge to which they had not been exposed. They also said that the course encouraged a new perspective on software systems. Some students wanted more emphasis on the process of architectural design and guidance in choosing an architectural idioms. The general opinion was that more could be added to the course, but not at the expense of current material.

The readings were generally viewed as a valuable part of the course. Students appreciated the incentive to read them regularly, and they particularly appreciated the absence of a final exam. They also liked having lectures serve to elaborate the readings rather than repeating them—something that is only possible when the instructor can assume that students have actually read the readings.

The course required a significant amount of work, but the students thought it was worth the effort. They noted that, unlike most courses, the load is fairly level.

They had to pay attention to the course regularly, but they didn't wind up with massive deadline crunches.

The team organization was also judged favorably. We received no complaints about unequal workload within a team, although some team members commented that getting a consensus, even on a small team, took time.

6.2 Changes to Consider

While we are generally satisfied with the course as taught, we see some areas that we plan to change the next time we teach the course.

Content. While the course did not suffer from a lack of material, a number of areas could be added to the curriculum. In particular, study of heterogeneous and integrated architectural idioms would be appropriate, as would more study and practice in architectural design and decision making. One way that room could be made for this material is by reducing the time spent on module interconnection languages.

Another improvement would be to develop a more consistent terminology in our lectures on architectures. Within the area generally termed software architecture, there is a bewildering diversity of terms for similar concepts. As the discipline evolves and the terminology stabilizes, we would expect this problem to diminish.

Format. There are a number of format changes which we believe would improve the coherency and conceptual integrity of the course. They are:

1. Concentrate on a particular idiom for a span of 3-4 lectures to give the students a deeper understanding of each class of architecture. A consistent format for the study of each idiom might be:
   (a) Introduction of idiom and survey of class
   (b) Related languages or tools
   (c) Formal model
   (d) Case study and analysis
   This could be complemented by an assignment for each idiom, to give a single, coherent presentation of an architectural style.
2. The assignments could be better planned to emphasize the architectural nature of the projects, and minimize the "hacking" necessary to build a system. Assignments should allow the students to create unsuccessful solutions as well as different but successful solutions to the same problem. More emphasis should be placed on analysis of the assignment, encouraging students to reflect on the choices made and the reasons for these choices.

   The only way we see to create reasonable projects is to provide collections of ready-made components. Unfortunately, reasonable "parts kits" are scarce, and most existing parts kits do not clearly illustrate an architectural style. Moreover, in many cases (such as in event systems), architectural styles require tools beyond those provided even by a carefully constructed parts kit. This infrastructure is likely to be different for each architectural style, compounding the problem when multiple architectural styles are presented. Generally, in order to effectively teach multiple architectural styles within the constraints of a single-semester course, we need architectural tools as well as parts kits.

3. The architectural analysis project should use examples that are familiar to the instructors and which have existing architectural documents for the students to start with.

4. The reports that the students produce from the architectural analysis project should emphasize the high-level structural and communications paradigms of the system, rather than specific functionality or detailed algorithmic analysis. To this end, the assignment of the project should specify the structure of the report, and provide good examples of existing architectural analyses.

6.3 Conclusions About Teaching Software Architecture

Software architecture is worth teaching. It can be taught in many ways. Based on our experience with the present course and previous experience with four semesters of graduate reading seminars in the area, we can draw some conclusions about teaching software architecture in any format.

- Architecture provides a bridge between theory and coding. In any program teaching system design, there are high principles of program construction which are difficult to relate to the small programming assignments that comprise the majority of the undergraduate experience. A course that presents students with the terminology of software architecture and that gives them concrete examples of systems to relate to specific architectural styles allows the students to relate these two disparate bodies of information more readily and concretely.

- Students seem capable of rapidly developing an aesthetic about architectures. They can identify systems in their own experience which match specific styles, and they can also identify flawed designs as examples of poorly-formed or poorly-understood architectures. They are quite capable of answering open-ended questions about the appropriateness of a specific architecture to a problem and defending their positions rationally and powerfully. Unity does not evolve among the students, however. Different students will promote different architectures for the same problem, depending upon their particular points of view.

- There is little concrete material available in any form to guide design decisions. Absent such material, students get little help in resolving point-of-view differences. Instructors should make every effort to present techniques for selecting among architectural alternatives, including even simple rules of thumb such as "consider an interpreter when you're designing for a machine that doesn't actually exist."

- There is enough substantive material to fill a course. The selection we made for this offering was based on the coverage of our graduate reading seminars. However, we recognize that there were a number of difficult choices in our selection which might well have gone another way. In our opinion, the field of software architectures is moving from a point where finding enough papers is difficult to one where the challenge is to select the appropriate complement of papers.

- We wish there were more organized surveys of the material than are currently present. Currently, the fragmented nature of the material requires that the students be carefully instructed on exactly which information within a given paper is appropriate to the subject at hand. This is compounded by the sheer size and disorganization of the current software architectures field. There are few papers which view problems from a purely architectural perspective, and the boundaries between architectural idioms are not always clear. We would like to see more papers presenting architectural analysis techniques, and more worked examples in specific architectures. We would also like to see more mature distributed systems architectures and more papers like Nii's [Nii86a, Nii86b] that survey a class of systems against a single architectural paradigm. We think this will come with a better understanding of the idioms that comprise software architecture.

- It is tempting to treat the subject of software architectures abstractly and present only idealized views of the various architectural idioms. Resist this. Students have weak intuitions about the high-level architectural abstractions. Every formal or abstract model must be related to a real example, so that the student not only learns the abstract view of the architecture, but also the characteristics of a concrete instance of that architecture.

- Practice in using models is important. Analyzing existing architectures without working within the specific architectural framework does not allow the student to recognize the strengths and weaknesses of individual architectural styles. It is not sufficient for a student to be able to recognize a specific idiom; the student must also be able to decide which idiom to apply to a particular problem. For that skill, analysis alone is not enough.

Acknowledgments

The authors would like to thank Robert Allen, Mario Barbacci, Marc Graham, Kevin Jeffay, Dan Klein, Reid Simmons, and Pamela Zave for participating as guest lecturers in the first offering of this course. We would also like to thank James Alstad for his participation in the development of the early curriculum of this course.

References

[AG92]   Robert Allen and David Garlan. A formal approach to software architectures. Submitted for publication, January 1992.

[And91] Gregory R. Andrews. Paradigms for process interaction in distributed programs. *ACM Computing Surveys*, 23(1):49–90, March 1991.

[Bac86] Maurice J. Bach. *The Design of the UNIX Operating System*, chapter 5.12, pages 111–119. Software Series. Prentice-Hall, 1986.

[BAP87] J. M. Bishop, S. R. Adams, and D. J. Pritchard. Distributing concurrent Ada programs by source translation. *Software—Practice and Experience*, 17(12):859–884, December 1987.

[Bis87] Judy M. Bishop. Ada profile charts in software development. *Journal of Pascal, Ada and Modula-2*, 8(2), October 1987.

[BO91]   Don Batory and Sean O'Malley. The design and implementation of hierarchical software systems using reusable components. Technical Report TR-91-22, Department of Computer Science, University of Texas, Austin, June 1991.

[Boo86]   Grady Booch. Object-oriented development. *IEEE Transactions on Software Engineering*, SE-12(2):211–221, February 1986.

[Boo87]   Grady Booch. *Software Components with Ada: Structures, Tools and Subsystems*. Benjamin/Cummings, Menlo Park, CA, 1987.

[BWW88]   M. R. Barbacci, C. B. Weinstock, and J. M. Wing. Programming at the processor-memory-switch level. In *Proceedings of the 10th International Conference on Software Engineering*, pages 19–28, Singapore, April 1988. IEEE Computer Society Press.

[D^{+}91]   Doubleday et al. Building distributed Ada applications from specifications and functional components. In *Proceedings of TRI-Ada'91*, pages 143–154, San Jose, CA, October 1991. ACM Press.

[DK76]   Frank DeRemer and Hans H. Kron. Programming-in-the-large versus programming-in-the-small. *IEEE Transactions on Software Engineering*, SE-2(2):80–86, June 1976.

[DSS90]   *Proceedings of the Workshop on Domain-Specific Software Architectures*, July 1990.

[Ear90]   Anthony Earl. A reference model for computer assisted software engineering environment frameworks. Technical Report HPL-SEG-TN-90-11, Hewlett Packard Laboratories, Bristol, England, August 1990.

[Fi87]   Bill Flinn and ib Holm Sorensen. *CAVIAR: A Case Study in Specification*. Prentice Hall International, 1987.

[Fis91]   Gary Fisher. Application portability profile -APP- The U.S. Government's open system environment profile. US Department of Commerce, April 1991. National Technical Information Service Special Report, 500-187.

[FO85]   Marek Fridrich and William Older. Helix: The architecture of the XMS distributed file system. *IEEE Software*, 2(3):21–29, May 1985.

[GD90]   David Garlan and Norman Delisle. Formal specifications as reusable frameworks. In *VDM'90: VDM and Z - Formal Methods in Software Development*, Kiel, Germany, 1990. Springer-Verlag, LNCS 428.

[GKN88]   David Garlan, Gail E. Kaiser, and David Notkin. On the criteria to be used in composing tools into systems. Technical Report 88-08-09, Department of Computer Science, University of Washington, August 1988.

[GN91]   David Garlan and David Notkin. Formalizing design spaces: Implicit invocation mechanisms. In *VDM'91: Formal Software Development Methods*, pages 31–44. Springer-Verlag, LNCS 551, October 1991.

[Gro91]   MIF Working Group. Master: A prototech module interconnection formalism. Draft of December 1991, 1991.

[H^{+}88]   Robert Harper et al. Introduction to Standard ML. Technical report, Laboratory for Foundations of Computer Science, Computer Science Department, University of Edinburgh, March 1988.

[HGN91]   A. Nico Habermann, David Garlan, and David Notkin. Generation of integrated task-specific software environments. In Richard F. Rashid, editor, *CMU Computer Science: A 25th Commemorative*, Anthology Series, pages 69–98. ACM Press, 1991.

[HK91]   Iain Houston and Steve King. Experiences and results from the use of Z in IBM. In *VDM'91: Formal Software Development Methods*, number 551 in Lecture Notes in Computer Science, pages 588–595. Springer-Verlag, October 1991.

[HR90]   Barbara Hayes-Roth. Architectural foundations for real-time performance in intelligent agents. *The Journal of Real-Time Systems, Kluwer Academic Publishers*, 2:99–125, 1990.

[I+83]   J. D. Ichbiah et al. Rationale for the design of the Ada programming language. *SIGPLAN Notices*, 14(16 (Part B)):8:1–16, 13:1–21, June 1983. Chapters 8 (Modules) and 13 (Generic Program Units).

[Joh86]   Stephen C. Johnson. YACC: yet another compiler-compiler. In *UNIX Programmer's Supplementary Documents*, volume PS1, pages 15:1–33. University of California, Berkeley, 1986.

[Lam84]   Butler W. Lampson. Hints for computer system design. *IEEE Software*, 1(1):11–28, January 1984.

[Lan90]   Thomas G. Lane. A design space and design rules for user interface software architecture. Technical Report CMU/SEI-90-TR-22 ESD-90-TR-223, Carnegie Mellon University, Software Engineering Institute, November 1990.

[Lin87]   Mark A. Linton. Distributed management of a software database. *IEEE Software*, 4(6):70–76, November 1987.

[LS79]   Hugh C. Lauer and Edwin H. Satterthwaite. Impact of MESA on system design. In *Proceedings of the Third International Conference on Software Engineering*, pages 174–175. IEEE Computer Society Press, May 1979.

[LS86]   M. E. Lesk and E. Schmidt. LEX—a lexical analyzer generator. In *UNIX Programmer's Supplementary Documents*, vol. PS1, pages 16:1–13. University of California, Berkeley, 1986.

[Nii86a]   H. Penny Nii. Blackboard systems Part 1: The blackboard model of problem solving and the evolution of blackboard architectures. *AI Magazine*, 7(3):38–53, Summer 1986. Reprinted with corrections by AI Magazine.

[Nii86b]   H. Penny Nii. Blackboard systems Part 2: Blackboard application systems and a knowledge engineering perspective. *AI Magazine*, 7(4):82–107, August 1986. Reprinted with corrections by AI Magazine.

[Par72]   D. L. Parnas. On the criteria to be used in decomposing systems into modules. *Communications of the ACM*, 15(12):1053–1058, December 1972.

[Pau85]   Mark C. Paulk. The arc network: A case study. *IEEE Software*, 2(3):61–69, May 1985.

[PCW85]   David L. Parnas, Paul C. Clements, and David M. Weiss. The modular structure of complex systems. *IEEE Transactions on Software Engineering*, SE-11(3):259–266, March 1985.

[PDN86]   Ruben Prieto-Diaz and James M. Neighbors. Module interconnection languages. *The Journal of Systems and Software*, 6(4):307–334, November 1986.

[Per87]   Dewayne E. Perry. Software interconnection models. In *Proceedings of the Ninth International Conference on Software Engineering*, pages 61–68, Monterey, CA, March 1987. IEEE Computer Society Press.

[PW91]   Dewayne E. Perry and Alexander L. Wolf. Software architecture. Submitted for publication, January 1991.

[RC86]   Sridhar A. Raghavan and Donald R. Chand. Applications generators & fourth generation languages. Technical Report TR-86-02, Wang Institute and Bentley College, February 1986.

[S+87]   Alfred Z. Spector et al. Camelot: A distributed transaction facility for Mach and the Internet - an interim report. Technical Report CMU-CS-87-129, Carnegie Mellon University, June 1987.

[S+88]   V. Seshadri et al. Semantic analysis in a concurrent compiler. In *Proceedings of ACM SIGPLAN '88 Conference on Programming Language Design and Implementation*. ACM SIGPLAN Notices, 1988.

On Teaching the Rational Design Process

Terry Shepard

Department of Electrical and
Computer Engineering,
Royal Military College of Canada,
Kingston, Ontario, K7K 5L0, Canada
shepard@qucis.queensu.ca

Dan Hoffman

Department of Computer Science,
University of Victoria,
P.O. Box 3055, Victoria, BC,
Canada, V8W 3P6
dhoffman@uvunix.uvic.ca

Abstract. In 1986, a rational design process for software was proposed [1]. This paper reports on experience teaching a course based on this process in an undergraduate computer engineering curriculum, with a companion course at the graduate level helping to feed the undergraduate course. Because the courses are for computer engineers, the emphasis is on real–time systems. The main issue is how to simplify the details of the steps so that all the steps can be learned and applied within the bounds of a one semester course. The culmination of the two courses is a project in which all the steps are used to create a working piece of software. In this paper, the steps as taught are described, with the aid of examples, and then some of the issues influencing the particular choice of material taught are discussed.

1 Introduction

For the past 6 years, a software engineering course based on the rational design process [1] has been offered at the University of Victoria [2]. The rational design process includes a specific sequence of steps: establish and document requirements; design and document the module structure, the module interfaces, the uses hierarchy, and the module internal structures; and write and maintain the programs. Many variations are possible on this theme, and iteration of the steps is usually needed before the final version of the results of each step can be produced, but with the increasing popularity of object based design (e.g. [3],[4]), the process with its variants comes close to being universally acceptable. On the other hand, there is nowhere near universal agreement on the details of what is to be done at each step. Also, the detailed activities proposed at each step, and even the steps themselves, are very different from conventional structured analysis and design practice (e.g. [5]) although that practice is evolving (e.g. [6],[7]) and being extended for real–time systems ([8],[9]). This creates some interesting challenges for the teaching of the rational design process. One common scenario is that there is one software engineering course in an undergraduate curriculum, and this is the only opportunity to address all the steps in the process.

For the course at the University of Victoria, specific selections were made of material to be taught in support of each of the steps in the process. Also, a module testing step was added as a specific part of writing and maintaining programs. One of the unifying assumptions of the course was that module interface specifications, program specifications, implementation and testing would all be embedded in and done using the C programming language. For undergraduate students, the use of a host programming language in this way has several advantages: the different versions of documentation belonging to different steps in the process are all quickly and easily available online in one file hierarchy, a single editor is used, and the students gain experience with the language and its environment. In the winter term of 1991/92, a version of this course was offered for the first time at the Royal Military College of Canada. While C was used for the first part of that course, versions of the interface and program specification steps were produced for Ada. Since Ada has more facilities to support modules and exception handling than C has, this caused some changes.

In the remainder of the paper, each of the steps in the rational process as taught is explained in turn. The steps are illustrated using the development of a naval battle simula-

[SG86]   Robert W. Scheifler and Jim Gettys. The X window system. *ACM Transactions on Graphics*, 5(2):79–109, April 1986.

[SG90]   Lui Sha and John B. Goodenough. Real-time scheduling theory and Ada. *Computer*, pages 53–62, April 1990.

[Sha85]   Mary Shaw. What can we specify? Questions in the domains of software specifications. In *Proceedings of the Third International Workshop on Software Specification and Design*, pages 214–215. IEEE Computer Society Press, August 1985.

[Sha90a] Mary Shaw. Elements of a design language for software architecture. Unpublished position paper, 1990.

[Sha90b] Mary Shaw. Toward higher-level abstractions for software systems. In *Data & Knowledge Engineering*, volume 5, pages 119–128. Elsevier Science Publishers B.V., North Holland, 1990.

[Sha91]   Mary Shaw. Heterogeneous design idioms for software architecture. In *Proceedings of the Sixth International Workshop on Software Specification and Design, IEEE Computer Society, Software Engineering Notes*, pages 158–165, Como, Italy, October 25-26 1991.

[Spi88]   J. Michael Spivey. *The Fuzz Manual*. Computing Science Consultancy, 2 Willow Close, Garsington, Oxford OX9 9AN, UK, 1988.

[Spi89a] J. M. Spivey. *The Z Notation: A Reference Manual*. Prentice Hall, 1989.

[Spi89b] J.M. Spivey. An introduction to Z and formal specification. *Software Engineering Journal*, 4(1):40–50, January 1989.

[SST86]   Steven A. Shafer, Anthony Stentz, and Charles E. Thorpe. An architecture for sensor fursion in a mobile robot. In *Proceedings of the IEEE International Conference on Robotics and Automation*, pages 2002–2010, San Franciso, CA, April 1986.

[Sta88]   John A. Stankovic. Misconceptions about real-time computing. *Computer*, Vol.21(10):10–19, October 1988.

[Tan81]   Andrew S. Tannenbaum. Network protocols. *ACM Computing Surveys*, 13(4):453–489, December 1981.

[WBJ90]   Rebecca J. Wirfs-Brock and Ralph E. Johnson. Surveying current research in object-oriented design. *Communications of the ACM*, 33(9):104–124, September 1990.

[Zav91]   Pamela Zave. An insider's evaluation of PAISLey. *IEEE Transactions on Software Engineering*, 17(3):212–225, March 1991.

tion game. The game consists of 2 opposing ships each controlled by a single player. The software runs simultaneously on two PCs connected via an RS–232 serial link. The game incorporates a colour graphics display on each PC providing information on the current status of the game, including objects visible to each player and the status of navigational, radar, armament, defence and EW control subsystems. Armament for each ship consists of surface–to–surface missiles. The ship defence system consists of one chaff launcher located on the stern of the ship. Objects visible to a player are either within visual range, detected by active radar, or detected as a result of passive reception of radar transmissions by the object.

2 Motivation and Steps in the Rational Design Process

One of the problems in teaching software engineering at the undergraduate level is that students are still in the process of becoming familiar with the basic tools of code development, and they tend to think that that is the main issue. To help motivate them at the start of the course, three papers are used ([1], [10], [11]). The specific techniques and circumstances discussed in these three papers, and the style of presentation, seem to be effective in making the students understand that there is more to software engineering than programming, cost estimation and project management. This background is needed to motivate some of the students to have faith in the need to learn so much explicit structure as part of the design process until they get to the second part of the course, where they have the opportunity to see how a larger project than they could do as individual students goes together.

The specific steps in the rational design process as taught are:

1. Requirements Specification
2. Module Decomposition
3. Module Interface Specifications
4. Program Specifications
5. Implementation
6. Testing

Each of these steps is explained. The first four will be illustrated with the aid of the naval battle simulation game.

2.1 Requirements

The requirements document is the least structured of all the steps as taught. There are many approaches to the specification of requirements, accompanied by much debate about how to handle the need for users (who are usually not computer literate) to review and comment on requirements. Solutions range from the very general to the highly structured (representative techniques for real–time systems, roughly in order, are: natural language, ([5] & [12]), ([8] & [9]), ([13] & [14])). Use of techniques of the complexity of ([13] & [14]) is impossible in an undergraduate overview course. Data flow diagram based techniques (e.g. [8]) or other visual techniques (e.g. [15]) could be taught, but it is not clear that they offer significant benefit over a structured natural language approach, and they certainly are a distraction in subsequent stages, since they suggest approaches to the rest of the design process which are at variance with the process actually taught. They also require more time than is available for the requirements portion of the course.

The solution adopted in the course was to provide a minimal structure for the requirements document, and explain that such documents can be written with much more precision, following more complex structure. The structure of the requirements document consists of the following headings:

Overview
Normal Case
Exception Handling
Expected Changes
Dictionary

In the case of the naval battle simulation game, headings under the normal case are application specific:

General Specifications
Ship Characteristics and Control
Radar Control Subsystem
Armament Control Subsystem
Defence Control Subsystem
EW Control Subsystem

Students in the undergraduate course are only asked to read requirements documents, but in a companion course at the graduate level at RMC, students have participated in writing and revising the requirements document for the naval battle simulation game. The requirements document for the naval battle simulation game is about 9 pages (single spaced: 2500 words), including a page of expected changes, a one page screen layout diagram, and a page and a half of configuration constants. The page of expected changes is interesting because it is there in theory to guide the rest of the design. In practice, in this particular case at least, some of the expected changes will require a re-design. Recording them serves two purposes. The first is justification of the simplifying assumptions that were made to make the project size feasible. The second is to keep a record of possible enhancements for future generations of students.

2.2 Module Decomposition

Deciding how to decompose a system into modules is difficult. The criteria to be applied are those laid down in [16], but minimal guidance is provided on how to apply the criteria. If requirements specifications are well structured (for example, using the techniques proposed in [13] and [14], some natural divisions into modules will suggest themselves, but other modules will be needed also. Those that do appear to be logical candidates need to be evaluated with care, using the expected changes as a guide. Normally other decompositions need to be considered as well. One consequence for the course is that little emphasis is placed on doing module decomposition, since the general principles available to constrain the actual choice of decomposition are relatively weak. This may be why decomposition into modules is only beginning to be widely used. Current trends are exemplified by the popularity of object oriented techniques, which still depend on examples and experience as the only mechanism for successful teaching of module decomposition. The concepts are taught using two simple but complete examples developed at the University of Victoria. One of the examples is a program to calculate the reachability set of a given set of nodes in a graph. It uses three modules. The other is a stack based simple calculator, which contains two modules.

The document described for this step is loosely based on the A7 module guide [17], in the sense that it does not enforce the recommended decomposition at the top level into hardware–hiding, behaviour–hiding and software decision modules, primarily because that decomposition is awkward for relatively small systems. Its structure is hierarchical, based on each module hiding some secret. Sub–modules of a module hide a portion of the parent module's secret. Modules are natural work assignments, since the decomposition based on secrets minimizes communication of details between module designers. Modules are also a primary mechanism for dealing with minor expected changes, since such changes are strong candidates to become module secrets. The module hierarchy for the naval battle simulation game is:

GAME DIRECTOR MODULE (ga)
GAME RULES MODULE
  Game Termination Rules Module (gt)
  Ship Rules Module (sh)
  Missile Management Module
    Missile Flight Sub–module (mf)
    Missile Control and Launch Sub–module (mc)
  Chaff Module (ch)
  Object Detection and Missile Guidance Module
    Visual Detection sub–module (vt)
    Ship's Radar and Module Guidance sub–module (sr)
    EW sub–module (ew)
COMMUNICATIONS MODULE
  Local Game Information Module (lg)
  Remote Game Information Module (rg)
  Computer to Computer Communications Module (cm)
    Clock Sub–module (cl)
USER INTERACTION MODULE
  Display Module
    Detected Objects Display Sub–Module (od)
    Panel Display Sub–Module (pd)
    Text Entry Display Window Sub–Module (td)
    Error/status Display Window Sub–Module (ed)
    Mouse Cursor Display Sub–Module (md)
  Input Module
    Mouse Input Sub–Module (mi)
    Text Input Sub–Module (ti)

Each of these modules is described under two sub–headings: *Service* and *Secret*. For example, the entries for the Ship Rules Module and Chaff Module are:

Ship Rules Module (sh)

Service: The Ship Rules module keeps actual position, speed and direction of the local ship, as well as values input by the local player for new speed and direction. It provides access calls to set new speed and direction. It holds constant values of Ship_Acceleration, Ship_Turn_Rate, and Max_Ship_Speed. At each period, it sends actual position and direction values to the Local Game Information module.

Secret: The details of the calculation of position.

Chaff Module (ch)

Service: Accepts calls to fire chaff in specific direction, and fires when legal to do so. Holds constants Chaff_Rounds_in_a_Load, Chaff_Fire_Interval, Chaff_Reload_Time, Max_Chaff_Distance. Provides calls to obtain position and bloom state of rounds of chaff that have been launched.

Secret: Details of the rules for launch, position, bloom size. Number of rounds of chaff available and in the air.

This simple structure is easy and straightforward to explain. The longest description of a module is about a page. Modules that take that much explanation are candidates for further decomposition. Undergraduate students are not asked to undertake any decomposition of systems into modules, but they do review such decompositions, which helps to reinforce the principle of inspection as a valuable tool in software development [10]. The graduate students participated in the module decomposition exercise, and will be able to do so on a more interesting basis in future years, in that it will be possible to consider variants on the established structure to a greater degree than was possible in the available time in the first version of the graduate course.

In the development of the next stage, we have found it useful to create an access program summary document as a transition tool. When the module decomposition is near completion, and the access program names and parameters are beginning to emerge, listing all the access programs, and for each module, listing the access programs which are used by that module, clarifies the module decomposition, and provides a firmer footing for the writing of module interface specifications. A more detailed uses hierarchy, relating each access program to the access programs it uses, can be developed once the module interface specifications have all been written, and is useful in guiding the choice of subsystems which can be developed independently [18]. In the courses, there was not enough time to do this.

2.3 Module Interface Specifications

This step determines the behaviour of the access programs that will be available to manipulate the data structures held by the module. The basis for the approach used is described in [19]. The syntax and semantics of the access programs are defined. Abstract types are used as the basis for describing module state, transitions, outputs and exceptions. The abstract types allowed are real, boolean, integer, string and character, which may be composed into more complex types using sequence, set and tuple operators. This type scheme may be viewed as simplified Z or VDM ([20],[21],[22]). Z and VDM are useful for professional designers, but again, the limitations of a single course dictate simplifications.

In theory, the interface specification step is independent of the programming language which will eventually be used for implementation. In practice, there are some dependencies. The first one is that syntax of the access programs is either described in language specific terms (in the C version) or in terms of the abstract types (in the Ada version). Even though abstract types are used in the Ada version, the interface specification is still embedded in an Ada package specification, primarily because this is a convenient way to keep the specification readily available at all times during development of the module. The program specifications are Ada based, which results in some changes in the package specifications when moving from the interface specification stage to the program specification stage. There are two reasons Ada declarations are not used at the interface specification stage: they tend to introduce unnecessary detail, and leaving the Ada declarations to the program specifications makes clearer to the students the purpose of having the two stages. There is another difference between Ada and C at this stage. Two of the modules in the game, the local game information module and the remote game information module have identical interface specifications. In Ada, this leads naturally to a generic package to implement two objects. In C, the logical solution would be to extend the language model to include C + +, but this is too ambitious for the course. Fortunately, the example only arises in the Ada based part of the course.

Two examples of module interface specifications using the Ada version are given in Annex 1 to illustrate the standard headings that are used and to show the approach used in general terms. They are the Ship Rules Module Interface Specification (sh) and the Chaff Module Interface Specification (ch). The standard headings are given below:

```
package interface_specification_template is
-- Syntax:
--   constants:
--   types:
--   access programs:
--   uses:
--   exceptions: bad_dir, bad_speed, bad_pos
-- Semantics:
--   Implementor's Assumptions:
--   State:
--   Transitions, Outputs and Exceptions:
```

```
--  Local Constants:
--  Local Types:
--  Local Functions and Procedures:
end interface_specification_template;
```

The syntax sections of all the modules are written before the semantics sections are written. The allows the 'uses' part of the syntax section of each module to be applied to checking the consistency and completeness of the set of access programs for the whole system. In the Ship Rules module, for example, the only call in the 'uses' section is to lg.s_ship, which is used to provide the information about ship position, heading and speed to another module (lg: local game) that is used by all the other modules in the game that need this information.

Everything in the syntax section is exported by the module. In the semantics section, rules of module behaviour are given under the heading 'Transitions, Outputs and Exceptions'. These rules are exported in the sense that users of the module must adhere to these rules if they expect to get the advertised services from the module, and if they expect exception–free execution. Module users must provide exception handlers. In C this must be explicit, while in Ada, many exceptions can be built in as range checks of subtypes, and can be turned off if it is known that exceptions will not occur. Local constants, types, and functions and procedures are invisible outside the module. Local functions and procedures can freely make use of the module state: there is no need to pass it to them as parameters.

In the Ship Rules module, the access program calls have been designed to make it impossible to set the ship's position arbitrarily except at the time of initialization of the game. Enforcement of this restriction could also be handled in the transition functions, if there was a reason to have a separate call to set ship position, for example by keeping a flag to indicate that set_position had been called, never allowing it to be called again, and requiring in the transition for s_update that the ship position be set prior to any update. In a more complex technique such as the trace specification technique [23], it is easy and direct to specify the legality of particular sequences of calls, but the benefits in courses like the ones under discussion are outweighed by the time needed to fully explain the technique.

The Ship Rules module makes no use of sequences or sets. Sequences and sets are interesting because they cause a greater variety of constructs in the target language than do tuples, so there tends to be a larger difference from the module interface specifications to the program specifications. For example, it is much easier to describe how to add and delete from both ends of a sequence in the abstract than it is to describe how to implement these operations using a circular buffer or linked list in a particular language. To illustrate these points, a second example of an interface specification, for the Chaff module, is given in Annex 1. Further discussion of the issues involved in converting abstract sequences to concrete state is postponed to the next section.

In the design of the access programs for the Chaff module, there is a synchronization problem in the use of s_chaff_launch, g_qty & g_bloom: if s_chaff_launch is used after g_qty but before g_bloom, the number of chaff blooms is no longer correct for determining how many times to call g_bloom. Several solutions are possible, but the main point in a teaching context is that it is useful to present the students with modules having subtle potential traps like this one, and to point out how much better it is to observe and fix such traps at this stage.

The students are introduced to interface specifications by example, using versions in C. In the undergraduate course, they are asked to work through, by hand, the effect of some traces of access program calls on the module state. In a later assignment, they are asked to write a module interface specification from a natural language description of the module similar to what might be inferred from the module guide and the requirements specification. They are then introduced to Ada based interface specifications in the second part of the course. The level of detail presented in this step and in the next one is determined in part by the students' ability to relate to the techniques presented. The skills required are related to programming skills, so it is easier for the undergraduate students to grasp and apply more of the details of these two steps than of the other 4 steps. The graduate students, with some guidance, wrote most of the module interface specifications for the naval battle simulation game without going through any of the preliminary exercises.

2.4 Program Specification

Program specification refers to the specification of the access programs of a module. The main differences from the interface specifications are the addition of an abstraction function and a state invariant, and the conversion of the abstract state to concrete state (called 'data reification' in VDM [21]) expressed in a particular programming language. The purpose of the first two is to assist in verification of correctness of the program specifications, both with respect to the interface specifications and in terms of internal behaviour. The purpose of the concrete state is to take one more step toward actual implementation.

Since Ada is used as the host language, it is natural to use package bodies to hold program specifications of modules. Some portions of the program specifications are embedded as comments, since Ada has no explicit provision for these constructs. The program specifications include the semantic information from the module interface specifications, expressed in terms of the concrete state. In Annex 2, two examples of program specifications are given, for the Ship Rules and Chaff Modules. Concrete Ada versions of abstract types used at the interface specification stage must be made visible to users of the package, and the only way to do this in Ada is to put the declarations in the package specification. The items to be inserted in the package specifications are listed in the first part of the program specifications given for the two modules. The format for a program specification is as follows:

```
package body program_specification_template is
-- abstraction function:
-- definitions:
-- concrete state:
--    state invariant:
--    declarations:
-- local functions and procedures:
-- access program transitions, outputs and exceptions:
end program_specification_template;
```

The sequence of declarations in the program specification is determined by the importance of the declarations to the reader and by the requirement that procedures and functions be declared prior to use. Thus, since the reader is presumed to have correctness as a first priority, the abstraction function and the state invariant are presented prior to the declaration of the concrete state. Local function and procedure definitions could be separated from their declarations, but these examples are simple enough that there is little point in doing so.

In the Ship Rules example, since there are no sequences or sets, the abstract state and the concrete state correspond very closely. There is still a significant increase in the level of detail in the program specification compared to the interface specification. This would be less true in C, so the interface specifications in C can be (and are) written using C specific declarations. The disadvantage of doing so is that the specifications are tied more closely to a single programming language. The advantage to having the students see interface specifications and program specifications in both Ada and C is that they then realize more clearly that the interface specifications are essentially language independent, even though it may be useful to embed them in a host language, but the program specifications are language dependent since they make declarations in the syntax of a specific language.

In Ada, the predefined exception constraint_error can be used to handle all of the exceptions in the Ship Rules Module, which raises the question of whether it makes sense both to declare types which explicitly contain range constraints and to include separate definitions of corresponding exceptions. The argument in favour of doing both is that the former is good programming practice, and, when it is known that all callers are trustworthy, it may be turned off using pragma suppress, while the latter may be important as a means of signalling a particular event to the calling program so that corrective action can be taken, for example by asking for a new input from the user. Exceptions in this latter category can never be turned off, since it is always possible that the user might make a data entry error.

The conversion of sequence to a concrete type is relatively straightforward in the Chaff module example, at the cost of shifting all the remaining live chaff entries left by one whenever one of the blooms disappears. If this inefficiency were judged to be unacceptable, the logical solution, supposing that chaff blooms die off in the same sequence in which they are created, is either a circular buffer or a queue. Either one might be implemented using one of the Booch Components [24], if there were time in the course to talk about reusable components! If chaff blooms do not die off in the same sequence as launched (which might be the case in some future more complex version of the game), then the concrete realization of a sequence might be a hash table indexed by an internal unique id for each round of chaff fired. The correspondence between this id and the id visible to the module user, which is always between 1 and Max_qty_live, would be complex. In any of these situations, the program specifications would be correspondingly more complex than the interface specifications.

As with the interface specifications, the students are introduced to program specifications embedded in C by example. In the undergraduate course they are asked to work through, by hand, the effect of some traces of access program calls on the concrete state expressed in C, and to calculate some values of the abstraction function for particular modules. They are asked to write a program specification from an interface specification. They do this before they are asked to write an interface specification of their own. In the second, Ada based, part of the course, they each write part of the program specification for a different module of the naval battle simulation game, and then write some of the code for that module. As with the interface specifications, the graduate students, with some guidance, write the rest of the program specifications for the naval battle simulation game without going through any of the preliminary exercises.

2.5 Implementation

Conversion of a set of program specifications embedded in either Ada or C (or in some other programming language) is straightforward, but is a useful exercise for students learning the language, which has been the case in the versions of the course taught to date. All of the students already have significant programming background in other languages, so learning basic programming skills is not one of the activities of the courses, although it does take some time to become familiar with two new languages and programming environments. This is offset by keeping the amount of actual coding that individual students must do to a minimum as a result of running a team project. In practice, it means that some students must pick up the slack for students who don't get their assignments done. On the other hand, because the software is so well defined by the time the implementation stage arrives, modified versions of previous implementations of modules can be used as well. In the RMC version of the course, because of the graduate course running in parallel, the undergraduate students act as implementors for a system described to the level of interface specifications, and partially described to the level of program specifications. This means that they review all documents up to and including some program specifications, write program specifications and code for some modules, and participate in integration of the whole system. The graduate students are also interested in learning as much Ada as they can, so they also participate in the implementation phase. The only awkward part of the implementation stage is that it is done on PCs, so modification of code during the integration phase creates some logistical problems, and an opportunity to demonstrate a shared network based software development environment is lost. On the other hand, given the time constraints on the course, learning the mechanics of such a shared environment might not be practical.

2.6 Testing

As part of the course, techniques for module testing are taught, along with the use of a C based language for describing tests to be applied and the results expected from tests [25]. Test harnesses are generated automatically and linked with the code for the module under test. Test results are written to files for later inspection. This approach is used in marking module implementations handed in by the students in the C part of the course. The intent is to teach a systematic approach to testing. It is emphasized that testing is only to be started after careful inspection of code, but time limitations prevent a formal inspection exercise. The distinction is made between white box and black box testing The undergraduate students are asked to write and use a test script to test one module. This is their last assignment prior to starting into the Ada based project.

The approach taught for testing a whole application emphasizes the need to start with modules whose behaviour is already known to be reliable, and the desirability of developing files of input and expected output to facilitate regression testing. Given the limitations of time, it is not possible to teach any of the details of software reliability assessment, although that would be desirable. Given the interactive nature of the application developed in Ada as a course project, its real testing in the course is by students playing the game. Since this happens at the very end of the course, there is little opportunity to explore the issues of more thorough and systematic testing of the application.

3 Some Issues in the Teaching of the Rational Design Process:

One could argue that a design process should be kept as independent as possible of the choice of programming language. In a teaching environment, this is not necessarily true. At both the University of Victoria and RMC, students need a slot in the curriculum where they can get some experience with C so they will have it available to them for other courses in their final year. The software engineering course can be a practical place to provide this experience. At RMC, the software engineering course is made somewhat less language dependent by teaching versions of the rational design process embedded in both Ada and C. This has the further advantage of giving the students exposure to two additional programming languages. Since there is no room in most computer engineering curricula for a required course on programming language paradigms, this is a useful opportunity. In future versions of the course at RMC, the students will already know both Ada and C at the start of the course. The most compelling reason for embedding the rational design process steps in a programming language is a practical one: it keeps three of the steps (interface specifications, program specifications and implementation) bound together in a common file and directory structure, and makes it easier for the students to see how it is possible to keep the documentation associated with all three of the steps consistent as the iterative process of development progresses. The actual experience they get is limited by the scale of project that is feasible in the course, and by the details of each students participation in the project. Ideally, an integrated environment would be available to the students to make all the documents and tools for the rational design process available at all times in a consistent and coherent fashion. While we wait for that nirvana, we must settle for what we have and can afford.

It is highly desirable to teach more complete and formal versions of the first two steps in the process, but part of the problem there is that the most widely used techniques for these two steps are mostly learned through experience. To put it another way, the body of knowledge on which these steps depends has yet to be codified in a manner which is fully acceptable in an undergraduate engineering curriculum. This suggests a conservative approach to teaching these two steps: outline some techniques, and leave the description based largely in natural language. It would also be desirable to teach variations on all of the steps, and even variations on the whole process, but some of the variations are not well codified yet, and in any case, the variations that can be taught in a single course are limited.

One of the issues that is left aside in the design process as taught in these courses is how to deal with concurrency and asynchronous external events. We may only hope that these issues will be dealt with in a subsequent course in real–time system development.

4 Conclusion

This paper has presented two courses organized around the application of a rational design process to a single software project. The feasibility of using a single project instance is largely determined by the number of students in each course. If there were more than about 5 graduate students, it would be hard to give them all exposure to all aspects of the design process without having more than one instance of a project. On the undergraduate side, since they spend less time creating and more time reviewing and inspecting, in a project of about 25 modules, a class size of up to about 25 can be accommodated on a single project. This places greater emphasis in the undergraduate course on the end result, but in a context in which they can appreciate the whole rational design process, and wish they had time to learn more of the details of all the steps.

The focus of the paper has been on the middle two of the six steps, and that is also the focus of the two courses, although module testing is also emphasized. The main limitation is the pressure of time, but that is also combined with the desire to make the steps in the process as concrete as possible to the students. This course, by teaching specific techniques for the purpose of illustrating general principles of software construction, avoids some of the pitfalls inherent in putting too much emphasis on project management There are aspects of project management that are unique to software engineering, but engineers in any discipline, at the undergraduate level especially, need to learn the technology of design and construction in their discipline. Part of the problem in the past has been that the technology for software engineering was relatively weak. It is getting much richer, which is what makes possible courses like the ones discussed here.

This paper is really about 2 problems: the need to have a well defined rational design process to teach to undergraduates, and the need to find space in undergraduate programs in computer science and engineering to teach such a process. In many such programs, especially in computer engineering, there is room for only one course on software engineering, which severely constrains what can be taught. Another constraint is that we are still waiting for general agreement on the details of many of the steps in a rational design process, which suggests that it may be too soon to consider teaching very many of the details of some steps, such as the specification of requirements, at the undergraduate level. Thus, although there is enough material in software engineering to justify more than one course in the core curriculum at the undergraduate level, it will be some time before there is widespread agreement on what the content of such additional courses should be. In the meantime, the course described in this paper is an attractive choice as the one core software engineering course.

References:

[1]   David Lorge Parnas and Paul Clements, "A Rational Design Process: How and Why to Fake It", IEEE Transactions on Software Engineering, V. SE–12, N. 2, February 1986, pp. 251–257

[3]   Grady Booch, Object Oriented Development, IEEE Transactions on Software Engineering, Feb 1986

[4]   Bertrand Meyer, Object–oriented software construction, Prentice Hall, 1988)

[5]   Tom DeMarco, Structured Analysis and System Specification, Prentice–Hall, 1978

[6]   Peter Coad and Edward Yourdon, "Object–Oriented Analysis", Yourdon Press Computing Series. Available from Object International in Austin, TX.

[7]   Paul Ward, How to Integrate Object Orientation with Structured Analysis and Design, IEEE Software, Mar. 1989, pp. 74–82

[8]   Derek Hatley & Imtiaz Pirbhai, Strategies for Real–Time System Specification, Dorset House, 1987

[9]   Paul Ward and Stephen Mellor, Structured Development for Real Time Systems, Vols. 1–3, Yourdon Press, 1985

[2]   Dan Hoffman, "An Undergraduate Course in Software Design", Proc. SEI Conf. Software Eng. Education, Apr 1988, pp. 164--168

[10] Glen W. Russell, "Experience with Inspection in Ultralarge–Scale Developments", IEEE Software, January 1991, pp. 25–31

[11] Fred Brooks, No Silver Bullet, IEEE Computer, Apr. 1987

[12] D. Marca & C.L. McGowan, SADT: Structured Analysis and Design Technique, McGraw Hill, 1988

[13] K.L. Heninger, "Specifying Software Requirements for Complex Systems: New Techniques and their Applications.", IEEE Trans. Software Engineering, SE–6, 1 (Jan 1980), 2–13 (reprinted in IEEE Tutorial on System and Requirements Engineering, 1990, pp. 555–566).

[14] A. John Van Schouwen, The A–7 Requirements Model: Re-examination for Real-Time Systems and an Application to Monitoring Systems (M.Sc. Thesis), QUCIS Tech.Rep. 90–276, Revision 3, January 1991

[15] Ray Buhr, Practical Visual Techniques in System Design, Prentice Hall, 1990

[16] David Lorge Parnas, "On the Criteria to be used in Decomposing Systems into Modules", Communications of the ACM, Vol. 15, No. 12, Dec. 1972, pp. 1053–1058

[17] Katherine H. Britton and David Lorge Parnas, "A–7E Software Module Guide", Naval Research Laboratories Report 4702, Dec. 1981

[18] David Lorge Parnas, "Designing Software for Ease of Extension and Contraction", IEEE Transactions on Software Engineering, Vol. SE–5, No. 2, March 1979, pp. 128–138

[19] Dan Hoffman, "Practical Interface Specification", Software Practice and Experience, Vol. 19(2), February 1989, pp. 127–148

[20] J.M. Spivey, The Z notation: A Reference Manual

[21] Cliff Jones, Systematic Software Development using VDM, Prentice Hall, 1986

[22] Ian Hayes, Specification Case Studies, Prentice Hall, 1987

[23] David Lorge Parnas and Yabo Wang, The Trace Assertion Method of Module Interface Specification, QUCIS Tech Report 89–261

[24] Grady Booch, Software Components with Ada, Benjamin Cummings, 1987 (components available in both Ada and C++)

[25] Dan Hoffman, "A CASE Study in Module Testing", 1989 Conference on Software Maintenance, October 1989, Miami, Florida

[26] R.C. Linger, H.D. Mills and B.I. Witt, "Structured Programming: Theory and Practice", Addison Wesley, 1979

Annex 1: Sample Module Interface Specifications

The interface specifications below can largely be read without explanation, but there are a few things that are not entirely self-evident.

A transition only needs to specify that portion of the state which is actually changed as a result of the call; if multiple components of the state are changed, a concurrent assignment statement is used. A concurrent assignment statement ([26], p. 48) is an expression of the form $v\_1, v\_2, ... , v\_n := e\_1, e\_2, ... , e\_n$, where the v_i's are distinct variables and each e_i is an expression of the same type as v_i. To evaluate the assignment statement, all of $e\_1, e\_2, ... , e\_n$ are first evaluated, and then e_i is assigned to v_i, for i in $[1,n]$. For example, the statement $x,y := y,x$ exchanges the values of x and y.

A *conditional rule* ([26], p. 29) is an expression of the form $C = (c\_1->r\_1 \mid c\_2->r\_2 \mid ... \mid c\_n->r\_n)$ where, for i in $[1,n]$, c_i is a boolean expression and r_i may be any expression. To evaluate a conditional rule C, evaluate c_1; if it is true, then r_1 is the value of C; otherwise, evaluate c_2; if it is true then r_2 is the value of C, and so on. Where no condition is true, C is undefined. For example, $(x <= y -> x \mid x >= y -> y)$ defines $min(x,y)$. Note that the conditions in a rule may overlap.

Exceptions cause the state to be left unchanged. The construct 'use init_coords' means prepend in what follows, so 'dir' becomes 'init_coords.dir', for example. Local functions in general need no parameters, as they have access to the state of the module, including the in parameters of the access programs that use them, provided there is no ambiguity. Append is a function that takes two sequences as arguments and appends the second one to the first.

Ship Rules Module Interface Specification (sh)

```
        package sh is                 -- Ship Rules

        -- Syntax:

        -- constants:
            Ship_Acceleration  : 0.1 -- knots/sec²
            Ship_Turn_Rate     : 0.1 -- (degrees/sec)/knot * Ship_Speed knots
            Max_Ship_Speed     : 30.0 -- knots
        -- types:
        --   coords : tuple of (
        --          dir   : real,
        --          speed : real,
        --          lat   : real,
        --          long  : real
        --          )
        -- access programs:
        --   s_init(   init_coords  : in coords );
        --   s_update;
        --   s_dir;
        --   s_speed;
        --   s_response( response  : in string );
        -- uses:
        --   lg.s_ship
        --   ed.s_display_msg
        --   ti.s_initiate_input
        --   ti.s_input_complete
        --   pd.s_indicator_display
        --   lg.g_game_speed
        -- exceptions: bad_dir, bad_speed, bad_pos

        -- Semantics:

        -- Implementors Assumptions:
```

```
--   s_init called exactly once at start or restart of game.
--   When the response from a user is bad, the user will continue to respond to each
--     prompt sent via ed.s_display_msg until a good response is input.
--   s_update is called once per second of game-time
-- State:
--   ship_coords    : coords
--   setting_dir    : boolean
--   setting_speed  : boolean
--   set_dir        : real
--   set_speed      : real

-- Transitions, Outputs and Exceptions:

--   s_init( init_coords : in coords ):
--   transition:
--     ship_coords, setting_dir, setting_speed := init_coords, FALSE, FALSE
--   exceptions:
--     use init_coords
--     (dir < 0 or dir > 360 -> bad_dir
--      | speed < 0 or speed > Max_Ship_Speed -> bad_speed
--      | lat < 0 or lat > Surface_Size
--        or long < 0 or long > Surface_Size -> bad_pos
--   s_update:
--   transition:
--     use ship_coords
--     dir,speed,lat,long := newdir, newspeed, newlat, newlong
--   exceptions:
--     none
--   s_dir:
--   transition:
--     setting_dir := TRUE
--   exceptions:
--     none
--   s_speed:
--   transition:
--     setting_speed := TRUE
--   exceptions:
--     none
--   s_response( response: in string );
--   transition:
--     (setting_dir and good_dir( response ) -> set_dir, setting dir :=
--                                        get_good_dir( response ), FALSE
--      |setting_speed and good_speed( response ) -> set_speed , setting_speed :=
--                                        get_good_speed( response ), FALSE
--   exceptions:
--     none

-- Local Constants:
-- Local Types:
-- Local Functions and Procedures:
--   newdir:
--     ( ship_coords.dir = set_dir -> return ship_coords.dir
--      |clockwise difference from ship_coords.dir to set_dir < 180
--        -> return min( (ship_coords.dir + Ship_Turn_Rate*ship_coords.speed) mod 360,
--                       set_dir)
--      |clockwise difference from ship_coords.dir to set_dir >= 180
--        -> return max( (ship_coords.dir-Ship_Turn_Rate*ship_coords.speed) mod 360,
--                       set_dir)
--   newspeed:
--     (ship_coords.speed = set_speed -> return ship_coords.speed
--      |ship_coords.speed  < set_speed ->
--              return min( set_speed, ship_coords.speed + Ship_Acceleration )
```

```
--      |ship_coords.speed > set_speed ->
--              return max( set_speed, ship_coords.speed - Ship_Acceleration )
--   newlat:
--     return ship_coords.lat + cos( ship_coords.dir ) * ship_coords.speed / 3600
--   newlong:
--     return ship_coords.long + sin( ship_coords.dir ) * ship_coords.speed / 3600
--   good_dir( response : string ) : real
--     convert response to real; if conversion fails or result is not between 0 and 360.0.
--     return FALSE; else return TRUE
--   get_good_dir( response : string ) : real
--     convert response to real and return value obtained
--   good_speed( response : string ) : real
--     convert response to real; if conversion fails or result is not between 0 and
--     Max_Ship_Speed, return FALSE; else return TRUE
--   get_good_dir( response : string ) : real
--     convert response to real and return value obtained

end sh;          --end of Ship Rules Interface Specification
```

Chaff Module Interface Specification (ch)

package ch is   **-- Chaff Module**

-- Syntax:

```
-- constants:
     Rounds_in_a_Load   : constant := 10;
     Fire_Interval      : constant := 20;   --seconds
     Reload_Time        : constant := 120;  --seconds
     Launch_Distance    : constant := 1000; --feet
     Max_Bloom_Radius   : constant := 500;  --feet
     Radius_Decay_Rate  : constant := 1     --feet/sec
-- types:
--   chaff_dir: set of {PORT,PORT135,ASTERN,STBD135,STBD}
--   bloom : tuple of (
--         lat  : real,
--         long: real,
--         dia  : real
--      ).
-- access programs:
--   s_init;
--   s_update;
--   s_chaff_launch( dir: in member of chaff_dir);
--   g_qty : integer;
--   g_bloom( id : in integer ): bloom;
-- uses:
--   ed.s_display_msg
--   pd.s_control_button_off
--   lg.g_ship
-- exceptions: not_exist, launch_illegal
```

-- Semantics:

```
-- Implementors Assumptions:
--   s_init called exactly once at start or restart of game.
--   s_update is called once per second of game-time
-- State:
--   chaff              : live_chaff
--   reload_time_count  : integer
--   fire_interval_count: integer
--   qty_remaining      : integer
```

-- Transitions, Outputs and Exceptions:

-- s_init:
--   transitions:
--   chaff.qty, reload_time_count, fire_interval_count, qty_remaining :=
--   0,0,0,Rounds_in_a_Load;
--   exceptions:
--   none;
-- s_update:
--   transitions:
--   update_live;
--   (fire_interval_count > 0 -> fire_interval_count := fire_interval_count - 1)
--   (reload_time_count > 0 -> reload_time_count := reload_time_count -1)
--   exceptions:
--   none;
-- s_chaff_launch(dir: in member of chaff_dir):
--   transitions:
--   launch_a_round;
--   exceptions:
--   (fire_interval_count > 0 or reload_time_count > 0) -> launch_illegal;
-- g_qty : integer;
--   output:
--   out := chaff.qty;
--   exceptions:
--   none;
-- g_bloom(id : in integer): bloom
--   output:
--   out := chaff.live[id];
--   exceptions:
--   not (id in [1,chaff.qty]) -> not_exist;

-- Local Constants: none
-- Local Types:
--   live_chaff : tuple of (
--   qty : integer,
--   live : sequence [1..qty] of bloom
--   );
-- Local Functions and Procedures:
--   update_live:
--   dead_cnt : integer := 0
--   for all id in [1,chaff.qty] begin
--   chaff.live[id].dia := chaff.live[id].dia - 2 * Radius_Decay_Rate
--   if chaff.live[id].dia < = 0 then
--   chaff.live := append(chaff.live[1..id-1],chaff.live[id + 1..chaff.qty]);
--   dead_cnt := dead_cnt + 1
--   end for
--   chaff.qty := chaff.qty - dead_cnt
--   launch_a_round:
--   if qty_remaining > 0 then
--   Get ship_pos from module lg;
--   Calculate lat, long from Launch_Distance, lg.g_ship.pos and lg.g_ship.dir.;
--   chaff.qty, chaff.live :=
--   chaff.qty + 1, append(chaff.live,(lat,long,Max_Bloom_Radius));
--   qty_remaining := qty_remaining - 1;
--   fire_interval_count := Fire_Interval;
--   call pd.s_control_button_off
--   else
--   reload_time_count := Reload_Time;
--   qty_remaining := Rounds_in_a_Load;
--   call ed.s_display_msg to post message "Chaff Launcher Reloading";
--   endif
end ch   --end of Chaff Module Interface Specification

Annex 2: Sample Module Program Specifications

-- Game_Types package includes the following declarations, among others:
Surface_Size   : constant : = 1000.0;   --Nautical miles
Max_Msg_Length : constant : = 60;   --characters
subtype Msg_String is string(1..Max_Msg_Length);

Ship Rules Module Program Specifications (sh):

-- Ada specific types: insert into sh package specification
  type Dir_Type is delta Ship_Turn_Rate range 0..360;
  type Speed_Type is delta Ship_Acceleration range 0..Max_Ship_Speed;
  type Dimension is delta 0.0001 range 0..Surface_Size;
  type Coords is
    record
      dir   :Dir_Type;
      speed :Speed_Type;
      lat   :Dimension;
      long :Dimension;
    end record;

-- Ada specific access program declarations: insert into sh package specification
  procedure s_init(init_coords : in Coords);
  procedure s_dir(dir   : in Dir_Type);
  procedure s_speed(speed   : in Speed_Type);

with lg, ed, ti, pd, Game_Types; use Game_Types;
package body Ship_Rules is
-- abstraction function
--   abstract.ship   : = concrete.Ship
--   abstract.set_dir   : = concrete.Set_dir
--   abstract.set_speed   : = concrete.Set_speed
-- definitions: none
-- concrete state
--   state invariant
--   use Ship_Coords
--   (dir > = 0 & dir < = 360 & speed > = 0 & speed < = Max_Ship_Speed)
--   declarations
      Ship_coords   : Coords;
      Setting_dir   : Boolean;
      Setting_speed : Boolean;
      Set_dir   : Dir_Type;
      Set_speed   : Speed_Type;
-- local functions and procedures:
--   newdir:
--   (Ship_coords.dir = Set_dir - > return Ship_coords.dir
-- |clockwise difference from Ship_coords.dir to Set_dir < 180
--   - > return min((Ship_coords.dir + Ship_Turn_Rate*Ship_coords.speed) mod 360,
--   Set_dir)
-- |clockwise difference from Ship_coords.dir to Set_dir > = 180
--   - > return max((Ship_coords.dir-Ship_Turn_Rate*Ship_coords.speed) mod 360,
--   Set_dir)
--   newspeed:
--   (Ship_coords.speed = Set_speed - > return Ship_coords.speed
-- |Ship_coords.speed > Set_speed - >
--   return min(Set_speed, Ship_coords.speed + Ship_Acceleration)
-- |Ship_coords.speed < Set_speed - >
--   return max(Set_speed, Ship_coords.speed - Ship_Acceleration)
--   newlat:
--   return Ship_coords.lat + cos(Ship_coords.dir) * Ship_coords.speed / 3600
--   newlong:
--   return Ship_coords.long + sin(Ship_coords.dir) * Ship_coords.speed / 3600

```
--   good_dir( response : Msg_String ) : real
--     convert response to real; if conversion fails or result is not between 0 and 360.0,
--     return FALSE; else return TRUE
--   get_good_dir( response : Msg_String ) : real
--     convert response to real and return value obtained
--   good_speed( response : Msg_String ) : real
--     convert response to real; if conversion fails or result is not between 0 and
--     Max_Ship_Speed., return FALSE; else return TRUE
--   get_good_dir( response : Msg_String ) : real
--     convert response to real and return value obtained


-- access program transitions, outputs and exceptions

    procedure s_init( init_coords : in Coords ) is
--   transition:
--     Ship_Coords := init_coords
--   exceptions:
--     use init_coords
--     (dir < 0 or dir > 360 -> bad_dir
--      | speed < 0 or speed > Max_Ship_Speed -> bad_speed
--      | lat < 0 or lat > Surface_Size
--        or long < 0 or long > Surface_Size -> bad_pos
    begin
     null;
    end s_init;
   s_update:
--   transition:
--     use Ship_coords
--     dir.speed.lat,long := newdir, newspeed, newlat, newlong
--   exceptions:
--     none
    begin
     null;
    end s_update;
    procedure s_dir is
--   transition:
--     Setting_dir := TRUE
--   exceptions:
--     none
    begin
     null;
    end s_dir;
    procedure s_speed is
--   transition:
--     Setting_speed := TRUE
--   exceptions:
--     speed < 0 or speed > Max_Ship_Speed -> bad_speed
    begin
     null;
    end s_speed;
    s_response( response : in Msg_String ):
--   transition:
--     (setting_dir and good_dir( response ) -> set_dir, setting dir :=
--                                 get_good_dir( response ), FALSE
--      | setting_speed and good_speed( response ) -> set_speed , setting_speed :=
--                                 get_good_speed( response ), FALSE
--   exceptions:
--     none
    begin
     null;
    end s_response;
end sh                   -- end of Ship Rules Module Program Specification
```

Chaff Module Program Specifications (ch):

    -- Ada specific types: insert in ch package specification
        type Chaff_dir is (PORT,PORT135,ASTERN,STBD135,STBD)
        type Dimension is delta 0.0001 range 0..Surface_Size;
        type Diameter_type is delta 2*Radius_Decay_Rate range 0..Max_Bloom_Radius
        type Bloom is
          record
           lat, long : Dimension;
           dia   : Diameter_type;
          end record

    -- Ada specific access program declarations: insert in ch package specification
    --   procedure s_init is
    --   procedure s_update;
    --   procedure s_chaff_launch(dir : in chaff_dir);
    --   function g_qty : integer;
    --   function g_bloom(id : in integer): bloom;

    with lg,ed,pd, Game_Types; use Game_Types;
    package body ch is   -- Chaff Module

    -- abstraction function:
        abstract.chaff.qty   := concrete.chaff.qty
        for all i in [1..chaff.qty] (abstract.chaff.live[i] := concrete.chaff.live(i))
        abstract.reload_time_count   := concrete.reload_time_count
        abstract.fire_interval_count   := concrete.fire_interval_count
        abstract.qty_remaining   := concrete.qty_remaining

    -- constants:
        Max_qty_live : constant := 20   -- function of 5 of the 6 package constants
    -- types:
        type chaff_qty_in_air is range 0..Max_qty_live;
        type live_chaff is
          record
            qty   : chaff_qty_in_air;
            live   : array(1..qty) of bloom;
          end record;
    -- definitions: none
    -- concrete state:
      -- state invariant:
      -- chaff.qty in [0..Max_qty_live]
      --   and for all i in [1..chaff.qty] (chaff.live(i).dia/2 in [0..Max_Bloom_Radius]
      --   and reload_time_count in [0..Reload_Time]
      --   and fire_interval_count in [0..Fire_Interval]
      --   and qty_remaining in [0..Rounds_in_a_Load]
      -- declarations:
        chaff   : live_chaff
        reload_time_count : integer range 0..Reload_Time
        fire_interval_count : integer range 0..Fire_Interval
        qty_remaining   : integer range 0..Rounds_in_a_Load

    -- local functions and procedures:
    --   update_live:
    --   dead_cnt : integer := 0
    --   for all id in [1.chaff.qty] begin
    --   chaff.live[id].dia := chaff.live[id].dia - 2 * Radius_Decay_Rate
    --   if chaff.live[id].dia <= 0 then
    --   chaff.live := append(chaff.live[1..id-1],chaff.live[id+1..chaff.qty]);
    --   dead_cnt := dead_cnt + 1
    --   end for
    --   chaff.qty := chaff.qty - dead_cnt

```
--    launch_a_round:
--      if qty_remaining > 0 then
--        Get ship_pos from module lg;
--        Calculate lat, long from Launch_Distance, lg.g_ship.pos and lg.g_ship.dir.;
--        chaff.qty, chaff.live : =
--            chaff.qty + 1, append(chaff.live.(lat,long,Max_Bloom_Radius));
--        qty_remaining : = qty_remaining - 1;
--        fire_interval_count : = Fire_Interval;
--        call pd.s_control_button_off
--      else
--        reload_time_count : = Reload_Time;
--        qty_remaining : = Rounds_in_a_Load;
--        call ed.s_display_msg to post message "Chaff Launcher Reloading";
--      endif

-- access program transitions, outputs and exceptions

      procedure s_init is
--    transitions:
--      chaff.qty, reload_time_count, fire_interval_count, qty_remaining : =
--            0,0,0,Rounds_in_a_Load;
--    exceptions:
--      none;
      begin
       null;
      end s_init;
      procedure s_update is
--    transitions:
--      update_live;
--      (fire_interval_count > 0 - > fire_interval_count : = fire_interval_count - 1)
--      (reload_time_count > 0 - > reload_time_count : = reload_time_count -1)
--    exceptions:
--      none;
      begin
       null;
      end s_update;
      procedure s_chaff_launch( dir  : in Chaff_dir) is
--    transitions:
--      launch_a_round;
--    exceptions:
--      (fire_interval_count > 0 or reload_time_count > 0) - > launch_illegal;
      begin
       null;
      end s_chaff_launch;
      function g_qty  : integer;
--    output:
--      out : = chaff.qty;
--    exceptions:
--      none;
      begin
       null;
      end g_qty;
      function g_bloom( id : in integer ): Bloom is
--    output:
--      out : = chaff.live[id];
--    exceptions:
--      not ( id in [1,chaff.qty] ) - > not_exist;
      begin
       null;
      end g_bloom;

end ch                -- end of Chaff Module Program Specification
```

Session 2:

University Perspective on Industry-Oriented Courses and Software Reuse
Moderator: Neal S. Coulter, Florida Atlantic University

Teaching an Industry-oriented Software Engineering Course
Bernd Bruegge, Carnegie Mellon University

Integrating Research, Reuse, and Integration into Software Engineering Courses
A. Jefferson Offutt and Roland H. Untch, Clemson University

Software Reuse in an Educational Perspective
Guttorm Sindre, Even-André Karlsson, and Tor Stålhane, Norwegian Institute of Technology

Teaching an Industry-oriented Software Engineering Course

Bernd Bruegge

School of Computer Science
Carnegie Mellon University
Pittsburgh, Pa. 15213

Abstract

Single project courses with a large number of participants are an excellent vehicle for teaching undergraduate students the problems of producing complex software systems. The emphasis placed on realistic development and delivery of a finalized product enables the students to appreciate software development as an engineering activity where cost/benefit decisions have to be made. In addition, students learn communication and project management techniques that are needed in many industrial settings.

In this paper we describe our criteria for the selection of projects that are complex enough to warrant large groups of developers but can still be developed in the limited time of a semester. We discuss our experience with different software development methodologies and process models, explore the problems of producing consistent and complete project documentation and describe an organizational and communicational structure that ensures a high chance of success.

The discussion is based on the experience with three project courses in which 12-30 students have designed, built and successfully delivered systems between 15,000 and 27,000 lines of code within a single semester.

1. Introduction

The primary objective of the undergraduate software engineering course at Carnegie Mellon University is teaching undergraduate students about the problems of building real-world software; groups of people must cooperate to understand what problem is being solved and then create and integrate a collection of software modules that solve the problem. The course is offered to junior and senior undergraduate students with a wide range of programming abilities but, in general, no experience in analysis and design techniques.

The student teams work on components of the product for a client, integrate their results and then attempt to pass an acceptance test set by the client. By carrying out the entire development cycle, rather than concentrating on a single phase alone, they observe or even learn how to execute all the roles that arise during the realization of such a project: planner, analyst, system designer, project leader, liaison and system integrator. Assigning all of the students to a single project adds real-world complexity to the communication aspects of software system development. An external ("real-world") client adds even more realism to the project. Students have to manage deadlines, interactions with a client, presentations of technical details and delivery of written documents. The emphasis on teamwork in a class project has a high positive impact on students and is becoming the preferred method for teaching project-oriented software engineering courses [Jacquot 90, Margo 90, Shaw 91].

The project styles differ from course to course, ranging from small projects, where the instructor divides the class into teams of 3 to 6 students [Knoke 91], to single large projects carried out by the entire class. A single project course has three main advantages over a course with several small project teams. First, it gives students a much more realistic exposure to the problems of teamwork and project organization; second, they have to analyze and design a system which is so complex that it cannot be developed by the heroic effort of a single programmer; and third, they have to deal with the problem of system integration and delivery in a realistic way. Successful single project courses involving 15 and more students have been reported [Bruegge 91,Tomayko 91] and our experience suggests that a single project course with up to 40 students can be taught.

In this paper we address some of the issues involved in running such a course successfully. The combined effect of dealing with beginners and the potential communication overhead makes the manageability of such a project questionable. Section 2 discusses the problem of finding topics for such a large team and we describe a class of realistic problems that fit very well into the classroom. The most important goal of our course is to give the students an appreciation of the problems of analysis and design of a large system. Section 3 describes the software development methodology and the process model used to achieve this goal. Section 4 specifies the set of deliverables that we ask the students to produce.

Sections 5 describes the project and communication structure we have chosen to make the project manageable and Section 6 summarizes our experience. Appendix I contains the syllabus of the undergraduate software engineering course currently taught at Carnegie Mellon University. Appendix II contains a sample of document templates handed out to the students during the course.

2. Finding a Project Topic

Finding a real problem for a single project course for 15 to 30 undergraduate students is one of the keys to running the course successfully. The problem is not to come up with a realistic topic per se. This is actually not difficult and some heuristics for finding topics have been published [Knoke 91]. But to be suitable for a large single project course the topic must have several important properties which are necessitated by the nature of the course: On the one hand, we want to have each of the students experience the complete software development process, in particular the system integration because we regard this as the most important aspect of a complex system. On the other hand, we can not assume that each of the students makes the same amount of progress.

The first property is that the problem should be decomposable into a set of modules which can be worked on by small groups of students. One of the problems with teaching software engineering to beginners is "flat staffing", that is, we immediately have to deal with 15 to 30 novice analysts and designers. By preempting part of the system design, we can reduce the initial problems due to the inexperience of the students. Assigning only a small group of students to each module also reduces the initial communication overhead.

Second, the modules should have a few but not too many dependencies (low coupling [Coad 92]) and they should be developed with the goal to be part of a single large system that solves the problem. If one of these modules is non-operational during system integration it should not prohibit the integration of the remaining modules. The system should still be demonstratable, if necessary with limited functionality.

Third, each of these modules should be balanced in terms of required resources and difficulty. Problems such as students dropping the course or unforeseen difficulties with a particular module have to be taken into account. One should not choose problems that are extremely hard to solve. In fact, the functionality of the individual modules should be relatively easy to implement.

Integrating Research, Reuse, and Integration into Software Engineering Courses

A. Jefferson Offutt* and Roland H. Untch

Department of Computer Science, Clemson University, Clemson SC, 29634-1906, USA

Abstract. This paper discusses a method for incorporating several important software engineering concepts that have been traditionally hard to teach
into courses at both the undergraduate and graduate level. We have created
a *project template* that can be instantiated in many ways to be tailored to
the level of a particular course, the number of students, the quality of students, and the goals of the course. We consider a "large" software project
to be one in which each programmer's contribution represents a small part
of the overall project (less than 10%). Our project template is a completed
software system, which, although too large for a semester project in its complete form, can be easily divided into coherent subsystems. The students are
provided with some subsystems, and asked to derive requirements for, design,
implement, and test the remaining subsystems. This approach allows the students to work in a large-project environment, reuse existing code, maintain
old code, and perform an integration of a significant system. This project
has been successfully used in undergraduate and graduate courses that have
completely diverging goals and purposes.

1 Introduction

One of the major difficulties with teaching software engineering, both at the undergraduate and graduate level, is that many of the engineering principles that are
so necessary with large-scale, multi-person development projects become hindrances
in projects that are small enough for students to complete in a single school term.
This makes it difficult not only to convince students that the engineering principles
are important, but also for students to internalize such principles through demon-
strations of the principles in realistic applications. In a previous paper, we reported
on a project organization that was successful in reaching some of these goals in an
undergraduate class [2]. We have since extended these ideas to realize other goals,
primarily related to research in software engineering.

We begin by presenting a list of educational goals for software engineering projects,
then discuss a *project template* that has been successfully used in both graduate and
undergraduate courses in several different forms. We define a project template to
be a system that can be instantiated into one of several projects supplying a large
amount of project support material while having the flexibility to be used to satisfy
a variety of goals.

---

* Current address: Department of Information Systems and Systems Engineering, George
Mason University, Fairfax VA, 22030, USA

Finally, the potential task should readily lend itself to the use of a good design methodology. Students should observe firsthand the ease with which a solution can be constructed if a good design methodology is used. The task has to be sufficiently complex that students can appreciate the difficulties involved in building a large system, especially if a design methodology is not applied. In fact, it should not be possible to solve the task by the heroic effort of one or two "hackers".

A good source for project topics fullfilling these requirements is the area of advanced information management systems such as multi-databases [Bright 92, Andleigh 92]. A multi-database can be seen as a browser interface to a set of different databases. This view lends itself easily to a design involving several database modules and a user interface. Each of the databases has to provide techniques for the storage, retrieval, manipulation and the display of data. The term "database" should be used in a loose way. It can be a simple file containing the phone numbers for the members of the department, a collection of satellite images, census files or an existing relational database. The problem statement should include queries involving the functionality of a single database as well queries accessing a subset or all of the databases. The goal is that each of the database modules can be developed and unit-tested mostly independently from the other modules, but that they have to be used together to answer more complex queries. The recommended approach for a user interface of a multi-databases is to build a graphical user interface (GUI) using toolkits such as X Windows (including Openlook, Motif, DECWindows and Interviews), IBM's Presentation Manager, NextStep, SunWindows or Microsoft Windows.

We have used the design and implementation of a multi-database as a project topic in three courses. In the Spring of 1991, we asked the students to build an interactive shared database browser, INTERACTIVE MAPS, that allows a user to "walk" through the CMU campus, enter class rooms and offices, and obtain schedule and personal information associated with the rooms' occupants. An important aspect of this project was the extensibility of the system. To prove the extensibility of the database browser, the client introduced an additional database at the middle of the semester. Part of the acceptance requirements was the successful integration of this unknown database into the student's design. The accepted system consisted of 15,000 lines of code and was written in C and Motif [Interactive Maps 91].

The project in the Fall semester 91, INTERACTIVE PITTSBURGH, allows a user to navigate through a shared database of visual and textual representations of the City of Pittsburgh, such as its streets, bus routes, landmarks and buildings. The amount and nature of the information to be displayed can be dynamically controlled by the user from a workstation with a graphical display. The students were asked to make their system backward compatible with INTERACTIVE MAPS. Starting with an existing system adds an important engineering component to the course, namely dealing with problems such as existing users. This adds even more realism to the project, because in many cases the first project a student will enter in industry is the maintenance of an existing system. The clients for the INTERACTIVE PITTSBURGH project were managers from the City Planning department and Port Authority of Allegheny County, who provided the project with digital maps of Pittsburgh's streets and bus stops. The system design was written in OMT [Rumbaugh 91a] and the accepted system consisted of 27,000 lines of code written in C++, C and Motif [Interactive Pittsburgh 91].

The project developed in the Spring semester 92, GEMS (Geographic environmental modeling system), is similar to INTERACTIVE PITTSBURGH but databases have been added to model changes in the environment. The system incorporates a model of the chemical processes involved in managing air

quality and enables the user to easily provide the information necessary for these calculations. Since a great deal of computational power is necessary to perform many of these calculations and a great quantity of data is needed as inputs and is produced as outputs, the students designed the system as a distributed database with different hosts handling different parts of the system. The underlying connections and the distribution of the databases are transparent to the user. An interesting aspect of the GEMS project was its increased emphasis on the use of tools. Instead of writing code from scratch the students were encouraged to use existing tools and software packages. The design of the user interface was done with MacroMind Director [MacroMind] and INTERVIEWS, a C++ toolkit for the rapid development of user interfaces [Linton 89]. OMT was chosen again as analysis and design tool, and FRAMEMAKER [Frame 90] was employed for the collaborative production of the documentation. The accepted system consisted of 20,000 lines of code written in C++, of which 9000 lines were written in Interviews [GEMS 92].

3. Managing the Process

Two central issues in the management of a project course are the selection of the software development methodology and the software process model. The software process model determines the order of the stages involved in software development and establishes the transition criteria for progressing from stage to stage. The software development methodology specifies how to navigate each of the phases of the software process model and how to present the phase products.

The Spring 91 course was taught with a software development methodology based on a mixture of two design approaches, data flow-oriented design [Yourdon 79] and object-based design using abstract data types [Liskov 86]. The requirements analysis and the design were done with the structured analysis and structured design tools available in StP [StP]. As instructors, we had problems using the SA/SD methodology. When teaching transform analysis as part of the transition from structured analysis to structured design, we found it difficult and time-consuming to convince the students that it is necessary to change not only the terminology but also the model when moving from analysis to design.

We are currently favoring an object-oriented software development methodology for consistent modeling during the whole development of the system. Among the software development methodologies supporting the involvement of a large group of designers, object-oriented methods are especially promising because by their nature they support the design of loosely coupled and cohesive modules. We are using the object modeling technique OMT because of its strong support for analysis and design as well as implementation and its support by a textbook [Rumbaugh 91a] and a tool [Rumbaugh 91b]. We chose OMT because it seems to strike the right balance between simplicity and expressive power, which makes it teachable within a semester and yet still be useful as a design tool for a single project course. We have had excellent experience with OMT. One of the major advantages of OMT is its ability to communicate a design without deep knowledge about the semantics of the notation. A comparison between the bulletin board communication patterns of the Spring 91 and Fall 91 classes indicates that the use of OMT led to a substantially smaller proportion of intergroup communication during system integration than did the use of a mix of SA/SD and object-based design [Bruegge 92].

To manage the development process, several methodologies are available for the teacher, ranging from the well-known waterfall model to various variants of prototyping. The DoD standard for software development essentially requires the use of the waterfall model [DoD-STD-2167A], but there is a general

agreement that this requirement continues to reinforce exactly the document-driven, specify-then-build approach that lies at the heart of so many software problems [Brooks 87]. Even though the disadvantages of the waterfall model are well-known it has one significant advantage. It is a good model for introducing software engineering concepts to novices, because it is possible to interleave the introduction of the deliverables in a simple way with the introduction of the development phases. Of course, a software life cycle with minimal iteration is possible only if the problem is well-defined. This is an important reason to pay careful attention to the selection of the requirements if a waterfall life cycle is used by the instructor.

Prototyping is an effective way of exploring alternative user interfaces for the system. And it is often the only way to extract requirements from a user who is not yet sure of the functionality of the system. One of the problems with early prototyping tools was that they were so inefficient that the prototype had to be thrown away after the user accepted it. This is no longer the case. Some of the prototyping tools available today allow for evolutionary prototyping where the prototype is already the seed for the final system. However, starting with evolutionary prototyping such as *"analyse a little, design a little, implement a little, analyse a little more, ..."* in an introductionary software engineering course is problematic. There are just too many issues that have to be taught simultaneously. Furthermore, students tend to neglect design issues when they start coding too early. Separating the implementation phase from the design phase makes them more aware of the importance of design and allows them to recognize design issues that they would not appreciate otherwise.

In our course we are now using a software process model consisting of a mix of prototyping and an object-oriented life cycle [Wirfs-Brock 90] with a large proportion, namely 9 weeks, spent on requirements analysis and design, 3 weeks for coding and 2 weeks for unit testing and system integration.

During the requirements analysis each of the teams specifies an analysis model for their module separately. Each analysis model is centered around the object model expressed in OMT, with additional methods supplied by the functional and dynamic models. For the specification of the dynamical model of the user interface we used state diagrams in the Fall 91 and screen forms in the Spring 92 semester. The Fall 91 user interface group had difficulties using the state diagram notation, which was generally regarded as too low-level. The Spring 92 students were much more at ease describing the user interface with sequences of screen forms, which were negotiated with the client and translated into code with the help of a user interface builder. We are now favoring this prototyping process to supplement the formulation of the dynamic model.

At the end of the requirements analysis the team specific object models are combined in a single object model placing the individual modules into separate OMTool sheets. In general this also involves some merges of the team specific models. The object models are a good medium for communication between and within the teams and with the client. In group meetings, different representations are discussed using different models on a white-board, and people take hard copies of their group's current document to other group meetings. They are also included in text form on bulletin boards and in the minutes of meetings.

During the object design phase, each group works on separate sheets of the object model. Signatures are generated from the model to form the basis of the code to be written by each group. At this point, the object model is taken under version control and managed by the configuration management group ("record keepers"), to ensure that the code is consistent with the object model. This technique helps to

reduce communication between the groups, since each group needs to look only at the object model to find out if changes have been made by other groups that could affect them.

Coding is strongly discouraged during the analysis and design phase. This makes students in general very uncomfortable, because they think that they have lost the touch with concepts they are familiar with. To make sure they are on firm grounds we tie the project phases intimately with homeworks and class lectures that show how analysis concepts such as classes and associations can be mapped into executable code. The ability of OMTool to generate C++ code from an object model supports this idea significantly and we repeatedly use it during the lectures on modeling. One implementation issue is the choice of the programming language. Because most of our students have extensive experience with the C programming language, C++ is an obvious choice. Most of the team members have been able to learn and use C++ productively within a semester.

We have had good experiences with review presentations describing the status of the project after each of the life cycle phases. The main goal of these reviews is to give *every* student the chance for an oral presentation. In general, a software engineering project course requires many lectures in the first few weeks of the course [Shaw 91], but not at the end of the semester. We used to schedule guest lectures on peripheral topics such as security or the job market to fill these slots [Bruegge 91], but we have now replaced them with the review presentations. A challenge for the teacher is the selection of the review presentation topics and assigning them to the students. We found that it works best to ask for volunteers for the initial presentations and assign the remaining talks to students who have not volunteered by the object design review deadline. We schedule a presentation dry run with each student to discuss the technical contents of the talk and make suggestions to the presentation style. We also send an e-mail feedback to each student after his or her presentation.

We place high emphasis on the timely delivery of the system, because we believe that this permits the students to experience the "engineering" aspects of software development. It forces the students to discuss many cost/benefit trade-offs and make decisions to deliver the system in time.

Our experience is that students can acquire the mechanics of software development in the process model scetched above and can then fully be exposed to a project requiring attention to system decomposition and changing requirements. Once the students have understood the distinction between "product" and "process", a different process model such as evolutionary prototyping *can and should be* employed. For example, all the software developers of the GEMS project, which used an evolutionary prototyping process model, had experience with the process model described above by participating in the INTERACTIVE PITTSBURGH project.

4. Managing the Deliverables

Our projects start with a problem statement handed out to the students at the beginning of the semester. An important aspect of the problem statement is the statement of the functional and global requirements for the system, in particular what constitutes a successful demonstration of the system at the end of the semester. It is desirable to formulate the system as a stand-alone service that the client wants to use.

Students should not be asked to develop the system from scratch. Using an existing system and extending the design in some aspects is an excellent opportunity to expose the students to large complex

systems. However, many existing systems are poorly documented and seldomly built with the software development methodology taught in the course, and therefore not many good examples are available to teach good design practice, so some trade-offs have to be made. A good solution is to start a modest project from scratch with one class and use the system produced by the class as the base system for succeeding classes. This philosophy has been applied successfully by several teachers [Jacquot 90]. The advantage is that the teacher becomes familiar with the system requirements and can guide the students during the development process.

To build a well-engineered system, our students have to produce deliverables throughout the semester. The deliverables correspond to the phases of the object-oriented software life cycle used by OMT [Rumbaugh 91a] covering analysis, system design, object design and implementation. We ask the students to produce documents for each of these phases. In addition the students have to produce documents after the planning phase, the unit testing phase and system testing phase, respectively. The final deliverable is a demonstration of the running system.

We treat the production of the technical documentation as a process that is very similar to the software development process [Levine 91] and we hand out templates for each of the documents before the corresponding development phase begins. These templates are seen as the "seed" for the full documents to be produced. The templates contain an outline of the topics and sentences or questions designed to trigger the writing process. Two examples of these document templates are given in Appendix II.

In the following we discuss each of the documents in more detail. The Software Project Management Plan (SPMP) is a detailed schedule for individual milestones of each module. The document sets up a schedule of activities for a group and specified personnel assignments using the Macproject project management tool [MacProject]. An SPMP is extremely useful because it helps to tie the members of the class together as part of a larger organism. Because it is unrealistic to expect the students to write a full-fledged SPMP at the beginning of the semester, we prepare major parts of the plan with a template based on the IEEE standard [IEEE 1058], leaving out several sections to be filled in by the students. If the project has a planner group, only a rough schedule is created and the planner group is responsible for the refinement of the schedule. Without a planner group, the instructor creates a much more detailed schedule.

The requirements analysis document is described to the students as a complete and consistent description of the problem statement, serving as the basis of the design. We found that Rumbaugh's OMT methodology supports requirements analysis in a way that can easily be understood by beginners. The students have to provide three descriptions of the system following Rumbaugh's methodology. The object model describes the static structure of the system, in particular the object classes and associations between objects. The dynamic model shows the behavior of the system using scenarios to describe typical and exceptional sessions. The functional model describes the functional decomposition of the system. Data flow diagrams are used to show the computation of output values as the result of input (and other) values.

The main difficulty for the students during requirements analysis is to get the basic understanding and definition of the problem domain. This step depends very much on communication skills, intuition and the experience level of the students. In an introductory software engineering course we don't expect the

students to be able to deal with incomplete requirements to be negotiated interactively with an external client. Instead, the students are given a fixed set of requirements which we don't expect to be changed significantly during the course. In an advanced software engineering course, however, the requirements can be incomplete and the students are expected to interact with the client for the full duration of the course to clarify and complete the requirements specified in the problem statement.

The system design document describes the design goals, decomposition of the system in terms of modules and layers, the identification of concurrency, hardware-software trade-offs, data and file management, implementation of control, and boundary conditions such as startup and finalization. It also shows that the system model (object, dynamic and functional model) from the requirements analysis adequately covers the queries mentioned in the problem statement[1].

The system design is the hardest phase for the students. While they understand the requirements analysis as a reformulation of the problem statement and are supported by the modeling tool OMTool, they experience more difficulties when attempting the design. The main reason is, of course, that the design activity is inherently difficult and there are usually many possible design solutions for any particular problem. The time limitation imposed by the course does not allow time for too many design iterations. Because of this reason the teacher should do a preliminary system design, in particular the system decomposition, before the beginning of the project. Despite the existence of this decomposition, the students should not be discouraged to look at different designs. In general, there are always some students who come up with alternative designs. In this case we schedule an extra class where the students have to present and discuss the design alternatives and a decision is then made which design to implement [Bruegge 91].

An important suggestion to make the design phase easier, is to treat the design document as a group document. In earlier courses we had asked each of the teams to produce their own requirement analysis and system documents. The underlying idea was to expose each of the students to the problems involved in describing a design. This documentation style fits well into a traditonal teaching environment, because it allows the instructor to grade the individual students according to their contribution to these documents. It is also easier for the students because of the reduced communication flow, but it has severe problems. It creates a flood of documents, none of which reflects the overall system. In addition, the students often do not have the time to understand or even discuss the documents produced by the other groups. In the Fall 91 course we switched to *single documents* for requirements analysis and for system design produced by a small group of volunteers representing the whole class. The advantage of such an approach is that project-wide unified documents are created for these important phases. The question is, of course, how to grade such a document. We have made a decision to give a single group grade for each of the documents and have had good experience with it. There are plenty of other opportunities in a course project to judge the students individually if necessary.

The remaining documents for the object design and unit test are module specific and can therefore be produced on a team basis. The object design document refines and possibly collapses classes and operations defined in the requirements analysis document. In particular, it contains a more detailed description of the object model in both graphical form (OMT diagrams) and textual form (class descriptions). The main purpose of the object document is to publish the signatures of public methods

---

[1]Rumbaugh makes this part of the requirements analysis but our experience is that it is better if placed into the system design

that can be invoked by other classes.

The unit test manual is produced during the coding phase. It specifies a set of tests for each module, and contains instructions on the application of those tests for a system maintainer, so that a given module's functionality can easily be tested and evaluated. The system test manual describes the overall system test plan, instructions for performing the tests, and metrics for evaluating them. We do not insist on an exhaustive description of test cases. Instead, we ask the students to select a few test cases which they think are representitive of the system and document these cases carefully.

In addition, the students are asked to produce a user's manual and an installation manual. In the Spring 92 semester we introduced technical writers whose primary responsibility was the production of the user manual. Our experiences with technical writers in a software engineering course are described in Section 5.

We also ask the students to produce a software configuration management plan. While the merits are known to every seasoned software engineer, introducing a configuration management document has its problems. Students tend to regard the insistence on configuration management as a bureaucratic obstacle. Adherence to the IEEE standard is good idea, but the teacher should make sure not to be too formal. We have dealt with this problem by asking the students to add a small chapter "Software configuration management" to the SPMP instead of producing a separate document. The emphasis in the chapter should be on the identification of configuration items and a description of the release policy. There is no need to insist on the formulation of a change control board in such a limited time frame.

Because of the temporal restrictions on the delivery of the system, we cannot insist on full consistency and completeness of the documents and we accept incomplete documentation in the following way. After a document is reviewed the first time we issue a document containing our comments (with extra care taken for the review of the requirements analysis and system design documents). The students are then asked to incorporate these comments into a new version which is baselined. If a baselined document requires more changes, we do not insist that the document be changed again. Instead, we view our new comments as a supplement to the existing documentation.

5. Managing the Students

We cannot expect the students to be familiar with project management and tackle these problems at the very beginning of the semester. To enable a successful delivery of the system within the given deadline, several decisions have to be made by the instructor. For example, as mentioned before, we provide the students with a rough decomposition of the problem, consisting of several modules. A group of students is assigned to each of these modules and is responsible for designing and implementing it as part of the system. Such a decomposition preempts decisions which, in a real project, should be made later during the system design phase. However, we believe that in a basic software engineering course these decisions have to be made before the project starts to give the project a good chance of success.

The decomposition of the modules should be done along functional aspects. In general we define groups that are responsible for each of the databases and for the user interface module. A good size for each of these groups is 4 to 6 students. Various aspects in the assignment must be considered, such as balance in experience, group size and preferences indicated by the students, but in general we have not experienced any difficulties with these assignments.

Within each software development group, six roles have to be filled: group leader (which is rotated among group members), group planner, liaison (the interface to the other groups), document editor, programmer, and record keeper. Aside from mandating that every student has to perform as group leader at some point during the project, we let each group assign roles as they see fit. This includes the possibility that people concurrently fill multiple roles (programmer being the most obvious example), in particular if the group size is smaller than six.

We advocate a system decomposition with 4 to 6 modules. If the class consists of more than 20 students, the instructor should consider the introduction of support teams instead of adding more database modules. We have already collected hands-on experience with several such teams, in particular with a tools group, a planner group, technical writers and a graphical designer. In the following we describe our experience with each of these groups.

The toolsmith as a new specific position in an object-oriented software development team was first advocated by Booch [Booch 91]. We introduced a tools group in the Fall 91 course, initially with the task of developing classes that apply to more than one database. Because of the newness of the concept, we experimented quite a bit and the tasks of the tools group were frequently redefined during the semester. For example, to support the information flow between the other groups and the tools group, we introduced "floating liaisons", who would attend each of the other groups' weekly meetings. This improved the communication between the groups, but increased the work load for the members of the tools group significantly. Our experience suggests that the tools group is an extremely useful concept for a single project course. However, the teacher should inform students before joining the tools group that they will experience a higher time involvement than students in the other groups.

The purpose of the planner group is to introduce the students to the problems of project management. The main task of the planners is the completion of the skeleton of the software project management plan (SPMP) handed out by the teacher. In the Spring 92 course, we added configuration management as another planner task. The specific task was the addition of a software configuration management plan following the IEEE guide [IEEE 1042] as an additional chapter to the SPMP. We encourage the planners to do *project tracking*, that is, to describe the progress of the project while it is being developed. We don't think *project planning* is achievable in our course. The goal is to have the students track the current project in such a way that they might be able to use the resulting project "plan" as a template for their next project.

In the Spring 92 course we included for the first time technical writers in our course. Having a technical writer team in the project has ensured consistency and completeness of the documentation in a manner unexperienced in the two previous courses where the software developers were also responsible for the documentation. The production of the documentation follows a prototyping model, with several interaction cycles between writers (editor) and developers (key writer and key reviewer) as shown in figure 5-1. For example, the user manual starts with a rapid prototype based on the dynamic model developed during the requirements analysis. The writers interact mostly with the user interface team and present the user manual at each of the project reviews during the project course. The technical writers are also given the responsibility for making project-specific changes to the document templates and for the version control of the documents.

FrameMaker [Frame 90] is used as the general document processing tool. For the students who are

- Editor plans document with key writer
- Editor reviews and updates document template
- Key writer creates first draft based on template
- Key writer and editor review first draft
- Key writer produces revision of draft
- Editor converts second draft into FrameMaker document
- The document is placed under version control (RCS)
- Key reviewer reviews second draft
- Editor edits second draft and produces base line version
- Key reviewer proofs base line version for accuracy
- Editor completes final proof of the document

Figure 5-1: The Interaction between Technical Writers and Software Developers

not familiar with FrameMaker or who are used to their own favorate text editors, the technical writers establish a standard specifying the submission of documents in "raw ascii".

Collaborative annotation of documents is also handled by the writers. We use traditional master copies with handwritten notes and bulletin board posts but we also started experimenting with *collaborative annotation* of documents: The documents were stored at a single location and were available for comments by each of the project members. Annotations were done with FrameMaker *markers* and *cross references* to indicate small changes to the document. Bigger changes were indicated by change bars (which can be removed only by the technical writers). Our experience with this annotation scheme has not been very good. One of the reasons is that most of the students are not familiar with FrameMaker and there is a high learning curve associated with the tool. Another reason is that the annotation mechanisms provided by FrameMaker are too-level for collaborative annotation. For example, annotations done with markers can easily be overlooked by the reviewer. Other approaches such as voice annotation [Neuwirth 90] are currently being evaluated.

A feature that was successfully used in the course to achieve consistency among documents is FrameMaker's *book* file, which lists the various project documents stored in separate files. This allows the technical writers to generate a table of contents and indices from all the documents in the book and ensures consistent formatting across documents. The book allows us also to tailor the documentation into various sets. For example, we defined a *project book* containing the complete project information. With network-wide access to the developer book, each of the project members could always get up-to-date information about the status of the documentation. Others books were tailored to the respective audience. For example, the *client book* contained the problem statement, SPMP and requirements analysis, but not the object design, unit testing and system testing documents. The *user book* contained only the user manual.

In addition to benefitting from the skills of technical writing students, we have also had good experience with the addition of a graphical designer to the course in the Spring 92 semester. The graphical designer, a student from Carnegie Mellon's design department, interacted with the software designer of the user interface group in designing the database menus, screen forms and reports. Because we could not

assume the graphical designer to be familiar with the OMT modeling methodology, we modified Rumbaugh's dynamic modeling process [Rumbaugh 91a] and used *illustrative prototyping* instead of state diagrams.   In particular, the dynamic model of the user interface was completely expressed with "storyboards", that is, sequences of screen dumps. These were initially produced by hand and later with the MacroMind Director tool [MacroMind].   The screen dumps were then translated by the software designer with the help of the Interviews tool kit. Both designers met regularly with the client to discuss and modify the look and feel of the user interface. The interaction between the graphical designer and the software designer of the user interface used in the GEMS project is shown in figure 5-2. We highly recommend this prototyping process to other instructors.

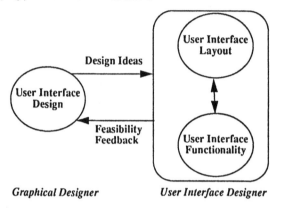

Figure 5-2: Interaction between the Graphical Designer and Software Designer of the User Interface

The formation of each of the teams mentioned above should be done at the beginning of the project. Students, once they have joined a team, are rarely mobile enough to switch to another group. In fact, they often associate themselves very deeply with the group, making a switch to another group almost impossible. We have tried several times to "load balance" groups in mid-semester, in particular after students dropped the course, but do not have good experience with it. We now think it is better to leave the initial group structure unchanged and reduce the functional requirements in a way that the smaller group can proceed.

The interaction of software engineering students with technical writers and graphical designers, exposed each of the students to new knowledge in areas which are not part of the traditional software education, but which are needed for the "engineering" aspects of the system. Given our experience with these groups, we advocate their inclusion into future software engineering courses.

6. Summary and Conclusions

Single project courses for a medium-sized problem with real data and real clients are an excellent vehicle to experience the problems associated with the production of complex software systems. In this paper we have described our criteria for the selection of complex projects that warrant large groups of 30 and more students, but can still be developed in the limited time of a semester. We have identified multi-databases as a rich source of topics for large project courses and presented a set of deliverables that can be realized by the students within the given time.

We have had good experience with an object-oriented life cycle model for the introduction of software engineering concepts. For the software development we advocate an object-oriented methodology such as OMT for consistent modeling during the whole development of the system.

To expose the students to the various software process models, we suggest two kinds of project courses, a basic and an advanced course. The basic course applies an object-oriented life cycle model, allowing the instructor to interleave the introduction of deliverables in a simple way with the introduction of the life cycle phases. The problem statement is formulated with a fixed set of requirements and a preliminary system design is done by the teacher before the start of the project. Once the students have understood the distinction between "product" and "process", they can take the advanced course which employs a different process model such as prototyping. In this advanced course the students actively participate in the negotiation and formulation of the requirements and in the system decomposition.

We have also experimented with the introduction of new groups in the project structure, in particular a designer group responsible for the look and feel of the user interface, a technical writer group for the production of the documentation and a tools group for the development and definition of reusable objects across teams. The involvement of students from other areas who are not software engineeering experts has increased the "engineering" component of our projects significantly. Our experience suggests that these groups enhance the chance of success in a large single project course.

7. References

[Andleigh 92] Prabhat K. Andleigh, Michael R. Gretzinger, Distributed Object-Oriented Data-Systems Design, Prentice Hall 1992.

[Booch 91] G. Booch. Object-Oriented Design with Applications, Benjamin Cummings, 1991.

[Bright 92] M. Bright, A. Hurson and Simin Pakzad, A Taxonomy and Current Issues in Multi-database Systems, Computer, Vol 25, No 3, pp 50-59, March 1992.

[Brooks 87] F. P. Brooks (1987), Report of the Defense Science Board Task Force on Military Software, Alexandria, VA: Defense Technical Information Center.

[Bruegge 91] B. Bruegge, J. Cheng and M. Shaw. A Software Engineering Course with a Real Client, Carnegie Mellon University, Technical Report CMU-SEI- 91-EM-4, July 1991.

[Bruegge 92] B. Bruegge, J. Blythe, J. Jackson and J. Shufelt, Object-Oriented System Modeling with OMT, Conference on Object-Oriented Programming Systems, Languages and Applications (OOPSLA '92), Vancouver, October 1992.

[Coad 91] P. Coad and E. Yourdon, Object-Oriented Design Prentice Hall, 1991.

[DoD-STD-2167A] Military Standard, Defense System Software Development, DoD, Washington D.C. 20301, February 1988.

[Frame 90] Frame Technology Corporation. FrameMaker Documentation, September 1990.

[GEMS 92] GEMS, a geographic environmental modeling system. 15-499 Advanced software engineering, System documentation submitted by the students, Carnegie Mellon University, May 1992.

[IEEE 1042] IEEE Guide to Software Configuration Management, in Software Engineering Standards, Spring 1991 Edition.

[IEEE 1058] IEEE. Standard 1058.1 for Software Project Management Plans, in Software Engineering Standards, Spring 1991 Edition.

[Interactive Maps 91]
Interactive Maps. 15-413 Software Engineering, System documentation submitted by

the students, Carnegie Mellon University, December April 1991.

[Interactive Pittsburgh 91]
Interactive Pittsburgh.   15-413 Software Engineering, System documentation submitted by the students, Carnegie Mellon University, December 1991.

[Jacquot 90]   J.P. Jacquot, J. Guyard, L. Boidot. Modeling Teamwork in an Academic Environment, in Software Engineering Education, J.E. Tomayko (ed.), Lecture Notes in Computer Science, Springer Verlag, pp. 110-122, 1990.

[Knoke 91]   P. Knoke. Medium Size Project Model: Variations on a Theme, in Software Engineering Education, J.E. Tomayko (ed.), Lecture Notes in Computer Science, Springer Verlag, pp. 7-24, 1991.

[Linton 89]   M.A Linton, J.M. Vlissides, P.R. Calder, Composing User Interfaces with Interviews, Computer, Vol 22, No 2, pp. 8-22, February 1989.

[Liskov 86]   B. Liskov and J. Guttag, Abstraction and Specification in Program Development, MIT Press, 1986.

[MacProject]   MacProject II V2.1. Project Management Tool, Claris Corporation, Santa Clara, CA.

[MacroMind]   MacroMind Director V2.0. MacroMind, Inc. San Francisco, Ca.

[Margo 90]   V. Margo, P. Feibig and D. Etter. Avoiding the tarpits - software's challenge, IEEE Potentials, pp. 9 - 12, February 1990.

[Mynatt 90]   B. T. Mynatt, Software Engineering With Student Project Guidance, Prentice Hall 1990.

[Neuwirth 92]   Neuwirth, C.M., Kaufer, D.S., Chandhok, R., Morris, J.H. (1990).   Issues in the Design of Computer Support for Co-authoring and Commenting. Proceedings of CSCW'90 Conference on Collaborative Work, pp. 183-195. Los Angeles, CA, October 7-10, 1990.

[Levine 92]   L. Levine, L. H. Pesante, S. B. Dunkle, Technical Writing for Software Engineers, Curriculum Module SE-CM-23, Software Engineering Institute, Carnegie-Mellon University, November 1991.

[Pfleeger 91]   S.Pfleeger. Software Engineering: The production of quality software, MacMillan, 1991.

[Rumbaugh 91a]   J. Rumbaugh, M. Blaha, W. Premerlani, F. Eddy and W. Lorenson. Object-Oriented Modeling and Design, Prentice Hall, Englewood Cliffs, NJ, 1991.

[Rumbaugh 91b]   J. Rumbaugh. Object Modeling tool (OMTool) User's Manual, GE Corporate Research and Development, Schenectady, NY, August 1991.

[Shaw 91]   M. Shaw and J. Tomayko. Models for Undergraduate Project Courses in Software Engineering, in Software Engineering Education, J.E. Tomayko (ed.), Lecture Notes in Computer Science, Springer Verlag, pp. 33-71, 1991.

[StP]   Interactive Development Environments. Software through Pictures (StP) User and Reference Manual, March 1990.

[Tomayko 91]   J. Tomayko. Teaching a Project-Intensive Introduction to Software Engineering, Software Engineering Institute, Carnegie Mellon University, Technical Report CMU-SEI-91-EM-6, July 1991.

[Wirfs-Brock 90]   R. Wirfs-Brock, B. Wilkerson and L. Wiener. Designing Object-Oriented Software, Prentice Hall, Englewood Cliffs, NJ 1990.

[Yourdon 79]   E. Yourdon and L. Constantine, Structured Design: Fundamentals of a Discipline of Computer Program and Systems Design, Prentice Hall, Englewood Cliffs, NJ, 1979. Press, 1992.

I. Course Syllabus

This appendix contains a revision of the syllabus for the undergraduate software engineering course taught at Carnegie-Mellon University in the Fall semester 1991. During the semester we made various changes to the syllabus handed out to the students in August 1991. These changes involved mostly reordering of lectures to improve the match between lectures and project phases.

The syllabus is grouped in three major parts. After two lectures about project planning, the modeling process is introduced in a bottom up fashion in the next six lectures. These lectures follow Rumbaugh's textbook very closely. Note that we do not include Chapter 4 in the course which deals with advanced object modeling concepts. The goal of the lectures is an understanding of the basic OMT modeling process. The advanced concepts are being taught in the project meetings if necessary. The middle part of the syllabus deals with requirements analysis and system design based on the OMT modeling methodology. Before we proceed to object design, we introduce Smalltalk and C++. The students are familiar with C, so the lecture on C++ deals mainly with the differences between C and C++. The third part of the syllabus introduces the backend of the life cycle, in particular unit and system testing, delivery and maintenance. These lectures are adapted from Pfleeger's textbook.

The purpose of the homeworks is to make the students fluent in the use of OMT. The first two homeworks are aimed at the completion of partially completed object diagrams, such as an air transportation system (Figure E 3.7 in [Rumbaugh 91a]) and the creation of the corresponding OMT diagrams with OMTool. After these homeworks the students should be able to work with the tool. The purpose of the third homework is to give the students the feeling that an OMT model leads naturally to an implementation in C++. This homework asks the students to take the object diagram on page 196 of Rumbaugh, loosely described in exercise 8.3 (a), and implement the objects in C++, so that small files can be sent between the sender and receiver objects. We require the code to be generated from OMTool. Because the students are generally not experienced in team work, we also ask them to work in groups of up to three people to solve this homework.

Software Engineering Fall 1991 Syllabus

People

Office Hours Office

Instructor:
  Bernd Bruegge
  bruegge@cs.cmu.edu
  Wed 4:30-5:00 pm
  Wean Hall 3206 x2567
Teaching Assistants:
  Jim Blythe
  jblythe@b.gp.cs.cmu.edu
  Tue 3:00-4:00 pm
  Wean Hall 8402 x3076

  Jeff Jackson
  jcj@a.gp.cs.cmu.edu
  Tue 10:30-11:30 am
  Wean Hall 8117 x2580

  Jeff Shufelt
  js@maps.cs.cmu.edu
  Wed 3:00-4:00 pm
  Wean Hall 3408 x8750
Secretary:
  Ava Cruse
  avac@b.gp.cs.cmu.edu
  Mon-Fri 8:30am-5:00 pm
  Wean Hall 4611 x3825

Aside from office hours and weekly project meetings please feel free to stop by and make individual appointments.

Objectives

Upon completion of this course, a student should

- Understand the difference between a program and a software product.

- Be able to reconstruct the analysis and design information in an existing software system.

- Be able to design and implement a module that will be integrated in a larger system.

Each student will have demonstrated the ability to

- Work as a member of a project team, assuming various roles as necessary,

- Create and follow project plans and test plans,

- Create the full range of documents associated with software products,

- Complete a project on time.

Administrative Matters

Meeting Times

Class meetings: Tuesdays and Thursdays 9:00-10:30 in WeH 5427.
Project Meetings: Weekly arranged by each team.

Textbooks

J. Rumbaugh et. al., *Object Modeling and Design*, Prentice-Hall 1991.
S. L. Pfleeger, *Software Engineering*, Macmillan Publishing Company, 1991.

Additional readings

G. Booch, *Object-Oriented Design with Applications*, Benjamin/Cummings, 1991.
M. Shaw, *Larger-Scale systems require higher-level abstractions*,
  Proceedings of the 5th International Workshop on Software Specification
  and Design, pp. 143-146, May 1989.

Computing

The project will be implemented as a service in Andrew.
If you don't have an Andrew account, we'll help you get one.
The course bulletin board is academic.cs.15-413 and various sub-bboards.
Subscribe to them.

In addition to the standard Andrew environment, the following tools will be used:
MacProject, a project management tool for planning and tracking the project.
OMTool, a workstation-based graphical tool for the preparation and maintenance of the object model.

Grading

Project: 60%
Equal weight (10 points) is given to each of the following :
Project plan, requirements analysis document, design documents (system and detailed design),
implementation, unit test manual, system test manual, user manual, installation guide.
Special incentive: If a complete product (working code and complete documentation)
with core functionality is delivered to the client as a joint effort of the course,
all students will receive at least 75 of the 80 project points.

Homework: 20%
5 points for each of 4 homeworks.

Quiz: 20%
1 point for short quiz on main points of reading at the beginning of each class
(except project meeting classes).

Instructors' evaluation: adjustment of up to 5%

Standards[2]

A: 110+
B: 100-109
C: 90-99, including at least 25 points from lectures and 70 points from project
D: 80-89, or 90-99 with wrong proportion of lecture and project points
R: less than 80

Course Schedule

Date	Lecture Topic	Readings	Homeworks	Deliverable
Aug 29	**Introduction** > Overview of course, > Introduction into project > *Project presentation by sponsor*			
Sep 3	**What is Software Engineering?** > Dealing with complexity > Software life cycle	Booch 1 Pfleeger 1		
Sep 5	**Project Management** > Software project management > WBS, planning and scheduling > SPMP template	IEEE Std 1058		
Sep 10	**Project Planning** > Cost estimation > Project management tools (Mac-Project)	Pfleeger 2		
Sep 12	**Software Development Concepts** > Software processes > Process vs Product > Software development methodologies > Standards (IEEE, MIL)	Rumbaugh 1 + 12		

---

[2]The project has 80 available points and the lecture 40.

Sep 17	**Object Modeling** > Objects, classes, links > Inheritance > OMT notation & Usage of OMTool	Rumbaugh 2 + 3	HW#1 out	Project Plan due
Sep 19	**Dynamic Modeling** > Event based model > State diagrams > Relation to object modeling	Rumbaugh 5		
Sep 24	**Functional Modeling** > Data flow diagrams > Constraints > Relation to object & dynamic modeling > SA/SD notation	Rumbaugh 6	HW#1 due	
Sep 26	**Requirements Analysis** > Combining object, dynamic & functional modeling > Requirements analysis template	Rumbaugh 8	HW#2 out	
Oct 1	**Requirements Analysis II** > Case study: CAD system	Rumbaugh 20.3		
Oct 3	**System Design** > Design goals > Breaking a system in subsystems > Concurrency, hardware/software trade-offs > Data management, control, boundary conditions > System design template	Rumbaugh 9	HW#2 due	
Oct 8	**Project review meeting** > Oral presentation of project plan and requirements analysis			Requirements Analysis, RED[3]
Oct 10	**Prototyping** > Illustrative, simulated, functional & evolutionary prototyping > Smalltalk > Building a user interface			
Oct 15	**Software Design II** > Architectural frameworks > Research on software architectures	Shaw 89		
Oct 17	**Introduction Into C++** > Features of OO languages > C vs C++ > Overloading > Compile time type checking > Base and derived classes > Calling mechanisms, exception handling > Inheritance and encapsulation		HW#3 out	System Design Document RED
Oct 22	**Object Design** > Obtain operations from models > Design algorithms, control, associations > Determine object representations	Rumbaugh 10+11		

---

[3]RED = Revisions of all Earlier Documents

> Package classes and links into modules

Oct 24	**Implementation** > Programming style Rumbaugh 13-15 > Translating a design into an implementation > Implementation with an OO language (C++)	HW#3 due	
Oct 29	*Project Review with Sponsor* > Oral presentation of project plan, requirements analysis, system design and prototype	RED	
Oct 31	**Unit & Integration Testing** > Unit & integration testing Pfleeger 7 > Regression testing > Estimating software quality > Test life cycle > Unit test plan template		
Nov 5	**System Testing & Test documentation** > Explanation of HW#4 Pfleeger 8 > Types of system testing > System tuning > α-β testing > System test plan template	HW#4 out	
Nov 7	**System Delivery and Maintenance** > Documentation Pfleeger 9 + 10 > Corrective, adaptive, preventive maintenance		Detailed Design Document due
Nov 12	**Configuration Management** > SCM Activities IEEE Std 1042 > Tailoring, conformance to SCM standard > SCMP template		
Nov 14	**Abstraction & Specification**		
Nov 19	**Project review meeting** Oral presentation of object design	HW#4 due	RED, Unit Test Manual due
Nov 21	**Examining the Development Process** > Reuse Pfleeger 11 Reengineering & Reverse engineering > CASE tools > SEI process maturity model		
Nov 26	**Software Law**		System Test Manual due,
Nov 28	*Thanksgiving*		
Dec 3	**Project meeting** > Dry run for project acceptance > Course evaluation		
Dec 5	*Project Acceptance by Sponsor* > Oral presentation of project.		User Manual & Installation Guide due
Dec 19	*Grades due.*		RED

II. Document Templates

We hand out templates for each of the documents to be delivered by the students. All of our templates are based on other documents or, if available, on existing standards and may be tailored to the project by the technical writers. The SPMP (Software Project Management Plan) and SCMP (Software Configuration Management Plan) templates are adapted from the IEEE Standards [IEEE 1058, IEEE 828]. The templates for the requirements analysis document merges suggestions from Rumbaugh [Rumbaugh 91a] and Mynatt [Mynatt 90]. Chapter 11 in Rumbaugh's textbook served as the basis for the system design and object document templates. Templates for the unit and system test manuals are adapted from Chapter 7 and 8 in Pfleeger's textbook [Pfleeger 91]. For space reasons we list only the templates for the requirements analysis and the system design documents, but FrameMaker and Scribe versions for each of the templates are available from the author.

Requirements Analysis Document Template

```
Primary Audience:              Developers
Secondary Audience:            Client
```

Abstract

<This document is a complete and consistent restatement of the problem statement for the proposed system and serves as a basis for the design. The document also includes design goals and comments on the feasibility of the proposed system.>

1 General goals

<Provide a prose description of the problem to be solved and the proposed solution. Write at a general introductory level>

2 Current system

<Refer to existing documentation or model the current system using object, functional and dynamic models if appropriate. Include a description of the current files and directory structure. If there is no current system, this section should be deleted.>

3 Proposed system

<Describe the models of the proposed system, its global requirements and feasibility.>

3.1 System model

<The system model consists of the object model, dynamic model and functional model of the proposed system.>

3.1.1 Object model

<Identify object classes, write a data dictionary, list the associations and attributes, identify inheritance. Describe the object model with figures created by OMTool. Consistency check: All items in the data dictionary should be defined in the object model>

3.1.2 Dynamic model

<This should include event scenarios, event traces, event flow diagrams, and a state diagram for each object with important dynamic behavior.>

3.1.3 Functional model

<This should include input and output values, data flow diagrams and a description of what each function does. Consistency check: All external files should be mentioned in the data flow diagram>

3.2 Global requirements

3.2.1 User interface and human factors
<This should include who the user will be, if training is required,whether or not it is particularly important that the system be easy to learn, and what sort of input/output devices for the interface are available.>

3.2.2 Documentation
<What kind of documents are required and who is the audience for each document?>

3.2.3 Hardware considerations
<Explain what hardware the system will be run on, including the memory size and auxiliary storage space.>

3.2.4 Performance characteristics
<List all the system constraints on speed, throughput, response time or size.>

3.2.5 Error handling and extreme conditions
<Describe how the system responds to input errors or extreme conditions.>

3.2.6 System interfacing
<Describe whether or not input is coming from or going to any other systems. List any restrictions on the format or medium of external input or output.>

3.2.7 Quality issues
<Include requirements for reliability, including the acceptable downtime, speed of recovery after failure,and also the requirements for portability of the system.>

3.2.8 System modifications
<What parts of the system are expected to be modified later and what are those modifications?>

3.2.9 Physical environment
<Explain where the target environment will be and whether or not the condition will be unusual in any way.>

3.2.10 Security issues
<Explain any security constraints that might apply, such as whether data access must be controlled, whether the system will be backed up, and who will be responsible for the back up.>

3.2.11 Resources and management issues
<Materials, personnel, computer time, knowledge by developers required to build install and maintain the system. Deadlines for system development. Say who is responsible for system installation and maintenance.>

3.3 Feasibility

<Estimate the projected size of the system and check if it is feasible with the provided resources. Specify if it can be completed within the proposed time range and budget.>

4 Customer Sign-off

Key writer: <Author>

Location of electronic file: <Full pathname of document>

System Design Document Template

Primary Audience: Developers

Secondary Audience: Project Manager, Client

Abstract
<This document will serve as the basis for the design of XXX. It describes how the proposed system is broken down into modules and layers and gives a high-level description of how the system will be implemented. It also describes the programming environment that will be used, and includes the design decisions made to date.>

1 Design Goals
<Describe the goals of the system >

2 System Architecture
<Describe the system architecture, if possible with a prototypical architectural framework (batch, interactive, simulation, real-time system, transaction based)>

2 System Decomposition

2.1 Layering
<Describe the system organization into subsystems, identify layers and partitions, specify the subsystem relationships. Specify if the architecture is open or closed. List services provided by the system>

2.2 Topology
<Show the information flow among the subsystems with a high level data flow diagram.>

3 Identification of Concurrency
<Identify which object must be concurrent. Identify mutual exclusion. Define thread of controls and specify folding of tasks into single threads of control.>

4 Hardware/Software Allocation
<Estimate the performance needs and the resources needed to satisfy them. Justify the choice of hardware or software implementation for subsystems, discuss trade-offs made. Describe allocation of subsystems to processors to satisfy performance needs and minimize communication.>

5 Data Management
<Specify the protocols, databases and files used to connect subsystems. Mention trade-offs between cost, access time, capacity and reliability.>

6 Handling Global Resources

<Identify global resources and determine mechanisms for controlling access to them>

7 Software Control

<Choose a control style for the whole system, specify external and internal control. External control is the flow of externally visible events among objects in the systems and can be one of the following: procedure-driven sequential, event-driven sequential or concurrent. Internal control is the control within one process using mechanisms such as procedure call, quasi-concurrent (RPC) or concurrent task calls.>

8 Boundary Conditions

<Describe the boundary conditions of the system when it is not in steady state.>

8.1 Initialization

<How is the system brought from initial state to steady state?>

8.2 Termination

<Do systems tasks release or clean up their resources when they terminate? Do they notify other tasks or subsystems?>

8.3 Failure

<How does the system behave when an error occurs? What kind of errors are recognized (user errors, exhaustion of system resources, external breakdown)?>

9 Trade-off Priorities

<Priorities which will be used to guide trade-offs during the rest of the design. Describe trade-offs not only with respect to the software, but with regard to the development process as well. Example: Timely delivery vs functionality. Look at problem statement for sources of priorities. Recognize and reconcile incompatible trade-offs.>

10 Unresolved Issues

<Describe the major issues that were discussed during the development of the design but were not resolved.>

11 Project Manager Sign-off

Key writer: <Author>

Location of electronic file: <Full pathname of document>

– Our primary goal for the undergraduate students is to let them work in a large-scale software development environment that is as realistic as possible. This means that the system being produced must be very large in relation to each programmer's contribution. Traditionally, this has been difficult because of the constraints of the semester, other classes, and the management problems associated with teams of students who have diverse and constantly changing schedules.

– One of the common shortcomings of undergraduate computer science education is that students seldom see software maintenance, and thus do not gain an appreciation for why sloppy software development leads to maintenance problems. Thus, another of our goals was to directly expose students to maintenance.

– Although a current goal of many software engineering development organizations is to reuse as much code as possible, few undergraduates have a chance to reuse old code (except when cheating), or the opportunities to see the issues and difficulties of reuse. Hence another goal is to require that students reuse existing code.

– Students are seldom forced to tackle the problem of integrating several software subsystems into one complete system. The integration process is a difficult task that has its own special problems, and will usually demonstrate any problems in the design or implementation that did not surface during testing. Thus, we set a goal of finding a way to incorporate an integration phase into our project.

– Although software engineering tools are becoming more widespread, most students still do not see many during their college education. Most commercially available tools are too expensive for universities, and require extensive training on the part of the students or the instructor. One of our goals was to give the students exposure to software development tools, both as tool builders and tool users.

– It is usually considered unfortunate that undergraduate students, even those who attend major research universities, are seldom exposed to research. One of our goals was to integrate a large research component into the software engineering project. The point of this is not necessarily to have the students actively solving current research problems, but to demonstrate some of the current research in software engineering.

– Although graduate courses typically deal with the results of research, few courses provide insight into research activities. For most areas of research it is difficult, except in specialized seminars, to do more than have the instructor present current research; the students usually do not have the background to actively participate in such research. Software engineering research, however, has the advantage that it focuses on issues with which graduate students can readily identify and understand. As practitioners themselves, these graduate students have the necessary background to participate in such research. We felt that a reasonable and worthwhile goal was to have the students become actively involved in the research process.

– Our final goal pertained specifically to a graduate software testing course. Such courses usually center on teaching theoretical concepts but offer little understanding or appreciation for how these concepts can be implemented and applied. Thus, our final goal was to demonstrate to the students how the testing techniques can actually be automated and used.

Although projects that realize any one of these goals are common, such projects typically take a large investment by the professor and often do not realize more than a few of the goals. We have created a multi-tool, multi-purpose project template that addresses all the goals listed above. This project template has been instantiated and used in two different courses (one undergraduate, the other graduate) in several different ways. By using the same project in so many different ways, the investment in time to create the project is justified. The key to our project is that we have the students redevelop portions of a system *that has already been implemented.*

2   IMSCU

For our project, we needed a system that was large enough to provide a significant challenge for the students, yet whose goals could be described in as little class time as possible. The project we chose is a software testing system based on *mutation testing.* We call our system *Instructive Mutation System from Clemson University* (IMSCU). In this section, we discuss the principles of mutation testing, then describe the project implementation in our classes, and close by describing how this project allows us to satisfy the goals listed in the previous section. Although the details of mutation and IMSCU are important to understanding our specific *project,* they are not crucial to understanding the *process* that we follow in this project, and most of our major points can still be understood if this section is skimmed and used as a reference.

2.1   Mutation Testing

Generating test cases that are effective at finding faults is one of the most technically difficult tasks of software testing. Mutation testing is a technique for generating test data that is based on *relative adequacy* as defined by DeMillo et al [4]:

Definition. If P is a program to implement function F and Φ is a collection of programs, then a test set T is adequate for P relative to Φ if P(t)=F(t) $\forall$ t$\in$T, and $\forall$ Q $\in \Phi$, Q $\neq$ F $\Rightarrow \exists$ t$\in$T such that Q(t)$\neq$F(t).

In other words, a test set is relative-adequate if it distinguishes the program being tested from a set of incorrect programs. *Mutation testing* can be regarded as a software analogue to the hardware fault-injection testing technique. Mutation testing systems apply a collection of *mutation operators* to the test program, each of which produces a set of executable variations, called *mutants,* of the original program.

Test cases are used to cause the mutants to generate incorrect output. Mutant programs that have been shown to be incorrect by a test case are considered "dead" and are not executed against subsequent test cases. Some mutants are functionally equivalent to the original program and cannot be killed. The goal of mutation testing is to find test data to kill all non-equivalent mutants. The assumption is that such test data will provide a strong test of the original program. The effectiveness of this approach is based upon a fundamental premise: if the software contains a fault, it is likely that there is a mutant that can only be killed by a test case that also reveals the fault.

A recent mutation system is Mothra [3], which allows a tester to examine remaining live mutants and design tests that kill them. The mutation operators used by Mothra [6] represent more than 10 years of refinement through several mutation systems.

When a program is submitted to a mutation system, the system first creates a set of mutant versions of the program. Next, a set of test data is supplied to the system to serve as inputs to the program. Each of these test cases is executed on the original program and the tester verifies that the output is correct. If correct, the test data is then executed on each of the mutant programs in turn. If the output of the mutant program differs from the original output, then that mutant is marked dead. Dead mutants are not executed against subsequent test cases.

If (as is likely) mutants are still alive, the tester can enhance the set of test data by supplying new inputs, usually to kill specific mutants that are left. This process of adding new test cases, verifying correctness, and killing mutants is repeated until the tester is satisfied with the number of mutants killed.

2.2   IMSCU Architecture

Although Mothra is a widely available, general purpose mutation system, we felt that Mothra had several shortcomings for this type of project. Specifically, Mothra was designed to be extremely flexible and general-purpose. Although this generality is useful for Mothra's purposes as a research and demonstration tool, the large number of choices that must be made to use it was felt to be too confusing for our purposes. Mothra also tests Fortran 77 programs, which was not considered ideal for our classes. Lastly, Mothra is very large (well over 50,000 lines of C code), and much of the bulk supports functionality that we did not need, or is code that provides portability and robustness. We felt that we wanted something that was more suited to academic purposes; a system with a small, tight design with limited flexibility, and that tests a modern language.

We based our system on the compiler project taught at Clemson that uses a Pascal-like language designed specifically for the class, called For Academic Purposes Only (FAPO). We modified that language slightly for our own purposes, and called it IMSCU Programming Language (IPL). IMSCU is designed as an interpretive system, and uses a postfix intermediate language called IPL Intermediate Code (IIC). To enhance separability of the IMSCU subsystems, mutation functions are implemented as separate programs that communicate through shared data structures. The seven tools of the IMSCU system are shown in Fig. 1.

Parse accepts an input program or subroutine and translates it to IIC, which is stored in two separate files, the symbol table file and the intermediate code file. *Inform* allows the tester to interactively define test case values for the variables in a main program or parameters of a subroutine. *GenMutes* creates representations for the mutant programs by generating, for each mutant, a *mutant descriptor record (MDR)* that encodes the changes to the IIC of the original program needed to produce the mutant. The mutants that IMSCU defines for IPL are based on the Fortran 77 mutations used by Mothra [6] and the C mutation operators defined by Agrawal et al [1]. *Interp* interprets the intermediate code using the test case values supplied through Inform. It executes the original program, or uses the MDR file to create and interpret mutant programs. *Decomp* decompiles the IIC code to a source program, and can display mutants as complete programs or by showing

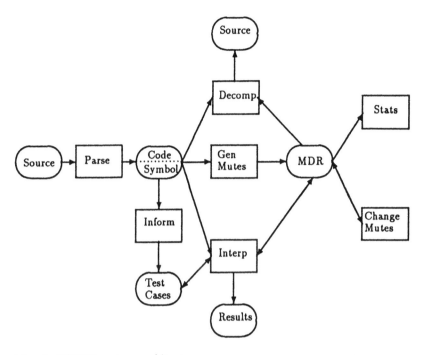

Fig. 1. IMSCU system architecture

the original program with mutated statements embedded after the corresponding original statement. *Stats* displays statistics about the current state of the mutants (percent killed, etc.), and *ChangeMutes* allows the tester to manually change the status of a mutant (principally to mark a mutant equivalent).

Because the mutation functions are implemented as separate programs that communicate through files, IMSCU has a high degree of independence and modularity among the tools. The shared files are accessed by each tool through independent modules that implement abstract data types for the symbol table, the IIC, the test cases, and the MDR list. Modularity and abstraction are crucial to the success of this project in a classroom setting. The first goal listed above was that of having the students work on a large project; by giving each team a separate tool to design and implement, they were able to solve a well-defined, complete problem that is very obviously part of a larger project. Because we began with large parts of the project already completed, the students were forced to perform some maintenance activities on pieces of the system to implement their portions, and were forced to reuse code that already existed. For example, one team in the senior level course usually is given the Inform program. To implement Inform, they have to use the routines provided by the symbol table module, and modify Interp to work with their output data structure.

3 A Senior Level Software Engineering Project

In our course, the students submit the following items to satisfy a rigid sequence of milestones:

1. a requirements document,
2. a design document, which is also orally presented to the class,
3. code and documentation,
4. a detailed unit level test report,
5. an integration report.

The requirements are derived from a statement of need and through interviews with users of the system, who are typically the instructor and former students of this class or the graduate class that uses IMSCU. Although these users are only modeling the system procurers that the students will see later, the users force the students to direct the interviews, and sometimes ask for ambiguous, conflicting, or infeasible functions. The users are also available for down-stream consulting such as acceptance testing.

Because building a complete mutation testing system would be impossible in a one semester software engineering course, we provide the students with portions of IMSCU, and have them build the rest. The most challenging subsystems of IMSCU are Parse and Interp, both of which require detailed knowledge of compilers to implement. Since most seniors do not have the background for these subsystems, we have always supplied the teams with Parse, Interp, and the modules for accessing the IIC and symbol tables. We supply the students with an architectural design (based on Fig. 1), divide them into teams of four or five, and assign each team to a subsystem. We also assign one team to building an interface to the system, and one team the job of system level integration (these two tasks are often assigned to the same team). Since the system level integration team is responsible for IMSCU as opposed to one subsystem, their requirement document contains requirements for IMSCU as a whole, their design is a system design and coding standards for the other teams, their implementation milestone consists of a user's manual and test standards, and their test report is replaced with an integration plan. The most important job of the integration team is to take charge during integration and ensure that the subsystems created by the other teams work smoothly together as one system.

Since the number of teams is controlled by the size of the class, the number of subsystems designed and implemented each semester varies. For example, GenMutes is usually not implemented (supplied in executable form), and we have also combined Stats and ChangeMutes on several occasions. The flexibility gained by having a completed system available makes it very easy to tailor the project to class size and even perceived skill levels. For example, we provide teams that are in serious danger of not completing the project with executable versions of their subsystems (but not the source). The data structures in IMSCU are viewed as "belonging" to one of the subsystems. For instance, the code and symbol tables belong to Parse, and the MDR file belongs to GenMutes. The test case file can belong to either Interp or Inform; although it is more logical to have it belong to Inform, we often consider it part of Interp and supply the source to the module. That avoids forcing the students to change Interp to suit their design of the test case module. In a more advanced class, or if the Inform team had extra people, asking them to design the module (and modify Interp) would be a valuable experience.

Having responsibility for the data structure modules often requires the students to perform maintenance on the modules. They usually wind up fixing some bugs (corrective maintenance), and modifying or adding new features to the modules in response to their own or other subsystem's needs (adaptive maintenance). There is usually no perfective maintenance involved in this project.

Having the subsystems implemented as separate programs that communicate through shared data structures not only makes for a clean separation of functionalities, but also lets the students see the value and difficulties of reusing other people's code. Additionally, basing the overall design of the system on data structures forces the students to internalize the data abstraction concepts that they have been learning during their previous three years. The most important element of this project, by far, is the final integration, where the subsystems designed, implemented, and tested by each team are hooked together into one unified system. We always have one team whose primary job is to oversee the integration. During the integration phase, they are assisted by one programmer from each of the subsystem teams, primarily for help in debugging interface problems. During this phase of the project, all the mistakes, inconsistencies, communication failures, and judgement errors become very obvious by showing up as integration problems. This one or two week period becomes the part of the course in which all the concepts become real and internalized. In fact, several students have claimed that participating in the integration for this project was the most important learning experience in their college career. By this point, the students invariably have developed a strong sense of team pride in the system and the project and they motivate themselves, sometimes (when problems arise) to extreme levels. Such an experience is not possible without having the students create a "large" project that has obvious applications.

Although success of the project is primarily dependent on what the students learn, some measure of the success can be gotten from how many functional requirements are satisfied. They have typically satisfied most of the requirements, and submitted a complete, usable system. There are invariably requirements that are too difficult to satisfy, are made difficult by the design, or that simply cannot be satisfied in the time constraints of a semester class. Recognizing and dealing with these problems turns out to be crucial to what the students learn from the project. They learn how to focus on the requirements that are essential to the system's functioning, and compromise on nonessential requirements. Because of this, we do not penalize the project for missed, nonessential requirements, *as long as they recognize and report the problems themselves.*

4 Providing Research Apprenticeship

Teaching graduate students how to perform research is hard. Research methodology courses are good at providing a survey of the research process, in showing *what* is done, but generally are unable to convey to the students any deep insight into *how* it is done. The how of research is taught by apprenticeship. Clearly the longer and more often students are involved in research the better. Unfortunately, such involvement in software engineering has usually been limited to students enrolled in advanced seminar courses and to those few students fortunate enough to work on an on-going research project.

Traditional engineering disciplines, such as mechanical engineering, have learned how to introduce such research apprenticeship into the classroom. Classroom design and construction projects are often used to develop students' research skills.

Consequently, more students are able to share in the research experience and have more opportunities to do so. Using a project template as described above allows software engineering educators to introduce the same sort of apprenticeship into the classroom.

We have used IMSCU as a component of our graduate software testing course in two ways. In one instantiation, IMSCU is used to simulate an on-going research project. Students enter this project "mid-stream" and reported feeling an immediate sense of project "momentum". In this version, portions of the project have been implemented but large portions are not only unimplemented, they are unspecified except in a general sense. Students are asked to form small teams of two or three, which are directed to complete the design and construction of the project.

Note how this differs from the use of IMSCU in the undergraduate setting described previously. There the students were able to work on a well-defined, complete problem that was part of a larger project. In this version, the graduate students must define many of the problems themselves. In doing so, the students must determine what are the applicable abstract principles. They must identify what are the research questions that will be asked and what elements of their work will help in answering those questions. As a bonus, working on the entire project forces the students to practice the project management skills they have previously acquired.

Typically, the translator (Parse) and the code and symbol tables are presented as implemented. Incomplete versions of the interpreter (Interp) and decompiler/pretty printer (Decomp) are provided. The proposed IMSCU system architecture (see Fig. 1) is sketched out.

At first, ideas are shared among the teams. This is important because students are initially unfamiliar with project goals and it gives the instructor an opportunity to identify and correct misconceptions. This also allows students to help one another understand what has "come before" in the project based on what they observe now.

After this initial stage, the students are directed to work independently. By acting as if they are the only team working on the project, each team is able to work at its own pace. Additionally, each team is free to develop and pursue their own ideas. It is important that each team recognize that there is not one right answer but rather many correct answers.

Interestingly, work on the project often intensifies student interest in certain lecture topics. Students apparently become quite involved with mutation testing. In discussing other testing techniques, spirited discussion and examination of the advantages and disadvantages of the other technique relative to mutation testing often ensue. The ability to use mutation testing as a point of comparison makes presentation of other techniques easier. Mutation testing provides a frame of reference for the students.

Of course, some problems do surface. Some teams report that implementing the somewhat involved GenMutes tool is tedious. As with all team projects, some teams have members that cannot or will not do the work. (Although this has not been necessary in the graduate class, we would handle this by emphasizing to the students involved that they will not be able to choose their partners in industry, and then reward the team members who do contribute with a higher percentage of the grade.)

IMSCU has also been used in a somewhat less successful manner. In this instantiation, the graduate students were expected to use the principles of constraint-based testing [5, 7] to create DATAGEN, an automatic test data generating system for IMSCU. As in the other approach, students were presented the scenario of a research project. A successful project instantiation, however, must present the character of a project underway. This was not done. Care was not taken to supply the proper project support material. Although all of IMSCU was made available to the students, none of the DATAGEN system was made available. The DATAGEN system was sufficiently independent of IMSCU that, rather than feeling like they were in a research project *in progress*, the students felt like they were *beginning* a research project. This lack of perceived "momentum" caused several problems. In particular, the students found it difficult to know where to begin. This was especially true of students who had only a weak grasp of the concept of abstract data types (and thusly of the integration principles for the project). Without the role models and examples that portions of DATAGEN could have provided, these students floundered. Providing portions of the DATAGEN system would have solved this problem.

Interestingly, giving them *less* of IMSCU would probably have solved the problem as well. If the students had been forced to design and write, say the decompiler/pretty printer Decomp, they would have understood the ideas of data abstraction better by having to use the Code/Symbol and MDR objects. They could have started the project earlier since the concept of a decompiler is easily grasped. Students would have been practiced in code reading, reuse, and maintenance. Finally, this would have gotten the teams a chance to get fired up and ready for the remainder of the project.

Eventually, with a great deal of instructor assistance, the DATAGEN system was completed. As before, it was very successful in helping students relate theoretical issues to practice. But our experience with this project only underscored the need to have of an existing system available for the students to use as a springboard.

5   Conclusions

In this paper, we have presented a project template for use in multiple undergraduate and graduate software engineering courses. More important than IMSCU itself, however, is the concept of a project template. Whereas a mutation testing system might not be appealing to some instructors as a project, the idea of having students develop subsystems of or extensions to a large, pre-existing system, is of general interest to anyone teaching a software project course. We feel that the essential characteristics of a successful software engineering project are:

- All or most of the project must already exist.
- The system must be clearly divided into modular subsystems that are complete in their own right, and that have well-designed interfaces with other subsystems.
- The system must be well designed to serve as a model for teaching design to the students.
- The project must be large in relation to each student's contribution.
- The goals of the system should be novel to the students, but understandable in a reasonably short time (by the end of the design phase, at least).

- Each instantiation of the project must provide the students with enough support material, *including code*, to feel momentum as soon as they start working.
- The project should have some research component.

The principle difficulty with our project template approach is that the project, including implementation details of the existing code, must be very familiar to the instructor or the TA. This is important for someone who wishes to use our approach, because it implies that the IMSCU system per se may not be the best choice. Part of the reason we chose IMSCU is because it was related to our own research; in fact, Offutt was one of the principal designers and implementors of the Mothra mutation system. Although IMSCU is available for use[2], another instructor may prefer to construct a system more related to his or her own research. This is not as daunting a task as it may sound, if the students are allowed to contribute to the ongoing development of the system. For example, our first version of IMSCU included only Parse, Interp, Inform, the modules for accessing the code and symbol tables and the test cases, and the *design* of the mutation operators. IMSCU was first used in the graduate testing class, where several groups built GenMutes and Decomp. We chose the best of those implementations to keep for use in future versions.

The use of project templates has been very successful in providing undergraduate students with an environment that is as close to an industry situation as possible. We have had numerous students come back to tell us how impressed industrial interviewers were with the comprehensive nature of this project; in fact, more than a few students have said that they were offered a job precisely because of their experience in this class.

One of the beneficial side-effects of this project is that *each student contributes something unique to the project*. This adds immensely to most student's confidence and good-feelings about the course; on the other hand, it means that students almost cannot cheat. There has been more than one student who came into the senior level class with good grades, only to not be able to contribute to this project. Usually, this is because the student never learned to program, but relied on other people's programs in previous courses.

Another unexpected benefit of using IMSCU as the project is that it turns out that using mutation is good testing training. Whether or not the students use mutation testing in their future work, the experience with the project teaches them a lot about what it takes to create a good test case, and how to design tests to find faults. This is a skill that employees find very appealing in our students.

Our one negative experience with our project template underscores what may be the most important aspect — project momentum. If students are provided with code that already exists, then they feel like they are joining something that is ongoing, with a history, and with a future, a feeling that gives them confidence that the project can be completed.

6 Acknowledgements

We would like to thank Stephen Lee for doing much of the programming on IMSCU, particularly for implementing the first version. We would also like to thank Dr. Joe

---

[2] IMSCU can be gotten through anonymous ftp from *hubcap.clemson.edu*.

Turner of Clemson's Computer Science Department for generously providing summer support for a research assistant and Dr. Harold Grossman for creating FAPO.

References

1. H. Agrawal, R. DeMillo, R. Hathaway, Wm. Hsu, Wynne Hsu, E. Krauser, R. J. Martin, A. Mathur, and E. Spafford. Design of mutant operators for the C programming language. Technical report SERC-TR-41-P, Software Engineering Research Center, Purdue University, West Lafayette IN, March 1989.
2. C. L. Bullard, I. Caldwell, J. Harrell, C. Hinkle, and A. J. Offutt. Anatomy of a software engineering project. In *Proceedings of the 1988 SIGCSE Technical Symposium*, pages 129–133, Atlanta GA, February 1988.
3. R. A. DeMillo, D. S. Guindi, K. N. King, W. M. McCracken, and A. J. Offutt. An extended overview of the Mothra software testing environment. In *Proceedings of the Second Workshop on Software Testing, Verification, and Analysis*, pages 142–151, Banff Alberta, July 1988. IEEE Computer Society Press.
4. R. A. DeMillo, R. J. Lipton, and F. G. Sayward. Hints on test data selection: Help for the practicing programmer. *IEEE Computer*, 11(4):34–41, April 1978.
5. R. A. DeMillo and A. J. Offutt. Constraint-based automatic test data generation. *IEEE Transactions on Software Engineering*, 17(9):900–910, September 1991.
6. K. N. King and A. J. Offutt. A Fortran language system for mutation-based software testing. *Software-Practice and Experience*, 21(7):685–718, July 1991.
7. A. J. Offutt. An integrated automatic test data generation system. *Journal of Systems Integration*, 1(3):391–409, November 1991.

This article was processed using the LᴬTEX macro package with LLNCS style

Software Reuse in an Educational Perspective

Guttorm Sindre,* Even-André Karlsson, Tor Stålhane†

Faculty of Computer Science, Norwegian Institute of Technology (NTH)
N-7034 Trondheim, NORWAY

Abstract

Software is largely developed from scratch, whereas other engineering disciplines tend to use mass produced, off-the-shelf components. Reuse still fails to have any massive impact in the software field beyond the low level functional libraries provided with various compilers.

We believe that this can partly be attributed to the neglect of reuse in the current software engineering education. This is illustrated by the contents of the computer science subjects at our university (NTH), which is believed to be representative of the international mainstream.

Based on our work in the REBOOT project, we divide the problems concerning reuse into a set of major topics which we think should be covered in a thorough software engineering education and discuss how reuse could be included in the curriculum.

1 Introduction

Compared to most other engineering disciplines, software engineering is rather ad hoc. This may partly be due to the fact that software engineering is more difficult than other engineering disciplines — there is no *one* method leading to good solutions in every case [1, 17, 15]. However, there are also weaknesses in the current practice. One commonly emphasized problem is that software is still largely developed from scratch, whereas other engineering disciplines tend to use mass-produced components. A current trend to mend this weakness is software reuse based on a library of components [9, 16, 2, 11, 5, 12]. This is also the approach that we have chosen in the REBOOT[1] project.

Reuse has often been promoted as allowing for an enormous increase in software engineering productivity. Compared to other engineering disciplines, there is the

---

*email: guttorm@idt.unit.no

†Stålhane is with SINTEF-DELAB.

[1]ESPRIT-2 project # 5327 REBOOT (Reuse by Object-Oriented Techniques) started September 1990 and has a duration of 4 years. The partners are Bull S.A. (prime, France), Cap Gemini Innovation (France), LGI at IMAG (France), SEMA GROUP S.A.E. (Spain), Siemens A.G. (Germany), Televerket (Sweden), Elektronikcentrum (Sweden), TXT (Italy) and SINTEF/NTH (Norway). The total planned effort is 124 man-years.

advantage that the duplication cost for software components is practically zero — software costs are development costs[2]. However, there are several problems which must be solved before we can reap the full benefits of reuse — it does not just happen by itself. In the software industry, both managers and developers are generally reluctant towards reuse, and ad hoc experiments with it have had a wicked tendency to fail. Reuse is more complicated than the optimists think, and we believe that its limited success so far is partly due to the low emphasis on reuse in current software engineering education.

The rest of the article is structured as follows: Section 2 illustrates how reuse is given very little attention in current education, with examples from the Norwegian Institute of Technology (NTH). Section 3 discusses what topics should be covered with respect to reuse. This section is inspired by our work in the ESPRIT project REBOOT. Section 4 discusses how reuse could be covered in a software engineering curriculum, either by means of a special course in reuse, or by means of integrating reuse in existing courses. Section 5 presents some conclusions.

2 The Status of Reuse in Education

As mentioned in the introduction, it is difficult to convince managers and developers in the software engineering field of the advantages of reuse. A common argument is that

- reuse of code is so troublesome that it is better to develop a component from scratch, even if one might have something which fits.

This argument is partly a myth, but for many people it is also based on hard-earned experience, and as such, it should be taken seriously by those promoting software reuse. The problem with failed attempts at reuse is usually that

- The components have been of low quality, e.g. their *reusability* has been low — because of weaknesses in the code or the documentation.

- It has been hard to find the right components for the right problem, i.e. the *tool support* for reuse has been insufficient and the base of components probably too limited.

The conclusion to be drawn from this is that the problems of more or less ad hoc systems development from scratch are not solved by moving on to ad hoc reuse — a systematic approach is required. However, systematic approaches to reuse are hardly taught today, and this may explain much of the current skepticism. Since people have only vague ideas about how to do reuse, most of them will not attempt it. And if they still do, their approach will be ad hoc and likely to fail, resulting in a bad experience which breeds even more skepticism.

---

[2]It should be noted, though, that the development of a reusable component will be somewhat more expensive than a similar non-reusable component, usually 20–25% [18]

The lack of reuse in a typical curriculum can be illustrated by the software engineering education at the Norwegian Institute of Technology (NTH). This is a 4.5 year university education with four years of study and approximately 40 courses plus a half year writing a Masters thesis. Many of the 40 subjects taken are basic subjects like mathematics, physics, chemistry, electronics, economy, and sociology — especially the first two years of study are dominated by such courses. The courses related to software engineering can roughly be divided in the following groups:

- *programming courses*, i.e. courses where the students learn to program in various languages and for various purposes. Some of these courses address programming in general (Programming (1st year), Algorithms and data structures, Programming methods (2nd year), and Logic programming (4th year)), focusing on different languages and levels of ambition. Others address the programming of certain applications: Computer graphics, Image processing, Discrete simulation, Systems programming.

- *basic software subjects*, i.e. teaching the structure of various kinds of basic software. Typical courses in this group are operating systems, compilers, expert systems, file systems, database systems[3]

- *systems engineering courses*, called Systems engineering 1, 2, and 3, discussing various modeling languages and analysis techniques, CASE-tools, systems and project administration, office information systems, document standards.

- *users courses*, i.e. learning to use various standard program packages.

Looking at the contents of these courses at NTH, the following observations can be made:

- *reuse* is not at all mentioned as a topic in the course summaries of the study plan. It is mentioned in the Systems Engineering 1 textbook, but no detailed treatment of the theme is given.

- *maintenance* is a topic in Programming methods and is also mentioned in Systems engineering 1. In both cases, however, it only counts for a very small part of the course. Considering the fact that maintenance currently makes up for about 70% of the total software life-cycle costs, a more thorough treatment could have been expected on how to maintain a system, and how to design systems components as maintainable as possible.

- *documentation*, which is essential both for reuse and maintenance, is mentioned in the introduction course on programming, but does not make up for an essential part of that course. Basically, students learn that it is wise to write documentation, and some hints about how, i.e. explain the purpose of the procedure, list and explain its in/out parameters, list the modules calling it and the modules it calls. But there is no thorough discussion about the problems

---

[3]although this course at NTH also has strong programming aspects, i.e. how to write SQL-queries

of documenting, and practical rehearsals are focused on making programs that work, not on documenting them. Practical experience with documenting comes in the group projects in the 2nd and 4th year, with little preliminary guidance. Whereas programming is recognized as difficult, the skill of documenting is assumed to come more or less by itself, maybe because it is done in a natural language.

All in all, we can conclude that

- The focus is on development from scratch. Reuse and maintenance are mostly neglected.

- The focus in the programming subjects is on making code that works, not on understanding existing code. Documentation, although its importance is stressed, is not taught in any detail, and exam questions in the programming courses typically concern writing programs, not documentation.

Some general knowledge relevant to reuse *is* acquired: orderly programming and use of comments will facilitate reuse, and so will good decompositions and a thorough analysis. However, most students leave the university without any mature ideas about how reuse can be done. The only students which are exposed to literature on reuse are those few who write Masters theses related to this topic.

The curriculum at NTH is supposed to be rather mainstream. It conforms to the recommended ACM Curriculum for Computer Science [3], which divides computer science into 9 areas. Fair enough, software reuse is not considered an area. More disturbingly, it is not even mentioned as a topic in the area where it would most appropriately fit in (area 6: software methodology and engineering). Thus, the ACM Curriculum has not contributed to improving the status of reuse in software engineering education.

Although we do not have detailed knowledge of the curricula elsewhere, we believe that the situation at most other universities is similar to that at NTH. To our knowledge, there is nowhere a special course on software reuse — at best it is mentioned in other subjects, and at that rather briefly. Neither have we heard of any specific course on maintenance. Why is this so? It *is* difficult to teach reuse — there is no recognized method. But there is no *one* recognized method for systems development from scratch either, and still it has been taught for decades.

3   What to Teach?

Our ideas concerning what to teach about reuse have been inspired by our work in the REBOOT project. The work package for technical transfer includes a substantial effort to develop course material and train industrial developers in object-oriented reuse.

Reuse is a complex issue which intersects with various other disciplines of computer science and related subjects. We have divided the reuse topics into two main groups:

- legal, economical, and organizational aspects of reuse.

- technical aspects of reuse.

The first group typically includes

- responsibility in case of component failure,

- how to pay for reuse,

- how to make reuse feasible,

- organizational incentives to motivate reuse among developers,

- how to convince people about the benefits of reuse,

- how to plan and organize reuse.

Although REBOOT is investigating all these issues, our work so far has been concentrated on the technical aspects. Since the technical aspects are also the most relevant for a typical computer science curriculum, we will concentrate on these in the rest of this section, stressing however, that the other aspects should not be overlooked.

In REBOOT, we have identified the four major technical problems of software reuse as follows:

Component qualification: What makes a component reusable? It is essential that the components in the library (including documentation) are of good quality, and some metrics must be established to ensure this. In other engineering disciplines, component quality can often be measured physically, and low quality will manifest itself through some physical damage or breakdown. For software components, quality control is much more problematic, and there is yet no recognized standard for software quality assurance.

Library organization: How do we facilitate the retrieval of components from the library? Unless the number of components in the base is fairly small, we need some structure to help the reuser find the right components. Compared to other engineering disciplines, software engineering has the problem that there is no standard terminology for component classification, and the components are diverse. Moreover, the domain is quickly evolving. Thus, whatever terminology there is, will be subject to continuous change.

Development methods for reuse: How do we develop reusable components? Reusable components can be developed from scratch, or by improving existing components through re-engineering. Development for reuse must also have a strong emphasis on component documentation.

Development methods with reuse: How do we develop a software system reusing components from a base? Both development for reuse and development with reuse will suffer from the general lack of sound development methods in the software engineering domain.

In our opinion, all these four topics should be covered in software engineering education at a university level. To indicate in more detail what could be taught, we present the REBOOT approach to these problems in sections 3.1–3.4. Notice that this does not mean that we expect everybody to start teaching the REBOOT approach — the purpose is only to illustrate what kind of material the topics would typically include.

3.1 Component Qualification

What is reusability? It is not trivial to decide exactly what makes a component reusable. Reuse requires something more than good component quality. In REBOOT we have used the factor-criteria-metrics model to define the two attributes quality and reusability for our components. The relationship between quality and reusability factors is shown in fig. 1.

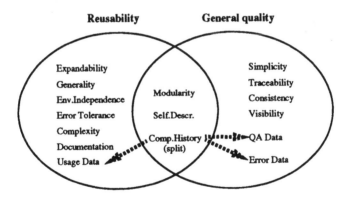

Figure 1: The REBOOT criteria for quality and reusability

Our factors for reusability are defined as follows:

- Portability: The ease with which software can be transferred from one computer system or environment to another.

- Flexibility: The term flexibility is usually used to denote the existence of a range of choices available to the programmer or implementer - the more choices, the greater the flexibility. Flexibility is also referred to as "generality" or "useful complexity".

- Understandability: A software product is understandable to the extent that its purpose is clear to the inspector.

- Confidence: The (subjective) probability that a module, program or system performs its defined purpose satisfactorily (without failure) over a specified time in an other environment than it was originally constructed and/or certified for.

These factors are split into criteria which are further decomposed into metrics for as shown in figure 2. Where there are two metrics for one criterion, we use the average. Checklists are filled in (yes/no) by developers and scores computed based on this.

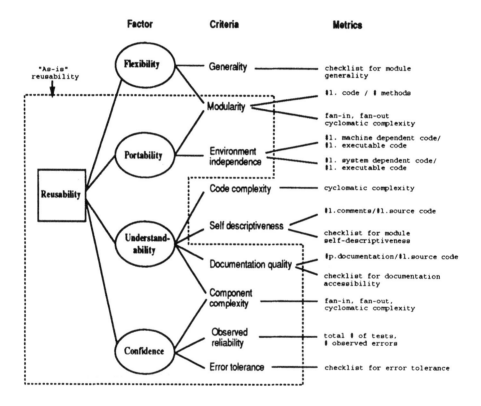

Figure 2: The REBOOT factor-criteria-metrics

Note that the reusability attribute is different for black-box ("as-is") and white-box reuse.

Experience estimates. The factors we defined through our a-priori model in the previous section can also be estimated after reuse. Before we define our estimators for the factors, we need to define the term productivity. The commonly used definition is:

$$\text{Productivity} = \frac{\# \text{ lines of code}}{\# \text{ person} - \text{days used}}$$

The number of lines of code that we consider will depend on the factor where the productivity is used.

The model shown in figure 2 shows that the factors flexibility, understandability, portability and confidence will influence the reusability. We have chosen to estimate these factors as follows:

$$\text{Flexibility} = \frac{\text{Change productivity}}{\text{Development productivity}}$$

$$\text{Understandability} = 1 - \frac{\# \text{ hours needed tounderstand component}}{\# \text{ hours needed to write component}}$$

$$\text{Portability} = \frac{\text{Porting productivity}}{\text{Development productivity}}$$

Our confidence is dependent not only on the ratio of successful reuse, but also on the total number of reuses done. In order to include this into our estimate, we will introduce a prior belief plus the assumption that Confidence is Beta distributed. If we have an information-less prior, this gives us the estimator shown below.

$$\text{Confidence} = \frac{(\# \text{ reuses with User Satisfaction} \geq (\text{maxscore} - 1)) + 0.5}{\text{Total}\# \text{ reuses} + 1}$$

From this list of estimators, we can now find numerical values for all the software factors suggested in the REBOOT model. This enables us to

- Check the quality of our prediction factor values, which are based on metrics.

- Improve our quality and reusability estimates for further REBOOT re-users.

3.2   Library Organization

With a small component library for in-house use, it is usually not necessary with any explicit structuring, except for some versioning and configuration management facilities to take care of library evolution. As stated in [18], most approaches with small libraries do fine just with some free text search facilities for component retrieval.

The need for a more elaborate organization of the library emerges when the number of components gets so large that the developers cannot know the library by heart, and is further increased if the library is supposed to support reuse *between* companies. Generally, the structuring of a reuse library must deal with the following three points:

- People use language differently, and thus, there may be a *terminology mismatch* between the person classifying a component and another person searching for it.

- In development with reuse, we might be interested in a component even if it is not identical to our request — if we can get away with rather small modifications, this might be better than development from scratch.

- People might not know exactly what they are looking for. This is particularly true in the early phases of development, i.e. if one attempts to reuse analysis and design results in addition to code.

All these points indicate that the querying mechanisms of ordinary databases are not quite appropriate for a large component library because they are based on *exact matching*. A query for a component will usually not have *one* right answer — it should rather yield a ranked list of components close to the request. These components must be evaluated in more detail by the reuser to pick the best candidate.

The dominating approach to dealing with these problems is *faceted classification*, introduced in [13] to classify books, and adapted to software by Prieto-Diaz [12]. The basic idea is to split the classification of the component into various orthogonal aspects. For each such facet, only a limited set of terms are available, thus preventing component developers from using an uncommon terminology at classification and reusers from using an uncommon terminology at search.

This faceted classification scheme has also been adopted by REBOOT. Whereas Prieto-Diaz concentrated on functional components, we work with object-oriented components (i.e. classes), which motivates some differences in the choice of facets. The REBOOT facets are:

Abstraction: Usually a component can be characterized by a noun, e.g. stack, flight manager.

Operations: Components provide operations, e.g. push, pop.

Operates On: This facet describes the objects the component acts on, e.g. integer, set, list, resource.

Dependencies: These are non-functional dependencies and characteristics which makes reuse of the component more difficult, e.g. C++-based, Unix-based, Hood-based.

As an example, we could have a stack (abstraction) of integer (operates on) written in C++ (dependencies) with operations push, pop, top, swap, i.e. it is possible to have more than one term filled in for each facet. A more detailed discussion of the REBOOT classification scheme can be found in [7].

In addition to the facets, a component will have other attributes, such as who developed it, when it was developed, how big it is etc. The distinction between facets and other attributes is that the facets encode the properties of the component which are most relevant in connection with reuse. The number of facets must not be too big — otherwise, the facets will easily become overlapping (i.e. not orthogonal), leading to the situation that one component can be classified in many different ways, which does not facilitate retrieval.

The problem of finding components close to a request is solved in REBOOT by organizing the terms of each facet in a weighted graph, so that the distance between a component request and the components available in the base can be calculated. More details about this approach, including heuristics to support the librarian with the maintenance of the library structure, are given in [6]. The details of the REBOOT classification scheme would not be appropriate to teaching, at least not in an overview course. However, a treatment of library organization should at least point out the special problems of large libraries, motivate the need for close matches, and give an introduction to faceted classification with structured term spaces, for instance discussing which facets would be appropriate for classifying various kinds of components.

3.3 Development for Reuse

Many guidelines for developing reusable components can be extracted from the qualification model, cf. section 3.1. A thorough introduction to the theme of developing reusable components should also discuss the following issues:

- *scope:* components can be made according to a general domain analysis, or as part of the development of a more specific application.

- *starting point:* components can be made from scratch or by re-engineering of existing code.

Techniques for each of these should be discussed. Additionally, one should stress documentation for reuse, which requires something more than ordinary documentation, in that one must explain in what contexts the component is intended to be reused without modifications and how it can possibly be modified to other contexts.

Components developed solely with one specific application in mind will usually have a rather low reusability. In adhering to the constraints of that specific application, the component will not fit other needs which are similar but not identical to the original one. In the ideal case, one should not focus on any specific application at all when making reusable components, but rather develop these according to a general domain analysis. A detailed analysis of a whole domain is an expensive and tedious process. For a company involved in day-to-day software development, with a need to meet certain dead-lines to make money, a domain analysis may not be feasible. Development for reuse can situate itself anywhere (except at the very left) on the continuous scale shown in figure 3.

Where to situate oneself on this scale depends on

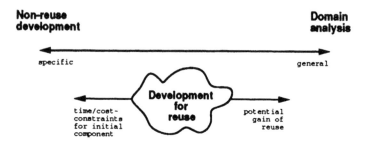

Figure 3: The specter from specific to general software development

- how fast we need the component for its initial purpose (a narrow time limit will lead to a less thorough analysis, and thus, probably, to a less general component),

- how many times we expect the component to be reused (if this number is high, the potential gain is larger, and thus, it is feasible to put more resources into analyzing the requirements for a general component)

The possibility for re-engineering existing code might be essential to the successful transfer of reuse methodologies to the industry, since they do not want to throw away all the code they have already got. Interesting techniques for re-engineering are design recovery from code and redesign for reuse. In REBOOT, redesign will be tightly connected to the qualification model, which will indicate weaknesses in the component.

The need for re-engineering may be signaled by the fact that there are many similar components in the library, in which case it could be interesting to make a more general component out of these. Also, due to the problem with narrow deadlines, people might not have the time to make components general when a project goes on. After the project is finished, they may go back and look at the components developed to try to make them more reusable. This approach is taken at the Norwegian company Taskon [14] which has been successful with reuse for ten years.

3.4 Development with Reuse

Development with reuse will be difficult to teach in isolation, since reuse must necessarily be integrated in some general development method. However, some general principles and life-cycle considerations could be presented. Given a specific development method including reuse, this could be taught in more detail.

REBOOT does not advocate any specific analysis and design method — the life-cycle model, of which the design phase is shown in fig. 4, should be possible to integrate with most existing methods based on some top-down refinement. The general pattern of work indicated in the figure is:

1. First, we do a general search in the base to get an idea of how many relevant components there might be. The result of this search will guide the choice of solution.

2. When specific component requirements have been identified, we search for these components.

3. If a component is found, it might need modification. In that case the modified component might be submitted to the library afterwards.

Components which have to be developed from scratch will implicitly have been classified by the requirements entered at search, and could be submitted to the reuse base when finished.

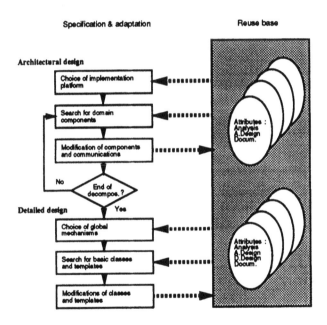

Figure 4: The REBOOT model of design with reuse

The major characteristics identified are that development for and with reuse are tightly connected, the development process will be a combination of top-down and bottom-up approaches [8], and the contents of the reuse base can be used to guide the choice of design, i.e. we go for the design which allows for the highest amount of reuse. The customer might even be willing to make slight changes to his requirements if the system is significantly cheaper that way.

In the analysis phase, components in the library can be used for rapid prototyping purposes, i.e. they may be useful even if they are quite contradictory to the customer's needs, because the prototype helps to eliminate misunderstandings between the user and the analyst.

4 How to Teach Reuse

There are several possibilities concerning how reuse could be included in a software engineering curriculum. At least, there are three questions to be answered:

- make a special course on reuse, or include reuse as a topic in existing courses?
- teach one specific approach to reuse in detail, or give a more shallow overview of several approaches?
- concentrate on theory or practice?

Choices here are not mutually exclusive. Especially for the last two questions, a combination might be the best (i.e. both overview and a more detailed account of at least one specific approach, both theory and practice). But this depends on the answer to the first question — if reuse is just one of many topics in a course, the time available might not be sufficient for detail and practical exercises. Below the various possibilities are discussed in some more detail:

Special course in Reuse: Going for this option, it might be best to make a course on "Reuse and Maintenance", since these two are related topics. Such a course should typically contain the following:

- motivation for reuse (and maintenance). Such a motivation should be rather thorough, i.e. more than the five standard lines introducing a typical reuse paper. If time allows it, one could go into cost models and reliability growth calculations, illustrating the potential benefits of reuse.
- clarification of the major problems of reuse (and maintenance).
- technical approaches to overcome the difficulties, i.e. what is required for a component to be reusable and maintainable, motivated by metrics, how to develop reusable components through domain analysis, re-engineering or by more traditional techniques, how to develop a system using reusable components, how to maintain a system, how to organize component libraries.
- some organizational and legal aspects.

Reuse in other courses: There are many courses where parts of the above mentioned reuse curriculum could fit in. For instance, a course on programming methods could introduce metrics explaining which factors make a component reusable. Courses in programming should generally give more attention to program reading and documentation, rather than focusing only on program writing. Library organization could fit in several places, for instance in a programming course or in a data base systems course. Systems engineering courses could discuss methods of development for and with reuse, as well as some organizational aspects. A course in information law could potentially touch upon the legal aspects.

For the status of reuse as a topic in its own right, it might be best if there was a special course. However, it should be noted that reuse alone does not solve any problems — it has to be used together with other techniques. Thus, it may be better to include it in existing subjects. This is also a more realistic way to go in terms of internal faculty politics, since it is usually not straight-forward to get resources for a new course.

Overview or detail?   Probably, a treatment of reuse should always be introduced by some overview, as indicated in our outline of the reuse course above. Thus, the question really is whether or not to include a more detailed treatment of one specific approach. We think that this would be an advantage, since a definite approach might be much more convincing to the students than just a collection of loose thoughts about problems and solutions.

Theory or practice?   A practical exercise in reuse which is not preceded by a thorough theoretical introduction, is likely to fail. Hence the question is not actually theory *or* practice, but whether the theory should be supplemented with practice. Indeed, practice would be good for really *teaching* reuse, rather than just talking about it. However, the exercise had better not fail. There are some problems with putting reuse into practice in education:

- To reveal the benefits of reuse, one would usually need a large target system for the exercise, as well as a large library of components. Thus, the challenge for the students is much greater than when they are merely hacking down small programs in isolation from everything else.

- The full cycle of reuse (development for, then development with) takes a long time.

Thus, it might be difficult to include all aspects of reuse in one practical exercise, even if it it lasts for a whole semester. A practical exercise would also require details about a specific approach in the theory part, and tool support for this approach would be a definite advantage.

In spite of the problems, reuse might lend itself fairly easily to practical experimentation in a university context. One of the problems in research projects on reuse is that it takes a long time to fill the reuse base with a sufficiently large number of components. However, in a course with hundreds of students, each student need only make a few components, and still, one will have a very large reuse base after some years. For instance, the students could do a practical project on "Development for reuse" in the spring, then continuing with a project on "Development with reuse" in the autumn, using the components resulting from the previous exercise. Universities have good opportunities to make reuse bases, in that they have the personnel resources for creating a large number of components without any pressure from narrow deadlines. There is a danger, of course, that many of the components developed will be of inferior quality. However, this is also an important part of the learning — to see which components are reusable and which are not. Besides, the reuse base should have a librarian which can remove bad components and take care of the long term development of the base. Acknowledged libraries such as COOL [4] and Interviews [10] have originated at American universities.

5 Conclusion

In this report we have discussed the status of reuse in the current software engineering education, with examples from the Norwegian Institute of Technology. Our conclusion is that reuse is given almost no attention. This is believed to be the case also at most other universities. Since reuse is an important issue in the goal of putting more engineering into software development, this neglect is a reason for worry.

We have suggested a set of topics which should be covered, inspired by our work in the REBOOT project. In REBOOT we are now developing courses in object-oriented development and reuse, to be followed by a more detailed course in the REBOOT methodology. These courses are directed towards software developers in European industry, and will contain theory as well as practical exercises with the REBOOT prototype reuse support environment. At our university we will try to include some REBOOT-inspired theory on reuse in the 2nd year course "Programming methods" the next semester, maybe accompanied by some practical exercises.

The reuse courses we have held for industry so far have been very well received, indicating a demand which has been overlooked by university education. More emphasis on reuse here is probably essential to removing the current skepticism towards reuse in most software development organizations. It is hard to achieve successful reuse on a large scale without educating people for it.

References

[1] Frederick P. Brooks jr. No silver bullet: Essence and accidents of software engineering. In H.-J. Kugler, editor, *Proc. Information Processing'86*. North-Holland, IFIP, 1986.

[2] Bruce A. Burton et al. The reusable software library. *IEEE Software*, pages 25–33, July 1987. The RSL is developed at Intermetics, Inc.

[3] Peter J. Denning et al. Computing as a discipline. *Comm. of the ACM*, 32(1):9–23, January 1989. Final Report of the Task Force on the Core of Computer Science, prepared for the ACM Education Board.

[4] Mary Fontana et al. COOL — C++ Object-Oriented Library. Technical report, Texas Instruments Inc., 1990.

[5] Sanjiv Gossain and Bruce Anderson. An iterative-design model for reusable object-oriented software. In *ECOOP/OOPSLA '90 Proceedings*, University Of Essex, UK, October 1990. ECOOP/OOPSLA.

[6] Guttorm Sindre, Even-André Karlsson, Patricia Paul. Heuristics for maintaining a term space structure for relaxed search. In *Proc. DEXA'92, Valencia*. Springer Verlag, 1992.

[7] Even-André Karlsson, Sivert Sørumgård, and Eirik Tryggeseth. Classification of Object-Oriented Components for Reuse. In *Proc. TOOLS'7, Dortmund*. Prentice-Hall, 1992.

[8] B. Langefors. *Theoretical Analysis of Information Systems*. Studentliteratur, Auerbach, first edition, 1973.

[9] John A. Lewis, Sallie M. Henry, Dennis G. Kafura, and Robert S. Schulman. An empirical study of the object-oriented paradigm and software reuse. In *OOPSLA 91*, 1991.

[10] Mark A. Linton, Paul R. Calder, John A. Interrante, Steven Tang, and John M. Vlissides. *InterViews Reference Manual, Version 3.0*. The Board of Trustees of the Leland Stanford Junior University, 1991.

[11] James Neighbors. The DRACO approach to constructing software from reusable components. *IEEE Transactions on Software Engineering*, 10(5):564–574, September 1984.

[12] Ruben Prieto-Diaz and Peter Freeman. Classifying software for reusability. *IEEE Software*, pages 6–16, January 1987.

[13] S. R. Ranghanathan. *Prolegomena to Library Classification*. Asia Publishing House, Bombay, India, 1967.

[14] T. Reenskaug et al. OORASS: seamless support for the creation and maintenance of object oriented systems. *Journal of Object Oriented Programming*, Summer 1992.

[15] H. Rittel. On the planning crisis: Systems analysis of the first and second generations. *Bedriftsøkonomen*, (8), 1972.

[16] Mary Beth Rosson and John M. Carroll. A view match for reusing smalltalk classes. In *Proceedings of CHI'91*, pages 277–283, 1991.

[17] Arne Sølvberg and Chenho Kung. *Information Systems Engineering*. Springer Verlag, 1992.

[18] Will Tracz. Software reuse myths. *ACM SIGSOFT Software Engineering Notes*, January 1988.

Session 3:

Panel Discussion
Moderator: Maribeth B. Carpenter, Software Engineering Institute

Industry Requirements for Academic and Continuing Education Programs in Software Engineering
Panel Moderator: Timothy J. Lulofs, Pacific Bell

Panel Discussion: Industry Requirements for Academic and Continuing Education Programs in Software Engineering

Moderator:

Timothy J. Lulofs
Technical Director, Software Engineering Training
Pacific Bell

Panel Members:

Lloyd Cole
Vice President, Information Systems Division
Charles Schwab and Company, Inc.

Elizabeth Comer
Senior Computer Scientist, COMSYSTEMS Quality Assurance Manager
Science Applications International Corporation

Eric Firdman
Executive Director, Strategic Information Systems
Pacific Bell

Robert L. Johnson
Manager, Information Technology Human Resource Development
Hewlett-Packard Corporation

Abstract. How well are graduates of university programs in software-related disciplines stacking up against industry expectations? How well prepared are such graduates to help solve real-world business problems? Are industry calls for "practical" skills too myopic, or are the emphases of academic programs irrelevant to the demands of industrial-strength software development? While not claiming representativeness, panel members identified what they see as current and emerging skill requirements, technical and otherwise, for successful software development in their fields; discussed ways in which existing deficiencies in these areas might be addressed through more extensive university-industry collaboration; and assessed the efficacy of software-engineering emphases in academic and continuing education programs. Position papers were distributed by the panelists at the conference.

Session 4:

Formal Methods and Engineering Instruction
Moderator: Keith R. Pierce, University of Minnesota, Duluth

Formal Methods and the Engineering Paradigm
Michael J. Lutz, Rochester Institute of Technology

Formal Methods for Software Engineers: Tradeoffs in Curriculum Design
David Garlan, Carnegie Mellon University

Teaching Protocol Engineering in Honours Year
Richard Lai, La Trobe University

Formal Methods and the Engineering Paradigm

Michael J. Lutz

Department of Computer Science
Rochester Institute of Technology
Rochester, New York

Abstract. The snail's pace of formal methods adoption disappoints those who believe such techniques are important for software engineering. My thesis is that the failure of formal methods to have much impact is a consequence of a general misunderstanding of the engineering paradigm. Most formal methods proponents have backgrounds in science or mathematics, where the rules for adoption of a new system are clear cut and unambiguous. The engineering method, however, is grounded in the use and application of heuristics, several of which relate to the application of science. This paper discusses the role of formal methods in the context of the engineering method. Several approaches to increase the use of formal methods are proposed based on this analysis.

1 Introduction

The stated theme of this conference is "Putting *Engineering* into Software Engineering." Consideration of this deceptively simple phrase uncovers a host of technical and philosophical questions: how do engineers solve problems, what is the role of science in engineering, and which computing concepts are essential for the education of a software engineer? This paper attempts to address some of these issues, using formal methods as a vehicle for illuminating the relationship between scientific theory and engineering practice. It also prescribes some activities that should take place if technologies such as formal methods are to have significant effect on practice.

Any discussion of formal methods should begin with a definition of this key term, so I propose the following:

A *formal method* is a mathematical system and associated rules of inference used to *model* and *reason about* some characteristic of a software system.

For good or ill, it is safe to say that formal methods are not standard industrial practice, at least not within the United States. This is distressing to those of us who hold that formal methods are one tool for improving quality and productivity. One recourse we have is to consider the use of formal approaches in other engineering disciplines.

If we are to use traditional engineering disciplines as guides for what we are doing, then the first order of business is to understand the *engineering method*. The focus here is less on what engineering *is* than what engineers *do*. That is, rather than concern ourselves with the goals of engineering endeavors, we should concentrate on the processes by which engineers achieve these goals. These processes are many and varied, but we will concentrate on the role of mathematics and science in the everyday activities of practicing engineers. In this way, we can determine if and how formal methods mirror these activities in the realm of software development.

Next, we must be more specific in categorizing formal methods. In particular, we need some way of assessing how formal methods can be applied and when particular methods are most appropriate.

Combining the investigation into engineering uses of mathematics and science with our taxonomy of formal methods, we can tackle the issue of how formal method technology can be of greatest benefit to software engineering practice. This, in turn, provides a backdrop against which we can consider the introduction of formal methods into software engineering curricula. In addition, it provides some guidance as to what needs to be done on the formal methods side of the fence to increase the rate of acceptance by practitioners.

Before continuing, however, readers should be aware of my background and biases. I have *not* received formal training as an engineer; my undergraduate major was mathematics, and my graduate work was in computer science, primarily systems software. It was with some trepidation that I started working with my colleagues on an undergraduate software engineering concentration. To gain a measure of confidence, I started reading the literature on the philosophical basis of engineering, especially the engineering method. In addition, my industrial experience in software development has led me to work with a variety of engineers, both capable and incompetent; this in turn has helped shape my views of how engineers really work. Finally, my engineering colleagues at RIT have participated in many stimulating (and heated) discussions as to what makes an engineer an engineer. While this background may not qualify me as an engineer, I believe I have a reasonable grasp of what defines professional engineering practice.

2 The Engineering Method

It is a rare engineer indeed who is both introspective and lucid enough to provide perspective on the philosophical foundations of the field.[1] Yet without such a perspective, it is presumptuous for non-engineers to speak to the appropriateness or utility of any concept to the practice of software development as an engineering discipline. Fortunately, there are a few engineering professionals who have spoken to these philosophical issues[7, 16, 19]. In addition, there has been some work by computer scientists trying to define the conditions under which software development can be classified as an engineering discipline[21].

A simple monograph by Billy Vaughn Koen[16] has had great influence on my thoughts. In this short work, Koen sets out to define the "engineering method" for professional engineers and the public at large. Space does not permit a full exposition of Koen's thesis and the consequences that flow from it. However, a short synopsis of the overall theme, followed by more detailed discussion of the role of science and mathematics, will provide a framework for judging the place of formal methods in software engineering.

---

[1] An RIT library search turned up 264 titles cataloged under both philosophy and science, whereas only 8 entries existed for philosophy and engineering. This ratio of roughly 30:1 was confirmed by scans of several other university libraries on the Internet.

Koen defines the *engineering method* as *the strategy for causing the best change in a poorly understood or uncertain situation within the available resources.* "Best" in this sense is not an absolute measure, but relative to the engineer's ability to assess and balance both technical and societal issues relating to the problem at hand. Koen then asserts that this method is identical to the use of appropriate engineering heuristics. The collection of heuristics available to an individual engineer at a given point it time is that engineer's "state-of-the-art" (or *sota*). The sota of the profession as a whole is the union of the sotas of the individual practitioners, again as a function of time. An engineer engages in *best practice* to the extent that the applicable part of his sota intersects with that of the profession as a whole.

Koen contrasts this pragmatic approach to that of science. Given two conflicting scientific theories, at least one is wrong; the winning theory in a scientific dispute is the one that best explains "the way things really are." Engineering heuristics, however, are never right or wrong. Instead, they are more or less applicable in a specific context. What is more, the engineering sota may harbor two conflicting heuristics, each of which is useful and applicable under different circumstances. This leads to two of Koen's key assertions:

1. There is not an absolute measure against which engineering practice can be evaluated, as the set of heuristics defining the state-of-the-art is in constant flux.
2. The choice of heuristics is dependent on factors other than pure technical merit (desires of society as a whole, cost/benefit analysis, etc.).

Thus a concept, technique, or approach is judged purely by its relevance to the task at hand. As the use of heuristics involves judgement, there is always a chance that things may go awry. What distinguishes engineering practice from random activity is the evolution of a body of heuristics that succeed much more often than they fail.

Koen goes on to discuss heuristics at various levels of detail. Some of these are specific to a given subdiscipline, such as "a properly designed bolt should have at least one and one-half turns in the threads." Software development, of course, has similar heuristics (avoid **gotos**, write short procedures, etc.).

What is of more interest are the higher-level heuristics shared by most engineering disciplines. Examples Koen mentions include *work at the margin of solvable problems, make small changes to the state-of-the-art,* and *allocate resources as long as the cost of not knowing exceeds the cost of finding out.* Many of these have direct applicability to software development. Most software organizations are conservative by nature, and leery of adopting radical new approaches (those that don't often rue their impetuousness[17]). Similarly, software teams are making greater use of prototypes to reduce risk prior to full-scale development.

For our purposes, however, the most relevant section of Koen's work addresses the use of science, and by extension mathematics, as part of the engineering method. In particular, Koen draws a sharp distinction between applied science on one hand and engineering on the other:

> The thesis that engineering is applied science fails because scientific knowledge has not always been available, is not always available now, and because, even if available, it is not always appropriate for use.

Instead, Koen states that "the engineer recognizes both science and its use as heuristics, although very important ones, to be applied *only when appropriate*" (emphasis mine). That is, science may be inapplicable because the cost of applying the knowledge cannot be justified.

While I used the work of Koen to lay out the principles of the engineering method, his thesis does not contradict (indeed, it is supported by) the writings of other commentators[1, 2, 7, 19]. Thus I think this provides a useful point from which to evaluate the possible role of formal methods in software engineering, the problems of introducing formal methods into industrial practice, and when and how formal methods should be incorporated in software engineering programs.

3   Categories of Formal Methods

This paper began with a short definition of formal methods. However, to assess the role of these methods in software engineering, we must develop a more detailed map of where and how they can be applied. To keep the presentation manageable, we will only discuss formal methods related to functional behavior. This is the area where the majority of work to date has been focused, and where, as a consequence, the mathematical models are most mature.

One possible categorization is by underlying mathematical philosophy. The clearest distinction is between the *model-based* approaches such as Z[22] and VDM[15], and *algebraic* (or equational systems) such as Larch[9, 10] and OBJ[8]. Model based systems assume an existing group of mathematical artifacts (sets, relations, sequences, etc.), and use these as building blocks for constructing product-oriented models. Algebraic systems are based on substitution of equal terms, and use equations to define the relationships between values of various *sorts*. In general, algebraic systems have been most successful in defining the attributes of abstract data types (ADTs), whereas the model-based approaches have typically been used for system-level definitions.

Another viewpoint considers the applicability of various methods to the traditional phases of software development. Thus, for instance, we can consider which formal methods are most suitable (as opposed to applicable) for use in specification, design, and implementation. Z is touted primarily as a specification tool, though it supports design activities as well. Similarly, VDM[15] also addresses specification and design, though in this case the emphasis is on the latter. Finally, the weakest precondition system of Dijkstra is used primarily to prove the correctness of algorithms developed from formal design specifications.

A third perspective is provided by two complementary aspects of any formal method: modeling and reasoning. While all formal methods exhibit both properties, there is a shift in emphasis from modeling to reasoning as activities proceed from specification to implementation. Systems like Z and VDM can be used to create clear, concise models of a software system, and this may in and of itself be of sufficient value to warrant the use of mathematics[11].[2] These same systems can also be

---

[2] Of course, the associated inference system can be used to uncover inconsistencies and ambiguities if desired.

used in conjunction with verified design[15, 20]. Here each design refinement is related to a previous, more abstract description by an abstraction or retrieve function. The modeling process is complemented by a rigorous reasoning process, wherein proof obligations are discharged to show that the refinement accurately captures the desired abstract functionality. When one reaches the implementation (coding) stage, where systems like Dijkstra's weakest precondition are employed[4], the modeling activity is implicit, while the inference rules drive the process of simultaneously creating algorithms and proving their correctness.

Finally, there is the role formal methods can play in cataloging and describing both systems and components. In this case, the use of formal methods is analogous to the use of mathematical descriptions in integrated circuit catalogs (e.g., state machines and timing diagrams). The purpose here is to provide a concise and accurate description of a component so that engineers can evaluate its fitness for their particular application. For example, the two-tiered Larch system[9, 10] can be used to describe the interface to packages written in C. Here again the emphasis is primarily on modeling, but as an aid to selection and evaluation.

The analysis above provides us with a four dimensional space for categorizing any formal method:

1. Underlying mathematical approach.
2. Relevant phase(s) of applicability.
3. Relative emphasis on modeling vs. reasoning.
4. Suitability for cataloging.

In all the methods, there is a common theme: the use of mathematics, specifically discrete mathematics, to precisely characterize the behavior of software products. The question we must ask is how significant these tools are in the practice of software development.

4 Formal Methods and Software Engineering

We can now discuss why formal methods have had little impact on industrial practice, where such methods might be used most productively, and how we might proceed to introduce formality into the process. A confession is in order: part of my attraction to formal methods is related to the mathematical elegance many of these systems possess. This, however, is essentially a scientific view; what's needed here is an engineering view. Specifically, what are the barriers to increasing the value of the heuristic "use formal methods" in software engineering?

One formidable barrier is the immaturity of the software development process in many organizations. Assuming the organizations represented by SEI process maturity data are representative of industry as a whole, the vast majority of firms in both the United States and Japan are still in the embryonic (read: chaotic) state[13]. As Humphrey has noted, for firms at this level, introduction of new technology may actually cause more harm than good[12].

However, even if we consider the case of more advanced development organizations, several impediments remain. Many of these simply reflect common engineering heuristics meant to reduce risk or cost. For instance, failure to adopt radically new approaches is in keeping with the heuristic "make small changes to the state-of-the-art." To gain wide acceptance, a new technology must prove itself in a variety settings. While this has happened to some extent with formal methods (e.g., CICS[14] and Cleanroom development[5]), the number of cases is still small, and much of the work is occurring in Europe. What is more, the natural conservatism of engineering is often compounded by a general uneasiness with respect to discrete mathematics.[3] As a result, formal methods have neither the visibility nor the acceptance necessary to make them standard practice.

The largest single obstacle to acceptance is one of perceived cost/benefit. Here we run up against the heuristic related to science: "apply science when appropriate." Many in industry believe that formal methods are inappropriate simply because the cost of their use is too high. Others assert that use of these methods leads to obsessive concern with correctness to the detriment of usability[3].

Even when the theoretical usefulness of formal approaches is conceded, the question of *engineering* appropriateness is still an open question. By way of analogy, consider the use of finite element analysis, which only recently has become a standard tool in civil and mechanical engineering. While the underlying mathematics were long understood, the wide-spread use of this technique had to await the advent of digital computers. The moral is that existence of a relevant theory does not necessarily imply its engineering suitability.

To increase the acceptance of formal methods, we must demonstrate that these systems can increase productivity, quality, or both, with acceptable cost. I suggest that the formal methods community work in three complementary areas to meet this goal:

1. Marketing: Concentrate on modeling rather than formal reasoning.
2. Technical: Develop "consumable" mathematical systems at the same level of detail as traditional engineering mathematics.
3. Education: Teach the basic principles to the next generation of professionals, both to prepare them for the future and to increase the adoption rate of formal methods.

The remaining sections expand on each of these topics.

5 Marketing of Formal Methods

Part of the reason that formal methods has such a bad name is that they are often confused with proving programs correct. While program proving is *one* aspect of formal methods, it is arguably the least significant. For one thing, it is only applicable at the latest stages of development, well after system specification and design. Most development organizations realize that the programming of algorithms is not the most error prone part of the process, especially if the overall architecture is well-conceived. When a system is precisely specified, and when its design is properly organized, the code for the individual pieces (e.g., procedures and functions)

---

[3] It has been my experience that many practitioners either feel that their mathematical skills have atrophied or that they are simply "not good in math."

is usually simple and straight-forward. The need for complex algorithms and their attendant correctness proofs is often an sign of poor design[5].

Thus the *real* benefits of formal methods emerge when they are applied to the early process stages. During specification, systems like Z can be used profitably to develop clear, concise specifications. While reasoning about these specifications may be advantageous, the simple act of precise modeling often provides the greatest benefit. Given the paucity of tools to support reasoning, it appears that advocates of formal methods should stress the advantages of modeling in its own right.

A second area where formal methods can be profitably applied is the specification of interfaces. For components forming part of a library, such specifications are the key to determining fitness for use (see above). But even in the case of system-specific components, a formal interface specification clearly indicates the rights and obligations of the module's clients and any of its implementations. As in the case of system specification, it is the modeling aspect of formal methods that comes to the fore.

Summary: to ensure wider acceptance of formal methods, apply the science to the area with the highest leverage, namely specification of systems and components. That is, using our categories from section 3, we should concentrate on those emphasizing specification, modeling, and cataloging.

6 Developing Consumable Mathematics

In the long run, of course, we should expect more of formal methods than simple modeling. By analogy to traditional engineering mathematics, we want to manipulate the model, draw conclusions, and evaluate consequences. Most formal methods currently available are inadequate in this regard. For one thing, there are few tools to aid in model assessment (e.g., proof assistants[6]). But there is another major hurdle: with few exceptions[5], most formal systems are not "consumable." That is, the depth of mathematical knowledge required to work with the system is much greater than for traditional engineering mathematics.

To be truly effective with most formal methods, one must be intimately knowledgeable about the inference rules of propositional and predicate calculus, as well as the specific mathematical system on which the formal method is based. This is a much greater level of detail than is common in traditional engineering. In these areas, the key mathematical results are identified, isolated, and packaged so as to be useful.

Few practicing engineers are conversant with the mathematical foundations of differential equations. Certainly no practitioner resorts to the limit definition of the derivative. But this is *exactly* the level at which the reasoning processes for most formal systems take place. We need the equivalent of the standard table of derivatives to go along with any formal method; short-hand laws whose preconditions are easy to understand and to evaluate, and whose results are of general benefit. Some work is being done in this area (e.g., the Z toolkit[22] and the Larch Shared Language handbook[10]), but more is required.

7   Educating Future Professionals

We close with a discussion of teaching formal methods to the next generation of software developers. In addition to the engineering method, we must consider the maturity level of undergraduate students and overall educational philosophy. At RIT, it is certainly the case that students entering the computer science program have attitudes closer to their peers in the College of Engineering than to those in the College of Science. This is further reinforced by RIT's tradition of career education (as seen in our cooperative education requirements). Our students are pragmatic, practical, and career-oriented – the hallmarks of engineering professionals. In particular, like developers in the industry, our students have little patience for theory if they cannot relate it to practice.

As a result, we do *not* introduce formality in the early stages of our program. For one thing, we still attract a considerable number of students who have little prior computing experience. To these students, everything is new, and layering formal mathematics on top of the basic concept development in algorithms and data structures would be counter-productive (i.e., we wouldn't have to worry about over-crowded sophomore classes). However, once the fundamentals of programming have been mastered, we can use these as a foundation for addressing larger issues in design. It is here, in the second year, that we introduce "semi-formal" methods.

Our sophomore course in design and implementation introduces the ideas of pre- and post-conditions, representation invariants, and abstraction functions. We do this in the spirit of Liskov and Guttag[18]. Precise English prose is used to define the properties of objects and procedures, though in our case the language is Modula-2 rather than CLU. The net effect is that our students begin co-operative education with a rudimentary idea of what constitutes a precise and concise specification.

For those upper-division students who elect the software engineering concentration, our course on specification and design introduces truly formal methods. Currently we use Z as our base language, though we also survey at least one algebraic system such as Larch. In line with the issues discussed above, we concentrate on specification and modeling, though we do introduce some of the inference rules in conjunction with deducing specification properties.

All the students in this course have at least some cooperative education experience, and they are generally well-versed in the problems of software development. It is heartening to see that the majority recognize the potential value of formal methods, though they do not believe they can apply them in practice. I address this question of applicability from two directions. First, I tell them that they are the vanguard of a new generation of developers who may well initiate the wider adoption of formal methods. Second, it is a safe bet that formal approaches will become more important as safety and reliability requirements become more stringent. Thus, students who have some grounding in formal methods will be better prepared when customers start making such demands.

8   Conclusions

In this paper, I argued that formal methods must be understood in the context of the overall engineering method. This method is characterized by the use of a set of heuristics defining the engineering state-of-the-art (or *sota*). In particular, meta-heuristics are used to evaluate the appropriateness and applicability of scientific and mathematical theories. Thus, if formal methods are to become part of the software engineering sota, we must address cost/benefit issues that attend to the use of any theory.

The final sections presented three ways to increase the use of formal methods:

1. We should be emphasize systems such as Z that support rigorous modeling at early development stages: this is where current methods are most effective. We should also promote algebraic systems like Larch as cataloging mechanisms, thus addressing one of the key issues in reusability: finding relevant components.
2. Second, we must concentrate on raising the level the reasoning component of formal methods. That is, we need consumable mathematics that can be reliably applied with the same way that traditional engineering uses calculus and differential equations. Proof assistants working at the level of the *engineer's* mathematical objects would help in this endeavor.
3. Finally, by integrating formal methods as part of a pragmatic approach to software engineering education, we both prepare out graduates for career growth, while slowly infusing this technology into industry. In this latter regard, we are like the Fabian socialists of the 19th century who promoted the continual evolution of socialist societies. With any luck, the Fabian formal methodists will be more successful in achieving their goals.

By moving forward on all these fronts, we will reduce the time until "use formal methods" is on the top shelf of the software engineering toolbox.

9 Acknowledgements

Much of what I know about engineering practice is the direct result working with dedicated engineers in industry and faculty associates in RIT's College of Engineering. In addition, wide-ranging discussions with my friend and colleague Henry Etlinger have been crucial in helping me clarify my thoughts. I gratefully acknowledge my debt to these professionals in forming my views on software engineering, while recognizing that any misunderstandings or misinterpretations are entirely my own.

References

1. Thomas Allen. Distinguishing engineers from scientists. In Ralph Katz, editor, *Managing Professionals in Innovative Organizations*. Ballinger Publishing, Cambridge, MA, 1988.
2. Mary-Frances Blade. Creativity in engineering. In Myron A. Coler, editor, *Essays on Creativity in the Sciences*. New York University Press, New York, 1963.
3. Nathaniel S. Borenstein. *Programming as if People Mattered: Friendly Programs, Software Engineering and Other Noble Delusions*. Princeton University Press, Princeton, New Jersey, 1991.
4. Edsger Dijkstra. *A Discipline of Programming*. Prentice-Hall, Englewood Cliffs, NJ, 1976.

5. Michael Dyer. *The Cleanroom Approach to Quality Software Development.* John Wiley & Sons, New York, 1992.
6. B. Fields and M. Elvang-Goransson. A VDM case style in *mural. IEEE Transctions on Software Engineering,* 18(4):265–278, April 1992.
7. Samuel C. Florman. *The Existential Pleasures of Engineering.* St. Martin's Press, New York, 1976.
8. Joseph Goguen. Parameterized programming. *IEEE Transactions on Software Engineering,* 10(5):528–543, September 1984.
9. John Guttag and James Horning. An introduction to LCL, a Larch/C interface language. Technical Report 74, Digital Systems Research Center, July 1991.
10. John Guttag, James Horning, and Andres Modet. Report on the Larch shared language. Technical Report 58, Digital Systems Research Center, April 1990.
11. Anthony Hall. Seven myths of formal methods. *IEEE Software,* 7(5):11–20, September 1990.
12. Watts Humphrey. *Managing the Software Process.* Addison-Wesley, Reading, MA, 1989.
13. Watts Humphrey, David Kitson, and Julia Gale. A comparison of U.S. and Japanese software process maturity. In *Proceedings of the 13th International Conference on Software Engineering,* pages 38–51, Austin, TX, May 1991.
14. Paul Johnson. Experience of formal development in CICS. In John A. McDermid, editor, *The Theory and Practice of Refinement,* pages 59–78. Butterworths, London, 1989.
15. Cliff B. Jones. *Systematic Software Development Using VDM.* Prentice Hall, Englewood Cliffs, N.J., 1990.
16. Billy Vaughn Koen. *Definition of the Engineering Method.* American Society for Engineering Education, Washington, D.C., 1985.
17. Burton Leathers. After the divorce: Reflections on using Eiffel at Cognos. In *Symposium on Object-Oriented Programming Emphasizing Practical Applications,* pages 66–80. Marist College, September 1990.
18. Barbara Liskov and John Guttag. *Abstraction and Specification in Program Design.* MIT Press, Cambridge, 1986.
19. Henry Petroski. *To Engineer Is Human: The Role of Failure in Successful Design.* St. Martin's Press, New York, 1985.
20. Ben Potter, Jane Sinclair, and David Till. *An Introduction to Formal Specification and Z.* Prentice-Hall, Englewood Cliffs, NJ, 1991.
21. Mary Shaw. Prospects for an engineering discipline of software. *IEEE Software,* 7(6):15–24, November 1990.
22. J. M. Spivey. *The Z Notation: A Reference Manual.* Prentice-Hall, Englewood Cliffs, N.J., 1989.

This article was processed using the LaTeX macro package with LLNCS style

Formal Methods for Software Engineers: Tradeoffs in Curriculum Design

David Garlan

School of Computer Science
Carnegie Mellon University
Pittsburgh, PA 15213

Abstract. While formal methods are becoming increasingly important to software engineering, currently there is little consensus on how they should be taught. In this paper I outline some of the important dimensions of curriculum design for formal methods and illustrate the tradeoffs through a brief examination of four common course formats. I summarize what I have learned from teaching courses in each of these formats and outline an agenda of educational research that will enable us to teach formal methods more effectively.

1 Introduction

As software engineering evolves into a true engineering discipline we can expect the role of formalism to play an increasingly important role. Mathematical modeling, abstraction, and analysis will help provide a scientific base for software systems in a similar way as it has done for other engineering disciplines. Signs of this are already apparent in the increasing use of formalism in areas such as testing, hardware verification, analysis of security, and fault tolerance.

An important component of this approach is the use of formalism for describing the behavior of software systems, and for developing software based on techniques of mathematical modeling and analysis – an area often referred to as formal methods. Formal methods have been advocated for many years under many guises, including program verification [Hoa72], rigorous program development [Gri81, Jon86], abstract specifications of modules [GH80], and modeling of concurrency [Hoa78]. But it is only recently that both the necessity and practicality of formal methods have become apparent. Necessity has emerged in applications involving safety critical systems [SIG91, MoD89], realtime scheduling [SG90], and protocol verification [MS91]. Practicality has been demonstrated in recent applications of formal methods to industrial software development [NC88, DG90, Bar89].

As formal methods become more important to software engineering, educators must find ways to educate software engineers in their use. Currently there is no clear consensus on how this should be done. Of course, it unlikely that a single approach to teaching formal methods will ever emerge. However, as we gain experience in teaching formal methods we *can* expect to understand the tradeoffs in curriculum design so that course materials and approach can be chosen to meet specific requirements of a software engineering program.

In this paper I outline some of the important dimensions of the space of curriculum design for formal methods and illustrate the implications of choices in this space. This is not meant to be an exhaustive taxonomy, but rather a reflection on lessons learned from having taught formal methods in four radically different ways: as a master's level survey course, as an in-depth master's level skills course, as an in-house industrial course, and as a graduate topics course. Each of these styles has its advantages and disadvantages, and it is the goal of this paper to illuminate the tradeoffs.

2 Basic Issues

The relative immaturity of software engineering has led to a wide variety of experimental approaches to teaching it. This is not all bad. Since many different purposes must be served, it is important that there be flexibility in choice of material and style of delivery. But at the same time, for topics such as formal methods there is relatively little accumulated experience to guide the would-be instructor in choosing appropriate ways of dealing with the material. Indeed, it is often not even clear what questions the course designer must answer in determining the nature of the course to be taught. Based on my experience eight key issues stand out

Target level: *What kind of expertise in formal methods do you expect students to acquire?*

Formal methods courses differ dramatically in their goals. At one extreme a course can familiarize students with a broad number of formal notations. At the other extreme a course can teach students to be fluent in one or maybe two notations. In the former case students come away with broad but shallow expertise; in the latter they gain deep but narrow skills.

There are obvious advantages and disadvantages to each approach. In the former case students may be able to determine which (if any) formal method would be appropriate to attack a given problem, but they may lack the skills to actually solve it. In the latter case students can be expected to solve a problem when it can be solved with the methods they have learned, but may lack the perspective to recognize the applicability of other methods.

Classes of system: *To what kinds of systems do you expect students to be able to apply formal methods?*

Formal methods differ dramatically according to the kind of system they are good at modeling. The most obvious distinction is between notations that were developed for sequential systems and those for concurrent systems. In the former case, there are relatively well established techniques and notational styles. (Model-oriented and property-oriented notations are the main alternatives.) But for concurrent systems, there is much greater variation. For example, Petri nets, temporal logic, and process algebras represent radically different approaches to concurrency.

There are also certain restricted classes of system that have specialized notations, such as state machines, protocols, and deadline-driven real-time tasks. By focusing on specific domains, specialized notations tend to have more power, but at the cost of generality. For the practicing software engineer, however, this may be a tradeoff worth making.

Engineering emphasis: *What aspects of formal methods are to be emphasized?*

Traditionally formal methods have focused on the problem of correctness: Given a formal specification of a system how can one produce an implementation that satisfies the specified properties. While the use of verification continues to be important for safety-critical systems, formal methods have recently found industrial applicability in a variety of alternative ways. They are being used to describe system interfaces as a means of precisely documenting the function of the system [NC88]. They are being used to characterize reusable system frameworks and software architectures [GD90, GN91]. They are being used to support the analysis of non-functional properties such as performance or real-time response [Zav82, SG90]. Many of these uses of formal methods more directly address industrial concerns, such as time-to-market and effective use of resources.

The choice of emphasis has a strong impact on the kind of analytical methods that are used in the course. Where correctness is a primary issue, verification-style proofs will play a central role. Where other uses formal methods are of concern, different kinds of proofs and techniques for analysis will be appropriate. For example, safety analysis and real-time schedulability typically require different analytical techniques from those used to prove correctness.

Use of case studies: *To what extent will case studies be used to present the material?*

Formal methods can be presented as purely mathematical systems. In such courses the underlying mathematical principles dominate. At the other extreme formal methods can be presented as a means to practical results. In such courses techniques for solving specific problems dominate. When the latter approach is adopted, formal methods are typically presented through case studies. These may be either pedagogical (for example, Library or Elevator problems [Cal86]), or based on industrial experience (for example, [NC88, BAR+91]). The advantage of the former approach is that it concentrates on underlying mathematical skills, while the advantage of the latter is that it focuses on practical skills.

Use of a project: *Will students undertake a project?*

A course in formal methods can require students to develop a formal specification of a non-trivial system as a course project. Projects permit in-depth exposure to a single problem and a single notation for dealing with it. The use of projects in a formal methods course has similar tradeoffs as the use of a project in an undergraduate software engineering course [ST91].

Level of formality: *What properties of mathematics are exploited?*

By definition, formal methods rest on mathematical foundations. But mathematics can be used in many different ways. One approach is to exploit the notational aspects of mathematics. Here mathematics is primarily used as a means of abstraction, precision, and conciseness. An alternative is to focus more on mathematical mechanisms, and in particular on the use of proof as a vehicle for analysis and reasoning. The kind of mathematical properties that are emphasized have a strong impact on the amount of instruction that is required to give students the mathematical skills for dealing with the notations. For example, if the use of proofs is to play a primary role, it is likely that the course will have to spend a reasonable amount of time on inference systems and purely mathematical proof. The amount of prerequisite mathematics required of students will also depend on the kind of mathematical system that is used. Systems based on set theory and first-order logic tend to require relatively few mathematical detours. Others – such those based on Scott domains, or category theory – may require considerable more mathematical training.

Use of tools: *What will be the role of tools?*

In the last few years many tools have been developed to support the use of specific formal notations. It is tempting to include these in a course – particularly a course with a practical focus. The advantages are obvious: tools make it easier to develop and analyze formal descriptions by mechanizing many of the low-level details.

Less obvious, however, are the disadvantages. First, the best tools may not be available for the best notations. The instructor is then faced with the unpleasant choice between teaching a less desirable method with good tool support, and teaching a preferred method with poor support. Second, there is often a significant learning curve associated with tools. The more sophisticated the tool, the steeper the curve. For example, most formal notations have a type checker that can be used with little or no effort. Other notations include proof checkers, document processors, and special-purpose editors, each of which may require several weeks for students to become proficient.

Interaction with other courses: *How will formal methods interact with other aspects of the curriculum?*

As techniques for exploiting formalism becomes more pervasive in software engineering it becomes more and more difficult to consider formal methods as a completely separate topic. Formalism associated with testing or verification may properly belong in a course on verification and validation, while formalism associated with reasoning about properties of concurrent systems (security, performance, process scheduling, etc.) may properly belong in a course on operating systems. Not only does this imply that it makes little sense to teach *all* formal methods in a single course, but it also suggests the possibility of using an entire curriculum as the forum for learning about formal methods. For example, the practical aspects of using formal methods for real systems might be taught as part of a project course. Further, by using formal methods in other courses, students will be more likely to view the material as an integral part of software engineering, rather than as an isolated topic. In the extreme case, a formal methods course *per se* may no longer be needed: formalisms are simply introduced as they become relevant to other parts of software engineering.

On the other hand, in-depth exposure to formal methods in a class specifically devoted to that topic has several important advantages. Students can build mathematical maturity and skills, they can make meaningful comparisons between different methods, and they gain exposure to the use of formalism over an extended period.

3   Course Models

The issues just outlined suggest a huge space of course alternatives. However, in practice several standard combinations predominate. I now briefly consider four such course organizations with which I have had some experience.

Master's level survey course:

Programs that lead to a Master's degree in Software Engineering typically teach formal methods in a semester survey course. A good example is the formal methods course of the SEI MSE program, developed by Mark Ardis, and distributed by the SEI through their education series. (Appendix A includes a syllabus for a version of this course, which I adapted to include more exposure to the Z specification language.) The course covers 10 different notations including ASLAN, Z, VDM, Larch, CSP, Petri Nets, Lotos, and Temporal Logic. On average, each method is allocated two weeks. This allows students just enough time to read one or two papers about the method and complete a simple assignment using it.

Although the treatment of each method in this kind of course is relatively superficial,[1] it is possible to for students to develop good intuitions about differences in expressive power. To achieve this goal it is particularly important to consider similar problems – both in homework and in lectures – for a collection of different methods. (In the case of the course outlined in the appendix, I have used the Library Problem [Kem85] and Spivey's birthday book example [Spi89] to illustrate methods for describing sequential systems. For concurrent systems I have used variations on traffic light and the elevator problems [Cal86].)

Reflecting on the success of this style of course, on the positive side students are exposed to a wide variety of notations and get a flavor for the ways they might be applied to a variety of problems. The course also seems to be accessible to most master's level students. In particular, the mixed mathematical backgrounds of students does not pose a serious problem because there is rarely time to delve into the deeper mathematical properties of the methods.

However, overall I have been dissatisfied with the attempt to cover a large number of methods and notations. It often seems that students just begin to understand one method, when it is time to move on to another. (As one student remarked, "If this is Monday, it must be Larch.") This leads to a situation in which students may be able to associate certain methods with certain kinds of problems, but are largely incapable of carrying out the solutions of those problems.

Master's level in-depth course:

An alternative to a survey course is an in-depth treatment of a small number of formal methods. I have experimented with such a course as an elective in the CMU MSE program. In it we consider only two formal notations: Z and Larch. The goal of the course is for students develop fluency in applying the notations to practical industrial problems. To accomplish these aims, course lectures rely heavily on case studies. Additionally, students complete two major projects. The first is carried out in Z as a system-level design problem. The second is carried out using the same problem, but expressed in Larch as a module-level design. (Most recently the students developed a formal model of a simple terminal air traffic controller. The description of the problem is included in Appendix B.)

In a course such as this it is practical – and desirable – to make the use of tools a central component since the length of exposure to each notation justifies the cost of learning to use the tools associated with it. Specifically, all students use the type checkers and document formatting tools associated with Z and Larch. Additionally, several students have used the Larch Prover to check simple proofs about their systems. Finally, the course brings in formal methods experts to talk about their experience using the formal methods taught in the class. These presentations can be quite detailed and technical since students can appreciate the problems at these levels.

Reflecting on the merits of this kind of course, I believe that it can be extremely effective. Students can learn to use formal methods effectively and with good taste. On the other hand, I have found that such a course is not for everyone. In particular, to really understand how to use a formal method effectively it is necessary to exploit the underlying mathematics. But not all students arrive with the necessary mathematical maturity or background to make this possible. Of course, it is possible – and often necessary – to spend time during class developing those skills. But this can be an uphill battle, and in the end perhaps not worth

---

[1] As Ardis puts it, "Students learn enough to be dangerous."

the effort for students who have little intention of applying formal methods in their practice of software engineering. The implication is that (a) formal methods should be an optional course, or (b) entry standards for an MSE program should be such that only students with suitable background in mathematics are accepted, or (c) students with weak backgrounds should be required to take remedial courses.

Industrial course:

The third kind of course with which I have had experience is one designed as an in-house industrial training course that was developed and taught jointly by Norman Delisle, Mike Spivey, and me at Tektronix, Inc. We had developed several formalizations of Tektronix products that were beginning to play an important role in certain product development efforts within the company. But outside of the research laboratory, engineers had virtually no training in formal methods. Our goal was therefore to give others an appreciation of the use of formal methods and to provide them with enough background to be able to read and understand the formal models that we had been developing. The course consisted of five hour and a half lectures, spread out over as many weeks. We provided optional homework assignments for each class. The lectures relied almost entirely on case studies. Where possible we chose examples that involved products and problems from local engineering domains. Several of these were formal models of Tektronix products.

The course was viewed as a success: overall it incurred relatively low overhead for the participants, and produced a several long-term benefits. Although it had relatively low aspirations – namely to develop a reading knowledge of formal specifications – it served to broaden the enthusiasm for the use of formal methods within the company. It also helped some engineers recognize ways to use the results of the specific models that we had developed for Tektronix product domains.

Graduate topics course:

The fourth course format is a graduate course in formal methods designed to give students a basic understanding of the potential of formal methods in preparation for research. The primary emphasis is the current state of the art, rather than the state of the practice. Assignments typically center around readings, many of which are current research papers. Usually there is no project, although students may take responsibility for presenting a case study or research paper to the rest of the class.

An important factor that determines how best to teach such a course is the fact that the students can generally be expected to have solid mathematical skills. They usually know how to carry out proofs of correctness for small programs. Typically they can reason formally about a problem, carrying out proofs, for example, by structural induction. It is therefore appropriate to consider deeper mathematical properties of the methods. For example, it may be worthwhile to discuss initial algebras when introducing algebraic notations, or type inference when presenting Z.

My experience with this kind of course, is that success depends on finding unifying mathematical themes with which to compare the different approaches. This allows students to obtain deep insight into the reasons why there are different formal notations and what kinds of analyses each will be appropriate for.

4   Some General Words of Advice

Packaging issues aside, over the years I have developed a number of opinions about what does and does not work well in teaching formal methods.

- **Iterate solutions to projects.** Few people can write elegant (or even tasteful) specifications the first time they try. In particular, learning to use the expressive power of logic and non-determinism is one of the most important but difficult lessons to teach. Students typically try to use a formal notation simply as a high-level programming language. When students undertake a project, it is therefore essential that they submit preliminary versions for critique and revision. Between the initial and final versions, it is not uncommon for students to cut their specifications in half, while at the same time improving readability and analyzability.
- **Use tools on projects.** If a project of any size is attempted it is usually worth the effort to teach students how to use simply-mastered tools for formatting, checking, and (perhaps) analyzing their formal models.
- **Interleave mathematical training with case studies.** It is tempting to try to teach all the mathematics that students might need to know as a single lump lesson, typically at the beginning of the course. My experience is that this is a mistake. It works much better to interleave mathematical training with the exposition of case studies. This not only helps motivate the mathematics, but helps guarantee that there is an appropriate balance between formalism and practical application. Moreover, it takes time to develop mathematical maturity: an interleaved approach allows students to gradually improve their skills.
- **Integrate industrial motivation.** Software engineers want to know how formal methods are actually being used in industry. It is tempting to teach this in a single section, typically at the end of the course (as illustrated in Appendix A). I have found this is much less effective that using industrial case studies throughout the course.
- **Stress families, not notations.** It is tempting to view each notation as defining a different method. This exacerbates the problems of understanding the field of formal methods, since their are hundreds of notations. Instead, concentrate on equivalence classes of methods. For example students, should be led to view VDM and Z as instances of the same family, while Larch and OBJ are instances of another.
- **Adopt "what can be analyzed" as a theme.** The fundamental differences between classes of formal methods can best be described by asking what properties of a system they make it possible to analyze. This provides a unifying theme with which to make comparisons, and it focuses on the essential differences between methods.
- **Interact with other courses wherever possible.** It is easy for students to view formal methods as a self-contained, separable topic, largely unrelated to the other more practical concerns of software engineering practice. This can be overcome by finding ways to apply formal methods in other courses.
- **Encourage informal use of formal notations.** There is a tendency to view formal methods as the province of mathematicians. As Hall has pointed out, it is possible to realize great benefits of formal methods even when they are used informally [Hal90]. This helps overcome the inertia of applying formal methods outside the classroom, and allows students to view formal methods as a cost-effective technique for gaining insight into design problems.

- **Show bad/flawed specifications.** To learn the difference between good and bad specifications, it is essential that students see examples of flawed or inelegant specifications. This can be partially accomplished through iteration on a course project, but it is also useful to do this in lectures and on homeworks. I typically give out at least one seriously flawed specification to my students, and ask them to critique it.
- **Encourage interactive use of formalism** There is a tendency to view the use of formal methods as a closet activity: the specifier emerges after a few days of isolation to reveal the perfect formal model. It is much more successful (and realistic) to engender the use of formal methods as a collaborative, interactive technique. This can be done by assigning group homework and by having students present their homework to the rest of class.
- **Concentrate on systems, not code.** The future of formal methods is in the development of entire systems, not individual algorithms or data structures. We must therefore teach our students how to use formal methods to attack systems engineering problems. In particular, this argues for a focus on engineering aspects of formalisms, not just mathematical elegance. Issues of reuse, scalability, automation, testability are as valid in the domain of formal methods as they are in other aspects of software engineering:

5 Agenda for Educators

The use of formal methods in software engineering education is relatively new. Not surprisingly therefore, there are a number of curricular materials that have not been well developed or disseminated. This represents a gap that should be filled by educators and practitioners of formal methods. I would include the following on my "wish-list" of materials that would greatly improve our ability to do an effective job of teaching.

- **Textbooks:** There are an increasing number of textbooks devoted to a specific formal method. While these are a welcome, there is also a strong need for textbooks that adopt a comparative view towards formal methods. Ideally such textbooks would make clear how different formal methods relate to each other and illustrate how they are appropriate for different kinds of problems.
- **Tools:** Although there are an increasing number of tools, few are engineered with students in mind. In particular, most tools developed for proof assistance are oriented towards researchers. The tools are often quite powerful, but also unnecessarily difficult to apply to the simple cases that students encounter.
- **Case studies:** Earlier I stressed the importance of using case studies. Regrettably there are very few published studies that can be used in a classroom. Moreover, there are almost no published case studies that (intentionally) illustrate mistakes, flaws, or stylistic problems.
- **Broader examples:** Where case studies in formal methods exist at all, they are typically presented in isolation from the system for which they were developed. To illustrate the connection with other activities in software engineering, it would be helpful to have complete examples that relate formalizations, code, documentation, testing, etc.

6 Acknowledgements

Although the opinions expressed in this paper are mine alone, the experience in teaching formal methods owes much to my collaborators in course development: Mark Ardis, Norman Delisle, and Mike Spivey. I would also like to thank the conference program committee and Mary Shaw for constructive comments on an earlier draft. Finally, the investigation into tools for teaching formal methods was made possible by a Faculty Development Grant from Carnegie Mellon University.

References

[Age79]   T. Agerwala. Putting Petri nets to work. *Computer*, 12(12):85–94, December 1979.

[AK84]   B. Auernheimer and R.A. Kemmerer. *ASLAN User's Manual*. Dept. of Computer Science, UC Santa Barbara, 1984.

[Bar89]   G. Barrett. Formal methods applied to a floating-point number system. *IEEE Transactions on Software Engineering*, 15(5):611–621, May 1989.

[BAR+91] W.C. Bowman, G.H. Archinoff, V.M. Raina, D.R. Tremaine, and N.G. Leveson. An application of fault tree analysis to safety critical software at Ontario Hydro. In *Conference on Probabilistic Safety Assessment and Management (PSAM)*, April 1991.

[BCM+90] J.R. Burch, E.M. Clarke, K.L. McMillan, D.L. Dill, and J. Hwang. Symbolic model checking: 10^{20} states and beyond. In *Proceedings of the Fifth Annual IEEE Symposium on Logic in Computer Science*, June 1990.

[Cal86]   Problem set for the fourth international workshop on software specification and design. ACM SIGSOFT Engineering Notes, April 1986, 1986.

[CHJ86]   B. Cohen, W.T. Harwood, and M.I. Jackson. *The Specification of Complex Systems*. Addison-Wesley, 1986. (Chapter 5: Model-based specification).

[CM78]   J.P. Cavano and J.A. McCall. A framework for the measurement of software quality. In *Software Quality and Assurance Workshop*, pages 133–139. ACM, November 1978.

[DG90]   N. Delisle and D. Garlan. A formal specification of an oscilloscope. *Software*, 7(5):29–37, September 1990.

[GD90]   David Garlan and Norman Delisle. Formal specifications as reusable frameworks. In *VDM'90: VDM and Z – Formal Methods in Software Development*, Kiel, Germany, 1990. Springer-Verlag, LNCS 428.

[GH80]   J.V. Guttag and J.J. Horning. Formal specification as a design tool. In *Seventh POPL*. ACM, 1980. (also in *Software Specification Techniques*, pages 187-207).

[GHM78]   J.V. Guttag, E. Horowitz, and D.R. Musser. Abstract data types and software validation. *Communications of the ACM*, 21(12), December 1978.

[GHM90]   J.V. Guttag, J.J. Horning, and M. Modet. Report on the Larch Shared Language: Version 2.3. Technical Report 58, Digital, Systems Research Center, 1990.

[GHW85]   J.V. Guttag, J.J. Horning, and J.M. Wing. The Larch family of specification languages. *IEEE Software*, 2(5):24–36, September 1985.

[GN91]   David Garlan and David Notkin. Formalizing design spaces: Implicit invocation mechanisms. In *VDM'91: Formal Software Development Methods*, pages 31–44. Springer-Verlag, LNCS 551, October 1991.

[Gri81]   D. Gries. *The Science of Programming*. Springer-Verlag, 1981.

[Hal90]   A. Hall. Seven myths of formal methods. *Software*, 7(5):11–20, September 1990.

[Hoa72]   C.A.R. Hoare. Proof of correctness of data representations. *Acta Informatica*, 1:271–281, 1972.

[Hoa78]   C.A.R. Hoare. Communicating sequential processes. *CACM*, 21(8):666–677, August 1978.

[ISO87]   ISO. Information processing systems – open systems interconnection – LOTOS – a formal description technique based on the temporal ordering of observational behaviour. Technical Report ISO/TC 97/SC 21, International Standards Organization, 1987.

[Jon86]   C.B. Jones. Systematic program development. In *Proc. Symposium on Mathematics and Computer Science*, 1986. (also in *Software Specification Techniques*, pages 89-108).

[Kem85]   R.A. Kemmerer. Testing formal specifications to detect design errors. *IEEE Transactions on Software Engineering*, 11(1):32–43, January 1985.

[MoD89]   Requirements for the procurement of safety critical software in defense equipment. U.K. Ministry of Defense, May 1989. Interim Defence Standard 00-55.

[MS84]   C. Carroll Morgan and Bernard A. Sufrin. Specification of the Unix filing system. *IEEE Transactions on Software Engineering*, 10(2):128–142, March 1984.

[MS91]   K. McMillan and J. Schwalbe. Formal verification of the Encore Gigamax cache consistency protocol. In *International Symposium on Shared Memory Multiprocessors*, 1991.

[NC88]   C.J. Nix and B.P. Collins. The use of software engineering, including the Z notation, in the development of CICS. *Quality Assurance*, 14(3):103–110, September 1988.

[OL82]   S. Owicki and L. Lamport. Proving liveness properties of concurrent programs. *ACM Transactions on Programming Languages and Systems*, 4(3):455–495, July 1982.

[PC86]   D.L. Parnas and P.C. Clements. A rational design process: How and why to fake it. *IEEE Transactions on Software Engineering*, SE-12(2):251–257, February 1986.

[Pet77]   J.L. Peterson. Petri nets. *ACM Computing Surveys*, 9(3):223–252, September 1977.

[Pou89]   D. Pountain. Occam II. *Byte*, 14(10):279–284, October 1989.

[SG90]   Lui Sha and John B. Goodenough. Real-time scheduling theory and Ada*. *Computer*, pages 53–62, April 1990.

[SIG91]   *Proceedings of the ACM SIGSOFT'91 Conference on Software for Critical Systems*, Software Engineering Notes, Volume 16, Number 5. ACM Press, December 1991.

[Spi88]   J.M. Spivey. The Fuzz manual, 1988.

[Spi89]   J.M. Spivey. An introduction to Z and formal specification. *Software Engineering Journal*, 4(1):40–50, January 1989.

[ST91]   Mary Shaw and James E. Tomayko. Models for undergraduate project courses in software engineering. In *Proceedings Fifth SEI Conference on Software Engineering Education*, October 1991.

[Ste88]   R.M. Stein. T800 and counting. *Byte*, 13(12):287–296, November 1988.

[Win90]   J. Wing. A specifier's introduction to formal methods. *Computer*, 23(9):8–26, September 1990.

[Zar91]   A.M. Zaremski. A Larch specification of the Miro Editor. Technical Report CMU-CS-91-111, Carnegie Mellon University, 1991.

[Zav82]   P. Zave. An operational approach to requirements specification for embedded systems. *IEEE Trans. on Software Engineering*, SE-8(3), 1982. (also in *Software Specification Techniques*, pages 131-169).

A Course Syllabus for Survey Course

Lecture	Topic	Subtopic	Reading
1	Overview	Introduction	
2	State Model	State-machine	[Win90]
3		ASLAN	[AK84],[Kem85]
4	Proof	Natural Deduction	[Gri81](Ch. 0-4)
5	Algebraic Models	Introduction	[GHM78]
6		Larch 1	[GHW85]
7		Larch 2	[GHM90]
8		Larch 3	[Zar91]
9	Abstract Models	VDM 1	[CHJ86]
10		VDM 2	
11		Z 1	[Spi89]
12		Z 2	[Spi88]
13		Z 3	[MS84]
14		Z 4	[DG90]
15		Z 5	[Bar89]
16		Z 6	[NC88]
17	MID-TERM EXAM		
18	Concurrency	Petri Nets 1	[Pet77]
19		Petri Nets 2	[Age79]
20		CSP	[Hoa78]
21		Occam	[Pou89], [Ste88]
22		Temporal Logic	[OL82]
23		Model Checking	[BCM$^+$90]
24		Lotos	[ISO87]
25	Practicalities	Lifecycle Issues	[CM78], [PC86], [Hal90]
26	Final Review		

B Description of a Course Project

The project for this semester's Formal Methods course is to produce a formal specification of the following system.

> A terminal air traffic control system (TATCA) handles the air traffic within a region of the country, which may include a number of airports. It schedules and controls the arrivals and departures of aircraft within the region, including having the aircraft "wait" in designated zones if there is insufficient runway capacity to land all of the aircraft. The TATCA interfaces with a number of en-route air traffic control systems. Aircraft are "handed-off" between these systems and the TATCA at a number of TATCA *gateways*. When aircraft land, they move from the gateway to a landing strip by traveling along a designated *glide path*, which takes them to one of several *approach paths* for the landing strip.

For this project we will consider a simplified TATCA, which schedules only landings and only for a single airstrip. The simplified TATCA has the following properties:

1. *Static Properties*
   (a) The TATCA schedules aircraft landing at a single airstrip of an airport.
   (b) The landing strip has a *fan* of approach paths into the landing strip.
   (c) There are a number of predetermined *glide* paths between each gateway and one or more of the approach points.
   (d) None of the glide or approach paths intersect, except at their endpoints.

2. *Dynamic Properties*
   (a) When an aircraft arrives at a gateway, the TATCA is notified of its identification and its arrival time at the gateway.
   (b) Aircraft must be scheduled into landing slots, which are fixed width time intervals.
   (c) To achieve optimal operation, the scheduler must wait to schedule aircraft waiting at a gateway until either:
      i. a number of as-yet unscheduled aircraft have entered its domain of operation ; or
      ii. a fixed interval of time has passed since the first as-yet unscheduled aircraft entered the TATCA.

The specification should contain enough explanatory prose to make the meaning of the specification clear to someone unfamiliar with the system being described. You should also elaborate on the design decisions you made in producing the specification. In particular, you should make clear where your specification resolves any areas of ambiguity, inconsistency, and incompleteness in the informal requirements.

Teaching Protocol Engineering in Honours Year

R. Lai
Department of Computer Science
and Computer Engineering,
La Trobe University,
Victoria, Australia 3083

Abstract

Protocol engineering is a branch of software engineering involved in the rigorous design, specification, verification, implementation and testing of communication protocols using formal methods. Teaching of protocol engineering in honours year (fourth year of the undergraduate course) at La Trobe University is conducted both by formal lectures and project supervision. A course by the name of "Protocol Engineering" has been taught since 1989. Students in their honours year have to do a substantial project under the supervision of a lecturer. This paper discusses the structure of the course, the experience of supervising honours projects in protocol engineering, and the improvements to be made in the future.

1 Introduction

Protocol specifications, written in English (informal specification), are subject to different interpretations and cannot be analysed for correctness. There is, therefore, a need for precise, unambiguous and consistent specification for these informal specifications. As such, the specifications need to be based on a mathematical or graphical language, called Formal Description Techniques (FDTs) so that they are unambiguous and can be analysed for correctness. Development of protocol using FDTs is called formal method. The availability of computer-aided tools for FDTs is a very important factor to their usefulness and applications.

Protocol engineering is a branch of software engineering involved in the rigorous design, specification, verification, implementation and testing of communication protocols using formal methods. Teaching of protocol engineering in honours year (fourth year of the undergraduate course) at La

Trobe University is conducted both by formal lectures and project supervision. A specialised course that focused on the development of communication protocols using formal methods, by the name of "Protocol Engineering", has been taught since 1989. While teaching formal methods in undergraduate courses is still not very common among universities all over the world, a specialised course on formal methods applied to communication protocol is the first of its kind among the universities in Australia. Honours students have to complete a major thesis as well as six other course subjects within a two semesters academic year, each being of thirteen weeks duration. The project is worth 35% of the honours course, with the other six course subjects constituting the rest 65%. Students work on the project under the supervision of a lecturer. Supervising students has proved to be a very effective way of teaching. A number of honours projects in protocol engineering have been completed successfully over the last few years.

This paper discusses the structure of the course "Protocol Engineering", the experience of supervising honours projects in protocol engineering, and the improvements to be made in the future. One of the main interests of this paper is about the teaching of analytical techniques that allow the prediction of safety of protocol, and the teaching of using formal methods for developing communication software systems in order to enhance their quality and reliability.

2 Protocol Engineering Methodology

A typical protocol engineering methodology for the development of reliable and quality communication software systems consists of the following steps :

- User Requirements - These are the communication requirements of the users. Examples are electronic mail, file transfer, directory services, and remote job processing.

- Informal Specification - The requirements of the users are studied. Some of the details include protocol model, services provided, reliability, and handling of errors. They are normally specified in English.

- Formal Specification - It is the specification using a FDT. This enables the specifications to be analysed.

- Protocol Verification - Based on the formal specification, it is to identify errors early in the development process. Should an error be detected, the specification is corrected.

- Protocol Implementation - This can be in the form of automatic implementation where a high-level compiler will take the formal specification as input to generate some intermediate code, say C. Then a C compiler can translate the intermediate code into executable codes.

- Conformance testing - It is the validation of the protocol implementation by testing against specifications or standards. The protocol is fed with a selected set of test inputs, and the outputs generated are observed and checked against specifications

- Interoperability Testing - It is the validation of the protocol implementation using implementations from different manufacturers. This ensures the protocol achieves the purpose of open communication.

- Maintenance - It is the phase that looks after the bugs after the software has been released as software is something that can hardly be bug-free regardless how it is developed.

With this methodology, there is a systematic approach to developing communication software. Errors can be eliminated at different stages before the products are released. The number of errors imbedded in the implementation will be significantly less. Subsequently, the cost for maintenance will be much reduced. These make the software more reliable. The methodology is summarised in figure 1.

3 Course Summary

In the course "Protocol Engineering" which is taught in the first semester, activities involved in the rigorous design of Open Systems Interconnect (OSI) protocols using formal methods are taught. The course objective is to teach practical software engineering technology for the development of reliable and quality communication software. The course comprises of the following seven major topics :

OSI Concepts. Concepts of communication protocols, the need for architecture, benefits of OSI, OSI reference model, OSI concepts like services, service access point, peer-to-peer communication, layer operation, protocol data unit and service primitives are discussed.

Protocol Engineering Methodology. Due to the nature of open systems and international standards being subject to different interpretations and implementations, there is a need for developing International Organisation for Standardisation (ISO) communication protocols using

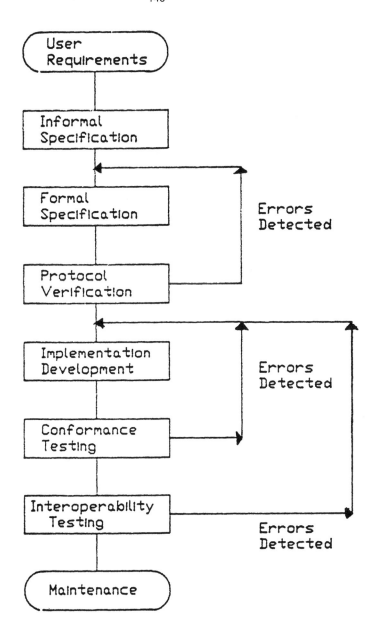

Protocol Development Process

Figure   1.

formal methods and a formal methodology. The methodology mentioned in section two is explained in details.

Formal Description Techniques. The motivation for using formal methods, like precision of expression, avoidance of ambiguity, possibility of rigourous analysis are discussed. This leads to the development of formal language, called formal description techniques by ISO. The different classes of FDTs are finite state machine, net, process algebra, and logic. Petri Nets, LOTOS, Estelle, and temporal logic are introduced. But only Petri Nets, in particular Numerical Petri Nets (NPNs) [36], and LOTOS are taught in details due to time constraints. The objectives of FDTs, namely, to enable unambiguous description of OSI standards, to allow such descriptions to be verified, to provide guidance to designers to implement OSI systems, and to act as a sound basis for conformance testing are discussed.

Petri Nets and Numerical Petri Nets. The concepts of Petri Nets, execution of Petri Nets, reachability graph (RG), Petri Net properties like deadlock, livelock, liveness, safeness, boundedness, and being strongly connected, are discussed. The limitations of Petri Nets in modelling communication protocols are addressed. This leads to the introduction of NPNs to overcome the limitations of Petri Nets. Petri Nets and NPNs are used to model the alternating bit protocol. The benefits of using NPNs over using Petri Nets are noted. The use of a place to represent a state or a data port of a protocol is compared. Using the global variable to represent the state of a protocol is also included. Petri Net and NPNs are taught before LOTOS because the concepts of Petri Nets are less abstract than those of LOTOS.

Protocol Verification. Verification objectives, methodology for verification, verification techniques, protocol properties, the need for verification tool, and some practical problems of verification, like state explosion, are discussed. For protocol properties, it is catergorised into two general properties : safety and liveness properties. The safety properties include deadlock freeness, livelock freeness, tempo-blocking freeness; whereas liveness properties includes termination and progress. The verification tool, PROTEAN[4], developed by Telecom Australia, is taught in details.

LOTOS. The syntax of LOTOS, different types of operators, value and variable declarations, data types including sorts, operations, parameterisation and actualisation, application to specify alternating bit protocol and simple example taken from the transport layer protocol are taught.

Conformance Testing. The topics covered in conformance testing are conformance criteria, protocol implementation conformance statement, different types of tests, test suite, analysis of results, test notation and language, and test architecture.

For topics of the protocol engineering methodology that have not been covered in details in the course, they are supplemented and complemented by the projects.

4 Textbooks and Handouts

There exists no text book that covers all the topics of protocol engineering. The reference texts on Petri Nets are [31,34]. The reference books that are used in the course are conference proceedings that are published as books. Some of the most useful ones are [1,32,33,35].

However, there are two recent texts that cover some useful topics of protocol engineering. The book by Tarnay [37] covers the areas of formal specification and conformance testing. FDTs discussed include Estelle, LOTOS, as well as Numerical Petri Nets for formal specification. The facts that it only covers two topics of the protocol engineering methodology and is priced over $100 make it not feasible to be adopted as text. The book by Holzmann [9] gives a good coverage on the design of protocol. But the FDTs and tool described in the book are specific to AT&T. So again it is not desirable to be adopted as text.

Papers that come from other sources, like journal and proceedings of other conferences, are also used in the course. Copies of the lecture notes, PROTEAN user manual, and transport layer protocol standard are available in the closed reserved library for students' references.

5 Assignments

Assessment of the course is by assignments and examinations, with both assignment and examination being worth 50%. There are two assignments. The first one, worth 30%, is on formal specification of an ISO protocol. The second one, worth 20%, is on the verification of the specification done in the first assignment. In the first assignment, students are given the opportunities to experience the inadequacies of specifications written in natural language They are required to convert the informal specifications to formal specifications in NPNs. In 1989 and 1990, students worked on the ISO ACSE [12] protocol. In 1991, it was on the ISO Transport layer protocol [10]. In the course of doing so, the students get to understand a ISO protocol in details.

This is of practical help when they enter the computer industry. The second assignment is on the verification of the protocol specified in the first assignment using the automated tool, PROTEAN. They are to use PROTEAN to verify the protocol against properties like deadlock freeness, livelock freeness, boundedness, termination and progress based on the technique Reachability Analysis [39].

The major reasons that NPN is chosen to be used in both assignments, instead of one of the internationally adopted FDTs, namely, LOTOS or Estelle, are as follow. The simpler concepts and graphical aspects of Petri Nets are very appealing to learning and teaching communication protocols as they provide visual clarity, whereas LOTOS and Estelle do not provide such features readily. Other reasons are its support for verification and the availability of the PROTEAN tool at La Trobe University, whereas the verification techniques and tools for LOTOS and Estelle are not as matured yet. An important aspect of Petri Net theory is that analytic techniques can be used to formally verify important properties of concurrent systems, like freedom from deadlock. In doing the second assignment, students have the practical experience to analyse such properties with the aid of PROTEAN. It thus makes NPN the inevitable choice to be used in both assignments.

6 Honours Project

Learning can be in the form of knowledge, skills, understanding, attitudes and values. Traditionally most courses place emphasis on acquiring knowledge. Skills and understanding must take a higher rating. For science, students must actually do something in order to understand it. Students must be active in learning. Listening to a lecture and reading a textbook are not enough [6]. Laboratory classes and project work are effective means of learning.

For all honours students (fourth year students), they are required to do a substantial project under a lecturer as supervisor. Supervision of honours project is an effective means of teaching. Good supervision provides guidance, and stimulation through the supervisor's own involvement in the project, while encouraging independence. While student's intellectual enterprise is encouraged, supervisor provides the regular and critical feedback on the work done. This is achieved through the frequent contacts with the students, as compared to the two hours of classroom contact. As a result, students learn more from the honours projects than from the course subjects. These justify to have a substantial project as a vital part of the honours course.

Over the last few years, a number of honours project in protocol engineering have been completed. All of them focused on a particular one or two stages of the protocol engineering methodology. The successes of such projects are evidenced by the facts that papers written about the work of a great majority of these projects have been refereed and accepted for publication in the proceedings of international conferences. This gives a measure of the good standards achieved by the students in the projects. The honours projects completed in protocol engineering are listed below.

Formal Modelling of ISO FTAM Protocol. In 1987, C. C. Ang did a modelling of a small section of the ISO FTAM[11] protocol using NPNs and verify the specifications using PROTEAN. The work was published in [2].

Formal Modelling of ISO ACSE Protocol. In 1988, V. Jordan specified the ISO ACSE protocol using NPNs and verify it using PROTEAN. It was published in [3].

Formal Methods for Conformance Testing H.S. Louie investigated the generation of test sequences from test tree for conformance testing purposes in 1989. The work was published in [26].

Specification and Verification of ISO JTM Protocol With the success of using NPNs and PROTEAN for the specification and verification of state-oriented protocol, E. Kok applied them to a procedural type of protocol, ISO JTM[15] in 1990. A number of inadequacies of NPNs in this application have been found and the results were published in [21].

Analysis of ISO FTAM Protocol Specified in LOTOS In 1990, A. Lo specified part of the ISO FTAM protocol and analysed its properties using LOLA [29], a LOTOS specification analysis tool developed by Technical University of Madrid, Spain. The properties analysed included deadlock freeness, livelock freeness and termination/progress. The results have been published in [22,23].

Automatic Implementation of ISO Protocol Specified in Petri Nets D. O'connor used a Petri Net based tool, PROMPT, developed by Telecom Australia , for the automatic implementation of ISO ACSE protocol in 1990. A paper on this project was published in [20].

A Simulation of ISO Virtual Terminal in LOTOS G. Galbiati specified the ISO Virtual Terminal Protocol [16] and simulated its behaviour using a LOTOS interpreter developed by University of Ottawa, Canada in 1991. A paper on the results has been accepted for publication in [24].

Automatic Implementation of Protocol Using TOPO ISO RTSE protocol [17] was specified in LOTOS by V. Shumanov in 1991. The specifications were then input to a tool, TOPO [27], developed by Technical University of Madrid, Spain, for automatic generation of executable code. A paper on this work has been submitted to [25].

Intelligent Backtracking Applied to Reachability Analysis The tool, NETVER, developed at La Trobe University, is for analysing Petri Nets specifications. To eliminate the unnecessary voluminous output of all possible sequences of transition firings, like those output by PRO-TEAN, programmed backtracking gives users full control over which sequences of transition firings are to be simulated. In 1991, the project of M. C. Wong is to extend the Netver tool to include intelligent backtracking in the reachability analysis.

Graphical Representation of ISO Protocol GROPE [28] is a tool developed by University of Delaware, USA. It displays a protocol specified in Estelle graphically. G. Holt in 1991 specified the ISO Common Management Information Protocol [19] in Estelle and used GROPE to display it graphically.

7 Opportunities for Improvement

In the course of teaching protocol engineering and supervising honours student projects, a few areas require further attention.

Explosion Problem The explosion problem of reachability analysis remains to be a practical problem in analysing ISO protocols specified in NPNs. The use of PROTEAN to verify protocols can be pushed back a great deal due to this problem. Since one is not interested in all the system states, one can restrict his attention to a manageable set of states. Possible future improvements in PROTEAN to address this have been suggested[38]. These strategies include finite representation of an infinite set of reachable states using some classical algorithms, partitioning of Petri Nets to enable more efficient reachability analysis and the idea of special colour types. These extensions to PROTEAN can also be of viable honours projects.

Query Language Further saving in time in analysing the RG is possible by implementing temporal logic as a query language on PROTEAN[7]. The analysis of the RG generated by PROTEAN is concerned with the structure of the graph. It does not deal with the information contained within each marking of the graph. The verification abilities can be enhanced by allowing users to inspect the specific details of the markings, groups of markings and sequence of markings. Using temporal logic as a query language on the graph enables the users to precisely express his queries about the graph.

Modelling Complex Data NPNs do not have the ability to model complex data types, like Abstract Syntax Notation one (ASN.1) [14], which LOTOS and Estelle would have more success with. Specification using NPNs is an attempt to model only the logical properties of the service definition. It does not model the actual parameter passing and the processing of those parameters as specified in the standards. The facts that LOTOS has been adopted as international standard and that it provides facilities to model data mean that it will have greater potential and influence in the scene of formal method. With the availability of the LOLA and CAESAR [8] tools for LOTOS verification at La Trobe University, it is planned that analysis of LOTOS specifications will be taught and that assignments will be set on LOTOS specification and analysis.

Automatic Implementation As for semi-automatic implementation of protocols, one needs to implement the actions of the protocols and also to include the data transferring between the end users. XNL, a high-level Petri Net language used by PROMPT, provides a way of specifying and implementing the actions which are to be performed. However there is no facility in XNL that supports encoding of PDUs specified in ASN.1. The next version of PROMPT that supports this facility has already been made available to La Trobe University. It is the project of another honours student in 1992 to investigate the use of PROMPT for automatic implementation that could include data handling.

Performance Evaluation. Performance evaluation is important because it helps in assessing a network's performance against overhead introduced, and in tuning a network's parameters to optimise its performance goals. Though it might not be practical to demonstrate performance measurement of communication protocols in the classroom environment, it is possible to have a model of how the system might perform. Recently the use of Generalised Stochastic Petri Net (GSPN) [30] techniques for the performance evaluation of communication systems has attracted wide interests and research. With the availability of the GreatSPN [5] software at La Trobe University, it is feasible to include performance evaluation using GSPN as part of the course in the future.

8   Conclusions

In this paper, the design and organisation of the course "Protocol Engineering" have been presented. The aims of the course are to teach an engineering methodology and analytical techniques based on formal description techniques to be able to address some of the unique problems of communication software development. The uses of Petri Nets and the associated verification techniques in the course enable the safety aspects of communication protocol to be demonstrated to the students and the correctness of the protocol to be verified. The teaching of protocol engineering is also complemented by project supervision in this area. Students have achieved good results in these projects in that the work, despite they are at undergraduate level, have been accepted for publications in the proceedings of some international conferences.

It is therefore concluded that teaching protocol engineering and supervising honours projects in such area at La Trobe University have been successful in educating undergraduates of applying formal methods to the development of communication protocol software.

References

[1] Advances in Petri Nets, Lecture Notes in Computer Science, Springer Verlag, 1983-1991.

[2] Ang, C.C., and County, E.J.P., "Modelling the OSI FTAM Protocol", Proceedings of the International Conference on Modelling and Simulation, Melbourne, Australia, Oct., 1987.

[3] Ang, C.C., Jordan, V., and Dillon, T.S., "Application of Petri Nets to Specify and Verify ISO CASE Protocols", Proceedings of the second International Symposium on Interoperable Information Systems, Japan, 1988.

[4] Billington, J., Wheeler, G.R., and Wilbur-Ham, M.C., "PROTEAN: A High-level Petri Net Tool for the Specification and Verification of Communication Protocols", IEEE Transactions on Software Engineering, Vol. 14, No. 3, March 1988.

[5] Chiola, G., "A Software Package for the Analysis of Generalised Stochastic Petri Net Models", Proceedings of International Workshop on Timed Petri Nets, IEEE Computer Society Press, 1985.

[6] Coes, L. "Science, Mathematics, and Student Values", Special Issue on Engineering Education, IEEE Communication Magazine, Dec., 1990.

[7] Everitt, H.J., "Temporal Logic as a Query Language for PROTEAN's Reachability Graphs", Switched Networks Research Branch Paper 147, Telecom Research Laboratories, 1988.

[8] Garavel, H., Sifakis, J.,"Compilation and Verification of LOTOS Specification", Proceedings of tenth International Symposium on Protocol Specification, Testing and Verification, North-Holland, 1990.

[9] Holzmann, G.J., Design and Validation of Computer Protocols, Prentice-Hall, 1991.

[10] ISO 8073, "Information Processing Systems - Open Systems Interconnection - Transport Service Protocol".

[11] ISO 8571, "Information Processing Systems - Open Systems Interconnection - File Transfer, Access and Management".

[12] ISO 8649, "Information Processing Systems - Open Systems Interconnection - Association Control Service Element".

[13] ISO 8807, "Information Processing Systems - Open Systems Interconnection - LOTOS - A formal description Technique based on Temporal ordering of observational behaviour".

[14] ISO 8824, "Information Processing Systems - Open Systems Interconnection - Specification for Abstract Syntax Notation 1"

[15] ISO 8832, "Information Processing Systems - Open Systems Interconnection - Specification of the Basic Class Protocol for Job Transfer and Manipulation"

[16] ISO 9041, "Information Processing Systems - Open Systems Interconnection - Virtual Terminal Protocol"

[17] ISO 9066, "Information Processing Systems - Open Systems Interconnection - Reliable Transfer Service Element"

[18] ISO 9074, "Information Processing Systems - Open Systems Interconnection - Estelle - A formal description Technique based on an Extended State Transition Model".

[19] ISO 9596, "Information Processing Systems - Open Systems Interconnection - Common Management Information Protocol Specification"

[20] Lai, R, O'Connor, D. "Automatic Implementation of Communication Protocols Based on Petri Nets", Proceedings of Second International Conference on Computer Network : Towards Network Globalisation, Singapore, G.S. Poo (Editor), pp103-107, World Scientific, Sept, 1991.

[21] Lai, R, Kok, E. "Specification and Verification Results for ISO JTM Protocol", Proceedings of Second International Conference on Computer Network : Towards Network Globalisation, Singapore, G.S. Poo (Editor), pp295-300, World Scientific, Sept, 1991.

[22] Lai, R, Lo, A. "Specifying ISO FTAM Basic File Protocol in LOTOS", Proceedings of Second International Conference on Computer Network : Towards Network Globalisation, Singapore, G.S. Poo (Editor), pp232-237, World Scientific, Sept, 1991.

[23] Lai, R., Lo, A., "An Analysis of ISO FTAM Basic Protocol Specified in LOTOS", Proceedings of Fifteenth Australian Computer Science Conference, C.D. Keen (Editor), World Scientific, 1992.

[24] Lai, R., Galbiati, G., "A Simulation of ISO Virtual Terminal Protocol Specified in LOTOS", accepted for publication in the proceedings of international conference on Communication Technology to be held in Beijing, China in Sept, 1992.

[25] Lai, R., Shumanov, V., "Automatic Implementation of Communication Protocol Using TOPO", submitted to Singapore International Conference on Communication Systems to be held in September in Nov, 1992.

[26] Louie, S., Lai, R., Dillon, T.S., "Test Sequence Generation for Conformance Testing of OSI Protocols", Proceedings of Second International Conference on Communication Systems, Communication Systems : Towards Global Integration, Singapore, S.P. Yeo (Editor), pp2.3.1-2.3.5, Elsevier Science Publishers B.V., Nov., 1990.

[27] Manas, J.A., de Miguel, T., "From LOTOS to C", Proceedings of first International Conference on Formal Description Techniques, North-Holland, 1988.

[28] New, D., Amer, P.D., "Protocol Visualization of Estelle Specification", Proceedings of Third International Conference on Formal Description Techniques, North-Holland, 1990.

[29] Quemada, J., Pavon, S., Fernandez, A., "Transforming LOTOS specification with LOLA: the parameterized expansion", proceedings of the 1st

international conference on FDTs, Stirling, UK, 6-9sept. 1988, North-Holland.

[30] Marsan, M.A., Balbo, G., Conte, G., "A Class of Generalised Stochastic Petri Nets for the Performance of Multiprocessor Systems,", ACM Transactions on Computer Systems, May, 1984.

[31] Petersen, J.L., Petri Nets Theory and Modelling of Systems, Prentice-Hall, Englewood Cliffs, N.J., 1981.

[32] Proceedings of the Second to Eleventh International Symposium on Protocol Specification, Testing and Verification, 1982-1991, North-Holland.

[33] Proceedings of the First to Fourth International Conference on Formal Description Techniques, 1988-1991, North-Holland.

[34] Reisig, W., Petri Nets : An Introduction, Springer-Verlag, 1985.

[35] Sifakis, J., Proceedings of First International Workshop on Automatic Verification Methods for Finite Systems", Lecture Notes in Computer Science, Springer-Verlag, 1989.

[36] Symons, F.J.W., "Modelling and Analysis of Communication Protocols using Numerical Petri Nets" PhD Thesis, Department of Electrical Engineering Science and Telecommunications, University of Essex, May, 1978.

[37] Tarnay, K., Protocol Specification and Testing, Plenum Press, 1991,.

[38] Tridgell, P.K., "A Study of Advanced Reachability Analysis of Numerical Petri Nets", Switched Networks Research Branch paper 110, Telecom Research Laboratories, Australia, 1987.

[39] Vuong, S.T., Cowan, D.D., "Reachability Analysis of Protocols with FIFO Channels", SIGCOM'83 Symposium, Communication Architectures and Protocols, ACM, pp. 49-57, March, 1983.

Panel Discussion
Moderator: Nancy R. Mead, Software Engineering Insitute

Across the Wire: Teaching Software Engineering at a Distance
Panel Moderator: Peter H. Lutz, Rochester Institute of Technology

Across the Wire:
Teaching Software Engineering at a Distance

Moderator:
Peter H. Lutz, Professor, Rochester Institute of Technology
Panelists:
Rolando Gabarron, Senior Software Engineer, Northern Telecom (NAS)
Roy Mattson, Academic Vice President, National Technological University
Michael Strait, Project Office for Research and Evaluation, Annenberg/Corporation for Public Broadcasting
Timothy Wells, Assistant Professor, Rochester Institute of Technology

Abstract:
There is growing experience with teaching technical topics at a distance. From this experience educators and purchasers of distance courses have derived a large number of questions and concerns. Among these are questions regarding the quality of instruction provided using a particular technology, the importance of real-time interaction, and the authentication of work performed by students whom the instructor never meets face-to-face.

Also of interest is how to deal with student apprehension and procrastination, and how to evaluate the effectiveness of instruction delivered in this manner. Related to this is the appropriate technology to use. Lower tech approaches tend to depend on ubiquitous devices (VCRs, telephones, etc.) which higher tech approaches demand more investment (video conference rooms, desk-top screen sharing, etc.) that limit the potential audience. How does one evaluate this trade-off and how does the decision evaluate the quality of instruction? Does more technology reduce or aggravate the problems for a student learning at a distance?

These topics will be touched on by short presentations by the panelists. Questions from the audience will be entertained.

Contacts:

Peter Lutz
Chairperson
Department of Information Technology
Rochester Institute of Technology
P.O. Box 9887
Rochester, N.Y.   14623-0887
(716) 475-6162
phl@cs.rit.edu   Internet

Rolando Gabarron
Senior Software Engineer
Northern Telecommunication Systems
97 Humboldt Street
Rochester, NY   14609-7493
(716)482-5000   x3018
rjg@sunsrvr1.cci.com   Internet
rjg@cs.rit.edu   (also) Internet

Roy Mattson
Academic Vice President
National Technological University
(303) 484-6050   fax: (303) 498-0601

Michael Strait
Project Office for Research and Evaluation
Annenberg / Corporation for Public Broadcasting
901 E Street NW
Washington, D.C.   20004
(202) 879-9649

Timothy Wells
Assistant Professor
Department of Information Technology
Rochester Institute of Technology
P.O. Box 9887
Rochester, N.Y.   14623-0887
(716) 475-7136
tjw@cs.rit.edu   Internet

Session 6:

Panel Discussion
Moderator: Gary Ford, Software Engineering Insitute

Issues in Licensing Professional Software Engineers
Panel Moderator: Donald Gotterbarn, East Tennessee State University

Issues in Licensing Professional Software Engineers

Donald Gotterbarn
East Tennessee State University
Johnson City, Tennessee 37614-0711

A movement toward licensing computing professionals is taking place in several state legislatures. This activity is being directed by politicians and consumer advocates. Furthermore, these same people are determining the standards for licensure and are populating the licensing boards. In other professions the movement toward licensing had a similar origin. But in other professions, engineering for example, the engineers set the standards and determined the licensing criteria. Because the professionals themselves took the lead, the credentialing standards fit the best technical standards of the profession being licensed. The issue of licensing software engineers is being addressed before the wrong audience. Because of the origin of the current movement toward licensing software engineering professionals, there are several potential risks. The problems and advantages of licensing need to be addressed by software engineers so that they might significantly influence any licensing process.

The panel, with participants from industry, education , and the military, will address the major issues of licensing *Professional Software Engineers* and the problems that arise from a failure of software engineering educators to be involved in licensing. Some of the topics to be discussed include: potential implementations of licensing similar to those used for professional engineers, minimal standards needed by licensed software engineer, malpractice monitoring, and risks involved in licensing such as freezing technology, limiting research, and causing the loss of jobs. The panel will also address the role of software engineering educators in this discussion and the roles they should have in the process when licensing comes about.

Participants:

Donald Gotterbarn	**Betty Nichols**	**Col. William Richardson**
East Tennessee State Univ.	IBM	United States Air Force Academy

Session 7:

Educating Practitioners
Moderator: Jorge Diaz-Herrera, Software Engineering Institute

Teaching Software Verification and Validation to Software Practitioners
Captain David R. Luginbuhl and Captain James E. Cardow, Air Force Institute of Technology

(Continuing) Education of Software Professionals
Ilkka J. Haikala, Tampere University of Technology and Jukka Marijarvi, Nokia Telecommunications

The Software Engineering - Patent Law Interface: A Practitioner's View
George M. Taulbee, Esq., Bell, Seltzer, Park, & Gibson, P.A.

TEACHING SOFTWARE VERIFICATION AND VALIDATION TO SOFTWARE PRACTITIONERS

Captain David R. Luginbuhl
Captain James E. Cardow

Air Force Institute of Technology

Abstract:

We describe the development and teaching of a two-week course in software verification and validation (V&V). The course is taught to Air Force software practitioners by faculty at the Air Force Institute of Technology (AFIT). We show that by organizing teaching materials using a framework involving interrelationships of activities throughout the software development life cycle, we were able to significantly enhance the development and teaching of the course. Such an organization is logical since V&V pervades *all* activities in *every* part of the life cycle.

1 Background

1.1 Introduction

As part of a U.S. Air Force continuing education curriculum in software engineering, we have developed a course in software verification and validation (V&V). During the development of this course, it became clear that a different overall structure was necessary to facilitate learning all that is involved in software V&V. With the help of U.S. Air Force Academy faculty members, we developed an approach to the course's organization that has been helpful both in creating and teaching course material. This paper describes the history of that process and its success.

1.2 History of the Software Professional Development Program

In 1989 the Air Force Deputy Assistant Secretary for Logistics, Lloyd K. Mosemann, requested a Broad Area Review (BAR) of Software Management within the Air Force. At that time he requested that the Commanders of the Air Force Systems, Logistics, and Communications Commands jointly chair the review. Specifically, Secretary Mosemann identified education and training needs to be a prime focus. During 1989 three formal reviews were held and a significant level of survey and staff work was performed to support the reviews. One important outcome of this effort was the realization of the need to educate large numbers of practicing professionals (Air Force military and civilians) in software engineering. The chairmen of the meeting were sufficiently convinced of this need that they agreed to accelerate the process by immediately providing the personnel positions and funding, rather than waiting for the normal budget process. With the decision made, the Air Force Institute of Technology (AFIT) was tasked with creating the Software Professional Development Program (SPDP), a Professional Continuing Education program in software engineering. Upon completion of the transfer of positions and funding, six Air Force captains were selected to develop courses and conduct the program.

The SPDP was to consist of five two-week courses: Software Engineering Concepts, Specification of Software Systems, Principles and Applications of Software Design, Software Generation and Maintenance (SGM), and Software Verification and Validation. The authors and one other faculty member were primarily responsible for the development and teaching of the SGM and V&V courses. As we have already explained, this article describes the V&V course (AFIT Course Number WCSE 475). For more information on the history of the SPDP and the other courses, see Mead91.

The first step in developing any educational material should be a consideration of the audience. The target audience for these classes consisted of software professionals, ideally with 4 to 8 years experience, working in software development, software maintenance, software acquisition, or software management. Each student must have earned a technical undergraduate degree (preferably in computer science or computer engineering), completed college work in data structures or algorithms, demonstrated math maturity by completing two courses beyond college algebra, and gained significant experience in a high order language.

With a mandate from the BAR, a general idea of our goal, and a knowledge of our target audience, we were ready to begin developing the courses. We turn now to the specifics of the V&V course.

1.3 Original Approach to the V&V Course

To begin development, it was necessary to determine three characteristics of the course: (1) the specific objectives, which would drive (2) the contents and (3) the internal structure.

We initially based the course objectives on three sources: a list of topics provided to the course developers for inclusion in the courses[*], the SEI Curriculum Module on Software Verification and Validation [Collofello88], and the 1989 SEI Report on Graduate Software Engineering Education [Ardis89a]. The latter two sources actually contained lists of objectives for a course in V&V; using these objectives and inferring objectives from the list of topics, we were able to construct a useful set of objectives for the V&V course. Appendix A contains a refined list of objectives for the original approach.

The SEI/CMU graduate course in V&V [Ardis89b] provided a framework for determining contents and structure. We tailored this framework appropriately to meet our stated objectives. The course would center on three major approaches to verification and validation: technical reviews, formal verification, and testing. We intended to present to the students several techniques relevant to each approach (e.g., for testing, we would discuss black-box and clear-box test case generation and integration testing among others). A finalized outline using the original approach is contained in Appendix B.

We were now ready to begin actual development of teaching materials. This involved research and discussions at the SEI for the first six months of the program and follow-on research at AFIT. In August of 1990, it was necessary to halt research for about nine

---

[*] As a result of the BAR, a group of representatives from various Air Force Commands gathered to discuss what should be included in the five courses. This list of topics was a result of that discussion.

months in order to prepare for and teach two other courses in the SPDP. Work resumed on the V&V course in May 1991 with a scheduled teaching date of December 1991.

1.4 Problems with the Original Approach

The challenge for this development effort was to take material, much of which was focused on graduate education, and tailor it for Professional Continuing Education of Air Force personnel. There were two major barriers: establishing a balance between theoretical content and practical content; and organizing the material to provide a smooth flow from one section to the next.

It was important to establish the right balance between theoretical and practical content because the students would want to be able to apply as much of this material as quickly as possible. They were thus less concerned with the "why" and more concerned with the "how." In fact, our experience with the earlier courses was that our students were resistant to more than a little theory. We recognized the importance of providing foundations for software development, which meant that we could not altogether ignore the theoretical aspects.

Even though much of the material in the V&V resources at the SEI could be considered practical in some sense, it did not completely address the needs of our audience. Specific techniques were addressed, but it was hard to fit them into the context our students were familiar with. The students would need to extrapolate these concepts to systems and working environments that they were used to.

The other barrier -- organizing material -- proved more difficult, and its remedy is the focus of the remainder of this paper. The problem was that structuring material around the three main approaches made it difficult to convey the material in a more practical context. Our major goal was for the students to see that V&V is not some activity that occurs at the end of software development; it is an ongoing process that begins when development begins and ends when the system is retired. For each technique we considered presenting, we knew the students would ask: "where in the life cycle does that apply?" or "how does the technique vary in different lifecycle activities?" (indeed, we found ourselves asking the same questions).

Even though we noticed this barrier early in our research, we continued gathering material in the hope that as we proceeded, it would become apparent how our original structure for the course would work. We concentrated on the content with the intent of being able to tie pieces together once everything was developed (the reader will note the unfortunate analogy to "big-bang" integration [Beizer84]).

Even before resumption of work in May, one member of the development team was transferred to another position, and we found it necessary to solicit outside help. We contacted Col. William Richardson, the Chairman of the Department of Computer Science at the U.S. Air Force Academy (USAFA) to see if any of his faculty could help us with the development effort. Several faculty members consented to look at our material and provide help, but they noticed the same organizational problem that we had noticed. They proposed that we abandon our original approach and present the material using a framework that captures the relationships of V&V activities throughout software development. That approach [Northrop91] is discussed in detail in the next section.

2   The   Framework

What's the best framework for presenting V&V material? Certainly a lifecycle approach is a good idea, but which life cycle gives the students the best view of all the activities and interrelationships between V&V techniques? Our first consideration was the waterfall model. It is a framework that students already understand, and it provides a sequence of activities defining the development process; however, it lacks easy adaptability to other models (e.g., spiral or incremental delivery). It also lacks refinability to define activities and relationships at lower levels of detail. A second consideration could have been the spiral model. However, the students are far less familiar with its implementation, and that would add an additional layer of learning to use the material, so it was never given serious consideration. In addition, the USAFA staff pointed out several shortfalls with any approach solely based on a software life cycle, the most damaging of which was the lack of detail for integrating all software development and maintenance activities. None of the conventional approaches appeared to meet the objectives of the course.

The USAFA staff offered an alternative framework. While the proposed framework was not a published, well-known model, it was being used in Academy courses as a means of connecting ideas related to software development. After lengthy discussions on the mechanics and philosophy, we decided to proceed with this framework, which we refer to as the "Richardson/Northrop Framework." The AFIT interpretation of the framework is described below.

2.1   Framework Structure

The Richardson/Northrop Framework is best viewed as a four dimensional structure. The vertical and horizontal dimensions are considered panes or *slices* of the framework. The vertical dimension is divided into two halves. One half represents products, the artifacts of software development and maintenance (e.g., code, documentation, and reports). The second half represents processes. Processes are defined as activities within the life cycle; for example, reviews or the design effort. The horizontal dimension is also divided into two halves. In this dimension, one half represents management, the other production. Management refers to activities or products that would, or should, be assigned to the senior software engineering staff. Technical management is probably a more accurate term. Production is meant to reflect the activities and products directly related to creation and maintenance of the software. A typical slice with example objects (*objects* are defined in the next section) is depicted in Figure 1.

The third dimension of the framework is the lifecycle model. In this dimension, any model appears to work well. For the purposes of the course we use the waterfall model in discussion because it is the most familiar and causes the least additional confusion. One special consideration for this dimension is that all representations start with a *slice* (i.e., a set of processes and products) referred to as *preparation*. Preparation involves the activities that determine the organization's policies and decision-making process for how to proceed with work. A representation of the framework's depth dimension using the waterfall model is shown in Figure 2. Note that slices occur throughout the depth of the model. At one point, the model was equated to a loaf of bread to explain the dimensions, hence the term *slice*.

171

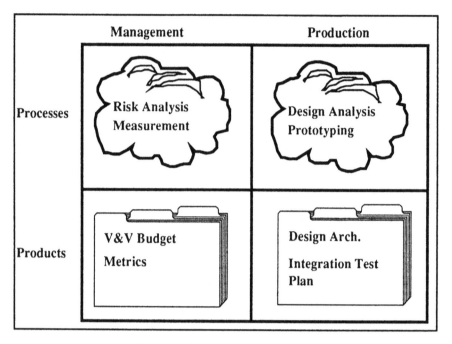

Fig. 1. Vertical and horizontal dimensions

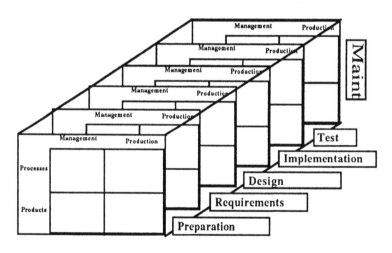

Fig. 2. Depth dimension

The fourth and final dimension is a wrapping around the model which represents the support or connection provided by tools and environments. Both tools and environments are pervasive across the life cycle. The framework deals with this concept of support by covering tools and environments for a single lifecycle step and those that support the connection and overlap between two or more lifecycle steps.

In addition to the four-dimensional structure, the framework also contains threads. Threads run through the slices to provide connectivity of objects. Objects and threads are explained below.

2.2. Framework Objects

Within the framework, processes and products are the objects that represent the work being accomplished and their results. As Figure 1 shows, processes are represented by cloud icons and products by folder icons. Processes are classified as being either management or production (although the distinction is often difficult), just as products can be either production or management. Figure 1 presents the management processes of *risk analysis* and *measurement*, the production processes of *design analysis* and *prototyping*, the management products of *V&V budget* and *metrics*, and the production products of *design architecture* and the *integration test plan*. This provides a convenient method for grouping the processes and products, but it is also important to show how they are interrelated. Figure 3 shows the connections resulting from Figure 1.

In Figure 3, the process of *measurement* results in the product of *metrics*, just as the processes of *design analysis* and *prototyping* result in the products of a *design architecture* and an *integration test plan*. So where are the products that start the processes? That is answered with the concept of *threads*. Most processes, and some products, are not limited to a single stage (or slice) of development; threads allow for continuity. V&V is especially reliant on threads. Test planning, as an example process, results in test preparation, test definition, test execution, and testing results, yet viewing all these in a single slice is wrong (not to mention bad software engineering). This is one of the biggest benefits of the framework.

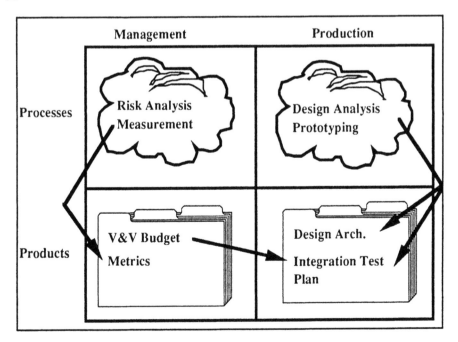

Fig. 3. Object connectivity

2.3 Framework Benefits

The Richardson/Northrop Framework seemed to meet our needs as the best framework for presenting V&V material. Flexibility is achieved through the interchangeability of the depth dimension (course examples of waterfall, spiral, incremental delivery, and change process are all used effectively). Because the waterfall model can be used, as an example, the learning curve is lessened. Lower levels of detail can be addressed by expanding on the objects and slices.

Finally, threads allow the continuity required to express the pervasive nature of V&V. Figure 4 is an example of the high level V&V activities and how connections occur through the depth of the model.

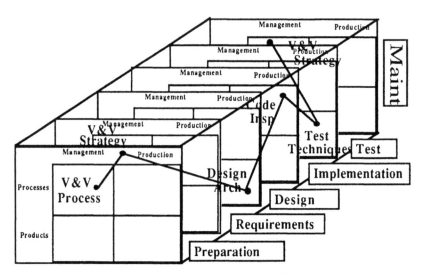

Fig. 4. V&V thread representation

3 The Framework in Development

Previous courses in the SPDP were essentially developed *by committee*. That is, the topics were selected and the assigned instructors divided up the topics, developed individual pieces, then came back together during *dry-runs* to see how it all worked out (generally resolving all problems at that time). This process often resulted in holes, overlaps, and inconsistencies. Software Engineering being far from standard practice, some disparity in course content was due to different opinions of the instructors. Under the original approach to the V&V course the same division of labor was planned, but working through the framework, we saw that it suggested a more effective approach. This new approach would reduce development time (an important consideration since there were now only two instructors) and would provide more consistency of material.

The first step of the approach was to look at the framework and address some basic questions. What information (topics) applied to each slice? How could the threads be best addressed? How could the connection between topics be integrated? The second step was to determine the approximate time for each major topic and the amount of time for each slice, given the topics to be covered. We applied this scheduling across the two-week format. The third step was to actually develop material.

We developed material using a *leap-frog* approach. We divided the material in half, and instructors developed alternating lessons (for the final course schedule, see Appendix C). Each instructor built on what the other had just developed. The first two lessons we developed were the explanation of the framework and the motivational material for learning V&V. These two lessons set the stage for all work to follow. Once a lesson was developed, both instructors would sit down and review that lesson, either agreeing that it was ready or recommending changes. With this approach, each instructor was never more than one lesson ahead or one lesson behind the other. This provided significant advantages.

The first advantage was consistency. It was very easy to draw on or expand the material from the last lesson. In fact, in many places actual slides could be copied over to show how later material applied to earlier material. A second advantage was continuity. For instance, V&V corporate policy is discussed in the Preparation slice. In the following slice, Requirements, the lesson takes the corporate policy and shows how to apply it to a project. A third advantage was in addressing threads. For example, in each slice there is a place for discussing the "threaded" activities of the software quality assurance and configuration management organizations. A fourth advantage was material planning. Each instructor could see where the course was going and could establish *footholds* to be used later. For instance, test planning is mentioned in early activities (requirements and design) without being specific, since later lessons cover black-box, clear-box, integration, and other specific test methods.

The greatest advantage was time savings. Our experience with developing previous courses in the SPDP was that fifty hours of development time (researching the topic, outlining the material to be covered, and preparing the presentation) were needed for one hour of lesson material. During the creation of the V&V course, development time was reduced to twenty hours per lesson hour. Admittedly, several external factors came into play, including experience with lesson development and amount of available material. However, the approach and the framework were significant contributors to the reduction in time. There was also a tremendous savings in time spent rehearsing course material (previous courses averaged about one week of dry-run per two weeks of lessons). This was eliminated by the instructor review after each piece was complete (about 15 minutes for one to two hours of lesson).

Bottom line for development: the framework improved the quality of the material developed while also increasing the productivity of the development effort. But how would the framework hold up for teaching the material?

4   The Framework in Teaching

4.1 What was Taught

As mentioned earlier, the first topics covered in the course are the motivation for V&V and description of the framework (see Appendix C). These help to set the stage and provide an overview of the course. After this introductory material, the remainder of the course is organized into blocks of instruction corresponding to the slices shown in Figure 2. In each block, we cover V&V activities and describe how they fit into the framework.

The first block describes Preparation activities. Preparation can be equated to establishing and refining the *corporate culture* of an organization; that is, determining the organization's approach to software development, including standards, policies, and acceptable processes. The prime topics covered in this part of the course are defining the V&V policy and understanding the generic aspects of reviews.

During the second block, Requirements, we explore the development of a V&V strategy and V&V plan for a specific project. Both the strategy and the plan look at the development life cycle to determine the entire suite of V&V activities to be applied. We also discuss evaluation of the requirements document as a V&V activity and development of acceptance criteria and acceptance and system test plans. By beginning to discuss test plans during the Requirements block, we help the students develop a mindset that testing must be considered very early in the life cycle.

The Design block covers the formulation of integration test plans as a natural step in system decomposition (planning how to put it together while you take it apart.) Another heavily emphasized topic in design is the introduction of metrics and measurement. Like other topics, measurement spans the life cycle but is covered in one slice and referenced in others. Because the developer typically produces module specifications during design, we use this block to introduce the students to black-box testing. The final major topic of the Design block is simulation and modeling as a V&V tool.

The Implementation block probably most resembles instruction as intended in our old approach. In this block, we cover code reviews, unit testing, formal verification, and clear-box testing.

We refer to the block on Testing as Testing Activities to reinforce the notion that test execution occurs during this period in development, but much of the test preparation has already occurred. Some of the specific topics addressed are integration and system testing, stress and recovery testing, and testing real-time systems. In this block, we also cover test management -- defining the purpose of testing, the organization's perspective on why testing is performed, and the expectations of results. We also address some critical threads that are mentioned throughout the course. These include security, safety, and reliability. Often during the course these are used as examples of items of interest, but at this point each is viewed in perspective across development.

Our final block of instruction covers Maintenance issues. Topics addressed during this slice naturally focus on regression testing and test planning as part of the normal change process. One of the key issues discussed during this block is the need to re-examine the organization's V&V strategy as part of the transition effort.

For each of the slices just mentioned, the course has a *management* section and a *production* section. One of the first charts in each of these sections is one similar to Figure 3 so that the connection to the framework and the other activities in the slice is always reinforced. All the slides similar to Figure 3 are contained in both the explanation of the framework and the summary to reinforce continuity. One additional note: although specification, design, and implementation are discussed with reference to related V&V activities , we do not focus in depth on these particular subjects since each is handled in a separate course in the SPDP.

Supporting the material presented in the lessons is a series of project activities. These are completed by small groups of students (five to seven per team). During the first week, parts of the project are tied to each slice. During Requirements, the student review a User's Requirements Statement and System Specification; they also develop acceptance and system test criteria. For Design, the students conduct a design review and plan integration strategies. As part of the Implementation block the students conduct a code walkthrough. In the second week, the project reinforces the higher-level issues of the course. The students are asked to define the V&V strategy for a specific project. This requires them to review all course material and examine its application to a specific need.

4.2 How it was Received

We were confident of the pedagogical value of the framework; that was the main reason for selecting it as the structure for the course. Nonetheless, it was rewarding to see it work in practice. As of June 1992, we have offered the course five times. Our experience with these classes has validated our choice of the framework. We can examine the success of the framework in the classroom from two perspectives: the instructor and the student.

It is clear that the framework enhanced our ability to present the material in a cohesive and clear manner. Because of the approach taken in development (discussed above), the instructors have a better understanding of how the lectures fit together, and course material is more consistent; therefore, instructors are able to build upon and reinforce V&V concepts presented earlier in the course. Because the course has been integrated so well, follow-on instructors will also benefit from the organization of the course.

The framework also provides a sturdy platform from which to launch important ideas. By continually referring back to the framework, we are able to present these ideas as part of a larger V&V process. Furthermore, by presenting V&V concepts in each slice of the life cycle, we are better able to show how V&V is an ongoing process, and not some concept tied to the end of development.

It is not as easy for us to judge the framework from the students' perspective. Our best metric is the course evaluation form provided to the students at the end of each course. From the evaluations of the offerings so far, it is apparent that a large number of students appreciate the framework as a teaching tool. One of the questions on the form asks the students to list what they liked best about the course. A significant number of respondents have indicated that one of the best things about the course is its organization or structure -- many of them have mentioned the framework *by name*. Several of them have commented positively on our teaching V&V as an activity that cuts across the life cycle.

Comments in the classroom and answers on the final (essay) exam also indicate that the students seem to grasp the concepts more easily because we use the framework to structure the information.

5   Conclusions

It is apparent that the framework has enhanced the way we teach V&V. It certainly helped in our development effort, and it has proved invaluable in the actual classroom environment.

Acknowledgements

We are grateful to Col William Richardson, Lt Col Larry Jones, and Dr Linda Northrop, all of the US Air Force Academy, for their help in establishing the organizational framework for this course. Dr Mark Ardis provided valuable guidance while the authors were at the SEI, and his V&V course provided an outstanding model for AFIT's own V&V course.

Appendix A Original Course Objectives

The object of this course is for each student to:

- Define the terminology commonly used in the verification and validation area
- Identify representative techniques for proof-of-correctness, technical reviews, and testing
- Explain the theoretical and practical limitations of V&V
- Describe the V&V objectives for typical products generated by the software evolution process
- Explain the complementary nature of black-box, clear-box, and error-oriented testing and analysis techniques
- Describe how the choice of testing and analysis criteria affects the selection and evaluation of test data
- Explain how V&V techniques fit in to the DoD framework
- Describe how software quality attributes can be measured
- Describe the role and limitations of testing
- Prove a small software module correct
- Plan and conduct a review
- Prepare an effective test plan
- Determine the applicability and likely effectiveness of V&V approaches for particular products of the software evolution process
- Analyze a test plan for completeness and usefulness
- Appreciate the need for verification and validation throughout the life cycle
- Respond very positively to established V&V techniques

Appendix B Original Course Outline

1   Introduction
2   Software Quality
3   Formal Verification
4   Reviews
    4.1   Walkthroughs
    4.2   Inspections

5   Testing
    5.1   Introduction to testing
    5.2   Levels of testing
    5.3   Types of testing
    5.4   Test planning
6   V&V Approaches to Software Reliability and Safety
7   Simulations and environments
8   Managerial aspects of V&V

Appendix C Current Course Outline

1   Introduction and motivation
    1.1   Examples of the effects of failed software
    1.2   A look at software errors
    1.3   Introduction to V&V
2   Course framework (Richardson/Northrop Framework defined)
3   Preparation activities
    3.1   V&V process and process models
    3.2   Organizational V&V policy
    3.4   Introduction to reviews and audits
4   Requirements slice
    4.1   Developing a V&V strategy and V&V plan
    4.2   Evaluating the requirements and specification
    4.3   Preparing for system and acceptance testing
    4.4   Requirements reviews
    4.5   Requirements prototyping
    4.6   Introduction to formal methods for V&V (formal specification)
5   Design slice
    5.1   Evaluating the design
    5.2   Design reviews
    5.3   Integration strategies and preparation for integration testing
    5.4   Black-box test case generation
    5.5   Simulation and modeling
6   Implementation slice
    6.1   Code reviews
    6.2   Unit testing
    6.3   Formal verification using the axiomatic approach
    6.4   Clear-box test case generation
7   Testing activities
    7.1   Higher level testing (integration, system, acceptance)
    7.2   Stress and recovery testing
    7.3   Real-time testing and simulation
    7.4   Security verification
    7.5   Software safety and reliability
    7.6   Management aspects of testing
8   Maintenance slice
    8.1   The change process and V&V
    8.2   Regression testing
    8.3   Maintenance implications for the V&V strategy
    8.4   Restructuring, re-engineering and V&V

(Continuing) Education of Software Professionals

prof. Ilkka J. Haikala
Tampere University of Technology
Software Systems Laboratory
P.O. Box 553
SF-33101, Tampere
Finland
internet: ijh@cs.tut.fi

Jukka Marijarvi
Quality Manager
Nokia Telecommunications
Cellular Systems
P.O Box 779
SF-33101, Tampere
Finland
internet: marijarv@tnclus.tele.nokia.fi

Abstract

The fields of computing and software engineering are evolving rapidly. Typically, a new generation of a software based product may require 5-10 times more effort than the previous one. This is causing an increasing need for software process improvement in software companies. The improvement is impossible without retraining existing personnel. On the other hand, there seems to be a mismatch between the software engineering education given by the CS departments at universities, and the requirements imposed by practical work in software projects. This problem is difficult, or even impossible to be solved by the universities alone: An active interaction between the software industry and the universities is required. This report describes our experiences with one form of such interaction; i.e. the Sofko project manager education program.

Keywords: Training, Data Processing Professional, Software Engineering, Project Manager

1. Background

During the last 30 years, the discipline of software engineering has moved from coding of programs of a few thousand lines to production of multi-million line systems. In parallel, producing software systems has changed from proofs of skill of single virtuosos to team work; i.e. software projects with several or even hundreds of people participating. Although the technical virtuosity is by no means obsolete, the most important success factor in such projects is skilful project management.

To be a successful, the project manager must master a wide spectrum of tasks, ranging from managerial and economical issues to design and construction of software systems. Also, he/she must often act as an 'interface' between the project group and the outside world; i.e. customers, marketing, and higher levels of management in the software company.

Lack of qualified project managers has been recognized as a major problem in Finnish software industry [1]. One reason is the extremely fast development of software technology that implies that constant work is required to maintain the professional skills. Another reason has its roots in the university education: there seems to exist an 'educational gap' between the software engineering education given by the CS departments, and the requirements

References

Ardis89a   Ardis, M. A. and Ford, G. 1989 SEI Report on Graduate Software Engineering Education. Technical Report CMU/SEI-89-TR-21, Software Engineering Institute, Carnegie Mellon University, Pittsburgh, PA, 1989.

Ardis89b   Ardis, M. A. *Software Verification and Validation.* Educational Materials AC-SVV-01, Software Engineering Institute, Carnegie Mellon University, Pittsburgh, PA, 1989.

Beizer84   Beizer, B. *Software System Testing and Quality Assurance.* New York: Van Nostrand, 1984.

Collofello88 Collofello, J. S. *Introduction to Software Verification and Validation.* Curriculum Module SEI-CM-13-1.1, Software Engineering Institute, Carnegie Mellon University, Pittsburgh, PA, Dec. 1988.

Mead91   Mead, N. R. and Lawlis, P. K. *Software Engineering: Graduate-Level Courses for AFIT Professional Continuing Education.* Proceedings of the Software Engineering Education Conference, Pittsburgh, PA, Apr. 1990. Springer-Verlag Lecture Notes in Computer Science, pp. 114-126.

Northrop91   Northrop, L. and Richardson, R. Personal communication, Aug. 1991.

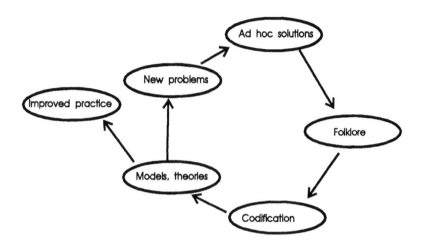

Fig. 1. Development of good software models [2].

imposed by practical work in software projects. Even worse, the gap has presumably grown wider during recent years, as the body of knowledge that one has to master in software projects is constantly enlarging.

The basic problem behind the educational gap is in the nature of current software engineering practices. It has been suggested that good models within software engineering develop as a result of the interaction between science and its practical applications, i.e. engineering [2]. A schematic view of this interaction is shown in figure 1 (adapted from reference [2]). First, we solve problems in any way we can. After some time we realize that some solutions seem to work on more than one problem, and they enter the folklore. Gradually, the folklore can be codified into written heuristics and procedures. Finally, the codification may be able to support models and theories that may lead to "improved practice".

Ideally, university level research and education should promote the "improved practice" based on "models and theories". However, most software engineering practices are still in the state of "folklore" or "codification". In spite of the lack of "models and theories" these practices are still important both from a practitioners and the university perspective, since they work better than "ad hoc solutions", and they should serve as input to research and development projects.

One way of reducing the educational gap is to maintain active interaction between the university and the software companies. From the company point of view the university can serve as a communication forum for exchanging of experiences and discussing new ideas, tools, and techniques. The university can accumulate this "folklore" knowledge, "codify" it and then utilize it in teaching and as a source for new research ideas.

We have been experimenting with several forms of industry-university co-operation, e.g. in technology transfer projects, practically oriented post graduate seminars, and continuing education courses. The experiences have been very encouraging and this co-operation has

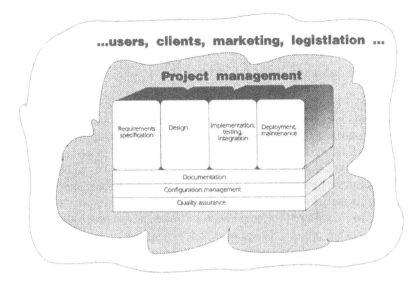

Fig. 2. The framework for course contents

had much influence on the regular software engineering education at our university. The rest of this paper will describe our experiences with one of these experiments, i.e. the Sofko project manager courses.

2. The Sofko Courses

Sofko is a special post graduate education program for software project managers, arranged in co-operation with Tampere University of Technology and the local software industry. The main objective of the program is to provide continuing education for software professionals. The university is responsible for course planning and organization, and the courses are supervised by a steering committee with members both from the software companies and the university.

Typically, the participants of the Sofko courses are software engineers with relatively long (5-10 years) experience in practical software work.

Each course consists of approximately 40 course days, with a time span of about one year. The course schedules are designed to keep the disturbance of regular work moderate: typically one 3-4 day period about once a month.

From April 1989 to February 1991 three Sofko courses, each with some 17-20 participants have been arranged (Sofko I, Sofko II, and Sofko III). Sofko I was our pilot course. Based on the experiences with the Sofko I course we designed two new courses; one for managers of product development projects (Sofko II) and one for management of tailored ADP-system projects (Sofko III).

After Sofko I we interviewed personally each participant. Although the feedback was mostly positive, a few changes were made. Especially, the attendees stressed that the 'soft side' of project management is the main problem area in their work. Therefore, we allocated more time for the 'human factors' part of the new courses. The following subsections describe shortly the planning principles, the course contents, and our experiences with these courses.

3. Planning Principles and Course Contents

The course syllabus is based on the idea that the course should be composed from a much wider spectrum of topics than typical staff training: in addition to the acute problems in the companies, the course should promote long term career development. The courses include both topics intended to be utilized in project managers daily work, as well as topics that will improve the project managers professional skills in general. As a starting point we used the framework presented in figure 1: The general theme is to proceed from outside to inner parts. The courses start with a period including presentation and communication skills, team work, and creativity. This is followed by corporate economics and project economics. After this we moved to software project management and then to life-cycle supporting functions (documentation, quality, and configuration management). Finally, we covered the software process (specification, design, implementation) and several (typically technical) special topics.

The Sofko II course was targeted to management of product development (e.g. embedded systems) software projects, and Sofko III to management of tailored ADP-system projects (e.g. financial systems). Although both courses have much in common, some of the topics covered are totally disjoint, and some have different emphasis in each case. For example, economics modules of the Sofko II course were targeted to economics issues of product development projects, and corporate economics portion was considered to be an informative section among other items, while on the Sofko III course product development issues were missing, and the main emphasize was on corporate economics. Another difference constitutes also the fact that in most product development projects the customer is not directly present, which makes it important to understand the role of marketing and customer needs. Also, the software methodology parts of the two course types were different: on Sofko II the main emphasize is on real time systems development, while on Sofko III the information management point of view was central.

The course contents were discussed extensively with the members of the steering committee. Also, several consulting companies, software houses, ADP departments of large companies, and software vendors were consulted. During this work, a plethora of additions to the proposal was suggested. The final programs are compromises between these educational needs and limiting the length of the course to an acceptable amount of lost work days.

The design process resulted in the following 7 modules for both courses.

1. Basics of Economics (**Econ**). The module provides background knowledge of economics; helping the participants to understand the underlying financial principles of software and product development in their own companies. It also gives a better understanding of the application area to those participants that develop financial systems. The theoretical background is explained in a few days, and practical examples are given by representatives of several companies. (Sofko II: 5 days, Sofko III: 4 days.)

2. Human factors (**Hum**). The goal of this module is to strengthen the knowledge of human issues that concern both the manager's own personal skills and the management of project

members for efficient project performance. In addition to this module, module 3 below contains a notable portion of material covering the "soft side" of the management of technical people. (Sofko II: 3 days, Sofko III: 4 days.)

3: Software project economics and management *(Mngmt)* The purpose of this module is to provide a good understanding of the role of a project in a company, and the management of project members for an efficient project. It contains the most important financial factors of a successful project followed by both technical and human issues. (Sofko II: 8 days, Sofko III: 7 days.)

4. Life-cycle supporting functions (Supp). This module contains submodules covering configuration management, quality control, and documentation. (Sofko II: 5 days, Sofko III: 3 days.)

5. Software development methodology *(Dev)*. The purpose of this module is to provide a good understanding of the main problem areas of software life-cycle phases. The main emphasize is on requirements specifications. (Sofko II: 7 days, Sofko III: 8 days.)

6. Special topics (Spe). This module contains miscellaneous issues that were recognized as important "every day" topics by the steering committee. (Sofko II: 4 days, Sofko III: 5 days.)

7. Technology update (Tech). The topics in this module were picked up as new and/or fast evolving exiting technology developments that a software engineer should be introduced to. (Sofko II: 8 days, Sofko III: 10 days.)

The modules consist of several submodules. The description of the submodules, accompanied with the duration of each submodule is given in the appendix.

In addition to the modules described above, the Sofko II course ended with a two day workshop to once more walk through the most important topics of the course (especially project management topics), and produced a "Project Managers Handbook". The handbook contains checklists, documentation guidelines, etc. This handbook was delivered to the participants of both courses.

Each course had some 30-40 instructors, and planning a successful mixture of instructors caused a lot of work. Typically, one instructor is responsible for one or more submodules, and others are used as 'visiting lecturers'. In addition to theoretical knowledge, most instructors should have sufficient experience in practical software development projects. This has limited the use of academic instructors in our program: most of the instructors come from consulting companies, or are experienced professionals. The role of the university is in organizing and tailoring a relatively consistent course from modules provided by the instructors; not in acting as a primary source of instructors. (On the other hand, it is extremely useful for an academic instructor to participate a Sofko course.)

4. Experiences

The Sofko II and Sofko III courses ended in February 1991. The enthusiasm and immediate feedback from the participants indicated that both courses were a success (the first of the authors of this paper attended almost all course periods on both courses as a representative of the university, and the second author participated the Sofko II course). Although most of

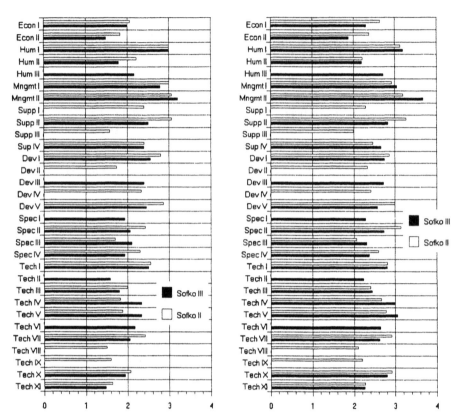

Fig. 3. Usefulness with respect to current task (Grade 1).

Fig. 4. Usefulness with respect to professional skills (Grade 2).

the participants were concurrently working in software projects with tight schedules, the average attendance percentage to course periods was more than 90%.

In order to evaluate our courses in retrospective, we conducted a survey among the participants of the Sofko II and Sofko III courses. The main goal of the survey was to detect, to which extent the courses did meet the original objectives, and also, to figure out what changes to the course syllabus of similar courses in the future are required. The study was carried out about half a year after the courses had finished. In the study the participants evaluated each submodule by giving three grades.

Grade 1: The usefulness of the module with respect to participants current work. This was rated from 1 to 4 (1 = the participant has no use for the topics in this module, 2 = some use, 3 = notably useful, 4 = very useful; the participant can utilize the module in his daily work).

Grade 2: The usefulness of the module with respect to participants professional skills in general. The rating was again from 1 to 4 (1=not useful, 4=the participant considers this topic very important).

Grade 3: The desired duration of the sub-module, rated from 1 to 5 (1=the submodule could be totally removed, 2=the submodule should be made shorter, 3=suitable length, 4=the submodule should be 1.5-2 times longer, 5=the submodule should be much longer).

A problem in the interpretation of the answers to the questions above is that the respondents tend to evaluate the merits of the instructor, not the importance of the subject. The respondents were explicitly warned about this, and they were asked to evaluate the subject, not the instructor. In spite of this, it is obvious that this problem cannot be totally eliminated.

Figure 3 and 4 display the average of grades 1 and 2 above for each submodule (the usefulness with respect to current work, and the usefulness with respect to professional skills, respectively). The standard deviations (not shown) ranged from 0.5 to 0.9. As expected, some of the human issues and project management submodules get high grades in figure 3, while some of the technology update submodules get notably low ratings. On the other hand, with grade 2 of these submodules (figure 4) this difference

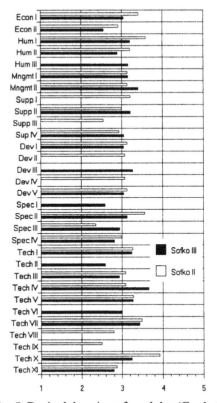

Fig. 5. Desired duration of modules (Grade 3).

is not as clearly visible. Anyway, the results are an indication about the problems that we had in fulfilling the aspirations of different participants in the Technology update module of the program.

Figure 5 displays the averages of grade 3. The participants have considered most submodules to be of suitable length.

After the submodule evaluation questions, the participants answered a few additional questions concerning the course contents. Among other things, the participants were asked to list the topics that should have been covered by the courses but were not. To this questions we got only a few suggestions, and marketing was the only topic that was mentioned in more than one reply form.

Another question queried proposals for submodules that could be removed, provided that we have to shorten the course notably. Most participants proposed several submodules, mainly from the economy and technology update modules. We also asked, what should definitely not be removed, and typical answers included submodules in the project management module and some of the submodules in the human aspects module.

5. A Participants View

Nokia Telecommunications/ Cellular Systems (NCS) took part in the planning of Sofko course. This was natural, since NCS has a fast growing subsidiary in Tampere (currently about 180 employees). Three NCS employees attended the Sofko II course. The business idea of NCS is to provide mobile phone switches and other cellular infrastructure to network operators. Most of the functionality in the products is realized with software, thus leading to large and complex software systems. This chapter is written from the point of view of the experiences gained by NCS in the course. However, most of the text reflects the situation in Finnish software companies, both small and large.

We believe, that the most substantial factor in producing high quality software is the quality of personnel. It is therefore important that software professionals are continuously educated even after their degree. Normally in Finnish software companies the personnel has good background education, usually a university degree. This benefits companies, since this often implies that these persons have already a sound theoretical background and are capable to learn new topics with ease. It is important from the company point of view that the newly hired personnel will acquire the work specific expertise level as rapidly as possible. But once the employees become productive, a more difficult problem arises: How to continuously educate software professionals?

Recent years have been an era of fast growth in software industry. It is therefore important to realize that the work practices must be subject to alteration all the time. Work processes that have worked well before, must be adapted to the requirements imposed by ever larger projects. This causes training needs of the personnel in charge of the software development processes, so that they can create new methods, and then also teach these new methods to the personnel.

Companies can train their personnel basically in two ways. One way is to give quick short term training, which is targeted to quick change of the work habits. The other possibility is to give broad education, where the benefits cannot be realized on short term.

Sofko course is an example of this broad education. It consists of basically everything one can desire; including most of the elements that have to be mastered in software engineering. Furthermore it included submodules (like "Basics of economics") that the participants would probably not have attended otherwise. As a whole, Sofko was a well planned and informative course.

A problem in this type of education is, that it is problematic to change the company practices: One or even more persons have limited capability to make improvements based on the theory adopted at the course. This problem is naturally connected to the company size and the job the attendee has in the company. Such areas as project management and management practices are especially difficult to change in a bottom-up fashion.

Basically, the problem lies in the difference of practices in software companies. Even though the Sofko course was a practical course, it did not contain examples of how to implement the methods in practice. There existed examples, but these examples were mainly to assist understanding of the theory. A lot of additional work and commitment is required in the companies to really fully utilize the contents of the course.

Somehow it is sad in the software engineering practices that even if one company has learned a lot when implementing new theories, this expertise stays in this company and is not being benefited by the software industry as a whole. Time after time all companies discover same things and perhaps waste their money in vain. One of the benefits of the Sofko course was that it brought together software experts from several companies, leading to numerous fruitful discussions and exchange of experiences. A more general conclusion is that perhaps the universities should adopt a role of a neutral communication link between different companies.

One conclusion we have made is that continuous education has many sides. The goal may be to increase the knowledge level of a certain person, or it may be improvement in the practices of the company. The latter can only be achieved if the key persons attend this education.

In Finland the turnover of personnel is relatively small. For example in the NCS, only two persons of the total 180 in Tampere have left the company in the four years of existence. So it is natural that companies seek long-term benefits from this kind of education. One goal is of course to develop personnel that have good education and broad experience to be used for executive positions later in the company.

6. Conclusions

The Sofko courses turned out to be beneficial not only for the participating companies, but also to the university. Especially, the courses have had a lot of fruitful impact on our standard software engineering classes. We are also considering possibilities to train one of our faculty members or teaching assistants on each of the Sofko courses in the future (provided that we are able to get government support for the courses).

The positive experiences have encouraged us to try to further increase the interaction between the software companies and the university. The goal is to use the university as a communication forum for the companies to exchange experiences and discuss new ideas, tools, and techniques. The university can accumulate this empirical knowledge and utilize it in teaching and as a source for new research ideas.

The participants of the Sofko courses have agreed that a yearly Sofko re-union seminar will take place. In these seminars, problems and different ideas will be discussed. The first two day seminar was arranged in January 1992. The participants were asked to describe (in written form) a practical example of utilizing the Sofko training in their work. After this, a balloting was arranged to select the best presentation. There were two winners with equal number of votes, and no surprise, both described successful supervision of software projects.

List of references

[1] Haikala, I.J. and Marijarvi, J., Academic/Industrial Collaboration in Project Manager Education Report published in: Lecture Notes in Computer Science, 376, Proceedings of the SEI Conference 1989, Pittsburgh, Pennsylvania, USA, July 18-21, 1989, pp. 124-130.

[2] Shaw, M., Prospects for an Engineering Discipline of Software. IEEE Software, (November 1990) pp. 15-24.

Appendix: Summary of course periods

The appendix describes the course outlines for the Sofko II (SII) and Sofko III (SIII) courses. Each course consists of 7 modules that are composed of several submodules. Most of the modules are common for both courses, although in some cases the emphasize and duration may be different. Some submodules are included only into one of the courses.

Following the description of each submodule we have added statistics collected from our query forms. They have the following format

$course$: [$duration, use1, use2, length$],

where $course$ is either "SII" or "SIII",
$duration$ is the length of the submodule in course days (8-10 hours),
$use1$ the average usefulness of the module with respect to participants current work,
$use2$ the average usefulness of the module with respect to participants professional skills in general, and
$length$ is the desired duration of the submodule.

The ratings given for modules are averages of the ratings given to its submodules, weighted by the duration of each submodule.

The standard deviation for answers is not given, but it ranged from 0.5 to 0.9.

Module 1: Basics of Economics
This module provides background knowledge of economics; helping the participants to understand the financial principles guiding software and product development in their own companies. It also gives a better understanding of the application area to those participants that develop financial systems. The theoretical background is explained in a few days, and practical examples are given by representatives of several companies.

    SII: [5,   2.0,   2.5,   3.2]
    SIII: [4,   1.8,   2.2,   2.9]

Econ I: corporate strategy, strategic management, basic components of investment analysis, information systems as investments, monetary management, principal applications, profitability, finance, pricing, budgeting, prospects of the information system for the economic management in the 1990's, principles of production management, production cost analysis, cash flow, flow of materials.
    SII: [3,   2.1,   2.6,   3.4]
    SIII: [2.5, 2,   2.3,   3.1]

Econ II for Sofko II: Managing and economics of product development projects, strategy, technology trends, economical considerations.

Econ II for Sofko III: "Software house" enterprise game.
    SII: [2,   1.8,   2.4,   2.9]
    SIII: [1.5, 1.6,   2.1,   2.6]

Module 2: Human factors

The goal of this module is to strengthen the knowledge of human issues that concern both the manager's own personal skills and the management of project members for efficient project performance. In addition to this module, the Project management module covers the "soft side" of the management of technical people to great extent.

```
SII:   [3,   2.7,   2.8,   3.5]
SIII:  [4,   2.5,   2.8,   3.1]
```

Hum I: presentation and communication skills.
```
SII:   [2,   3.0,   3.1,   3.6]
SIII:  [2,   3.0,   3.2,   3.2]
```

Hum II: creativity and group work methods.
```
SII:   [1,   2.2,   2,2,   3.2]
SIII:  [1,   2.0,   2.2,   2.9]
```

Hum III: dealing with difficult/uncomfortable/awkward people. This submodule was added to Sofko III as a result of the requests of the participants.
```
SIII:  [1,   2.2,   2.5,   3.2]
```

Module 3: Software project economics and management

The purpose of this module is to provide a good understanding of the role of a project in a company, and the management of project members for an efficient project. It contains the most important financial factors of a successful project followed by both technical and human issues issues of project management.

```
SII:   [8,   3.1,   3.1,   3.1]
SIII:  [7,   3.2,   3.6,   3.4]
```

Mngmt I: cost analysis, budget planning with follow up actions, acquisitions.
```
SII:   [2,   3.0,   2.9,   3.1]
SIII:  [1,   2.8,   3.1,   3.2]
```

Mngmt II: management of software project team members, project planning, project management issues, project scheduling, project staffing, multiproject environment, resource allocation, tools.
```
SII:   [6,   3.1,   3,2,   3.1]
SIII:  [6,   3.2,   3.7,   3.4]
```

Module 4: Life-cycle supporting functions.

This module contains introductions to supporting functions are present in all life cycle phases, i.e. configuration management, quality control, and documentation.

```
SII:   [5,   2.5,   2.7,   3.0]
SIII:  [3,   2.5,   2.8,   3.2]
```

Supp I: Configuration management: configuration management methods, problems and tools. (This was not included into the Sofko III course, a mini-introduction to this topic was embedded into Supp II submodule of the Sofko III instead)
```
SII:   [1,   2.4,   2.3,   3.2]
```

Supp II: Quality, quality assurance: the role of quality and other quality issues, methods, standards, metrics.

SII: [2,   3.1,   3.3,   3.0]
SIII: [2,   2.5,   2.8,   3.2]

Supp III: Software metrics and measurements, measurement driven quality management, establishing a metrics program.

SII: [1,   1.6,   2.0,   2.5]

Supp IV: Most useful SE standards and their use as documentation guides, ISO9000.

SII: [1,   2.4,   2.5,   2.9]
SIII: [1,   2.4,   2.7,   3.1]

Module 5: Software development methodology

Due to the different backgrounds of the participants, no specific development methodology was chosen for the course, and the topics in this module were covered in a relatively method independent way. Also, in this module the aspirations of the different courses were most notably different from each other. The purpose of this module is to provide a good understanding of the main problem areas of software production phases.

SII: [7,   2.5,   2.7,   3.1]
SIII: [8,   2.4,   2.7,   3.2]

Dev 1: Introduction to methods, feasibility studies, requirements, specification, design, implementation, and CASE-tools.

SII: [2,   2.8,   2.9,   3.1]
SIII: [2,   2.6,   2.8,   3.1]

Dev II: an introduction to formal methods.

SII: [1,   1.8,   2.3,   3.1]

Dev III: Use of modern analysis techniques in commercial ADP-system development (information engineering accompanied with a case study).

SIII: [4,   2.4,   2.7,   3.3]

Dev IV: Practical applications of software development methodologies (presentations from 4 companies).

SII: [2,   2.3,   2.4,   3.1]

Dev V: testing methods and strategies, problems, and tools, deployment, operational issues, maintenance. Especially the operational issues and maintenance parts were much different for each course.

SII: [2,   2.9,   3.0,   3.1]
SIII: [2,   2.4,   2.6,   3.1]

Module 6: Special topics
This module contains miscellaneous issues that were recognized as important "every day" topics by the steering committee.

    SII: [4,   2.2,   2.7,   3.1]
    SIII: [5,   2.0,   2.5,   2.9]

Spe I: Legal issues in financial systems, inspections, audit trail.
    SIII: [1,   1.9,   2.3,   2.6]

Spe II: Legal issues pertaining software, current legislation, trends, copyright and liability issues, writing contracts, implications of legislation to software system design, software and taxes, legislation issues of European Community and common software markets,, criminal legislation.
    SII: [2,   2.4,   3.1,   3.6]
    SIII: [2,   2.1,   2.7,   3.1]

Spe III: Security and protection, fault tolerance, protection against hackers and viruses. On Sofko II the main focus was in security of embedded systems and on Sofko III on security of financial ADP-systems.
    SII: [1,   1.7,   2.1,   2.4]
    SIII: [1,   2.1,   2.3,   2.9]

Spe IV: Human aspects in use of computers, human interface problems, dialog planning, use of colours.
    SII: [1,   2.3,   2.6,   3.0]
    SIII: [1,   1.9,   2.4,   2.8]

Module 7: Technology update
The topics in this module were picked up as new and/or fast evolving exiting technology developments that a software engineer should be introduced to.

    SII: [8,   1.9,   2.5,   3.1]
    SIII: [10,   2.0,   2.7,   3.1]

Tech I: graphical user interfaces, Windows, Motif, Open Look.
    SII: [1,   2.5,   2.8,   3.3]
    SIII: [1.5, 2.5,   2.8,   3.3]

Tech II: the user interface of the future, hypertext, interactive video, the data glove and beyond.
    SIII: [1,   1.5,   2.2,   2.5]

Tech III: CASE-tools, what is available and what to purchase. Different tools were presented for each of the courses (Sofko II: SA/RT -tools, Sofko III: information engineering tools).
    SII: [1,   2.0,   2.4,   3.1]
    SIII: [1,   1.8,   2.4,   2.9]

Tech IV: Relational databases, problems, solutions, networking.
    SII: [1,   1.8,   2.6,   3.1]
    SIII: [1,   2.3,   3.0,   3.6]

Tech V: Client/server-based systems, software architectures in local area networks, application development, strategies, methodologies, software architecture, development tools.
    SII: [1,   1.8,   2.7,   3.2]
    SIII: [2,   2.3,   3.0,   3.2]

Tech VI: Electronic document interchange, introduction, example systems, economics (EDI).
    SIII: [1,   2.2,   2.6,   3.0]

Tech VII: LAN-technology, including ethernet, fiber optics, protocols, gateways, routers, bridges etc.
    SII: [0.5, 2.4,   2.9,   3.5]
    SIII: [0.5, 2.0,   2.6,   3.4]

Tech VIII: Networking in embedded systems, field busses, vehicle busses, protocols.
    SII: [1,   1.5,   2.1,   2.8]

Tech IX: Real time operating systems, multiprocessing, distributed real time operating systems.
    SII: [1,   1.6,   2.2,   2.5]

Tech X: Object oriented methods, analysis, design and programming. Tools and deployment.
    SII: [1,   2.1,   2.9,   3.9]
    SIII: [1,   2.0,   2.8,   3.3]

Tech XI: Expert systems, basics, tools, practical examples.
    SII: [1,   1.6,   2.3,   2.9]
    SIII: [1,   1.5,   2.3,   2.8]

Workshop: a two day workshop for Sofko II to produce a "Project Managers Handbook".

THE SOFTWARE ENGINEERING - PATENT LAW INTERFACE: A PRACTITIONER'S VIEW

by

George M. Taulbee, Esq.
BELL, SELTZER, PARK & GIBSON, P.A.
Charlotte and Raleigh, North Carolina

TABLE OF CONTENTS

THE SOFTWARE ENGINEERING - PATENT LAW INTERFACE:
A PRACTITIONER'S VIEW

by

George M. Taulbee, Esq.
BELL, SELTZER, PARK & GIBSON, P.A.
Charlotte and Raleigh, North Carolina

I.   INTRODUCTION

In the "early" days of the computer age, hardware was the primary focus and software was an afterthought, custom designed for each application, with relatively limited distribution. The large emphasis placed on hardware greatly reduced the costs (regardless of how "costs" are defined) of hardware engineering. While the costs of hardware engineering were steadily decreasing, the costs of designing and developing software remained high. Eventually, attention shifted to reducing the costs of software design and development. "Seat of the pants" trial and error techniques for designing and developing software dedicated solely to a single application was no longer cost effective. Rather, it became necessary to reduce the cost of designing and developing software while at the same time expanding the applications of the software. As a result, the design and development of software evolved from a "seat of the pants" art for which few systematic methods existed to a highly disciplined field of engineering. The field of software engineering was born.

Patent protection for early computer systems was directed to the hardware because software often was considered an afterthought, and in most cases, was customized for the individual application or to execute on particular hardware. Software related inventions were generally protected only as special purpose hardware patents, whose broad claims would also apply to a general purpose computer running a stored program. Few, if any, patents issued solely for software related inventions. However, as emphasis on software design and development increased, so too did concern over protection, and in particular, patent protection, for software related inventions.

This paper is directed to software engineers from academia, industry and government to provide a practical understanding of the interface between software, software engineering, and the patent laws, including obtaining patents relating to software engineering and software. At the outset, general definitions of software and software engineering are presented followed by an overview of patent law and patent law practice before the United States Patent and Trademark Office and the relationship between software and software engineering, and patent law and the Patent and Trademark Office. Thereafter, one of the major obstacles, namely the notorious "mathematical algorithm" problem, to obtaining patent protection for software is discussed. This discussion will include a look at the significant legal opinions and the rules of practices before the United States Patent and Trademark Office. Finally, some examples of software patents will be presented.

II. SOFTWARE AND SOFTWARE ENGINEERING - AN OVERVIEW

A. Definition of Software

Software can be defined in an unlimited number of ways. Although many of these definitions may be similar, it is helpful for purposes of discussion to provide a general definition of software. One general definition of software is the following:

1) instructions (computer programs) that when executed provide desired function and performance;

2) data structures that enable the programs to adequately manipulate information; and

3) documents that describe the operation and use of the programs.

R.S. Pressman, _Software Engineering: A Practitioner's Approach_, Second Edition, McGraw-Hill Book Company, 1987, p. 5. In addition, software may be referred to as being applicable to any situation for which a "previously specified set of procedural steps (i.e., an algorithm) has been defined." _Id._ at p. 11. Special note should be taken of "procedural steps (i.e., an algorithm)" because it is not the same as a "mathematical algorithm" referred to by the courts as discussed below.

B. Classification of Software

Software may be classified in numerous ways. The following classifications of various types of software will help the reader identify the subject matter of the patents and patent applications discussed later. Pressman classifies the various types of software as follows:

1) system software;

2) real time software;

3) business software (including information and database systems);

4) engineering and scientific software (including "number crunching" software and computer aided

design, system simulation, and other interactive application software);

5) embedded software (including software for controlling products and systems for consumer and industrial applications);

6) personal computer software (including software that ranges across other classifications); and

7) artificial intelligence software (including expert system, pattern recognition, and game playing software).

Id. at pp. 12-13.

C.   Definition of Software Engineering

Similar to software, software engineering can be defined in numerous ways. However, for purposes of discussion, it is helpful to provide one definition of software engineering. Software engineering can be defined as

The establishment and use of sound engineering principles in order to obtain economically software that is reliable and works efficiently on real machines.

Id. at p. 19, citing Naur, P., and B. Randell, *Software Engineering: A Report on a Conference Sponsored by the NATO Science Committee*, NATO, 1969.

D.   Evolution of Software and Software Engineering

The evolution of software engineering has basically paralleled and been necessitated by the evolution of software and computer systems during the computer age. Pressman has broken the evolution of software and computer systems into the four eras identified below. See Pressman, pp. 2-4.

The first era ranged from the late 1940s to the mid 1960s and was directed to batch orientation, limited distribution and custom software. The second era, which ranged from 1960 to the mid 1970s, primarily focused on multi-user, real time, database and product related software. The third era stretched from the early 1970s to the late 1980s and was directed to software such as distributed systems, embedded "intelligence", low-cost hardware and consumer impact software. Finally, the fourth era began in the mid 1980s and is expected to stretch into the early 21st century and includes computer systems in the nature of expert systems, artificial intelligence machines and parallel architectures.

The fourth era of software and computer system evolution has resulted in a number of problems in the area of software design and development. These problems, include, but are not limited to:

1) the fact that hardware sophistication has outpaced the ability to build software that can utilize the hardware's potential;

2) the ability to design and develop new programs does not keep pace with the demand for new programs; and

3) the ability to maintain existing programs is threatened by poor design and inadequate resources.

Id. at p. 4.

The solution to these problems is the application of principles and methods of traditional engineering disciplines to the design and development of software. This is often referred to as software engineering and is particularly appropriate since software is developed or engineered and not manufactured in the traditional sense.

Keeping these basic concepts of software and software engineering in mind, attention is now directed to patent protection, in general, the interface between software/software engineering, practice before the United States Patent and Trademark Office and patent protection for software, in particular.

III. AN OVERVIEW OF PATENT LAW

A.   Patents In General and the Software
     Engineering - Patent Interface

Patents are simply one type of intellectual property, i.e. a piece of property created by the human intellect. Intellectual property includes patents, trademarks, copyrights, mask works, and trade secrets. All forms of intellectual property protection should be considered for integrated protection of software.[1]

Patents provide protection for "inventions." The United States Constitution expressly authorizes the Federal statute for protecting "inventions" and provides, in part, as follows:

"Congress shall have the power ... to promote the progress of science and useful arts, by securing for limited times to authors and inventors the exclusive

---

[1]   This paper is restricted to patent protection for software in order to provide a more detailed discussion of the practical considerations for protecting software through the patent law.

right to their respective writings and discoveries."
Article 1, Section 8, Clause 8.

In accordance with this clause of the Constitution, the United
States Patent Act specifically defines what is considered to be
patentable subject matter. The Patent Act provides:

> Whoever invents or discovers any new and useful process,
> machine, manufacture, or composition of matter, or any
> new and useful improvement thereof, may obtain a patent
> therefor, subject to the conditions and requirements of
> this title. 35 U.S.C. §101.

These classes of invention are often referred to as "statutory
subject matter."

In light of the above, it follows that any discovery resulting
from software engineering, as defined above, falls within the
intent of the Federal statute for protecting "inventions" as
authorized by the United States Constitution. In addition,
software engineering, similar to other engineering disciplines,
produces "new and useful processes, machines, and manufacturers."
Therefore, any resulting product or discovery based on
implementation of software engineering principles and methods
should be considered statutory subject matter.

B. Patent Rights

There are several types of patents, including utility patents,
design patents[2] and plant patents.[3] Utility and design patents
last for a period of seventeen (17) and fourteen (14) years,
respectively. Utility patents are the particular type of patents
generally referred to when the term "patent" is used and for
purposes of discussion, only utility patents will be considered.

A patent grants the right to exclude others from making, using
or selling the invention claimed in the patent. In other words,
others may be prevented from trespassing on the property. A patent
does not, however, grant the right to make, use or sell the
patented invention.

---

[2]   Design patents are directed to the aesthetic appearance
of a product which is new and different from the aesthetic
appearances of prior products of the same general type. Although
design patents may be relevant to some aspects of software
inventions, including user interfaces, the scope of this paper is
primarily directed to utility patents.

[3]   Plant patents are directed to new and distinct
varieties of plants. Plant patents are irrelevant to the present
discussion.

The rights of a patent are defined by its claims. A patent is, in effect, a contract between the patent owner and the public for these exclusive rights in return for a disclosure to the public of the invention claimed in the patent and the use by the public of the patent after the seventeen (17) year period expires and the patented invention passes into the public domain.

United States patents are obtained by filing a written application in proper form with the United States Patent and Trademark Office. However, no patent right is obtained upon filing the patent application in the Patent and Trademark Office. Rather, a substantive examination by a patent examiner in the Patent and Trademark Office is required before patent rights are granted. This phase of obtaining a patent is often referred to as "prosecution" of the application.

Preparation of a patent application is complex and extensive and has often been described in the legal profession as the most difficult legal document to prepare. It involves a detailed technical description of the invention, usually accompanied by drawings, which discloses to one with ordinary skill in the art the best mode of practicing the invention. The technical description must also be capable of being understood by a non-technical judge and jury, if the patent is later litigated, and by non-technical management people, if the patent is licensed. The application concludes with claims which define the legal rights being sought in the patent application. The claims are the yardstick on which subsequent infringement by others is measured and the yardstick for measuring the value of the patent rights when licensing to others. For machines and articles of manufacture, the claims are generally in the form of a combination of interrelated elements, while for processes the claims are generally in the form of a combination of interrelated steps.

An invention must be novel, non-obvious, and useful in order to be patentable. The first criteria for patentability is that an invention must be novel; in other words, it was not known or used by others before the invention by the applicant for the patent, and the invention was not disclosed or published in a printed publication (including a prior patent), was not in public use and was not sold or offered for sale more than one (1) year prior to the date the patent application was filed in the United States Patent and Trademark Office.[4] 35 U.S.C. §102. The second criteria for patentability is that an invention must not have been obvious to a person having ordinary skill in the art at the time the

---

[4]   The requirement that the application must be filed within one year from the time the invention is first sold, offered for sale, publicly used, disclosed or published is a critical requirement for filing an United States patent application. It should be noted that foreign countries allow no grace period at all, and an application must be on file before any publication, sale or public use.

invention was made. 35 U.S.C. §103. Finally, the criteria of "utility" for patentability is generally met by software related machines and processes and does not usually play a particularly strong role in the determination of patentability of these inventions. Proof of utility, however, is often critical for chemical and pharmaceutical inventions.

C.   Remedies for Infringement of a Patent

In order for an accused device or process to be deemed to infringe the claims of a patent, the accused device or process must contain every element (or step) of a patent claim or its substantial equivalent. There are two types of infringement of patent claims, namely literal infringement and infringement under the doctrine of equivalents. Literal infringement requires that the accused device embody every element of the claim. Thus, omission of even a single element recited by a claim avoids literal infringement. Even if no literal infringement is found, an accused device or process may infringe the claims of a patent under the doctrine of equivalents. In order for an accused device or process to infringe the claims of a patent under the doctrine of equivalents, the accused device must perform substantially the same function in substantially the same way to obtain substantially the same result as the claimed invention.

Once infringement is found, a patentee may be entitled to a number of remedies. One possible remedy is injunctive relief. A patentee may be entitled to an injunction, preliminary or permanent, to prevent an infringer from further making, using or selling the invention claimed in the patent. 35 U.S.C. §283. A second remedy is damages for infringement. Damages for infringement are measured by the injury to the patent owner/ licensee. The patent owner/licensee is entitled to damages based upon the profits lost by the patent owner/licensee but no less than a reasonable royalty. 35 U.S.C. §284. A patent owner/licensee may also be entitled to prejudgment interest. 35 U.S.C. §284. Such interest is awarded regardless of whether damages are based upon lost profits or on a reasonable royalty. Interest on a reasonable royalty runs from the time the royalties should have been paid. Similarly, interest on lost profits runs from the date when the profit was lost and not from the date of last infringement.

In addition, a patentee may be entitled to an award of treble damages when a court concludes that the infringement was willful. 35 U.S.C. §284. Finally, a patentee may recover attorney fees and costs. 35 U.S.C. §§284-285. Recovery of attorney fees and costs is at the court's discretion and is only awarded in extraordinary cases when there is a finding of unfairness or bad faith (willfulness) in the conduct of the losing party. The purpose of awarding fees and costs is to compensate the prevailing party for costs that it would not have incurred but for the conduct of the losing party. It should be noted that the prevailing party may be either the patent owner/licensee or the accused infringer.

D.   A Patent Is A Form Of Intangible Personal Property

A patent is a form of intangible personal property. That is, it is an asset which can be bought, sold or licensed, either exclusively or non-exclusively, dependent upon the field of use, market region, size of CPU, or other factors. Owning a patent allows a great deal of flexibility in business dealings. In addition, a security interest (lien) in a patent can be perfected.

IV.   UNITED STATES PATENT AND TRADEMARK OFFICE -
       REGISTRATION AND CLASSIFICATION

Concern over the patenting of software related inventions is expressed by participants in the software field, including those from industry, government and academia, on almost a daily basis. A great deal of the concern relates to the technical aptitude and training of patent attorneys and patent examiners, as well as the availability and consideration of prior art during the patent application examination process in the United States Patent and Trademark Office. The discussion in this section provides a brief overview of the registration requirements for practicing before the Patent and Trademark Office (which are the same as those for becoming a Patent Examiner) and the classification of patents in the Patent and Trademark Office, and changes made by the Patent and Trademark Office to the registration requirements and classifications as an attempt to address the concerns expressed by individuals and groups in the software field.

A.   Registration to Practice

In order to practice before the United States Patent and Trademark Office, it is necessary to be registered either as an attorney or as an agent. With few exceptions, applicants seeking to register must write a patent examination. However, prior to being permitted to write the examination, an applicant must meet the necessary scientific and technical requirements. The Patent and Trademark Office recognizes undergraduate degrees, or the equivalent thereof, in a number of subjects. Degrees that relate either directly or indirectly to software and which are recognized by the Patent and Trademark Office as meeting the necessary scientific and technical training requirements include electrical engineering and computer engineering. However, it should be noted that degrees in computer science, software engineering, mathematics, and other software related fields are not accepted.

If an applicant does not possess one of the accepted degrees, an applicant may nonetheless qualify to write the examination by meeting one of four options. The option which is directed to those individuals who have scientific and technical training in computer science, software engineering or other software related curricula requires a combination of courses in chemistry, physics, biological science and engineering. Computer science courses that are computer engineering in nature are accepted. The Patent and Trademark Office has defined these type of courses to include courses that provide in-depth knowledge of computer science, including digital computer system architecture and system software organization, representation and transformation of information structures, and the theoretical models for such representations and transformations. Courses directed to linear circuits, logic circuits, networking, fundamentals of computer science, algorithms, data structures, software design, programming languages, operating systems and computer architecture are also accepted as being oriented towards scientific and technical training. Many of these courses are required courses in computer science and software engineering curricula. The author, who has a Bachelor of Science degree in Computer Science from Virginia Polytechnic Institute and State University and a Master of Mathematics degree in Computer Science from the University of Waterloo was able to become registered to practice before the United States Patent and Trademark Office using this approach.

This elaborate definition of computer science courses that are computer engineering in nature and thus directed to scientific and technical training was included in the Patent and Trademark Office registration requirements in 1991. Prior to that time, the long list of accepted courses was not included.

The definition of accepted courses is of particular importance because the requirements necessary to register to practice before the Patent and Trademark Office are the same requirements which must be met by a potential patent examiner. Prior to the defining of acceptable computer science courses, much concern existed in the technical and patent law communities regarding the technical training of the patent examiners who examine applications for software related inventions. By including this definition of computer science courses, the Patent and Trademark Office has taken a step in the right direction towards hiring examiners who possess the necessary scientific and technical training in the software field. Therefore, the concern of the technical and patent law communities, to a large extent, has been overcome. This concern could be fully overcome by recognizing computer science, software engineering and other software related degrees as fully meeting the necessary scientific and technical training requirements.

B.   Classification of Patents in the United States
     Patent and Trademark Office

Patents are classified in the United States Patent and Trademark Office according to subject matter. Patent classification is necessary in order to permit not only prior art searches to be conducted by inventors or their representatives, but also to permit the patent examiners to conduct their own pre-examination search of the prior art which is required by the Patent Office examining guidelines (Manual of Patent Examining Procedure). Prior to November 5, 1991, the majority of computer technology related patents, and in particular, application independent software patents, were classified under a single subclass entitled "General Purpose Programmable Digital Computer System" (Class 364, Subclass 200). Several other subclasses existed including those entitled "Artificial Intelligence" (Subclasses 513-513.5), "Control of Data Presentation" (Subclasses 518-523) and "Miscellaneous Digital Processing Systems" (Subclass 900).

The size of the subclass for General Purpose Programmable Digital Computer Systems was enormous, to say the least, and made searching of prior art patents difficult, if not impossible. Thus, the patent law community determined that it was necessary to reclassify patents for general purpose computer systems. The reclassification became effective on November 5, 1991 and is identified as Class 395. Class 395, which is entitled "Information Processing System Organization", replaced Class 364, Subclasses 200, 513-513.5, 518-523 and 900. It is directed to digital processing systems and corresponding methods for performing information processing functions and methods for controlling operation of such processing systems. Class 395 also encompasses artificial intelligence. Artificial intelligence is meant to include systems or methods which have the capacity to perform one or more of the functions of recognition, speech signal processing, knowledge processing (i.e., propositional logic, reasoning, learning self-improvement), complex operations of manipulation (e.g., robot control), or inexact reasoning (e.g., fuzzy logic). Class 395 for digital processing systems also includes methods or apparatus for processing data for static presentation (hard copy) or display, wherein the processing of data for display includes the creation or manipulation of graphic objects, such as artificial images, or text by a computer prior to use with or in a specific display system.

Class 395 for digital processing systems and corresponding methods has 19 subclasses at the present time. These subclasses are as follows:

1) Artificial Intelligence (Subclass 1);

2) Data Presentation/Computer Graphics (e.g., image graphics, text) (Subclass 100);

3) Transmission of Information among Multiple Computer Systems (Subclass 200);

4) Buffering Functions (Subclass 250);

5) I/O Processing (Subclass 275);

6) System Interconnections (Subclass 325);

7) Instruction Processing (Subclass 375);

8)   Storage Address Formation (Subclass 400);

9)   Storage Accessing and Control (Subclass 425);

10) Compatibility, Simulation, or Emulation of System Components (Subclass 500);

11) Timing (Subclass 550);

12) Reliability (Subclass 575);

13) Database or File Management System (Subclass 600);

14) Processing (Task) Management (Subclass 650);

15) System Utilities (Subclass 700);

16) Access Control Processing (Subclass 725);

17) Power Control (Subclass 750);

18) Internal Control (Subclass 775); and

19) Processing Architecture (Subclass 800).

Although the majority of patents for application independent software related inventions are now classified in Class 395 directed to digital processing systems, some application independent software patents may be assigned to one of a limited number of other classes, including Class 364 which contains patents directed to computer applications, Class 340 containing patents directed to displays and communications and Class 371 directed to error detection, correction and recovery patents.[5]

Thus, in light of the reclassification of computer technology related patents, including software related patents, in the United States Patent and Trademark Office, and the redefining of the requirements to register to practice before the Patent and Trademark Office or become a patent examiner, practice before the Patent and Trademark Office directed to software related inventions has been greatly improved. Although this is not a total answer to the question of inadequate examination of patents, including lack of ability to identify the best prior art, it certainly is a step in the right direction.

Now that the reader has a basic understanding of patents, in general, and practice before the Unites States Patent and Trademark Office, the issue of patenting software, and in particular, whether

---

[5]   Application specific software patents are often times classified by application, e.g. engine control or manufacturing systems.

a software related invention is statutory subject matter, will be discussed.

V.   PATENTING SOFTWARE

The main issue in patenting a software related invention is whether or not the software invention is considered statutory subject matter under 35 U.S.C. §101. In other words, whether the software related invention is considered to be "any new and useful process, machine, manufacture, or composition of matter, or any new and useful improvement thereof." 35 U.S.C. §101. This section is directed to the case law and the United States Patent and Trademark Office's position on whether software inventions are statutory subject matter. The discussion that follows is not an attempt to discuss every software related patent case, but rather, to provide a practical outline for software engineers directed to the question of patenting software. Although each software invention must be considered on a case by case basis and in some circumstances, a particular court decision may be more applicable on a factual basis than those discussed below, only the most important cases concerning the question of patenting software are presented for discussion.

A.   History of Patenting Software

In considering the history of patent protection for software related inventions, it is helpful to give a brief overview of the early court decisions. The "early cases" discussed below provide the reader with a background for understanding the subsequent decisions by the Supreme Court.

1.   The Early Cases

The early court cases dealt with overcoming the "mental steps" doctrine. The mental steps doctrine in computer related cases relates to whether the computer merely practices a mathematical process which can be carried out by a human, albeit much more slowly. Patent protection for software, as in the case of any invention, which precludes practice by humans is not statutory subject matter.

One of the first cases in this area was *In re Prater*, 415 F.2d 1393 (CCPA 1969). The patent application at issue had both apparatus and process claims for spectrographic analysis using linear equations run on a digital computer. The claimed invention processed spectrographic data obtained in the form of a spectrogram to produce a quantitative spectrographic analysis of a qualitatively known mixture, for example, a mixture of gases, by which the unknown component concentrations could be determined with minimum error. The Court initially held that the mental steps doctrine did not preclude patent protection. On rehearing, the

Court concluded that the mental steps doctrine was inapplicable to the application for spectrographic analysis because an apparatus for implementing the process without human intervention was not disclosed.

A later case, *In re Bernhart*, 417 F.2d 1395 (CCPA 1969), involved an invention for a digital computer solving a set of equations and a method of projecting three-dimensional figures onto two-dimensional surfaces. The Court of Custom and Patent Appeals reaffirmed the rule that a general purpose computer programmed to perform a claimed process was statutory subject matter. In reaching this conclusion, the Court reasoned that a machine which is "programmed in a new and nonobvious way" is "physically different" from that which is not so programmed. *Id.* at 1400.

The Court of Customs and Patent Appeals continued to follow this trend in *In re Musgrave*, 431 F.2d 882 (CCPA 1970). *Musgrave* was concerned with a process of establishing weathering corrections in geophysical exploration using a digital computer. The Court extended statutory subject matter to include computer programmed processes and concluded that the mental steps doctrine did not apply merely because some or all of the steps which were carried out on a digital computer could also be carried out with human aid. In reaching this conclusion, the Court stated that all that was necessary for a sequence of operational steps to be statutory subject matter is that it be "in the technological arts so as to be in consonance with the Constitutional purpose to promote the progress of 'useful arts'." *Id.* at 893.

This line of cases regarding the mental steps doctrine resulted in many applications being filed for software related inventions. In these applications, the claims were directed to special purpose hardware inventions, whose broad claims would also apply to a general purpose computer running a stored program. The claims were drafted in this manner in order to overcome the "mental steps" doctrine.

2. Supreme Court Decisions

The Supreme Court, subsequent to the early cases discussed above, addressed the question of whether software related inventions were statutory subject matter. In particular, the Supreme Court focused on the "mathematical algorithm" problem. According to the Supreme Court, a mathematical algorithm is not patentable, *per se*, because it is just like a law of nature which cannot be patented. However, an application of a mathematical algorithm or law of nature to a statutory process is statutory subject matter, i.e., can be patented. The Supreme Court cases which address the "mathematical algorithm" problem are *Gottschalk v. Benson*, 409 U.S. 63 (1972), *Parker v. Flook*, 437 U.S. 584 (1978), and *Diamond v. Diehr*, 450 U.S. 175 (1981). These cases are discussed below.

a.   *Gottschalk v. Benson, 409 U.S. 63 (1972)*

Gottschalk applied for a patent on a method for converting numerical information from binary coded decimal ("BCD") representation to binary representation for use in programming a general purpose digital computer. The Court held the invention was not statutory subject matter because it was only a series of mathematical calculations. In reaching its holding, the Court called the invention a generalized formula for converting numbers from one form to another, i.e., an "algorithm." *Id.* at 65. The Court was primarily concerned that the claims for the conversion of BCD to binary were broad enough to encompass not only the embodiment of the disclosed digital computer but any conversion process. In particular, the Court stated that:

> Here the "process" claim is so abstract and sweeping as to cover both known and unknown uses of the BCD to pure-binary conversion. *Id.* at 68.

The Court, however, specifically noted that it was not holding that there could not be a patent for any program servicing a computer. *Id.* at 71. It is important to note that although the Court concluded that the generalized formula for converting numbers from one form to another was an "algorithm" and therefore not statutory subject matter, the definition of an algorithm used in this case (procedure for solving a given type of mathematical problem) for patent purposes as defined by the Supreme Court is not so broad as to encompass any fixed step-by-step procedure for accomplishing a given result, i.e., an algorithm in the software or computer science sense.

b.   *Parker v. Flook, 437 U.S. 584 (1978)*

Parker dealt with an application for a method for updating "alarm limits" during a catalytic conversion process. The Court concluded that the invention was not statutory subject matter because the only novel feature was a mathematical formula used on a computer.

In reaching this conclusion, the Court rejected the applicant's arguments that his method was not applicable to all updating processes but only to those related to the catalytic conversion process and that his recited post solution activity of adjusting the alarm limit based on the outcome of the process would make his claim statutory. The Court stated that the claimed invention did not include any monitoring of the process, setting off of an alarm or adjusting of the alarm (only adjusting of the alarm limit). Although the Court again stated that an algorithm or a mathematical formula is not patentable, it noted that a "process is not unpatentable simply because it contains a law of nature or a mathematical algorithm." *Id.* at 590. In addition, the court stated that the tying of a specific end use does not make a method of calculation patentable. "The process itself, not merely the mathematical algorithm, must be new and useful." *Id.* at 591.

c. *Diamond v. Diehr, 450 U.S. 175 (1981)*

Despite the fact that the Supreme Court in *Benson* and *Flook* stated that the decision should not be interpreted to deny protection to all computer programs, *Diehr* was the first case in which the Supreme Court held a software related invention to be statutory subject matter. Diehr applied for a patent on a process for curing synthetic rubber in a mold, including several steps which used a known mathematical formula relating to the time for curing. A digital computer was used in determining the length of curing time and for opening the mold.

The Court restated its earlier decisions by stating that mathematical formulae cannot be the subject in a patent. However, a claim drawn to statutory subject matter is not made nonstatutory because it uses a mathematical formula, computer program or computer. In *Diehr*, the invention continuously measured the temperature inside a rubber mold and applied these measurements to a computer which repeatedly calculated the cure time by use of an equation. When the recalculated time equaled the actual time since the mold had closed, the computer caused the mold to open.

In reaching its decision, the Court distinguished the earlier *Benson* and *Flook* decisions on the basis that the *Benson* and *Flook* claims were directed to an algorithm programmed for execution by a general purpose digital computer which, like a law of nature, cannot be the subject of a patent. On the other hand, the *Diehr* claims were drawn to subject matter otherwise statutory and did not become nonstatutory simply because they used a mathematical formula, computer program or digital computer. Thus, unlike Benson and Flook, Diehr sought a patent on a process for curing rubber using a mathematical formula and not on the formula itself.

3. Interpretation of the Supreme Court Decisions – Development of the Two-Step Test

Subsequent to the decisions of the Supreme Court in *Benson*, *Flook* and *Diehr*, the Court of Custom and Patent Appeals considered the "mathematical algorithm" problem in light of software related inventions. Numerous cases were decided. The three major cases which developed a "two-step" test that is applied to software related inventions are *In re Freeman*, 573 F.2d 1237 (CCPA 1978), *In re Walter*, 618 F.2d 758 (CCPA 1980) and *In re Abele*, 684 F.2d 902 (CCPA 1982). The evolution of the "two-step" test, often referred to as the *Freeman-Walter-Abele* test, is discussed below.

a. *In re Freeman, 573 F.2d 1237 (CCPA 1978)*

The "two-step" test was first formulated in *In re Freeman*. Freeman dealt with an application for a system for typesetting information using a computer-based control system in conjunction with a conventionally designed phototypesetter. The court upheld the claims as being directed to statutory subject matter. In reaching this holding, the Court stated the following two-step test based upon *Gottschalk v. Benson* for determining whether a software related invention is statutory subject matter:

1) Determine whether the patent claim directly or indirectly recites an "algorithm" in the *Benson* sense of the term, i.e., a procedure for solving a given type of mathematical problem; and

2) Analyze the claim to ascertain whether in its entirety it wholly preempts that algorithm.

Id. at 1245.

The Court reached its conclusion by reasoning that the "local positioning algorithm" of *Freeman* was a step-by-step procedure for solving a problem and not a mathematical algorithm in the *Benson* sense, i.e., a procedure for solving a given type of mathematical problem, and that the claimed invention did not directly or indirectly relate to a mathematical algorithm.

b. *In re Walter, 618 F.2d 758 (CCPA 1980)*

The *Walter* Court restricted the scope of the second step of the two-step test. Walter's application was directed to a method and apparatus of seismic prospecting and surveying by processing seismic exploration data using known mathematical operations. The steps included transmitting seismic source waves into the earth, sensing, and converting the reflected waves to a more useable form by a "method of correlating". The Court affirmed the rejection of the application as claiming nonstatutory subject matter. Although the Court used the *Freeman* two-step test as a basis for its conclusion, it rewrote the second step as follows:

> Once a mathematical algorithm has been found, the claim as a whole must be analyzed. If it appears that the mathematical algorithm is implemented in a specific manner to define structural relationships between the physical elements of the claim (in apparatus claims) or to refine or limit claim steps (in process claims), the claim being otherwise statutory, the claim passes muster under §101. If, however, the mathematical algorithm is merely presented and solved by the claimed invention, as was the case in *Benson* and *Flook*, and is not applied in any manner to physical elements or process steps, no amount of post-solution activity will render the claim

statutory; nor is it saved by a preamble merely reciting the field of use of the mathematical algorithm. *Id.* at 767.

In other words, the *Walter* Court restated the second step of the two-step test to be defined as follows:

If the mathematical algorithm is implemented by providing a structural relationship between the physical elements of an apparatus claim or refining or limiting the steps in a process claim, then the mathematical algorithm is not preempted and the claim is patentable.

Thus, the Court emphasized structural relationships between the elements of apparatus claims or limitations of the steps in the process claims as a test for whether an invention is statutory subject matter. In doing so, the Court concluded that Walter's claim elements directed to "correlating" were essentially mathematical in nature. In addition, the Court also concluded that the data gathering steps and the "post solution activity" of outputting partial product signals did not render the claims statutory subject matter.

c. *In re Abele, 684 F.2d 902 (CCPA 1982)*

The court in *In re Abele* further defined the second step of the two-step test. Abele filed an application for an improved computerized axial tomography (CAT scan) which utilized a computer to implement several mathematical calculations and then display an image representing a transverse slice or section of a patient's body. An x-ray source and a sensor were used for generating x-rays and detecting the x-rays passing through the body, respectively. The claimed invention used a weighting function to process the output of the sensor.

The *Abele* Court concluded that the process and corresponding apparatus claims for producing, detecting and displaying x-ray attenuation data generated by a computerized tomography scanner, as well as the process and corresponding apparatus for an improved method of CAT scan image processing were statutory subject matter. However, the Court also held that a method and corresponding apparatus for displaying data comprising calculations and displaying the differences between specified values were not statutory subject matter. In reaching its conclusion, the *Abele* Court used the two-step test defined by the *Freeman* Court and further restricted by the *Walter* Court. However, the *Abele* court rewrote the second step of the two-step test as follows:

If the claim would be otherwise statutory, albeit inoperative or less useful without the algorithm, the claim likewise presents statutory subject matter when the algorithm is included. *Id.* at 907.

In applying its rewritten second step of the two-step test, the court considered two claims. Method claim 6 required x-ray attenuation data. The Court stated that:

> [T]he specification indicates that such attenuation data is available only when an x-ray beam is produced by a CAT scanner, passed through an object, and detected upon its exit. Only after these steps have been completed is the algorithm performed, and the resultant modified data displayed in the required format. *Id.* at 908.

The Court went on to state that were they to view the claim absent the algorithm:

> the production, detection and display steps would still be present and would result in a conventional CAT scan process. *Id.* at 908.

Therefore, the Court concluded that production and detection could not be considered mere antecedent steps to obtain values for solving the algorithm and that this claim was statutory.

However, in contrast, the Court concluded that a claim (Claim 5) which presented no more than the calculation of a number and display of the result, albeit in a particular format, was directed to nonstatutory subject matter. *Id.* at 909. In addition, the Court stated that the specification provided no greater meaning to the "data in a field" than a matrix of numbers regardless of the method by which the data was generated. *Id.* at 909. Thus, the algorithm was neither explicitly nor implicitly applied to any certain process and therefore Claim 5 was not statutory.

B.   Present State of the Law

Subsequent to 1982, courts and the United States Patent and Trademark Office have applied the *Freeman-Walter-Abele* two-step test to numerous cases and applications. The discussion below addresses the decisions of the United States Court of Appeals for the Federal Circuit and the guidelines of the United States Patent and Trademark Office.

1.   Court of Appeals for the Federal Circuit

In 1989, the United States Court of Appeals for the Federal Circuit[6], the court with appellate jurisdiction over patent law

---

[6]   The United States Court of Appeals for the Federal Circuit is the successor court to the United States Court of Customs and Patent Appeals whose decisions have been adopted as binding precedent by the Court of Appeals for the Federal Circuit. See *South Corp. v. United States*, 690 F.2d 1368, 1370

cases, decided two cases in the area of software related inventions, namely, *In re Iwahashi*, 888 F.2d 1270 (Fed. Cir. 1989), and *In re Grams*, 888 F.2d 835 (Fed. Cir. 1989). A third significant decision, namely, *Arrhythmia Research Technology, Inc. v. Corazonix Corp.*, 22 USPQ2d 1033 (Fed. Cir. 1992), was handed down by the Federal Circuit in 1992, relating to patenting software inventions.

a. *In re Iwahashi*, 888 F.2d 1370 (Fed. Cir. 1989)

Iwahashi described his invention generally as a device for pattern recognition and in particular as a voice recognition device. The *Iwahashi* Court applied the *Freeman-Walter-Abele* two-step test to the invention claimed in an application for an apparatus for an auto-correlation unit useful in pattern recognition to obtain auto-correlation co-efficients. The Court held the invention patentable and confirmed the two-step test for determining whether a claim containing a mathematical algorithm qualifies as statutory subject matter. In reaching its conclusion, the *Iwahashi* court confirmed that the two-step test included:

(1) a determination as to whether a mathematical algorithm exists in the claim; and

(2) analysis of the claim as a whole to determine whether the mathematical algorithm is implemented in a specific manner to define structural relationships between the physical elements of the claim (in apparatus claims) or to refine or limit claim steps (in process claims).

Id. at 1374-75.

In essence, the *Iwahashi* Court held that the claim in question recited specific structural limitations including a read-only memory and explicit means-plus-function recitations that directly corresponded to well-known digital circuits. The Court concluded that these structural limitations made the claim statutory.

b. *In re Grams, 888 F.2d 835 (Fed. Cir. 1989)*

The Court of Appeals for the Federal Circuit decided *In re Grams* on the very same day that it decided *In re Iwahashi*. The *Grams* Court considered whether claims directed to a computerized method of diagnosing abnormal conditions in complex systems recited statutory subject matter.

(Fed. Cir. 1982) (in banc).

The application claimed the method of diagnosing a plurality of parameters to detect a normal or abnormal condition in an individual, the parameters being obtained from a series of clinical laboratory tests which measure the levels of chemical or biological constituents of an individual. Although the claims were directed to a human, the applicants stated in the patent specification that their invention was applicable to any complex system, whether it be electrical, mechanical, chemical, biological or combinations thereof. The method consisted of steps such as conducting tests on individual instances of the system, comparing resulting values with values for normal individuals and conducting further successive tests in an attempt to determine the cause of the abnormality.

In concluding that the invention was nonstatutory, the Court held that the presence of a physical step in a claim to obtain input data (data gathering step) for use by a mathematical algorithm claimed in the remaining steps does not render a claim to be directed to statutory subject matter. Thus, a preliminary data gathering step or token post-solution activity will not convert a nonstatutory claim into a statutory claim.

It is interesting to note that, in reaching its conclusion, the *Grams* Court appears to have followed its own narrowing of the second step of the *Walter-Freeman-Abele* test. In a footnote, the *Grams* Court narrowed the second step by stating the following:

> We do not read the last sentence of this quote [*In re Abele*, 684 F.2d at 907] as declaring patentable any claim that is statutory without the algorithm. We read it consistently with the previous sentence, and with *Walter*, as requiring (to meet the *Walter* test) not only that the physical steps in the claim (without the algorithm) constitute a statutory process, but, also, that the algorithm operates on a claimed physical step. *Id.* at 839, footnote 4.

Thus, the *Grams* Court concluded that the claim was nonstatutory by applying the otherwise statutory standard and determining that the algorithm did not operate on a claimed physical step. It should be noted, however, that although the court held that a claim containing only a data gathering step in addition to steps implementing a mathematical algorithm to be nonstatutory, the Court expressly declined to decide whether a claim would be directed to nonstatutory subject matter in every case where the physical step of obtaining data for the algorithm is the only other significant element in a mathematical algorithm claim.

c. *Arrhythmia Research Technology, Inc. v. Corazonix Corp.*, 22 USPQ2d 1033 (Fed. Cir. 1992)

Arrhythmia Research unlike *Iwahashi* and *Grams*, was an appeal from the trial court for an infringement action on an issued patent, United States Patent No. 4,422,459 to Simson ("the Simson patent"). The trial court ruled that the Simson patent was invalid for failure to claim statutory subject matter because the claims of the Simson patent were nothing more than a mathematical algorithm. The Federal Circuit reversed the finding of the trial court and upheld the validity of the Simson patent.

The Simson patent claims an apparatus and a method for analyzing electrocardiographic signals in order to determine certain characteristics of the heart function to identify heart attack victims that have a high risk of ventricular tachycardia, an acute type of heart arrythmia. The claims of the Simson patent included steps (of method claims) and elements (of apparatus claims) for converting signals from analog to digital, processing the resulting digital signal via a digital high pass filter, calculating certain arithmetic values, and comparing the resulting arithmetic values with a predetermined level.

The Federal Circuit applied the *Freeman-Walter-Abele* two-step test and found that the claims of the Simson patent contained a mathematical algorithm. As a result, the Federal Circuit proceeded to the second step of the test and concluded that the claims of the Simson patent were directed to statutory subject matter under the second step of the test.

The Federal Circuit based its conclusions on a number of factors. The preamble for the method claim was a "method for analyzing electrocardiograph signals to determine the presence or absence of a predetermined level of high-frequency energy in the late QRS signal." The Court stated that this claim limitation, like every claim step, is important to the analysis of whether a claim is directed to statutory subject matter. In addition, the Court found that the steps of converting, applying, determining, and comparing are "physical process steps that transform one physical, electrical signal into another." *Id.* at 1038. Finally, under the guidance of the decision in *Grams, supra*, the *Arrythmia Research* Court concluded that Simson invented a "method of analyzing electrocardiograph signals in order to determine a specified heart activity." *Id.*

The *Arrythmia Research* Court followed a similar analysis with respect to the apparatus claim in the Simson patent. The use of mathematical formulae to describe electronic structure and operation does not render a claim nonstatutory, and moreover, it is appropriate to use mathematical terms when they are the standard way of expressing certain functions or apparatus. *Id.* at 1039. Further, the Court stated that although the result (final output) of the claimed apparatus and method is numerical, it is not a mathematical abstraction, but rather, a measure in microvolts of a specified heart activity which is an indication of ventricular tachycardia. *Id.*

In essence, the *Arrythmia Research* Court held that, based on: (i) the limitations in the preamble of the claims, (ii) the specific physical process steps and structural limitations recited by the claims, and (iii) the fact that the result of the process and final output of the apparatus was not an abstract number, but rather an indication of the risk of ventricular tachycardia, the claims of the Simson patent were directed to statutory subject matter.

2. United States Patent and Trademark Office Guidelines

In 1989, the United States Patent and Trademark Office issued guidelines regarding the patentability of computer programs and computer processes. See United States Patent and Trademark Office Rules, 1106 United States Patent and Trademark Office Official Gazette 5, September 5, 1989. These guidelines are summarized below:

a. Definition of "Mathematical Algorithm"

The United States Patent and Trademark Office follows the *Gottschalk v. Benson* definition of "mathematical algorithm." As defined above, with respect to the discussion of *Benson*, a "mathematical algorithm" is a "procedure for solving a given type of mathematical problem." This definition does not extend to algorithms in general which are step-by-step procedures to arrive at a given result.

b. Mathematical Algorithms - Per Se Nonstatutory

Mathematical algorithms per se are nonstatutory subject matter. This is because mathematical algorithms are considered to be the "basic tools of scientific and technological work," *Benson*, 409 U.S. at 67, and should not be the subject of exclusive rights. However, a "claim drawn to subject matter otherwise statutory does not become non-statutory simply because it uses a mathematical formula, computer program, or digital computer." *Diamond v. Diehr*, 450 U.S. 175, 187-88 (1981).

c. United States Patent and Trademark Office Follows the *Freeman–Walter–Abele* Two-Step Test

The United States Patent and Trademark Office follows the *Freeman–Walter–Abele* two-step test for analyzing mathematical algorithms/statutory subject matter cases. The two-step test used by the Patent and Trademark Office is as follows:

(1) Step 1 - Determine whether a mathematical algorithm is directly or indirectly in the claim, regardless of form.

(2) Step 2 - Determine whether the mathematical algorithm is applied in any manner to physical elements or process steps -- if so, view the claim without the mathematical algorithm to determine whether what remains is otherwise statutory subject matter.

There are several guidelines which assist in the interpretation and application of Step 2 of the *Freeman-Walter-Abele* test. These guidelines are identified below.

(i) Post Solution Activity

If the only claim element other than the mathematical algorithm is insignificant or non-essential post solution activity, the claim does not encompass statutory subject matter. Examples of insignificant post solution activity are provided below[7]:

Post Solution Activity	Reason for Nonstatutory
Adjusting an alarm limit (as a final step)	Simply determining a pure number is insignificant post solution activity, (*Parker v. Flook*, 198 USPQ 193 (CCPA 1978))
"Means for processing said windshear signal to provide an indication representing magnitude thereof"	Displaying of an indication is insignificant post solution activity (*Safe Flight*)
"Display the value of said difference as a signed gray scale at point in a picture which corresponds to said data point"	Displaying the value is insignificant post solution activity (*Abele*, supra)

---

[7] This table of examples was adapted from Fleming, Michael R., *Patentability of Claims Involving Mathematical Algorithms and Computer Programs - An Examiner's Perspective*, American Intellectual Property Law Association Mid-Winter Institute, The Law of Computer Related Technology, La Quinta, CA, January 22-25, 1992, Volume I, pp. D-9 and D-10.

Post Solution Activity	Reason for Nonstatutory
Recording the last result of the calculation on a magnetic tape	Merely recording a pure number after calculation is insignificant post solution activity (*Walter*, supra)
"Constructing said obstruction with the actual open channel at the specified adjusted location indicated by the mathematical model"	A lack of nexus between the previous calculating steps and the post solution step renders the post solution step to be considered insignificant post solution activity (*In re Sarker*, 200 USPQ 132 (CCPA 1978))
"Transmitting electrical signals representing said sequence of coordinates calculated in step (b)"	Transmitting an electrical signal alone is considered insignificant post solution activity (*In re de Castelet*, 562 F.2d 1236 (CCPA 1977))

It should be noted that the particular order of the steps is not determinative of the statutory subject matter inquiry.

(ii) Field of Use Limitations

Limitations in a claim which limit the use of a mathematical algorithm to a particular technological environment do not convert an otherwise nonstatutory process or apparatus into a statutory process or apparatus. For example, in *Parker v. Flook*, attempts to limit the application of the claimed method to a "process for the catalytic chemical conversion of hydrocarbons" did not serve to render the method statutory. A further example was the subject of *Walter*, in which the court held that although the claim preambles related the claimed invention to the art of seismic prospecting, the claims themselves were not drawn to methods of, or an apparatus for, seismic prospecting.

(iii) Data Gathering Steps

The rejection of claims as being directed to mathematical algorithms is often based upon a position by the patent examiner that the additional non-mathematical algorithm steps in a claim are merely data gathering steps. The addition of steps which merely gather data for determining values of variables used by mathematical formulae for making calculations does not convert an otherwise nonstatutory process or apparatus into a statutory process or apparatus. Presence of a physical step in the claim to derive data for the algorithm will not render a claim statutory. However, it should be noted that if data gathering steps are not dictated by the algorithm but by other limitations which require certain antecedent steps, a claim may be directed to statutory subject matter.

(iv) Transformation of Something Physical

It is often helpful to consider whether a claim recites the transformation of something physical into a different form. Transformation of something physical into a different form, such as transforming physical "signals" from one physical state to a different physical state, is statutory subject matter. However, transformation of "data" i.e., mathematical manipulation of "data", is nonstatutory subject matter. It is left to the reader to formulate a distinction between "signals" and "data" in the age of digital signal processing. The following represent attempts by the courts to do so.

For example, conversion of substantially spherical seismic signals into a form representing the earth's response to cylindrical or plane waves is a statutory process. Also, conversion of amplitude-versus-time seismic traces into amplitude-versus-depth seismic traces is statutory.

On the other hand, calculation of airborne radar boresight correction angles from a plurality of signal sets is not statutory. In addition, conversion of BCD numbers into pure binary numbers is also not statutory.

It is important to note that the statutory nature of the subject matter is independent of labels, such as "signals" or "data."

(v) Structural Limitations in Process Claims

Although structural limitations in process claims are not improper, they generally are not given patentable weight by a patent examiner. Claims to nonstatutory processes are not necessarily made statutory by incorporating references to an apparatus.

d. Additional Exceptions to Statutory Subject Matter

Additional exceptions to statutory subject matter may include "methods of doing business" and "mental steps" which may not be "true" computer processes but merely implementations of nonstatutory subject matter on a computer. It should be noted that although "methods of doing business" per se are nonstatutory subject matter, "a method of operation on a computer to effectuate a business activity" has been held to be statutory subject matter.

VI. REASONS FOR AND AGAINST PATENT PROTECTION FOR SOFTWARE

A number of factors should be considered in deciding whether or not to seek patent protection for software inventions. Although each invention must be evaluated on a case-by-case basis, the following factors should be considered. It is important to note that for any individual invention, a factor which is listed as "favoring patent protection" may actually turn into a "factor against patent protection," and vice versa.

A. Factors Which Generally Favor Patent Protection For Software

1. Popular

Many individuals and companies are obtaining patents on software. This is evident from the backlog in the Patent and Trademark Office, the number of newly issued patents listed in official publications, and mass circulation publications containing articles referring to software patents.

2. Broad Protection

A patent protects an underlying system or method. In addition, independent creation is no defense to an allegation of infringement. Finally, protection is generally not limited to a specific programming language or hardware environment. As illustrated by the patents identified in Section VII below, protection for software patents are generally not limited to any particular class or category of software.

3. Favored by the Courts

Patents are favored by the courts and can be vigorously enforced. The courts will grant injunctions (preliminary and/or permanent), large damage awards, prejudgment interest, and in extreme circumstances, treble damages as well as attorney fees and costs.

4. Flexible Exploitation

Patents can be licensed in a number of ways. For example, patents may be licensed on a claim-by-claim basis. In addition, software patents can be licensed to distinct hardware and software licensees. The license can be based on particular field of use, size of CPU, or other sub classifications of the claimed invention.

5. Cross License

Patents are often obtained so that the patent owner can obtain freedom from an infringement action by another. This is accomplished by using the patents as leverage in a cross license with another patentee who owns a blocking patent.

6. Detection of Infringement

Although detection of infringement of software patents may be difficult if reverse engineering is necessary to detect the infringement, often a simple examination of the display screens of user interfaces during operation will provide evidence of infringement.

7. Likely Infringer/Licensee

It is important to consider whether the likely infringer is a small user or a big customer. In other words, in asserting patent rights, consider whether the likely infringer has a shallow pocket versus a deep pocket.

8. Ownership

Ownership of a patent lends credibility to a business. It can attract venture capital or other forms of outside investment, and lends credibility in establishing relationships with hardware vendors.

9. Assets

Patents are considered to be assets of a company. As such, they can be bought, sold or licensed. In addition, security interests in patents can be perfected. Often patents are the only real asset of a business.

10. Recognition

A patent is valuable to an inventor because they permit public recognition of the inventor's achievements and contributions to the field.

B. Factors Against Protection

1. Cost of Obtaining

The cost of obtaining patents on software inventions can often be relatively high. This is due not only, in part, to the complex technology, but also because the patent attorney must understand the invention in order to prepare the patent application. Moreover, the patent attorney must have a sufficient understanding of the invention in order to be able to describe the invention so that not only a patent examiner but also a judge and a jury made up of lay people can understand the invention if the patent is litigated.

2.   Cost of Enforcement

Patent infringement litigation is extremely expensive. This is especially true for software patents where judges and juries are lay people who lack familiarity with most kinds of technology. However, cost of enforcement should not necessarily deter one from seeking patent protection because many companies are more likely to license a patent than to litigate.

3.   Full Disclosure Required

A patent is granted in exchange for a full disclosure of the invention. Although it is not necessary or desirable to disclose the source code, it is often necessary to disclose at least high level flow charts or other forms of block diagrams. It is important to note that to the extent any information is disclosed, trade secret protection is precluded after the patent issues.

4.   Delay in Issuance

The backlog in the United States Patent and Trademark Office is substantial. With respect to applications for software patents, the backlog in the Patent and Trademark Office can result in a delay of more than two years between the filing date of the application and the issue date of the patent.

5.   Changing Technology

Rapid advances in software technology may make the invention obsolete before the seventeen (17) year exclusive right terminates.

6.   Prior Sales or Disclosure

The United States has a one (1) year grace period in which a patent application must be filed. If the invention was publicly disclosed, publicly used, sold, published, or placed on sale more than one (1) year prior to the filing of the application in the Patent and Trademark Office, patent protection is precluded. It is also important to note that use of the (1) one year grace period in the United States may adversely affect the possible patent protection in many foreign countries.

VII. EXAMPLES OF SOFTWARE RELATED PATENTS[8]

Patent No.	Title	Date
4,646,256	Computer and Method for the Discrete Bracewell Transform	02-24-87
4,788,538	Method and Apparatus for Determining Boundaries of Graphic Regions	11-29-88
4,811,199	System for Storing and Manipulating Information in an Information Base	03-07-89
4,825,358	Method and Operating System for Executing Programs in a Multi-Mode Microprocessor	04-25-89
4,876,735	Method and Apparatus For Character Recognition Systems	10-24-89
4,888,812	Document Image Processing System	12-19-89
4,922,432	Knowledge Based Method and Apparatus for Designing Integrated Circuits Using Functional Specifications	05-01-90
4,924,521	Image Processing System and Method Employing Combined Black and White and Gray Scale Image Data	05-08-90
4,931,769	Method and Apparatus for Controlling the Operation of a Security System	06-05-90
4,931,931	Method and a System for Processing Logic Programs	06-05-90
4,955,066	Compressing and Decompressing Text Files	09-04-90
4,956,777	Automatic Vehicle Control System	09-11-90
5,038,211	Method and Apparatus for Transmitting and Receiving Television Program Information	08-06-91

---

[8] The first page of each patent identified in Section VII is attached hereto at Appendix A.

Patent No.	Title	Date
5,043,988	Method and Apparatus for High Precision Weighted Random Pattern Generation	08-27-91
5,050,090	Object Placement Method and Apparatus	09-17-91
5,054,774	Computer-Controlled Muscle Exercising Machine Having Simplified Data Access	10-08-91

VIII. CONCLUSION

The above discussion has considered the software/software engineering - patent law interface. Software engineering is a discipline that is covered by the United States Patent Act as stated by the United States Constitution. In addition, the requirements to write the examination to practice before the Patent and Trademark Office include most, if not all, areas of study within the software engineering field. Finally, the classification of patents in the United States Patent and Trademark Office has been revised to clearly define areas of software related inventions.

Software, the product resulting from implementation of software engineering techniques, is considered statutory subject matter and subject to patent protection. However, software containing mathematical algorithms may be deemed nonstatutory and, therefore, not subject to patent protection. Determination as to whether a software invention is statutory is based upon the *Freeman-Walter-Abele* two-step test. The first step is to determine whether a mathematical algorithm is directly or indirectly recited. The second step is to analyze the claim as a whole to determine whether the mathematical algorithm is implemented in a specific manner to define structural relationships between the elements of the claim or to refine or limit claim steps. However, despite this two step test, a patent examiner, will, in the final analysis, reject a claim that contains a mathematical algorithm as being directed to nonstatutory subject matter if the claim is so broad that it will encompass any and every apparatus capable of performing the recited mathematical algorithm.

Patents for software related inventions are currently being issued by the United States Patent and Trademark Office in record numbers. The software engineer who develops new software, is strongly encouraged to consider the merits of obtaining patent protection for the software engineering development, prior to publishing, commercializing or otherwise disclosing the development.

United States Patent [19]

Bracewell

[11] Patent Number: **4,646,256**

[45] Date of Patent: **Feb. 24, 1987**

[54] **COMPUTER AND METHOD FOR THE DISCRETE BRACEWELL TRANSFORM**

[75] Inventor: Ronald N. Bracewell, Stanford, Calif.

[73] Assignee: The Board of Trustees of the Leland Stanford Junior University, Palo Alto, Calif.

[21] Appl. No.: 590,885

[22] Filed: Mar. 19, 1984

[51] Int. Cl.⁴ G06F 15/31
[52] U.S. Cl. 364/725
[58] Field of Search 364/725, 726, 727

[56] **References Cited**

U.S. PATENT DOCUMENTS

3,821,527	6/1974	Kang	364/727
4,093,994	6/1978	Nvssbaumer	364/726
4,156,920	5/1979	Winograd	364/726
4,385,363	5/1983	Widergren et al.	364/725

OTHER PUBLICATIONS

Cochran et al, "What is the Fast Fourier Transform?"- *Proceedings of the IEEE* vol. 55, No. 10, Oct. 1967, pp. 1664–1674.
Kolba et al "A Prime Factor FFT Algorithm Using High-Speed Convolution" *IEEE Trans. on Acoustics Speech & Signal Processing* vol. ASSP-25, No. 4, Aug. 1977, pp. 281–294.
Cooley et al "An Algorithm for the Machine Calculation of Complex Fourier Series" *Math of Computation* vol. 19, Apr. 1965, pp. 297–301.

Bracewell, *The Fourier Transform and its Applications* McGraw-Hill, Inc. 2nd Ed. 1978, p. 179.

Primary Examiner—David H. Malzahn
Attorney, Agent, or Firm—Fliesler, Dubb, Meyer & Lovejoy

[57] **ABSTRACT**

Disclosed is a special purpose computer and method of computation for performing an N-length real-number discrete transform. For a real-valued function $f(\tau)$ where τ has the values $0,1, \ldots ,(N-1)$, the Discrete Bracewell Transform (DBT) H (v) is as follows:

$$H(v) = (N^{-1}) \sum_{\tau=0}^{N-1} f(\tau)\cos(2\pi v\tau/N)$$

where,

$$v = 0,1, \ldots ,N-1$$

$$\cos\theta = \cos\theta + \sin\theta.$$

The DBT is performed without need for employing real and imaginary parts, and in efficient embodiments, is executed efficiently and in less time than the Discrete Fourier Transform (DFT). The process steps for the original transform and the inverse retransformation are the same.

41 Claims, 3 Drawing Figures

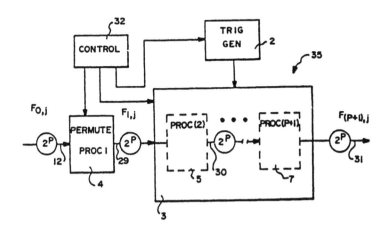

United States Patent [19]

Klein et al.

[11] Patent Number: 4,788,538

[45] Date of Patent: Nov. 29, 1988

[54] METHOD AND APPARATUS FOR DETERMINING BOUNDARIES OF GRAPHIC REGIONS

[75] Inventors: Stephen A. Klein; David A. Rolfe, both of Pasadena; William T. Gross, La Canada; Lawrence S. Gross, Santa Monica, all of Calif.

[73] Assignee: Lotus Development Corporation, Cambridge, Mass.

[21] Appl. No.: 42,161

[22] Filed: Apr. 24, 1987

Related U.S. Application Data

[63] Continuation-in-part of Ser. No. 931,678, Nov. 17, 1986, abandoned.

[51] Int. Cl.^{4} G09G 1/14
[52] U.S. Cl. 340/747; 340/744; 340/728; 340/709
[58] Field of Search 340/703, 706, 709, 710, 340/723, 728, 747, 789

[56] **References Cited**

U.S. PATENT DOCUMENTS

4,368,463	1/1983	Quilliam	340/744
4,626,838	12/1986	Tsujioka et al.	340/728
4,646,078	2/1987	Knierim et al.	340/747
4,698,625	10/1987	McCaskill et al.	340/709

Primary Examiner—Gerald L. Brigance
Attorney, Agent, or Firm—Blakely Sokoloff Taylor & Zafman

[57] **ABSTRACT**

The present invention provides apparatus and methods for determining the boundaries of arbitrarily shaped regions on a computer display system having a central processing unit (CPU). The CPU is coupled to a display having a plurality of selectively enabled and disabled display elements arranged in a matrix, whereby each display element is identified by a unique X,Y address. A memory coupled to the CPU includes a plurality of memory cells, wherein the cells correspond to a display element on the display. An initial X,Y address is selected on the display by a user employing a cursor control to identify an area on the display where the boundaries of a region are to be determined. The initial X,Y address selected by the user is defined as a seed cell. The CPU determines if the initial seed cell corresponds to a disabled memory cell and blank (disabled) display element, and in such event increments the initial X,Y address to search outwardly a predetermined maximum distance to adjacent memory cells until an enabled (non-blank) cell is located. This enabled cell is set as a new seed cell. The CPU then searches radially outward in M directions from the new seed cells X,Y address for N consecutive disabled (blank) memory cells and sets in each of these directions the last non-blank (enabled) memory cell prior to the N consecutive disabled cells, as boundary cells. An initial rectangular region is defined through at least two of these boundary cells, and the CPU determines if P consecutive rows and columns of blank (disabled) memory cells bound the initial rectangular region. If not, the CPU selectively extends the boundaries of the initial rectangular region in X and Y directions until the region is bounded by P consecutive rows and columns of disabled cells. Accordingly, the boundaries of a region on a display are determined.

35 Claims, 7 Drawing Sheets

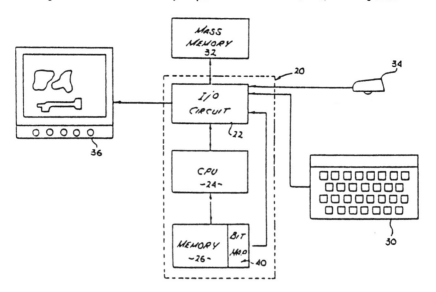

United States Patent [19]

Kuechler et al.

[11]	Patent Number: **4,811,199**
[45]	Date of Patent: **Mar. 7, 1989**

[54] **SYSTEM FOR STORING AND MANIPULATING INFORMATION IN AN INFORMATION BASE**

[76] Inventors: William L. Kuechler, No. 3 Rum Row, Hilton Head, S.C. 29928; David W. Kuechler, 1618 Beacon Ridge Rd., No. 605, Charlotte, N.C. 28210

[21] Appl. No.: 47,703

[22] Filed: May 8, 1987

[51] Int. Cl.⁴ G06F 1/00
[52] U.S. Cl. 364/200; 364/300
[58] Field of Search 364/200, 300, 900

[56] **References Cited**

U.S. PATENT DOCUMENTS

4,012,720	3/1977	Call et al.	.... 364/200
4,267,568	5/1981	Dechant et al.	.... 364/200
4,270,182	5/1981	Asija	.... 364/900
4,587,670	5/1986	Levinson et al.	.... 381/43

OTHER PUBLICATIONS

"A Bit-Mapped Classifier", pp. 161–172, *Byte*, by Frey (Nov. 1986).
"Finding Rules in Data", pp. 149–158, *Byte*, by Thompson and Thompson (Nov. 1986).
"Predicting International Events", pp. 177–190, *Byte*, by Schrodt (Nov. 1986).
"Retrieval on Secondary Keys", pp. 551–567, *The Art of Computer Programming*, vol. 3, Sorting and Searching, by Knuth (1973).

Primary Examiner—Raulfe B. Zache
Attorney, Agent, or Firm—Bell, Seltzer, Park & Gibson

[57] **ABSTRACT**

The present invention provides a system for the input, retrieval, manipulation and analysis of stored information in an information base. The system comprises an input device, a storage device, and an output device each capable of handling information elements. Each of the attributes of the information elements is processed to produce a compact symbol or code corresponding to predefined ranges of values of an attribute. These codes are then stored in correspondence with the information elements which gave rise to them. The result of this processing is a topological map of the attributes of the information elements. These topological maps may be retrieved and later processed to efficiently retrieve stored information elements, given any general unprogrammed query as input to the system. These topological maps may also be utilized in a process to determine correlations among the various attributes of the information elements.

28 Claims, 1 Drawing Sheet

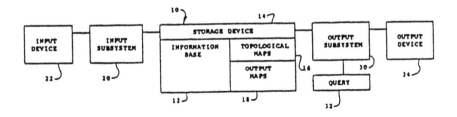

United States Patent [19]

Letwin

[11] Patent Number: **4,825,358**

[45] Date of Patent: **Apr. 25, 1989**

[54] **METHOD AND OPERATING SYSTEM FOR EXECUTING PROGRAMS IN A MULTI-MODE MICROPROCESSOR**

[75] Inventor: **James Letwin, King County, Wash.**

[73] Assignee: **Microsoft Corporation, Redmond, Wash.**

[21] Appl. No.: **64,117**

[22] Filed: **Jun. 18, 1987**

Related U.S. Application Data

[62] Division of Ser. No. 722,052, Apr. 10, 1985, Pat. No. 4,779,187.

[51] Int. Cl.⁴ G06F 9/46
[52] U.S. Cl. 364/200; 364/232.9; 364/280
[58] Field of Search ... 364/200 MS File, 900 MS File

[56] **References Cited**

U.S. PATENT DOCUMENTS

4,519,032	5/1985	Mendell	364/200
4,590,556	5/1986	Berger et al.	364/200
4,679,166	7/1987	Berger et al.	364/900

Primary Examiner—Gareth D. Shaw
Assistant Examiner—Debra A. Chur

Attorney, Agent, or Firm—Seed and Berry

[57] **ABSTRACT**

Improved methods and operating systems for use with a multi-mode microprocessor enable efficient operation in a multi-mode environment. Preferred embodiments for use with microprocessors which were not designed to switch from each mode to another mode enable multi-tasking of a mixture of programs written for different modes using the mode switching methods of the present invention. Frequently used portions of the operating system are stored in memory at locations which can be commonly addressed in all modes. Means for handling device drivers and interrupts in all modes are also provided. Preferred embodiments for use with computer systems using microprocessors such as the Intel 80286 include means for storing the operating system routines to maximize performance of the system in real mode. Auxiliary protection hardware and I/O masking hardware are also provided in alternate preferred embodiments to enhance protection during real mode operation of such systems. Means for handling interrupts in a mode switching environment and alternate embodiments to eliminate problems caused by hooking programs in a multi-tasking environment are also provided.

21 Claims, 11 Drawing Sheets

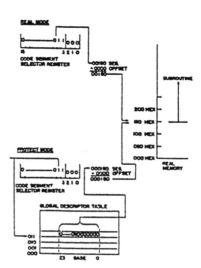

United States Patent [19]

Martin et al.

[11] **Patent Number:** **4,876,735**

[45] **Date of Patent:** **Oct. 24, 1989**

[54] METHOD AND APPARATUS FOR CHARACTER RECOGNITION SYSTEMS

[75] Inventors: William C. Martin; Gene D. Rohrer, both of Charlotte, N.C.

[73] Assignee: International Business Machines Corporation, Armonk, N.Y.

[21] Appl. No.: 134,729

[22] Filed: Dec. 18, 1987

[51] Int. Cl.⁴ G06K 9/00

[52] U.S. Cl. 382/57; 382/7; 382/39; 382/62

[58] Field of Search 382/57, 62, 7, 39, 38

[56] **References Cited**

U.S. PATENT DOCUMENTS

RE. 31,692 10/1984 Tyburski et al. 382/57
3,496,543 1/1967 Greeniy 382/9

3,641,495	2/1972	Kiji	382/38
3,876,981	4/1975	Welch	382/62
3,938,089	2/1976	McGregor et al.	382/62

Primary Examiner—David K. Moore
Assistant Examiner—Yon Jung
Attorney, Agent, or Firm—Bell, Seltzer, Park & Gibson

[57] **ABSTRACT**

The present invention employs a method of choosing between the output of two different character recognition systems to improve the rate at which characters are recognized, without significantly increasing the number of undetected substitution errors. If the first recognition system cannot recognize a character, a random probability generator is used to determine whether to use the output of the second recognition system, or alternatively to generate a reject character.

10 Claims, 1 Drawing Sheet

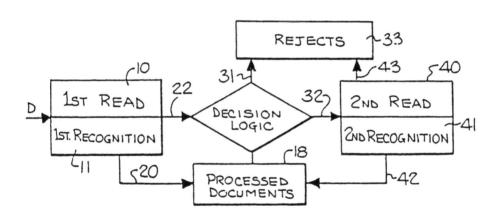

United States Patent [19]

Dinan et al.

[11] Patent Number: 4,888,812

[45] Date of Patent: Dec. 19, 1989

[54] **DOCUMENT IMAGE PROCESSING SYSTEM**

[75] Inventors: Raymond F. Dinan, Mint Hill, N.C.;
James F. Dubil, Lake Wylie, S.C.;
Jerald R. Malin, Charlotte, N.C.;
Robert R. Rodite, Matthews, N.C.;
Clair F. Rohe, Charlotte, N.C.; Gene
D. Rohrer, Concord, N.C.

[73] Assignee: International Business Machines
Corporation, Armonk, N.Y.

[21] Appl. No.: 134,734

[22] Filed: Dec. 18, 1987

[51] Int. Cl.⁴ G06K 9/00; G06K 7/14
[52] U.S. Cl. 382/7; 382/57;
235/379; 364/200
[58] Field of Search 382/7, 57; 235/379;
364/200 MS File

[56] **References Cited**

U.S. PATENT DOCUMENTS

3,832,682	8/1974	Brok et al.	340/146.3
4,096,472	6/1978	Mercier	382/57
4,205,780	6/1980	Burns et al.	235/454
4,369,430	1/1983	Sternberg	340/146.3
4,538,182	8/1985	Saito et al.	358/280
4,538,183	8/1985	Kanno et al.	358/280
4,538,184	8/1985	Otsuka et al.	358/283
4,551,768	11/1985	Tsuchiya et al.	358/283
4,553,261	11/1985	Froessl	382/57
4,574,351	3/1986	Dang et al.	364/200
4,590,606	5/1986	Rohrer	382/54

Primary Examiner—David K. Moore
Assistant Examiner—Yon Jung
Attorney, Agent, or Firm—Bell, Seltzer, Park & Gibson

[57] **ABSTRACT**

Documents, such as bank checks, are processed at a high rate of speed on an image processing system which optically scans the documents and converts optically perceptible data on the documents into video image data. The video image data from the scanner is compressed by data compression techniques and the compressed data is sent over a high speed data channel to a high speed mass storage device which receives and temporarily stores the data. A lower speed mass data storage device, such as an optical disk, is connected for receiving at a lower data transfer rate the compressed video image data and for storing the video image data for subsequent retrieval. The system also includes real-time quality control systems for monitoring the quality of the image data to detect the existence of unacceptable image quality data and for generating a signal which can be used for immediately stopping the generation of unacceptable quality image data.

34 Claims, 2 Drawing Sheets

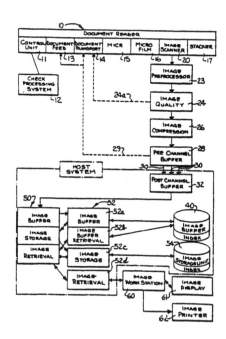

United States Patent [19]

Kobayashi et al.

[11] Patent Number: 4,922,432

[45] Date of Patent: May 1, 1990

[54] KNOWLEDGE BASED METHOD AND APPARATUS FOR DESIGNING INTEGRATED CIRCUITS USING FUNCTIONAL SPECIFICATIONS

[75] Inventors: Hideaki Kobayashi, Columbia, S.C.; Masahiro Shindo, Osaka, Japan

[73] Assignees: International Chip Corporation, Columbia, S.C.; Ricoh Company, Ltd., Tokyo, Japan

[21] Appl. No.: 143,821

[22] Filed: Jan. 13, 1988

[51] Int. Cl.⁵ G06F 15/60
[52] U.S. Cl. 364/490; 364/489; 364/488; 364/521
[58] Field of Search 364/488–491, 364/521, 300, 513

[56] References Cited

U.S. PATENT DOCUMENTS

4,635,208	1/1987	Coleby et al.	364/491
4,638,442	1/1987	Bryant et al.	364/489
4,648,044	3/1987	Hardy et al.	364/513
4,651,284	3/1987	Watanabe et al.	364/491
4,656,603	4/1987	Dunn	364/488
4,658,370	4/1987	Erman et al.	364/513
4,675,829	6/1987	Clemenson	364/513
4,700,317	10/1987	Watanabe et al.	364/521
4,703,435	10/1987	Darringer et al.	364/488
4,803,636	2/1989	Nishiyama et al.	364/491

FOREIGN PATENT DOCUMENTS

1445914	8/1976	United Kingdom	364/490

OTHER PUBLICATIONS

"Verifying Compiled Silicon", by E. K. cheng, VLSI Design, Oct. 1984, pp. 1–4.
"CAD System for IC Design", by M. E. Daniel et al., IEEE Trans. on Computer-Aided Design of Integrated Circuits & Systems, vol. CAD-1, No. 1, Jan. 1982, pp. 2–12.
"An Overview of Logic Synthesis System", by L. Trevillyan, 24th ACM/IEEE Design Automation Conference, 1978, pp. 166–172.
"Methods Used in an Automatic Logic Design Generator", by T. D. Friedman et al., IEEE Trans. on Computers, vol. C-18, No. 7, Jul. 1969, pp. 593–613.
"Experiments in Logic Synthesis", by J. A. Darringer, IEEE ICCC, 1980.
"A Front End Graphic Interface to First Silicon Compiler", by J. H. Nash, EDA 84, Mar. 1984
"quality of Designs from An Automatic Logic Generator", by T. D. Friedman et al., IEEE 7th DA Conference, 1970, pp. 71–89.
"A New Look at Logic Synthesis", by J. A. Darringer et al., IEEE 17th D. A. Conference 1980, pp. 543–548.
Trevillyan—Trickey, H., Flamel: A High Level Hardward Compiler, IEEE Transactions On Computer Aided Design, Mar. 1987, pp. 259–269.
Parker et al., The CMU Design Automation System—An Example of Automated Data Path Design, Proceedings Of The 16th Design Automation Conference, Las Vegas, Nev., 1979, pp. 73–80.
An Engineering Approach to Digital Design, William I. Fletcher, Prentice-Hall, Inc., pp. 491–505.

Primary Examiner—Felix D. Gruber
Assistant Examiner—V. N. Trans
Attorney, Agent, or Firm—Bell, Seltzer, Park & Gibson

[57] ABSTRACT

The present invention provides a computer-aided design system and method for designing an application specific integrated circuit which enables a user to define functional architecture independent specifications for the integrated circuit and which translates the functional architecture independent specifications into the detailed information needed for directly producing the integrated circuit. The functional architecture independent specifications of the desired integrated circuit can be defined at the functional architecture independent level in a flowchart format. From the flowchart, the system and method uses artificial intelligence and expert systems technology to generate a system controller, to select the necessary integrated circuit hardware cells needed to achieve the functional specifications, and to generate data and control paths for operation of the integrated circuit. This list of hardware cells and their interconnection requirements is set forth in a netlist. From the netlist it is possible using known manual techniques or existing VLSI CAD layout systems to generate the detailed chip level topological information (mask data) required to produce the particular application specific integrated circuit.

20 Claims, 12 Drawing Sheets

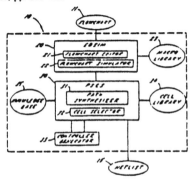

United States Patent [19]

Dinan et al.

[11]	Patent Number:
[45]	Date of Patent:

4,924,521

May 8, 1990

[54] **IMAGE PROCESSING SYSTEM AND METHOD EMPLOYING COMBINED BLACK AND WHITE AND GRAY SCALE IMAGE DATA**

[75] Inventors: Raymond F. Dinan, Mint Hill, N.C.; James F. Dubil, Wylie, S.C.; John R. Hillery, Charlotte, N.C., Robert R. Rodite, Matthews, N.C., James M. White, Charlotte, N.C.

[73] Assignee: International Business Machines Corporation, Armonk, N.Y.

[21] Appl. No.: 134,733

[22] Filed: Dec. 18, 1987

[51] Int. Cl.^{5} G06K 9/54
[52] U.S. Cl. 382/54; 382/56; 382/42; 358/133; 358/135
[58] Field of Search 382/54, 56, 42; 358/133, 135

[56] **References Cited**

U.S. PATENT DOCUMENTS

4,032,977	6/1977	Liao	358/280
4,280,144	7/1981	Bacon	350/280
4,399,461	8/1983	Powell	382/54
4,558,371	12/1985	Rallapalli et al.	358/261.3
4,665,436	5/1987	Osborne et al.	358/135
4,776,026	10/1988	Shimura	382/56
4,817,181	3/1989	Kamiya	382/54

OTHER PUBLICATIONS

Troxel et al., "Bandwidth Compression of High Quality Images" ICC'80 1980 International Conference on Communications 8-12 Jun. 1980. 31.9/1-5.
Troxel et al., "A Two Channel Picture Coding System-Z-Real Time Implementation" IEEE Transaction on Comm. vol. Com-29, No. 12, Dec. 1981 p. 1841-1848.
Paul G. Roetling, "Visual Performance and Image Coding", Proceeding of the S.I.D., vol. 17/2 Second Quarter 1976, pp. 111-114.
Jack DiGiuseppe, "A Survey of Pictorial Data-Compression Techniques", The University of Michigan Technical Report 16, Concomp. Mar. 1969.
J. M. White, "Recent Advances in Thresholding Techniques for Facsimile", Journal of Applied Photographic Engineering, 6, No. 2, pp. 49-57 (1980).
James M. White, "Image Sampling, Resolution, and Gray-Scale", IBM Report Summarizing Presentation to the Image Quality Workshop, Mar. 26-27, 1984, in Yorktown, N.Y.

Primary Examiner—Leo H. Boudreau
Assistant Examiner—Yon Jung
Attorney, Agent, or Firm—Bell, Seltzer, Park & Gibson

[57] **ABSTRACT**

In order to reduce data storage and transmission bandwidth requirements, a high resolution gray scale image is represented in two separate image forms, namely, a high resolution, high sampling density black and white image and a lower resolution, lower sampling density gray scale image. Generating separate black and white and gray scale image data allows the use of either image form independently. The high resolution black and white image data and the low resolution gray scale image data may be recombined subsequently to produce reconstructed high resolution gray scale image data representing the image.

8 Claims, 3 Drawing Sheets

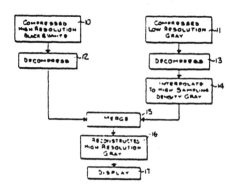

United States Patent [19]

Phillips et al.

[11] Patent Number: 4,931,769

[45] Date of Patent: Jun. 5, 1990

[54] METHOD AND APPARATUS FOR CONTROLLING THE OPERATION OF A SECURITY SYSTEM

[75] Inventors: Kirk B. Phillips, Wilkesboro; Peter Kastan, Hickory, both of N.C.

[73] Assignee: Moose Products, Inc., Hickory, N.C.

[21] Appl. No.: 271,009

[22] Filed: Nov. 14, 1988

[51] Int. Cl.⁵ G08B 13/00
[52] U.S. Cl. 340/541; 340/825.32; 340/506
[58] Field of Search 340/541, 540, 505, 506, 340/712, 825.32, 825.31, 826.34; 341/22, 23; 235/382.5; 364/225.2

[56] References Cited

U.S. PATENT DOCUMENTS

4,021,796	5/1977	Fawcett, Jr. et al.	340/500
4,023,139	5/1977	Samborg	340/506
4,186,871	2/1980	Anderson et al.	340/825.31
4,333,090	6/1982	Hirsch	341/23
4,425,627	1/1984	Eibner	341/23
4,502,048	2/1985	Rehm	340/825.31
4,532,507	7/1985	Edson et al.	340/541
4,538,138	8/1985	Harvey et al.	340/521

4,570,217	2/1986	Allen et al.	364/188
4,602,246	7/1986	Jensen	340/521
4,724,425	2/1988	Gerhart et al.	340/539
4,766,746	8/1988	Henderson et al.	70/63

OTHER PUBLICATIONS

Ademco, Ademco's Alpha Vista. 1988.

Primary Examiner—Joseph A. Orsino
Assistant Examiner—Geoff Sutcliffe
Attorney, Agent, or Firm—Bell, Seltzer, Park & Gibson

[57] ABSTRACT

A security system includes a display for displaying user prompts to select from a set of alternative options for controlling the system, so that the user may respond by selecting one of the options. If further information is necessary, second and subsequent sets of options are displayed for user selection. If an authorization code is required, a prompt for an authorization code is displayed. The sets of options are preferably displayed adjacent a keypad, so that an option may be selected by actuating the key adjacent the selected option. Sequences of commands need not be memorized by a user, and complicated keyboards are not required to control the security system.

26 Claims, 5 Drawing Sheets

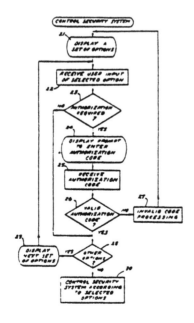

United States Patent [19]

Syre et al.

[11] **Patent Number:** 4,931,931

[45] **Date of Patent:** Jun. 5, 1990

[54] METHOD AND A SYSTEM FOR PROCESSING LOGIC PROGRAMS

[75] Inventors: Jean-Claude Syre; Harald Westphal, both of Munich, Fed. Rep. of Germany; Max Hallperin, Hayward, Calif.

[73] Assignee: European Computer-Industry Research Centre GmbH, Munich, Fed. Rep. of Germany

[21] Appl. No.: 70,818

[22] Filed: Jul. 2, 1987

[30] Foreign Application Priority Data

Jul. 8, 1986 [EP] European Pat. Off. 86109342.5

[51] Int. Cl.⁵ G06F 9/00
[52] U.S. Cl. 364/300; 364/200; 364/275; 364/259
[58] Field of Search ... 364/200 MS File, 900 MS File, 364/300

[56] References Cited

U.S. PATENT DOCUMENTS

4,775,934 10/1988 Houri et al. 364/300
4,811,210 3/1989 McAulay 364/200

OTHER PUBLICATIONS

J. H. Chang, A Despain & D. DeGroot-And-Parallelism of Logic Programs Based on a Static Data Dependency Analysis, In IEEE 1985, *Digest of Papers*. pp. 218–225.

Peter Borgwardt. "Parallel Prolog Using Stack Segments on Shared Memory Multiprocessors". In IEEE (editor), 84 *Int. Symposium On Logic Programming*. pp. 2–11, Feb. 1984.

J. H. Chang & Doug DeGroot. "AND-Parallelism of Logic Programs Based on Static Data Dependency Analysis". In *Draft Proc. Afcet85*, p. 11. Oct. 1984.

A. Ciepielewski, B. Hausman and S. Haridi. "Initial Evaluation of A Virtual Machine for OR-Parallel Execution of Logic Programs". In J. V. Woods (editor),

Fifth Generation Computer Architectures. pp. 81–99. Royal Institute of Technology, Sweden, 1986.

J. Crammond. "A Comparative Study of Unification Algorithms for OR-Parallel Execution of Logic Languages". In D. DeGroot (editor), *Int. Conf. on Parallel Processing*. pp. 131–138. IEEE, St. Charles, Ill., Aug. 1985.

Seif Haridi & Andrzej Ciepielewski. "An Or-Parallel Token Machine". In Nucleo de Inteligencia Artificial. Universidade Nova de Lisboa (editor), *Proc.* 1983 *Logic Programming Workshop*. pp. 537–552. Stockholm Sweden, Jun. 1983.

K. Kumon, H. Masuzawa, A. Itashiki. "Kabu-Wake: A New Parallel Inference Method and is Evaluation". *In Proc. IEEE Compcon* 86, pp. 168–172. San Francisco, Mar. 1986.

Yukio Sohma, Ken Satoh, Koichi Kumon, Hideo Masuzawa, Akihiro Itashiki. "A New Parallel Inference Mechanism Based on Sequential Processing". In UMIST (editor), *IFIP TC*-10 Working Conf. on Fifth Generation Computer Architecture. Manchester, Jul. 15–18, 1985.

Primary Examiner—Gareth G. Shaw
Assistant Examiner—Debra A. Chum
Attorney, Agent, or Firm—Bell, Seltzer, Park & Gibson

[57] ABSTRACT

In a method for processing logic programs—especially in Prolog-like languages—using at least one processor, which allows parallelism—also retroactively—by an existing process, called "father", creating at optional OR-parallel nodes at least one process, called "son", standing in an OR-parallel relationship to the father, a deep-binding list, called "hash-window" is created only for the newly created son in which—while processing the split-off OR-parallel branch—it performs bindings to variables commonly accessible to it and its father, called "commonly accessible variables."

8 Claims, 8 Drawing Sheets

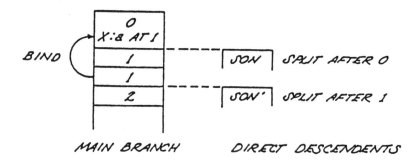

United States Patent [19]

Notenboom

[11] Patent Number: 4,955,066

[45] Date of Patent: Sep. 4, 1990

[54] COMPRESSING AND DECOMPRESSING TEXT FILES

[75] Inventor: Leo A. Notenboom, Woodinville, Wash.

[73] Assignee: Microsoft Corporation, Redmond, Wash.

[21] Appl. No.: 421,466

[22] Filed: Oct. 13, 1989

[51] Int. Cl.^{5} G06K 9/00
[52] U.S. Cl. 382/56; 382/40; 358/261.1; 358/427
[58] Field of Search 382/40, 56; 358/261.1, 358/427

[56] References Cited

U.S. PATENT DOCUMENTS

4,494,150 1/1985 Brickman et al. 358/260
4,626,829 12/1986 Hauck 340/347

Primary Examiner—Leo H. Boudreau
Assistant Examiner—Daniel Santos
Attorney, Agent, or Firm—Seed and Berry

[57] ABSTRACT

A method of compressing a text file in digital form is disclosed. A full text file having characters formed into phrases is provided by an author. The characters are digitally represented by bytes. A first pass compression is sequentially followed by a second pass compression of the text which has previously been compressed. A third or fourth level compression is serially performed on the previously compressed text. For example, in a first pass, the text is run-length compressed. In a second pass, the compressed text is further compressed with key phrase compression. In a third pass, the compressed text is further compressed with Huffman compression. The compressed text is stored in a text file having a Huffman decode tree, a key phrase table, and a topic index. The data is decompressed in a single pass and provided one line at a time as an output. Sequential compressing of the text minimizes the storage space required for the file. Decompressing of the text is performed in a single pass. As a complete line is decompressed, it is output rapidly, providing full text to a user.

12 Claims, 4 Drawing Sheets

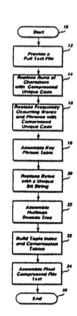

United States Patent [19]

Cearley et al.

[11] Patent Number: 4,956,777

[45] Date of Patent: Sep. 11, 1990

[54] AUTOMATIC VEHICLE CONTROL SYSTEM

[75] Inventors: Thomas W. Cearley, Clemmons; Michael F. Donovan, Advance; Raymond A. Gardes, II, Winston-Salem; Kolleen C. Hughes, King; William R. Hunt, III, Mt. Airy; William R. Jarvis; Marvin R. Martin, both of Winston-Salem, all of N.C.; Aftab Shamb, Clay, N.Y.; Michael D. Shepard, Winston-Salem, N.C.; William F. Summers, Mocksville, N.C.; David C. Twine, Winston-Salem, N.C.; Lonnie M. Utt, Jr., Mt. Airy, N.C.

[73] Assignee: R. J. Reynolds Tobacco Company, Winston-Salem, N.C.

[21] Appl. No.: 204,336

[22] Filed: Jun. 9, 1988

[51] Int. Cl.³ C06F 15/50
[52] U.S. Cl. 364/424.02; 180/168; 180/169
[53] Field of Search 364/424.01, 424.02; 364/513; 180/167, 168, 169; 371/9.1

[56] References Cited

U.S. PATENT DOCUMENTS

4,284,160 8/1981 DeLiban et al. 180/168

4,361,202 11/1982 Minovitch 364/424.02
4,630,216 12/1986 Tyler et al. 180/168
4,780,817 10/1988 Lofgren 180/168
4,791,570 12/1988 Sherman et al. 364/424.02

OTHER PUBLICATIONS

"A Distributed System for Digital Signal Processing and Computation for Automated Vehicle Guidance", by Goddard et al., IEEC & E, Oct. 1981.

Primary Examiner—Gary Chin
Attorney, Agent, or Firm—Grover M. Myers

[57] ABSTRACT

The system includes a first computer for communicating with automatic guided vehicles on a guided vehicle loop and storing information related to vehicle position. A second computer determines vehicle destinations. The first computer and the second computer maintain separate databases. Information in the data of the first computer relating to vehicle position is copied into the database of the second computer to assist in making vehicle destination determinations and the vehicle destination information stored in the database of the second computer is copied into the first computer. The invention also includes a unique fast and slow polling routine to insure that data transfer to the vehicles requiring it most is achieved in any polling cycle.

19 Claims, 4 Drawing Sheets

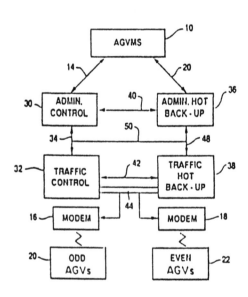

United States Patent [19]

Hallenbeck

[11] **Patent Number:** 5,038,211

[45] **Date of Patent:** Aug. 6, 1991

[54] **METHOD AND APPARATUS FOR TRANSMITTING AND RECEIVING TELEVISION PROGRAM INFORMATION**

[75] Inventor: Peter D. Hallenbeck, Efland, N.C.

[73] Assignee: The SuperGuide Corporation, Shelby, N.C.

[21] Appl. No.: 375,829

[22] Filed: Jul. 5, 1989

[51] Int. Cl.⁵ H04N 7/08
[52] U.S. Cl. 358/142; 358/146; 358/903
[58] Field of Search 358/142, 146, 147, 84, 358/86, 143, 310, 903; 380/10, 20

[56] **References Cited**

U.S. PATENT DOCUMENTS

3,440,427	4/1969	Kammer .
3,493,674	2/1970	Houghton .
3,833,757	9/1974	Kirk, Jr. et al. .
3,891,792	6/1975	Kimura .
3,996,583	12/1976	Hutt et al. .
4,016,361	4/1977	Pandey .
4,026,555	5/1977	Kirschner et al. .
4,052,719	10/1977	Hutt et al. .
4,096,524	6/1978	Scott .
4,134,127	1/1979	Campioni .
4,139,860	2/1979	Micic et al. .
4,161,728	7/1979	Insam .
4,170,782	10/1979	Miller .
4,203,130	5/1980	Doumit et al. .
4,205,343	5/1980	Barrett .
4,218,698	8/1980	Bart et al. .
4,231,031	10/1980	Crowther et al. .
4,233,628	11/1980	Ciciora .
4,249,211	2/1981	Baba et al. .
4,261,006	4/1981	Weintraub et al. .
4,264,924	4/1981	Freeman .
4,270,145	5/1981	Farina .
4,288,809	9/1981	Yabe .
4,337,480	6/1982	Bourassin et al. .
4,337,483	6/1982	Guillou .
4,344,090	8/1982	Belisomi et al. .
4,390,901	6/1983	Keiser .
4,412,244	10/1983	Shanley, II .
4,413,281	11/1983	Thonnart .

4,420,769	12/1983	Novak .
4,425,581	1/1984	Schweppe et al. .
4,449,249	5/1984	Price .
4,456,925	6/1984	Skerlos et al. .
4,477,830	10/1984	Lindman et al. .
4,488,179	12/1984	Krüger et al. .
4,495,654	1/1985	Deiss .
4,496,171	1/1985	Cherry .
4,496,976	1/1985	Swanson et al. .
4,547,804	10/1985	Greenberg .
4,566,034	1/1986	Harger et al. .
4,595,951	6/1986	Filliman 358/142
4,595,952	6/1986	Filliman 358/142
4,620,229	10/1986	Amano et al. .
4,691,351	9/1987	Hayashi 358/142
4,694,490	9/1987	Harley 358/142
4,707,121	11/1987	Young .
4,751,578	6/1988	Reiter et al. .
4,768,228	8/1988	Clupper 380/20
4,908,707	3/1990	Kinghorn .... 358/142·X

FOREIGN PATENT DOCUMENTS

0041121 12/1981 European Pat. Off. 358/142

Primary Examiner—Victor R. Kostak
Attorney, Agent, or Firm—Bell, Seltzer, Park & Gibson

[57] **ABSTRACT**

An online television program information system extracts from a broadcast datastream of television program information only that program information for those shows which meet predetermined selection criteria, and stores only the extracted information. By not storing all broadcast television information, memory size for information storage is reduced and a high performance processor is not required for subset searches of the entire stored datastream for programs of interest. A low cost online television program information system is thereby provided, which may store large amounts of useful program information. Content selective storage is facilitated by transmitting and receiving the television program information in three groups, with the first group comprising event data, the second group comprising titles and the third group comprising descriptions.

34 Claims, 6 Drawing Sheets

United States Patent [19]

Brglez et al.

[11] **Patent Number:** **5,043,988**

[45] **Date of Patent:** **Aug. 27, 1991**

[54] **METHOD AND APPARATUS FOR HIGH PRECISION WEIGHTED RANDOM PATTERN GENERATION**

[75] Inventors: **Franc Brglez**, Cary; **Gershon Kedem**, Chapel Hill; **Clay S. Gloster, Jr.**, Raleigh, all of N.C.

[73] Assignees: **MCNC**, Research Triangle Park, N.C.; **Northern Telecom Limited**, Montreal, Canada

[21] Appl. No.: **398,772**

[22] Filed: **Aug. 25, 1989**

[51] Int. Cl.⁵ G01R 31/28
[52] U.S. Cl. 371/27; 364/717
[58] Field of Search 371/27, 22.3, 25.1; 364/717

[56] **References Cited**

U.S. PATENT DOCUMENTS

3,633,100	1/1972	Hellwell et al.	371/25.1
3,636,443	1/1972	Singh et al.	371/25.1
3,719,885	3/1973	Carpenter et al.	371/27
4,546,473	10/1985	Eichelberger et al.	371/20.3
4,687,988	8/1987	Eichelberger et al.	371/22.3
4,688,223	8/1987	Motika et al.	371/22.3
4,730,319	3/1988	David et al.	371/68.3
4,745,355	5/1988	Eichelberger et al.	371/22.3
4,754,215	6/1988	Kawai	371/22.3
4,782,288	11/1988	Vento	324/158 R
4,801,870	1/1989	Eichelberger et al.	371/22.3
4,807,229	2/1989	Tada	371/27
4,817,093	3/1989	Jacobs et al.	371/22.3

FOREIGN PATENT DOCUMENTS

59-160236 9/1984 Japan .

OTHER PUBLICATIONS

Gloster, Clay S. and Brglez, Franc. "Boundary Scan with Built-In Self-Test", *IEEE Design & Test of Computers*, Feb. 1989, pp. 36–44.

Lisanke et al., "Testability-Driven Random Test-Pattern Generation", *IEEE Transactions on Computer-Aided Design*, Nov. 1987, pp. 1082–1087.

Primary Examiner—Charles E. Atkinson
Attorney, Agent, or Firm—Bell, Seltzer, Park & Gibson

[57] **ABSTRACT**

A high precision weighted random pattern generation system generates any desired probability of individual bits within a weighted random bit pattern. The system includes a circular memory having a series of weighting factors stored therein, with each weighting factor representing the desired probability of a bit in the weighted random pattern being binary ONE. The random bits from a random number generator and a weighting factor are combined to form a single weighted random bit. The random bits and weighting factor are combined in a series of interconnected multiplexor gates. Each multiplexor gate has two data inputs, one being a bit from the weighting factor, the other being the output of the preceding multiplexor gate. The random number bit controls the output of the multiplexor. For example, when the control input (random bit) is high, the multiplexor output is the weighting factor bit. When the control input (random bit) is low, the multiplexor output is the output of the preceding multiplexor. The output of the final multiplexor gate in the series is the weighted bit.

31 Claims, 2 Drawing Sheets

United States Patent [19]

Golub et al.

[11] **Patent Number:** **5,050,090**

[45] **Date of Patent:** Sep. 17, 1991

[54] **OBJECT PLACEMENT METHOD AND APPARATUS**

[75] Inventors: Alexander J. Golub, Lewisville; Oscar F. Garza; C. Pat Joiner, both of Winston-Salem; Alan W. Neebe, Chapel Hill, all of N.C.

[73] Assignee: R. J. Reynolds Tobacco Company, Winston-Salem, N.C.

[21] Appl. No.: 331,621

[22] Filed: Mar. 30, 1989

[51] Int. Cl.⁵ G06F 15/20
[52] U.S. Cl. 364/478; 414/273
[58] Field of Search ... 364/478, 468, 300, 200 MS File, 364/900 MS File; 414/902, 900, 922, 286, 791.6, 799, 273, 275

[56] **References Cited**

U.S. PATENT DOCUMENTS

4,641,271 2/1987 Konishi et al. 364/478
4,692,876 9/1987 Tenma et al. .... 364/478 X

OTHER PUBLICATIONS

"AALPS–A Knowledge Based System for Aircraft Loading," Debra Anderson & Charles Ortiz, IEEE Expert, vol. 2, No. 4, Winter, 1987, pp. 71–79.
CAPE Container Loading I & II, CAPE Systems & Consulting Servs., Div. of Spectrum Planning Inc., Richardson, TX; undated
CAPE Multiproduct Loading, CAPE Systems & Consulting Servs., Div. of Spectrum Planning, Inc., Richardson, TX; undated.

Primary Examiner—Joseph Ruggiero
Attorney, Agent, or Firm—Bell, Seltzer, Park & Gibson

[57] **ABSTRACT**

An object placement method and apparatus which obtains efficiency and optimized placement by providing a library of object placement patterns, each pattern in said library representing a plurality of objects filling a pattern line or series of pattern lines of a three-dimensional space. For each pattern line, a first type object (for example, a first size object) to be placed is selected and the pattern which minimizes the portion of the three-dimensional space used to place a number of first type objects, subject to at least one constraint factor, is determined. A representation of the objects in the rows according to the determined pattern may be provided. According to another aspect of the invention, linking restrictions between the objects of differing sizes may be provided. The linking restrictions are patterns from the library which may not be employed with objects of differing types in a line of the three-dimensional space. The linking restrictions may reject patterns that lead to irregular pattern geometries, inefficient use of space, unstable characteristics or any other undesirable configuration of the two object types in a single pattern line. The element placement technique of the present invention determines the patterns which minimize the portions of the three-dimensional space used to place the objects consistent with at least one constraint factor without violating the linking restrictions.

44 Claims, 18 Drawing Sheets

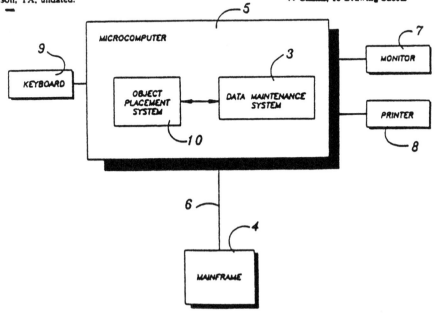

United States Patent [19]

Belsito

[11] Patent Number: 5,054,774

[45] Date of Patent: Oct. 8, 1991

[54] COMPUTER-CONTROLLED MUSCLE EXERCISING MACHINE HAVING SIMPLIFIED DATA ACCESS

[75] Inventor: Anne W. Belsito, Chattanooga, Tenn.

[73] Assignee: Chattecx, Hixson, Tenn.

[21] Appl. No.: 537,039

[22] Filed: Jun. 12, 1990

[51] Int. Cl.⁵ A63B 23/04; A63B 24/00
[52] U.S. Cl. .... 272/130; 272/DIG. 5; 272/DIG. 6; 340/712; 128/25 R
[58] Field of Search .... 272/129, 130, DIG. 5, 272/DIG. 6; 73/379; 128/25 R, 25 B; 434/247, 392; 340/712

[56] References Cited

U.S. PATENT DOCUMENTS

4,235,437	11/1980	Ruis et al.	272/134
4,408,613	10/1983	Relyea	272/670
4,544,154	10/1985	Ariel	272/129
4,566,692	1/1986	Brentham	272/130
4,586,035	4/1986	Baker et al.	340/712
4,601,468	7/1986	Bond et al.	272/130
4,637,607	1/1987	McArthur	272/129 X
4,691,694	9/1987	Boyd et al.	128/25 R
4,711,450	12/1987	McArthur	272/129
4,714,244	12/1987	Kolomayets et al.	272/72
4,765,613	8/1988	Voris	272/129
4,779,080	10/1988	Coughlin et al.	340/712
4,817,940	4/1989	Shaw et al.	272/93
4,828,257	5/1989	Dryer et al.	272/DIG. 5
4,842,274	6/1989	Oosthuizen et al.	272/129
4,848,152	7/1989	Pratt, Jr.	73/379

OTHER PUBLICATIONS

LIDO Active Isokinetic Rehabilitation System Operations Manual Loredan Biomedical, Inc., 9/1988.
Dynatrac Strength Rehabilitation brochure by Med-Ex Diagnostics of Canada, Inc.

Primary Examiner—Richard J. Apley
Assistant Examiner—L. Thomas
Attorney, Agent, or Firm—Bell, Seltzer, Park & Gibson

[57] **ABSTRACT**

A data access method and apparatus for computerized control of a muscle exercising machine, allows large amounts of data to be stored and retrieved with minimal computer skill. The muscle exercising machine displays a window or "scroll box" on its display device in response to an appropriate selection of a first type of data to be retrieved. The window contains a list of at least some of the names of the first type of data to be retrieved and a selection area for highlighting one name in the list of the first type of data in the window. The list can be scrolled in the up or down direction via a touch screen to locate a data file within a selection area of the window or scroll box.

The window and up/down selection options may be used to simplify storage and retrieval of patient data. In response to a selection command, at least some of the names of users are displayed and one name is selected. Then, at least some of the dates of exercise for the selected name are displayed and one date is selected. Then, at least some of the exercises performed by the selected name on the selected date are displayed. One of the exercises may be selected, and the exercise machine may be controlled to perform the selected exercise.

The muscle exercise machine may be controlled using the window and up/down option to permit exercising of standard exercises including isokinetic, isotonic and isometric exercises. The exercise machine may also be controlled to permit creation and retrievals of customized exercise protocols, based on previously defined protocols. The protocols are defined using the touch screen interface as well as the window or scroll box.

60 Claims, 60 Drawing Sheets

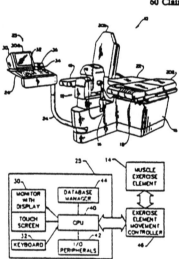

Session 8:

Integrating Software Engineering with Computer Science

Moderator: Anneliese von Mayrhauser, Colorado State University

A Joint Master's Level Software Engineering Subtrack
Don Epley, The University of Iowa

Planning for Software Engineering Education Within a Computer Science Framework at Marshall University
James W. Hooper, Marshall University

Integrating Object-Oriented Software Engineering in the Computer Science Curriculum
Raj Tewari and Frank Friedman, Temple University

A Joint Master's Level Software Engineering Subtrack

Don Epley
Department of Computer Science
The University of Iowa
Iowa City, Iowa 52242
email: epley@cs.uiowa.edu

The Departments of Computer Science and Electrical and Computer Engineering at the University of Iowa are establishing a 12 semester hour sequence of courses or subtrack in software engineering within their established Master's programs. Students completing the subtrack receive a special designation on their transcript. The design of the subtrack is discussed and comparisons of the resulting Masters programs with programs for separate Master degrees in software engineering are made. Surprisingly, the differences are not as large as one might expect. Moreover, the specific differences provide insight into the relationship between the subtrack approach and the separate degree approach. A possible evolution of a subtrack into a complete degree program is also made evident. With the current shortage of resources for starting new degree programs, this subtrack approach should be attractive to many other universities.

Background

The Department of Computer Science at Iowa has a long tradition of attempting to include the applications and practice of computer science within its theoretically based graduate programs. Most of the time, the lack of resources has curtailed the size of these attempts but not the fervor or the modernity of the instruction. Over the years since 1966, the coursework has evolved from a computation laboratory with students working at the University Computer Center to a problems in computer science course(1969), to a programming laboratory in which structured programming methodology and software engineering concepts were introduced (1978), to a one-semester software engineering course (1982), and finally, to a two-semester software engineering sequence (1990). Thus, the new software engineering subtrack has some deep roots.

The Electrical and Computer Engineering Department's interest in software engineering evolved from a faculty member's involvement in the design and implementation of simulation systems at the University's Center for Computer-Aided Design (CCAD) and the addition of a faculty member with interests in software reliability analysis.

Our software engineering courses, both the one-semester and two-semester versions, have always been organized around multi-person team projects but have also incorporated discussions of fundamental software engineering principles. Typical textbooks are Sommerville[1] and Ghezzi et. al.[2].

Subtrack Courses

Catalog descriptions of the subtrack courses are given in the Appendix. Topics are typical of software engineering courses at the first-year graduate level but note that each course is prerequisite to the following course. The fifth course described in the Appendix is a software engineering elective not included in the required subtrack. The role of this course is discussed later.

Fundamentals of Software Engineering   *3 s.h.*
Formal Methods in Software Engineering   *3 s.h.*
Software Engineering Project I   *3 s.h.*
Software Engineering Project II   *3 s.h.*

One major difference between our subtrack and the SEI Master of Software Engineering (MSE) Curriculum[3,4] is that the subtrack is a sequence of four core courses while the SEI MSE Curriculum has no prerequisites among the six core courses.

With regard to philosophy, the subtrack emphasizes the problem-solving view of software engineering which has been clearly and wonderfully discussed by Blum[9] at the sacrifice of the management-oriented viewpoint.

With respect to pedagogy, the subtrack is intended to support two continuing themes: the project nature of software engineering and the foundational importance of formal methods. Every course in the subtrack has a project component. The fundamentals course has a small "toy" project strongly defined, specified, and controlled by the instructor. But this limited project setting still allows demonstration of the stages in the software life cycle, confronts the students with issues of project scheduling, technical communication within teams, presentations of team and project results to nonteam members, and provides a "first project experience" which gives the students background for improvements in the management of later projects. The formal methods course includes multiperson projects on construction of formal specifications, thereby allowing more experience with intrateam communication and presentations to external groups. Multiperson projects also allow assignment of more complex and "real" examples of construction of formal specifications. The final two courses in the subtrack form a sequence which is a combination of a capstone project, which uses one of the formal methods studied in the formal methods course, and a more indepth discussion of principles and methods used in the stages of the software process. This sequence also provides a fuller project lifecycle experience than the one done in the fundamentals course.

The placement of the formal methods course as the second course in the subtrack sequence was the key design decision. There are several reasons for this decision. Firstly, it allows use of formal methods in the terminal project sequence. Secondly, the practical experience of having performed the fundamental course project without having formal methods provides stronger motivation for their study and small concrete examples which the student can use to assist in understanding the formality. Thirdly, it allows reinforcement and extensions of some methods, such as data flow diagrams and finite state machines, used in the fundamentals course.

The two distinct but equally important objectives of the formal methods course should be emphasized: (1) to provide understanding and the ability to apply a formal method which depends upon automated tools for use on real applications; this type of formal method will be used in portions of the capstone project: VDM and Z are examples; and (2) to provide the ability to rigorously use operational specification methods such as data flow diagrams, finite state machines, and Petri nets, on smaller applications which do not require automated tools. As one of our colleagues has expressed it, the discipline, precision, and rigor of formal methods and models is applicable to "software-engineering-in-the-small." Not *all* important software engineering applications are large projects.

Finally, as indicated in the description, the formal methods course will emphasize the use of formalisms and precise models in *all* phases of the software engineering lifecycle. In particular, the recent efforts to formalize flow diagram models used in the early stage of requirements analysis[10] and to formally model the overall software process[11] will receive attention.

Complete Master's Programs

In this section, *typical* overall Master of Science degree programs will be described. Students in the software engineering subtrack are first admitted to the graduate program of either the Computer Science (CS) Department or the Electrical and Computer Engineering (ECE) Department. Official admission to the software engineering subtrack occurs after the student has completed the foundations and the formal methods courses. These courses may also be used as electives by students not entering and completing the subtrack.

The CS program contains four required courses while the ECE program contains a more flexible requirement of six courses from an approved list. Both programs require a minimum of 36 s.h.

Computer Science

SE Subtrack	12

Required

Operating Systems	3
Prog. Lang. Foundations	3
Advanced Computer Architecture	3
Computation Theory	3

Elective

Computer Networks	3
Distributed Computing	3
Database Systems	3

(SE) Software Engr. Project Management	3

Total	36

Electrical and Computer Engineering

SE Subtrack	12

Required

VLSI Design	3
Advanced VLSI Design	3
Design Automation	3
Computer-Based Control Systems	3
Intro. to Robotics	3
Computer Networks	3

Elective

Distributed Computing	3

(SE) Software Reliability Analysis	3

	36

The computer networks course is jointly offered by the two departments but the other listed courses are not. Distributed computing and software reliability analysis are advanced courses offered by ECE, and the software engineering project management course, which is described in the Appendix, is offered by CS.

Software Engineering Electives

As typical of academic environments, the total interests of the faculty determine the availability of courses. The distributed computing and software reliability courses listed in the typical programs reflect the interests of ECE faculty members. Within computer science, the following courses which are suitable for software engineering electives are available for the same reason:

Data: Abstractions, Types, and Structures
Topics in Object Oriented Programming and Human Interfaces
Topics in Realtime Systems
Topics in Discrete Distributed Simulation

Comparison of Subtrack Core and MSE Core

After the subtrack was designed and approved by both departments and our Graduate College, a detailed comparison with the SEI Recommendations for a Master's in Software Engineering [3,4] was made. Of course, all of the members of the SEI Recommendations as a starting point. Instead, the Committee concentrated upon the local faculty resource constraints, the collective experience that four of the Committee members had acquired in teaching the local software engineering courses, and the specific interests of the faculty who would be offering the subtrack.

The SEI Recommendation identified twenty distinct MSE Curriculum Units. These are listed in Table 1. The SEI Recommendation then suggests a possible packaging of nineteen units, with Technical Communication omitted because it is incorporated as a consistent theme within the Curriculum, into six core courses.

Table 1. SEI MSE Curriculum Units

MSE Curriculum Units	Sommerville	Subtrack
1. Software Engineering Process	Yes	Yes
2. Software Evolution	Yes	Yes
3. Software Generation	No	No
4. Software Maintainence	Partially	Partially
5. Technical Communication	--------	Throughout
6. Software Configuration Man.	Yes	Yes
7. Software Quality Issues	No	Light
8. Software Quality Assurance	Partially	Light
9. Software Project Organization and Management Issues	Yes	Yes
10. Software Project Economics	Yes	Light
11. Software Operations Issues	No	No - Systems
12. Requirements Analysis	Yes	Heavy
13. Specification	Yes	Heavy
14. System Design	No	No - Systems
15. Software Design	Yes	Heavy
16. Software Implementation	Yes	Heavy
17. Software Testing	Yes	Yes
18. System Integration	No	No - Systems
19. Embedded RealTime Systems	No	No - Systems
20. Human Interfaces	Yes	Light

As a consistency check on our comparison of subtrack contents with the MSE Curriculum core courses, the second column of Table 1 indicates how the contents of a typical textbook[1] used in our courses compares with the MSE Curriculum Units. The third column contains an evaluation of the subtrack content relative to the MSE Curriculum Units. Note that the contents of the subtrack course occur in two forms or styles because of the inclusion of projects: (1) study of software engineering principles separate from projects; (2) study of topics which directly support project work and independent study of project-related material. This partitioning of style of coverage seems to exist in all software engineering courses containing project work. Both forms of study are included in the third column of Table 1.

Table 1 makes clear the omissions of our subtrack: systems engineering topics in Units 11, 14, and 18; light or partial treatments of the fundamental topics of Software Quality (Units 7,8) and Software Project Economics (Unit 10), and the technical topic of Software Generation (Unit 3). Embedded RealTime Systems and Human Interfaces are Units omitted from the subtrack but available in elective CS courses. On balance, the subtrack and available electives adequately cover thirteen of the twenty MSE units and lightly cover three of the other seven.

It seems clear that a four-course subtrack cannot provide any additional coverage while also providing a significant project experience. It should be noted that the SEI MSE Recommendation contains six core courses plus a two-course project experience component.

Comparison of Overall Degree Programs

A superficial global view of the SEI MSE Curriculum indicates eight software engineering courses, the six core courses plus the two-course project experience, and four electives outside of software engineering. Our MSCS and MSECE Curriculua contain four required software engineering courses with the *potential* for up to four software engineering electives. In the case of ECE, achieving this potential requires the faculty to allow some software engineering courses to be included in the approved list of courses. Referring to the typical ECE program given previously, two of the software engineering electives would be in the Required course section and two in the Elective section. In the case of CS, the faculty would have to allow all electives to be software engineering courses.

Our conclusion is that if sufficient faculty resources are available to allow the offering of more software engineering courses within either one of the departments or jointly, our subtrack can evolve into a program very compatible with the SEI MSE Recommendations. A separate degree at the Master's level is not needed to provide a complete and sound education for software engineers.

As a consistency check on this conclusion, a comparison of our subtrack degree program with the graduate degree programs at other schools [4,5] was made. There is a wide variety of names for programs but a commonality of structure exists: a number of required core courses, a project requirement, and restrictions on elective courses. Perhaps the only uniqueness to our subtrack is the blending of project activities with the core material thereby leaving some of the core material to be covered in supplementary or advanced electives. The advanced Software Engineering Project Management course described in the Appendix is a good example of this difference. Students in this course enter with the experience of the subtrack and thus are far better prepared to study the subtleties of project management within a context that they have already experienced.

Our comparison with other degree programs does identify one basic difference which goes beyond simple naming. The *professional* degree programs of Master of Software Engineering at Seattle University and Carnegie Mellon University require at least two years of professionial software experience for admission. Master of Science degree programs such as ours require only an undergraduate degree and satisfaction of the usual graduate admission standards.

Local Evolution -- Some Possibilities

One of the side effects of our comparison of the current subtrack degree program and more fully developed separate degree programs is the identification of several possible directions for the development of our program.

Firstly, the inclusion of the omitted core material as represented by the SEI MSE Curriculum Units could be done in nontraditional instructional formats. The "short course" format often favored by industry may well play a role here if the scheduling problem can be solved. For example, a local industry, Rockwell International, has a deep interest in and commitment to software engineering [6]. It would seem possible to make some arrangement where students in the software engineering program could have some access to Rockwell-supported short courses. In particular, the important omissions of the Software Quality and Software Project Economics Units and the systems engineering units could perhaps been supplied in that manner.

Secondly, the business side of software engineering is one in which CS and ECE departments are least prepared to cover with some perspective. Faculty in our College of Business, in particular the MBA program, have already expressed an interest in the possbility of their students having access to at least a part of the software engineering subtrack. If the reverse access problem of allowing software engineering students to study the particularly relevant portions of the MBA program can be solved, there would be a benefit to both programs.

Finally, the notion of "advanced" electives which deliberately build upon the student experience gained in the required subtrack seems educationally important. The Software Engineering Project Management course is but one example. Another intriguing one is a course in "Evaluation of Software Design". The software development studio in the Carnegie Mellon program[7] has a sizable component devoted to this kind of evaluation work. One of the vexing problems in software engineering education is the one of adding depth. As the SEI Curriculum designers [3,4] indicated, there is no linear ordering among the fundamentals and principles of software engineering, but a way of adding depth to software engineering curriculua must be found if software engineering is to mature as an academic discipline.

Conclusions

The future and, in particular the rate, of the evolution of software engineering education is somewhat uncertain. There is a well-established need for such programs as the work of the SEI and other workers have shown[8]. Indeed, the slow growth in the number of software engineering academic programs is disappointing and a cause for national concern. Many CS and ECE departments would probably like to implement a software engineering initiative but have been held back by lack of faculty resources. The "good news" reported here is that it is possible to make a start if local departments are willing to cooperate and to make joint efforts. Surprisingly, very little compromise seems necessary, and the result is very comparable to existing separate degree programs.

Acknowledgements

The comparisons and conclusions expressed here are the responsibility of the author. However, the design of the subtrack was truly a team effort of an ad hoc commitee. The author would like to thank the committee members, Jon Kuhl and Michael Lyu from ECE and William Decker and Mahesh Dodani from CS. Don Alton from CS also contributed advice and counsel. The enthusiastic administrative support of Sudhakar Reddy from ECE and Jon Simon from CS is gratefully acknowledged. The source of the terminology 'software-engineering-in-the-small' was Doug Jones of CS.

References

1. I. Sommerville,*Software Engineering*,Third Edition,Addison-Wesley, Reading, Mass.,1989

2. C. Ghezzi, M. Jazayeri, and D. Mandrioli,*Fundamentals of Software Engineering*,Prentice-Hall,Englewood Cliffs, New Jersey,1991

3. G. A. Ford and N. E. Gibbs,A Master of Software Engineering Curriculum,*Computer*,vol. 22,9,59-71,September 1989

4. M. Ardis and G. A. Ford,"1989 SEI Report on Graduate Software Engineering Education",Technical Report CMU/SEI-89-TR-21,Software Engineering Institute, Carnegie Mellon University, Pittsburgh, Pennsylvania,June 1989

5. L. E. Deimel,Ed.,*Software Engineering Education: SEI Conference 1990 Proceedings*,145-156,Pittsburgh, Pennsylvania,April 1990

6. H. E. Romanowsky et. al.,The Rockwell Avionics Group Software Engineering Training Program,*Software Engineering Education: SEI Conference 1989 Proceedings*,131-140,Pittsburgh,Pennsylvania,July 1989

7. N. E. Gibbs et. al.,The Carnegie Mellon University Master of Software Engineering Degree Program,*Software Engineering Education: SEI Conference 1990 Proceedings*,152-154,Pittsburgh, Pennsylvania,April 1990

8. N. E. Gibbs and R. E. Fairley,*Software Engineering Education: The Educational Needs of the Software Community*,New York, NY,1987

9. B. I. Blum,*Software Engineering: A Holistic View*, Oxford University Press, New York,1992

10. Y. Tao and C. Kung,Formal Definition and Verification of Data Flow Diagrams,*Journal of Systems and Software*,vol. 16,29-36,1991

11. B. Kramer and Luqi,Toward Formal Models of Software Engineering Processes,*Journal of Systems and Software*,vol. 15,63-74,1991

Appendix: Subtrack Course Descriptions

22C:180 Fundamentals of Software Engineering   3 s.h.

Introduction to software engineering process: problem analysis, requirements definition, specification, design, implementation, testing/maintenance, integration, project management; human factors; managment and technical communication; design methodologies;   software validation and verification; group project experience. Prerequisite: senior standing in computer science or electrical and computer engineering. Same as 55:180.

22C:181 Formal Methods in Software Engineering   3 s.h.

Study of formal models and methods and their application in all phases of software engineering process; operational, algebraic, model-based and property-based specification methods; verification of consistency and completeness of specifications; verification of properties of software; exercises in specification construction and verification using method-based tools. Prerequisite: 22C:180.   Same as 55:181.

22C:182 Software Engineering Project I   3 s.h.

Team project work on software engineering of real software product; estimation, risk analysis, scheduling, tracking and control, software metrics; CASE tools and project management techniques. Students must register for 22C:183 in the following semester. Prerequisite: 22C:180 and 22C:181. Same as 55:182.

22C:183 Software Engineering Project II   3 s.h.

Continuation of 22C:182, which is prerequisite. Same as 55:183.

22C:189 Software Engineering Project Management   1-2 s.h.

Resource requirements estimation, planning and managment; risk analysis; scheduling, tracking and control; personnel supervision, training, evaluation; process determination and management including change control and configuration management; technical project leadership and assessment. Students register for two consecutive semesters and assist in supervision of teams in concurrent offerings of 22C:182 and 22C:183. Prerequisite: 22C:182.22C:183 and consent of instructor.

Planning for Software Engineering Education

Within a Computer Science Framework

At Marshall University

James W. Hooper

Department of Computer and Information Sciences
Marshall University
Huntington, West Virginia 25755
Telephone: (304) 696-2693
Fax: (304) 696-4646
email: CIS010@marshall.wvnet.edu

Abstract. This paper presents an overview of the planning process undertaken at Marshall University, to update and strengthen the undergraduate computer science program, and to introduce a strong emphasis in software engineering. An Advisory Panel of senior computing managers from the region was formed, and has provided valuable input to the "requirements determination" phase of the planning process. Based on the Panel's input, and guided by current curriculum design recommendations and accreditation standards, the computer science faculty--with the participation of other colleagues--has undertaken a total revision of the curriculum, addressing other issues as well, such as laboratories and staffing. Summaries are provided of the Panel's input, and of the current draft status of the evolving curriculum.

1 Introduction

Marshall University has for some years offered the B.S. degree in computer science, with emphasis in either information systems (business-oriented) or "main stream" computer science. There has also been a Business Information Systems (BIS) major in the BBA degree program. The Department of Computer and Information Sciences (CIS) has been within the College of Business since its creation as a department. The main stream computer science degree was patterned along the lines of the 1978 ACM curriculum, but did not emphasize science courses, and did not strongly emphasize mathematics. The information systems degree has been lighter still in mathematics emphasis, and has required a different set of computing courses at the junior and senior level. The BIS program has placed less emphasis on computing courses and greater emphasis on business courses.

The relationship of the department to the College of Business and other business departments has often been uneasy at best. It has been difficult to bring about acceptance of strong science and mathematics emphasis among business-oriented students, and there has often been a mismatch of viewpoints and expectations between CIS faculty and other College of Business colleagues. The teaching loads have been heavy (nominally twelve hours per semester), and it has thus been very difficult for the faculty to conduct research and publish. A significant manifestation of these problems has been the high turnover of CIS faculty. Also, there has been a concern among some area employers that some graduates of these degree programs were not able to be productive soon after employment.

Discussions were held on campus during the summer of 1991 concerning a possible move of the CIS Department to the College of Science. Both of the Deans (Business and Science) and the Provost came to agree that the proposed move was likely to benefit the students in the CIS programs. The transfer became a reality in late September, when President J. Wade Gilley--newly-appointed president of Marshall University (MU)--wrote a letter approving the transfer of the Department and programs to the College of Science. Dr. Gilley came to MU from George Mason University (GMU) where he was Senior Vice President; an engineer by education, he was very much involved in the growth and development of GMU, including engineering programs, computer science, and software engineering. He made known his desire that the transfer of CIS should include curriculum updating and strengthening, and that software engineering should be emphasized due to the needs of the region. The author came to MU in late August of 1991 as a visiting professor--on leave-of-absence from the University of Alabama in Huntsville. The position (The Arthur and Joan Meyer Weisberg Chair in Software Engineering) was endowed by a successful civic-minded couple with business connections to a Huntington-based software engineering firm, who were aware of the need to strengthen the computer science programs at MU. The author was appointed as Chairman of the Transition Planning Committee for Computer Science, tasked with "effecting an orderly transition of the department". The Acting Chairman of the CIS Department continued in that position, administering the on-going programs.

2 Planning Approach

The first step in the planning process was to form the Transition Planning Committee for Computer Science. The committee consists of all members of the CIS faculty (seven full-time faculty), the Associate Director of the Computer Center, an engineering professor active in planning for a manufacturing sciences degree program, and a management professor from the College of Business having a strong management information systems (MIS) background. It was also considered critically important to establish effective interrelationships with computing organizations/professionals in the region. To this end, a number of senior computing managers from the "Tri-State" area were invited to join the Computer Science Advisory Panel. Current members are from Ashland Petroleum Co., Inco Alloys International, Inc., State Electric Supply Co., Strictly Business Software Engineering, and Union Carbide Chemicals and Plastics Co., Inc. All of these managers have manifested a very strong interest in improving computer science education at MU, and have actively and thoughtfully participated in strategy sessions. They have all had experience with MU computer science students, as interns/coops or regular employees. Monthly meetings of the Advisory Panel have been held beginning in November 1991; the Dean of the College of Science and the author have participated in all meetings. Numerous working sessions have been held by the faculty, at various times also including other Transition Planning Committee members.

It is understood that the faculty has "the last word" on curriculum planning. However, the faculty has welcomed the active participation of others both within MU and outside MU, recognizing the importance of their input in building and sustaining a high-quality academic program. It is the motivating objective of the faculty to develop a strong academic computer science program, with software engineering emphasis, whose graduates will be well prepared to function as computing professionals in a diversity of organizations. The opportunity to participate in achievement of this objective has been accepted with enthusiasm by the faculty.

The scope of activities necessary to achieve the overall objective includes more than curriculum, of course. The following list of necessary planning activities was developed, characterizing the scope/responsibilities of the Transition Planning Committee:

* Determine long-term instructional, research, and service goals for computer and information science programs at MU

* Plan revised B.S. curriculum, including emphasis on software engineering, and taking into account interrelationships with other existing and planned curricula and MU research thrusts

* Determine a (longer-term) plan for an M.S. degree program; take these preliminary requirements into account while planning the B.S. curriculum

* Determine resources necessary for the revised B.S. program

* Develop a transition plan for introducing the revised B.S. program(s) and phasing out the existing B.S. programs; this should include feasible schedules, and should document assumptions about availability of resources

* Determine a strategy for increasing research activities in the department, including specific research thrusts, and prospective funding sources

* Develop a strategy for faculty development, recruitment, and retention, based on anticipated program redirection and growth

Most of these activities are in progress at the time this paper is written. Greatest emphasis so far has been given to curriculum development, and most of the following discussion focuses on that activity.

3 Curriculum Planning

The Advisory Panel was requested to provide insight to MU concerning their viewpoint of the characteristics we should seek to bring about in the B.S. program in computer science. (I.E., we sought their input to the requirements determination process!) After discussion sessions and reviewing a previous draft, the Panel provided the Mission/Vision and Standards Statements shown as Figure 1.

MISSION/VISION

The Computer and Information Science (CIS) Advisory Panel was created to provide a vehicle for dialogue between the College of Science and the business community regarding Marshall University's Computer and Information Science program. The Mission and Vision of the Advisory Panel follows:

The Mission is:

o   To provide leadership and technical expertise in identifying and communicating to the College of Science appropriate programs and curricula that will result in a highly developed Computer and Information Science graduate suitable for regional employment.

o   To enhance the overall competitive position of Marshall University in attracting faculty, research grants and support of the business community for the CIS program.

o   To suggest programs and strategies in accordance with our Mission that will accelerate the accomplishment of the Vision.

When the Mission is accomplished, it is our Vision that:

o   The CIS program at Marshall will exceed student's expectations and graduates will be highly sought by the employers.

o   Marshall University will have achieved a competitive advantage in attracting faculty and business support for the CIS program.

(continued on next page)

Figure 1. Advisory Panel Mission/Vision and Standards Statements

o   Lasting alliances between the business and academic community will have been established in support of the CIS program.

STANDARDS

The standards, outlined below, are the definitive milestones that measure our progress toward the Vision.

o   The CIS program at Marshall will be linked to the business community and be driven by requirements of regional enterprises.

o   The CIS program will consistently provide high-quality graduates.

o   The CIS program will be accredited by the appropriate accrediting organization(s).

o   Partnerships will be established between the business community and the University to establish student work programs, faculty research projects and technology transfer.

o   The University can attract and tenure professors in the field of computer science.

o   The CIS program will attract top area students because of its reputation for excellence.

Figure 1.   Advisory Panel Mission/Vision and Standards Statements (Continued)

We also asked the Panel to provide input concerning their viewpoint of the characteristics a computer science graduate should possess to be successful in the workplace. Their response is summarized in Figure 2. The author's own long-term experience with government and industry software projects leads to strong concurrence with the emphasis given by the Panel to personal communication skills, and also to project management considerations. In other words, technically-oriented college graduates need to be more than "techies"--they must be able to organize and communicate ideas, understand management principles, have a "system view" of development and maintenance, and understand principles relating to cost and trade-off analysis.

Based on the Advisory Committee's input, the faculty's knowledge of other computer science curricula (including the author's long-term participation in the University of Alabama in Huntsville's accredited B.S. program in computer science), and recent guidance on curriculum design (especially [CC91], [CSAB], [FORD90]), we undertook an extensive B.S. curriculum revision. We established the following (preliminary) list of goals for the B.S. program:

* Meet the CSAB quantitative requirements
* Meet the Computing Curricula 1991 CS requirements
* Have a strong software engineering emphasis
* Provide students practical experience participating in:
  * Team-oriented software projects
  * Development and maintenance of large software systems
  * Formal treatment of life cycle activities--including creation and documentation of requirements, designs, and code, participation in formal reviews, change control boards, ...
* Place strong emphasis on the "systems approach" to software development, beginning with the very first freshman-level course
* Provide background and experience in systems engineering as it relates to software--i.e., embedded systems, hardware/software tradeoffs; simulation, queuing theory, for use in determining requirements feasibility, performance evaluation, etc.
* Emphasize management methods, cost analysis, quality assurance, decision support systems
* Seek a synergistic relationship with Manufacturing Science
* Emphasize supervised teaching laboratories as part of some courses

---

COMMUNICATION
  Oral Expression--Competent in:
    Vocabulary use (general business, specific technical)
    Speaking and presentation (including use of audio-visual aids)
  Written Expression--Competent in:
    Organizing and representing thoughts clearly
    Using word processing or desktop publishing tools
    Graphical representation and graphics tools
  Listening

ANALYTICAL
  Mathematics
  Problem solving--Competent in:
    The use of problem prevention and solution methodologies
    The use of statistical analysis tools
  Modeling
    Problem decomposition, process flow, context, data
  Decision theory

(continued on next page)

Figure 2. Advisory Panel Capabilities List for Success in a Working Environment

TECHNICAL
  Data types, structure, organization, dictionaries,
    languages, algorithms, operating systems,
    hardware, communications,
    standards, security, documentation,
    CASE concepts, prototyping concepts

PROJECT
  Competent in software engineering life cycle concepts:
    analysis, design, construction, testing, implementation,
    change management

PERSONAL
  Personal behavior management
  Meeting planning and leading
  Group techniques and team processes
  Organizational behavior

Figure 2. Advisory Panel Capabilities List for Success in a Working Environment (Continued)

Pascal had been for many years the introductory teaching language at MU. While it has served well in that role, it is a "dead end" relative to use in development of large software systems. Thus we decided to use Ada as the primary teaching language, beginning with an appropriate subset (essentially equivalent to Pascal) in the first freshman-level course. We consider Ada to be the best available language for encouraging good software engineering and programming principles. We believe that its use as the primary teaching language will help enforce and facilitate good practices from the beginning, and will also provide the graduates working knowledge of a language that can be used in professional practice. We also feel an obligation to ensure that the graduates are familiar with the C language, due to the demand by prospective employers, but believe it is best to defer its use until programming methods and skills have been established by use of Ada. We are strongly committed to provide concepts and experiences to the students different from the "toy problem" approach of most current computer science courses, which are usually solved by a student working alone. Many of us are well aware of the laments of employers of computer science graduates who must give new graduates extensive training before they are capable of performing as professional software engineers. This revised curriculum emphasis must include participation in developing and maintaining large software systems, following a well-defined software process, and working as part of teams.

Figure 3 summarizes briefly the current draft status of the evolving curriculum. We emphasize at this point that this draft material is presented to give a general understanding of our current curriculum emphasis and planning status, but that any of the specifics of the curriculum are subject to change as we proceed. We have proposed that the name of the Department be changed to reflect the increased emphasis on software engineering, while still reflecting the emphasis on a solid computer science base. The name under current consideration is "Computer Science and Software Development"; thus the course designations use "CSD" as a prefix. We are planning to delete all existing CIS courses; even though some are similar to replacement courses, we want to institute a new numbering scheme and impose different prerequisites in many cases.

We are planning no separate information systems option in this program; it is our opinion, supported by the Advisory Panel, that a good quality program with a software engineering emphasis should be applicable to business and management applications, as well as to engineering and scientific applications. We believe that all students, of all majors, should be exposed (if not already in high school) to word processing, spread sheets, databases, control statements, electronic mail, and some fundamental concepts about programming and a programming language. Exactly how each college at MU will approach such computer literacy is still under discussion.

We have included one course each in management, economics, and accounting, to help prepare the students for software engineering practice, and to help develop a working knowledge of business-related concepts and terminology for use in possible future computing applications. Speech and technical writing courses are included to help develop communication skills. Courses in physics and chemistry are specified to help develop a necessary foundation for industrial computing applications (numerous chemical industries operate in the Tri-State region, for example).

4 Conclusion

Much work remains, including completing detailed curriculum planning and implementing the new courses, upgrading laboratories, recruiting faculty, and strengthening research. We are planning to gradually phase in the new courses, beginning in the Spring semester of 1993, culminating in the offering of the Senior Team Project Sequence in academic year 1994-95. The first increment of the proposed curriculum has been reviewed and approved by college and university-level curriculum committees, and awaits approval by the Faculty Senate. We plan to report on further phases of the work as it proceeds. We are very much encouraged by the enthusiasm of the participants in this process, and by the strong support from the MU administration. Most of all, we believe that the real "winners" from this effort will be the young people of the region who graduate from the resulting program.

************************* PLEASE NOTE: *****************************
   THE FOLLOWING IS A BRIEF SUMMARY OF THE CURRENT
   STATUS OF THE PROPOSED CURRICULUM. SOME CHANGES
   MAY OCCUR AS DETAILED PLANNING IS COMPLETED AND
   APPROVAL REVIEWS OCCUR.
****

CSD 100 Fundamentals of Computing (i.e., computer literacy)
   * 3 sem. hours: 2 hours lecture, 2 hours supervised laboratory
   * CSD majors may not receive credit hours for this course

REQUIRED COURSES (38 Sem. Hrs)

CSD 119, 120 Introduction to Computing I, II
   * PR: CSD 100 or equiv. knowledge, CSD 119, respectively
   * 4 sem. hours each: 3 hours lecture, 2 hours supervised lab.
   * Introduce the software life cycle, placing software design, coding, unit
     testing, in that context; reading, alteration of existing code; reuse;
     design/programming using Ada; data structures emphasis in 120. Team
     concepts, experiences; use of simple CASE-like tools. Social, ethical,
     professional issues
   * see CD 101/102 in Computing Curricula 1991 (CC91)

CSD 212 Introduction to Computer Engineering
   * PR: CSD 120
   * 3 sem. hrs.: 2 hours lecture, 2 hours supervised lab.
   * Essentially equiv. to "Switching Theory"
   * See CD 201 in CC91

CSD 222 Computer Organization and Assembly Language Programming
   * PR: CSD 212
   * 3 sem. hrs. `
   * Register level architecture of a specific processor, assembly language
     programming for that processor; data representation, I/O devices, bus
     transactions
   * See CD 301 in CC91

CSD 240 Analysis and Design of Algorithms
   * PR: CSD 120, Discrete Structures
   * 3 sem. hrs.

(Continued on next page)

Figure 3. Draft Curriculum Summary

* Includes advanced data structures coverage; intro. to object-oriented design; complexity, recursive algs., computability; relationship to software eng. / large software systems; continued use of Ada.
* See CD 202 in CC91

CSD 313 Intro. to Systems and Software Engineering
  * PR: CSD 240
  * 3 sem. hrs.
  * The complexity of large systems; the systems approach; life cycle activities; methods and tools of systems engr.; requirements determination, trade-off studies, cost estimation; tools and methods of systems engr., quality assurance, human engineering
  * The relationships of systems engr. and software engr.; systems engr. in embedded-systems applications; allocations to softw., hardware, communications, people; CASE tools (Computer-Assisted Systems Eng./ Softw. Eng.): e.g., RDD 100; management approaches, risk analysis
  * The Softw. Engr. life cycle / software process
  * Team project that provides experiences in sys. eng. combined with softw. engr.

CSD 322 Computer Architecture
  * PR: CSD 222, CSD 240
  * 3 sem. hrs.
  * Design alternatives, instruction set architectures, memory organization, interfacing, alternative computer architectures
  * See CD 306 in CC91

CSD 325 Intro. to Programming Languages
  * PR: CSD 222
  * 3 sem. hrs.
  * Emphasis on programming language principles, illustrated by syntax and semantics of constructs in current languages
  * Imperative and functional languages; concurrency; logic-based approach; object-oriented approach
  * See CD 304 in CC91

CSD 333 Software Engineering
  * PR: CSD 313
  * 3 sem. hrs.

(continued on next page)

Figure 3. Draft Curriculum Summary (Continued)

* Further experience in requirements analysis and specification; functional and object-oriented design, user interface design, implementation in Ada, verification and validation issues, systems integration; maintenance; reuse; real time; safety; configuration management
* Team project experience, large software system
* See CD303 in CC91

CSD 338 Operating Systems
   * PR: CSD 222, CSD 240
   * 3 sem. hrs.
   * Process management, device and memory management, security, networking, distributed operating systems
   * File structures, UNIX emphasis, programming in C
   * See CD 305 in CC91

CSD 493,494 Senior Team Project Sequence
   * PR: CSD 333, CSD 322
   * 3 sem. hours each
   * A two-consecutive-semester course sequence providing a realistic experience in team-based software development. Student teams will perform requirements analysis and specification, design, implementation, testing and integration. In-class reviews will be conducted by the teams. The project is to be of significant size and complexity. Project management will be stressed, including costing and scheduling.
   * See CG407,408, CC91

ELECTIVE COURSES
(A student will select three courses to complete major, totalling 47 sem. hrs.)

CSD 345	Software Development for Business/Management (COBOL)
CSD 356	Scientific Computing / Supercomputing (FORTRAN)
CSD 367	Systems Programming (C, Unix emphasis)
CSD 409	Computer Information Systems for Health Care
	(not available as part of major for computer science majors)
CSD 419	Decision Systems
CSD 429	Intro. to Computer Graphics
CSD 439/539	Intro. to Artificial Intelligence

(continued on next page)

Figure 3. Draft Curriculum Summary (Continued)

CSD 442/542	Communic. Networks and Distributed Systems
CSD 449/549	Formal Languages and Automata Theory
CSD 457/557	Database Systems
CSD 459/559	Computer Simulation and Modeling
CSD 467/567	Compiler Design
CSD 470/570	Intro. to Applied Automation

OTHER REQUIREMENTS (Tentative)

Freshman English	6 sem. hours
Speech	3
Technical Writing	3
Literature	3
Classics, Philosophy, or Religious Studies	3
Microeconomics	3
Social Science	12
Chemistry	10
Physics	5
Mathematics	21
Calc./Analyt.I,II 9	
Discrete Struct. 3	
Linear Algebra 3	
Numerical Analy. 3	
Prob./Stat. 3	
Princ. of Accounting 3	
Princ. of Management	3
ELECTIVES (to bring to a total of 128 sem. hours)	6

Figure 3. Draft Curriculum Summary (Concluded)

Acknowledgement

Appreciation is expressed to the continuing participants in this process, and to the MU administrators who encouraged it from the beginning and strongly support it. Advisory Panel members: Larry Cassity, Tom Pressman, Jim Roma, Bob Shields, Mike Workman. At Marshall University: Dr. Wade Gilley, President; Dr. Alan Gould, Vice President for Academic Affairs; Dr. Steve Hanrahan, Dean of Science; CIS Faculty Dr. Hamid Chahryar, Dr. Jamil Chaudri, Dr. Akhtar Lodgher, Prof. Elias Majdalani, Dr. Wlodek Ogryczak, Dr. Dave Walker; other MU participants Dr. Dick Begley, Mr.

Allen Taylor, Dr. John Wallace. Dr. Akhtar Lodgher's participation in curriculum development has been exceptionally helpful and enthusiastic. The author expresses personal appreciation to Art and Joan Weisberg for their generosity in endowing the Weisberg Chair, a recent example of their long-term interest in and support for education of the young men and women of the Tri-State region.

References

[CC91] Computing Curricula 1991: Report of the ACM/IEEE-CS Joint Curriculum Task Force; ACM Press/IEEE Computer Society Press.

[CSAB] 1990 Annual Report for the year ending September 30, 1990; Computing Sciences Accreditation Board, Inc.

[FORD90] 1990 SEI Report on Undergraduate Software Engineering Education, CMU/SEI-90-TR-3.

Integrating Object-Oriented Software Engineering in the Computer Science Curriculum*

Raj Tewari and Frank Friedman

Temple University, Philadelphia, PA 19122

Abstract. The recent ACM/IEEE *Computing Curricula '91* report identifies important and recurring concepts that pervade computer science. These include complexity of large programs, the concept of binding, abstract data types, evolution of requirements, levels of abstraction, and the importance of software reuse. We present an improved curriculum for the software oriented courses that better addresses these concepts. The major objective of the proposed curriculum is the introduction of the concept of components as building blocks for creating solutions to software design problems. Component-based software engineering is currently best facilitated by the object-oriented approach through reuse of available class libraries and application frameworks. Based on our experience in the use of the object-oriented approach for the introductory programming courses as compared to past instruction using a predominantly procedural-oriented point of view, we feel that our approach can be successfully integrated into the computer science curriculum with proper planning and availability of resources.

1 Introduction

There is a growing awareness among computer science educators that the software content of the undergraduate computer science curriculum needs to be re-examined in the light of new reports on the nature of the *Computing Discipline* [4], and the recent comprehensive ACM and IEEE reports on *Computing Curricula* [5, 18, 19]. Undergraduates in most institutions are being prepared to think about algorithms and writing small programs, but they do not learn enough about existing systems and software, about the incorporation of components into a large program, or about the complete software development lifecycle.

One of the important distinctions made in [13] between routine engineering design problems versus innovative, is that routine problem solving relies on well established and codified procedures (essentially through reuse of components). Innovative engineering problems, on the other hand require creative problem solving approaches. This distinction is well established in engineering disciplines such as mechanical, electrical, civil and chemical engineering, where most design problems fall into the routine category in which prior solution procedures can be reused.

On the other hand, current instruction in software engineering, all too often emphasizes a craft-based approach, relying on building software essentially from scratch. As pointed out in [13]:

---

* The planning and design phases of the work reported herein are being partially supported by National Science Foundation Grant # USE 9156079.

Computer science teaching and research emphasizes innovative, green-field, once-used designs created by individuals. Software development and software engineering practice, however, involves work that frequently should be routine, that is most often enhancement of previous work, that is normally instantiated in many variants, and that involves large teams.

Some of the fundamental and recurring concepts in computing that have been identified in [18] are: complexity of large programs, the concept of binding, abstract data types, evolution of requirements, levels of abstraction, and the importance of software reuse. We present an improved curriculum with respect to these concepts. This curriculum will enable students to better tackle the complexities of programming and design in a variety of application areas, provide them with a better foundation to take advanced undergraduate and graduate level courses, and provide a good background for reading and understanding contemporary computer science literature.

The major objective of the new curriculum is the introduction of the concepts of components as building blocks for creating solutions to design problems. This approach adapts the engineering aspects from older, more established engineering disciplines, and is a first step towards putting the engineering back into software engineering and for that matter into the general computer science curriculum. Component based software engineering is currently best facilitated by the object-oriented approach through reuse of available class libraries and application frameworks.

A revised, three-course sequence of programming courses is described first and some early results of our experiences in these courses are presented. Experiences in the use of the object-oriented paradigm in these early courses are compared to past instruction using a heavy procedural-oriented point of view.

We have also had some experience in building on the early emphasis on object-oriented approaches when teaching some advanced courses. We include a section on these experiences as well, limited to courses in Programming Languages, Compiler Design, and a senior level introductory survey course in Software Design. Our experience in the introductory course sequence and the three advanced courses indicates that our objective can be achieved by integrating component-based software engineering concepts in the undergraduate curriculum, rather than creating a separate software engineering major. This finding reinforces the ideas presented previously by one of the authors, Friedman[7] and more recently by Wulf[20], Freeman[6] and Shaw[15], where a case was made that a separate software engineering degree might be harmful for the undergraduate curriculum.

2 Inadequacies of Existing Curricula

One of the most important decisions facing educators today is the choice of the programming language paradigm and the choice of a specific language to support the chosen paradigm. As suggested in [9], the choice of the first teaching language is critical because it impacts the kinds of abstractions that can be built by students, as mentioned in [9]:

> Just as the choice of available materials and technology affects both the architect's vision of what can be built and the constructions that are actually

attempted, so language constrains the programmers ambitions and abilities. The choice of the first teaching language is therefore critical ....

Recent changes in the existing introductory curriculum that we are considering have been relatively minor. The situation in the software market, advanced undergraduate courses, and graduate education has undergone considerable change. There is a need to better equip students for performing more effectively in an increasingly competitive marketplace, and to face the increasing rigors of advanced undergraduate and graduate studies as the computing field matures. We will identify several emerging trends that necessitate a revision of the curriculum.

As pointed out by Shaw [14], there has been a shift in research attention in computing in each of the last three decades. The primary software engineering paradigm that could be identified in the decade 1960 ± 5 was *programming any-which-way*, characterized by small programs, elementary understanding of control flows, emphasis on representing structure and symbolic information, and a state space that was not very well understood. The tools and methods of this decade were assemblers and core dumps. The decade of 1970 ± 5 emphasized *programming-in-the-small*, characterized by algorithms and programming, data structures and types, simple input/output specification, small and simple state space, individual effort. The tools and methods were programming languages, compilers, linkers and loaders. The 1980 ± 5 decade witnessed the shift to *programming-in-the-large*, characterized by interfaces, long-lived databases (symbolic and numeric), systems with complex specification, a large structured state space, team efforts and system lifetime maintenance. The tools and methods were environments, integrated tools and documents.

We extend Shaw's framework to the 1990 ± 5 decade. Characteristic environments in this decade include multi-windowed user interfaces incorporating multi-media, large relational and object-oriented databases, distributed and real-time computing, highly complex system specifications, large structured and unstructured state spaces, and group effort. The tools and methods are windowed source code debuggers, integrated program development environments, hypertext encoded documents (active documents), heterogeneous systems integration, and windowing toolkits. These represent an opportunity for us at universities to revise our curricula to emphasize new tools, techniques, and paradigms.

If we place our programming courses in the above context, we find that we are teaching students technology that is essentially *programming-in-the-small*. We are currently lagging two generations, and we suspect that there are a large number of computer science departments in the country that are in a similar situation, teaching based on the *programming-in-the-small* paradigm. By assigning small isolated problems based on individual programming effort, we are perpetuating the craft nature of software, instead of focusing on the realities of the software market that demand mastering the complexities of intricate toolkits and *programming-in-the-large*. The reasons for this in the past may have been lack of faculty expertise, lack of modern computing facilities, and a lack of suitable tools such as low cost compilers, debuggers, profilers, and integrated development environments.

Shaw in [13] points to five flaws prevalent in many software curricula:

- too much emphasis on programming from scratch;

- too much emphasis on the study of a final software product (the code), and not enough on the analysis, design, and testing that resulted in this product;
- considerable abstract discussion but not enough complete illustrations of techniques and principles of good software development practice;
- too much time devoted to coding and debugging at the expense of all other aspects of the software development process;
- far too many short, "throw-away" exercises as opposed to projects that may start small, but are grown over one or more semesters.

We feel that this is a specially good time for revising the curriculum to address some of the above problems through innovative instructional techniques such as those discussed in Section 6. Optimizing compilers for several languages that emphasize good software engineering principles and software reuse are becoming widely and inexpensively available on a variety of platforms from PC's to Unix workstations. In addition, integrated program development environments, large general and special purpose class libraries, both commercial and public domain, are becoming widely available. We are currently integrating these tools in our courses. Faculty expertise in object-oriented concepts and languages is now adequately developed in our department through a combination of research and teaching interests, and attendance in conferences such as the ACM Conference on Object-Oriented Programming, Systems and Languages, and Applications (OOPSLA)[17].

3 The Object-Oriented Approach and Software Reuse

In a special issue of IEEE Software on *Software Challenges*, Lewis and Oman [10] present the results of a focus group of fifteen eminent academic and industry professionals assembled to identify software challenges in the 1990's. Three of the most important trends identified by this group [10] are:

- Rise of the Graphical User Interface (GUI): the pervasiveness of graphical user interfaces, including speech and other ways to interact with a computer, is a clear sign that all software must address the user's need for ease of use.
- Development Environments: completely integrated development support environments are on the rise as a part of the reusable-components movement.
- Object-oriented programming: object-oriented design and programming are rapidly moving into practice. This 20-year old technology has finally come of age. Object-oriented features are being added to traditional languages like C, Pascal, and Fortran.

There is also growing evidence from industry that object-orientation has resulted in faster product development cycles, better and more reliable software, and improved responsiveness to market demands. One prominent software company that has made a shift exclusively to the object-oriented paradigm is Borland Inc. As a result, it has been the first to market with innovative new products, and is now the market leader in programming language compilers and databases in the PC segment. To quote Borland's chief executive, Philippe Kahn[8]:

The potential of object-oriented technology accounts for a wealth of industry support from not just Borland but from giants such as IBM, DEC, Hewlett-Packard, Apple, and Sun Microsystems, as well as software companies like The Whitewater Group and ParcPlace. Object-oriented technology is the focus of the Object Management Group, an active industry organization whose roster of member companies is growing rapidly.

In a landmark article[2], Brooks observes that building software will always be hard because the complexity of software construction is the essence of the process of building software, not an accidental property. Brooks further contends that no silver bullet is likely to be forthcoming for software engineering, even though a succession of technologies have promised to abstract away the complexity of software construction. The inherent properties that make up the irreducible essence of modern software construction are complexity, conformity, changeability, and invisibility of software.

It is worth noting that of the several modern technologies mentioned by Brooks as potentially useful in attacking the essence of software engineering, the most important is object-oriented programming and design. Other promising technologies such as artificial intelligence, expert systems, automatic programming, graphical programming, program verification, environments and tools, and modern workstations are viewed by Brooks as attacking only part of the problem of software development. Only object-oriented techniques used with component-based reuse methodologies is seen as the most promising approach. We list below some of the important techniques for attacking the essence of software engineering pointed out by Brooks and applied in the object-oriented context by us:

- **Buy versus build**: this can be viewed as constructing large software systems out of readily available, high quality software components. This principle has been recognized for some time, and limited reuse is a part of the software engineer's bag of tools. However, software reuse has been hitherto limited to procedure libraries, that are suitable for specific tasks such as mathematical subroutine libraries. More general application frameworks are just becoming available. If the kind of software industrial revolution envisaged by Cox[3] is to take place, more general and reliable software components must become widely available. We assert that this process is just beginning to take place, with the recent announcements of high quality class libraries such as the Borland Application Frameworks, the Microsoft Foundation Classes, and the AT&T Standard Components Library.
- **Requirements refinement and rapid prototyping**: the object-oriented approach facilitates this process by making possible development of software through generalization and specialization of class hierarchies, allowing creation of software modules through inheritance. This task is also aided by information hiding in the object-oriented paradigm.
- **Incremental development**: the principle here is to grow, not build software. This is the common currently prevalent paradigm in most other engineering disciplines, where specialists construct the pieces of a structure, and a general contractor, manufacturer, or assembler puts them together to create a useful end product. If we are to put the engineering into software engineering, incremental development is the right way achieve that objective.

– **Great designers**: students of software engineering can learn most effectively from following design practices of great designers. This is most prevalent in the field of architecture, where designs of famous architects are widely emulated, and improved upon by successive generation of architects, thereby building a cumulative tradition. This is also the focus in the architecture curriculum. Software construction is more close to architecture than traditional engineering disciplines. Perhaps, we can learn something from them. This point has been recently enforced through experimental studies reported by Linn in [11], where it is reported that students perform much better in programming tasks if they are given a case study approach, complete with experts solutions and a summary of the experts thinking process.

Given this background, we are of the opinion that it is time to start introducing component-based software engineering in the computer science curriculum, to redress some of the extant problems in the curriculum. The current time frame is particularly important since the "Computing Curricula '91" report has just been published, and educators across the country are re-evaluating their curriculum in the light of this report.

A few educational institutions have very recently begun to introduce object-oriented thinking and languages in their introductory courses[16, 12]. However, to the best of our knowledge no institution has done a major curriculum overhaul for the three course introductory sequence in a coordinated manner for introducing the object-oriented paradigm.

4 Goals

A recent report of the Computer Science and Technology Board (CSTB) of the National Research Council [1], titled *The National Challenge in Computer Science and Technology*, identifies some grand challenges in computer sciences that have an urgent priority for investigation and funding. The first grand challenge identified in the report (pages 33-34) is "Technology for large correct, software systems":

> The major component of the cost of computation is now the development and maintenance of software. Not only is the cost high, but so is the uncertainty; it is exceedingly difficult to know whether a piece of software is correct... This challenge calls for tools, methods, and predefined components that will allow development at reasonable, predictable cost for large software systems (i.e. systems that require a million lines of code) that are knowably correct when released and that admit of modification at a cost proportional to the magnitude of the change.

The CSTB report goes on to say that one of the important future directions of software progress is to find effective ways of improving the productivity of the software development process, e.g. through automation of the software development process, reuse of existing software components, or new type of software architectures.

The choice of the first language for teaching computer science is heavily influenced by personal preferences of decision makers, and in some cases seems to be almost a religious issue. Proponents of a particular language paradigm will in most cases have a strong conviction that they should teach their favorite language paradigm and their favorite language. It is, however, now time to reexamine some of their assumptions and reevaluate the choice of the programming paradigm to address some of the problems we mentioned in Section 2.

We prefer the object-oriented approach[2] (exemplified by C++, Smalltalk etc.) as an alternative to the procedural approach (exemplified by Pascal, C etc.), because we believe it is best suited to addressing the issues discussed in Section 3.

The goals and objectives of our revised curriculum are:

1. Introduce students to key software development concepts such as modularization, abstraction, information hiding, separation of concerns, and software reuse, early in the introductory curriculum to enable them to learn good software engineering concepts. This is accomplished through a combination of case study examples and programming assignments. The assignments vary in scope from those requiring from-scratch development to those that involve corrective maintenance and/or the augmentation of a basic system to one of enhanced capability.
2. Promote component-based software engineering to bring software engineering closer to traditional engineering disciplines.
3. Integrate software engineering concepts in the existing curriculum with appropriate modifications of the curriculum, rather than create a separate software engineering major.

5 Course Work and Laboratories

In this section, we summarize those aspects of the Temple CIS undergraduate curriculum that have changed as a result of the introduction of the object-oriented paradigm. The discussion is limited to the first three programming courses, and to three advanced courses, one each in Programming Languages, Compiler Design, and Software Design. The changes described have also impacted undergraduate independent study courses taken by our students.

We have chosen the object-oriented approach using the C++ language as the primary vehicle for case study preparation and engineering practice at Temple. Clearly there are other approaches (Scheme, Smalltalk, Ada...) which may work as well as the one we propose. Our choice is based upon a number of factors:

1. The great majority of Temple students will immediately join the workforce upon graduation. Aside from COBOL and fourth generation skills, C (and we presume soon, C++) and UNIX clearly have become established as preferred areas of skill and experience.
2. C alone, in our view, still presents too many practical drawbacks when used as a supporting language for the early instruction in the principles of abstraction, problem solving, and program design.

---

[2] There is a debate in the object-oriented camp about the benefits of pure object-oriented languages such as Smalltalk, over hybrid languages such as C++, and vice-versa. We are of the view that recent versions of these languages provide comparable capabilities, albeit with differing ontologies.

- C's return-value argument passing mechanism makes it difficult to introduce the fundamental concept of modularization at a sufficiently early stage in the first course.
- C provides no facility for the convenient implementation of abstract data types. In our experience, this detracts substantially from any efforts to imbue introductory students with an appreciation of data abstraction.
- There is still far too great an emphasis on programming with pointers. We are sensitive to the historical factors governing the use of C (and the writing of C texts). Nevertheless, we agree that pointers have their place in higher level languages and that their indiscriminate use outside this domain is to be strongly discouraged.
- Finally, C provides no facility for "format free" input and output, a feature which we prefer in the early stages of the first course.

We are aware of several universities using Ada in a first course. Recent Department of Defense pronouncements notwithstanding (see for eg. [20]), we find Ada to be a distant also ran as the language of preference in our upper division undergraduate courses and in local industry. While this may simply be indicative of an all-too-typical slow reaction of academia and non-DoD industry, it is nonetheless an important factor in our decision. Further, we have a clear preference for the C++ class facility (with templates) versus the Ada package for teaching students about building new types and developing type hierarchies using inheritance. The extensive library facilities and inexpensive development environments rapidly appearing on the C++ market further fuel the C++ focus. All the remaining difficulties with C++ notwithstanding, we are yet to be convinced that Ada is a practical alternative for our students at the introductory level.

The choice of C++ versus Smalltalk or Scheme is strictly a compromise driven by the practicalities of the market place and our upper division courses. This may seem inappropriate and unfortunate to some who feel that the focus should be upon the best tools for the job rather than other, more practical considerations. Given the rapid emergence of improved C++ programming environments, documentation,and support tools, we are convinced that on balance, for our purposes, C++ is more than adequate for the task.

In the first course, procedural abstraction is introduced in two stages. The first stage is presented early in the course, even before the rudiments of decision structures and loops. Midway through the course, data abstraction is covered. The advantages of being able to define new abstractions (new data types) are presented even before students are introduced to the fundamental structured data forms.

Software engineering concepts such as structured programming (top-down design, modularization, limited module coupling, cohesive modules, etc.), encapsulation, information hiding, object definition, and component generality and reuse are stressed throughout the course, especially in the second half. By this time, students have the tools necessary to study examples of the development of systems illustrating these concepts and to practice such development themselves. A subset of the C++ language is used for illustration and laboratory practice.

The second course builds on this foundation, focusing on concepts of software reuse through function and class libraries, and introducing the basic concepts of programming-in-the-large through integrated software development environments. The concept of type hierarchies (implemented using inheritance) is introduced. There is an increased emphasis on good engineering practice as opposed to the old focus on data structures and algorithms. The study, understanding and reuse of data structures (lists, trees, graphs etc.) and the operations on these structures is stressed, rather than the from-scratch development of these data structures and related algorithms. Some introductory material on algorithm analysis is also presented.

By the time students have reached the third of the three-course programming sequence, the concepts introduced in the first two courses can be put into practice in software maintenance, enhancement and development projects of moderate complexity. This work is carried further into more advanced courses, such as those on the comparative study of some classical software design techniques.

These courses are all project-oriented and therefore provide ample opportunity for the application of the engineering guidelines and concepts studied in the first two courses. Example projects include translators, loaders and interpreters for simple, pseudo assembly codes, compilers and interpreters for subsets of Pascal or C, applications using graphical user interfaces, and game simulations.

Issues of complexity and performance are discussed in the context of reusable software as well as traditional design of algorithms. The emphasis on student dexterity with algorithms is reduced in keeping with the philosophy that students should be taught about what exists, and when and how to use it, so that they need not spend hours in class and in the lab recreating these algorithms. The issue of what to take out of the present curriculum, in order to include the new proposed concepts, is one of the important questions that we have to address.

6 Innovative Instructional Methods

The object-oriented approach using C++ is a primary enabling factor for the innovative instructional approach being pursued. It provides the supporting tools necessary for the introduction of the fundamental software development concepts required for the effective practice of component-based software engineering. The advantages of this approach address important instructional issues raised in [13] as follows:

- *Study good examples of software systems*: This requires development of good case studies that incorporate experts design processes, in addition to a suggested solution using software components. The object-oriented approach also allows assignments that are extensions to case examples discussed by the instructor, since extending object-oriented solutions is typically easier than procedural solutions.
- *Learn more facts*: In the object-oriented approach we can interpret this principle to mean that students should have an opportunity to learn about existing class libraries, before they start on a solution, so that they do not reinvent what is available. In addition, the object-oriented approach allows modification of available software components, before their use in a solution. This is not possible with a procedural approach where function libraries are constrained to be used as given, without any modifications.
- *Modify and combine programs as well as create them*: The component based object-oriented approach provides maximum flexibility to achieve this princi-

ple. Existing components can be reused with slight modifications through the inheritance mechanism.

– *Provide good reference material:* Modern state-of-the-art workstations with integrated development environments are striving to provide on-line context sensitive help facilities, together with features such as program profilers that allow performance benchmarking, interactive source code debuggers that facilitate the debugging process, smart linkers and source code management tools that maintain interdependencies between modules, and class hierarchy browsers that allow programmers to browse class hierarchies providing them with an effective way of learning what is available, thereby facilitating component based software reuse.

A recent experimental study by Linn and Clancy [11] points out the value of using case studies in the instructional process. The case studies used by them incorporated a description of design experts problem solving process, to provide an insight into the design of the solution to the problem. Student comprehension was found to markedly increase when the case studies were supplemented with an outline of the decision taken by the expert designer and the reasoning for each decision. The important case study principles identified in this study are listed below, with an explanation of how our component based approach allows better application of the principles:

The Recycling Principle: This principle concerns reuse of ideas, specifically templates for design. Object-oriented languages such as C++ in the current AT&T version 3.0 support the concepts of templates to allow creation of parameterized software, resulting in more reusable software components.

The Multiple Representation Principle: Multiple representations of each design template should be explained to students for a better understanding. These include class hierarchies, CRC (Classes, Responsibilities, and Collaborators) diagrams, Booch diagrams, and pseudocode in the case of component based design.

The Alternative Paths Principle: Alternative design approaches should be explained. This is facilitated by object-oriented component based approaches, for example using the class libraries that come with Borland C++ 3.0, an application can be constructed with a class hierarchy of components that do not use the template mechanism, and another solution can be constructed using the template mechanism. This is feasible because Borland C++ 3.0 comes with two class libraries with equivalent functionality, one without templates, and the other with templates.

The Divide-and-Conquer Principle: Incremental design of the solution is possible using the component based approach, with function prototypes as stubs during the development process. Furthermore, reusable components are perhaps the best examples of the divide and conquer approach. A well designed class library is a working example that provides students with access to a large amount of well-designed code.

7 Observations on Early Experiences

Our efforts to date have been hampered by the lack of suitable computer systems support for student labs and projects, and by the lack of a uniform student population in our courses. Only a few of the Temple CIS faculty are using the C++

object-oriented development focus at the undergraduate level. As a result, even our advanced courses have a wide variation in the backgrounds of registrants, ranging from those who have had two semesters of experience with object-based concepts, to those who have had no exposure to these ideas. The implications of this variation are even more severe at the advanced level than in our introductory courses. A considerable investment in time and energy is required to bring those with no background up to speed. While many of our students are able to make up this deficiency with minimal additional lecture attention to these subjects, still a sizeable portion of class time is needed to provide an even playing field for as many students as possible.

We have found it much easier to get across the basic concepts of abstraction and good program development practice earlier in the curriculum than to have to do it later, after students have had two years of practice with the procedural paradigm alone (or worse, two years of practice in the any-which-way approach). However, instruction at the introductory level is not without its problems.

We introduce procedural abstraction and the modular composition of programs (using C++ functions) even before the rudiments of repetition and decision structures. Although the need for argument passing is much easier to motivate in C++ than in Pascal (we utter nary a word about global variables), students still have some difficulty understanding the argument passing mechanisms until late in the first course. The independence of function name and data space also creates problems in the early going.

Functions are revisited again immediately after the treatment of the fundamental decision and repetition structures; here the use of arguments for returning values is introduced. The concept of data abstraction and definition of abstract data types are presented even before structured data types are introduced. The C++ class is used to illustrate these ideas, which are then repeatedly illustrated through the treatment of structured data types, recursion, and an introduction to dynamic storage structures. Two or three small projects are initiated early in the semester and carried through to the end using maintenance tasks and problem specification enhancements designed to illustrate new concepts and their realization in C++. Program structure charts and textual descriptions of the attributes and operations associated with classes are the primary development tools currently used to support our approach. Graphical tools for describing classes and program structures appear to be around the corner. For maximum effectiveness, such tools must be easy to use and should generate C++ code templates from class and function definitions.

Except in rare cases, students clearly cannot fully appreciate the importance of what they are learning. They can repeat back what they read and are told, but their experiences do not scale up to large enough projects. Yet it is clear that even after two semesters, students who have rigorously practiced a more data/type oriented approach to problem solving are considerably far ahead of those who have not. Along with this practice comes a better understanding of some of the durable concepts in computer science:

- information hiding; effectively practiced using classes and private data and low-level functions;
- the notion of state — of tracking the history (simple as it may be to this point) of the transformations on program data stores;

- interface minimization, controlled use of global data, and maximally cohesive procedural components, all plainly visible as a result of the data-oriented approach using classes for implementation;
- reuse of software components, especially class and function templates, and the composition of new software systems from existing components;
- separation of concerns and information access limitations, again almost automatic by-products of the class implementation;
- an introduction to the notion of type hierarchies, realized through the inheritance mechanism of C++.
- the idea of language extensibility and the advantages of raising (through user defined types and type hierarchies) the level of the platform on which a new system may be built.

On the downside, students who have taken this path through the first two programming courses perhaps have little in the way of products of the strictly procedural oriented approach to which to compare their own results. Yet this problem is easily remedied in the second course even with just a single, small system "restructuring" exercise (an exercise we do not recommend in a first course).

The benefits, however, are significant. By the time students reach advanced courses, either in programming techniques, compiler design, data bases, the comparative study of programming languages, operating systems, networking, real-time systems, graphics and image processing, or the comparative study of software design techniques (all offered at Temple), they are prepared to apply what they have learned to projects of at least some minimal complexity (simple compilers, assemblers, loaders, and interpreters, and object-based graphics, image processing, operating systems and networking support systems). Each such project provides not only insights into the course material at hand, but also further experience with the object-oriented paradigm and the more advanced aspects of the C++ language.

Our experiences in initially developing the data/type-based approach at the advanced (junior or senior) level are admittedly limited, but nonetheless interesting. Among other things, we have found a surprising amount of student confusion regarding the concepts of types, attributes, and objects. This may in part be due to our own pedagogic approach (or to our inability to adequately explain this approach).

We ask students to first analyze the problem specification and problem domain environment to identify those objects that are relevant to the required software. We then encourage them to model these objects by first abstracting out their essential features and looking for commonalities among the objects. This provides a first pass view of the classes (types) they may want to define and their attributes. Perhaps some type hierarchy relations may begin to emerge at this point as well.

Once this view has been documented, a procedural-oriented analysis of the required system functionality is performed. It is expected that additional data types may emerge from this analysis and that numerous changes will be made to the initial abstract data types defined in the first stage. A clearer picture of inheritance-based type hierarchies should also emerge at this stage.

Students with a limited background with data/type based concepts find it extremely difficult to separate procedural and data-oriented concepts when focusing on abstract views of new types and type hierarchies. Some seemingly obvious types are omitted in their analysis. In addition, we often see early designs suggesting highly innovative type hierarchies, possibly based upon procedural views or entity relationships having nothing to do with inheritance. These problems may well be due to our own instructional failures rather than student backgrounds. Yet those of our students who have had a two semester introduction to the data/type focus of program design do not seem to be similarly afflicted. Perhaps we have moved too fast with the others, or inadvertently assumed they knew as much as the group that suffered with our biases for two previous semesters.

8 Conclusion

Admittedly, we have more questions than answers at this point. Nonetheless, we are convinced that more of the foundational concepts of good software development practices can be introduced and illustrated in the first two courses than we had previously thought. We are also convinced that this transition does not come easily. Even those of us who believe it is important have struggled with the new curriculum development. Old methods die hard, especially when the software tools available to support the new approaches are either not sufficiently mature or are far to complex (from a user interface point of view) to be useful in an introductory setting. Here, an analogy to the industrial revolution may be appropriate [3]. It took over a hundred years for industries to make the transition to standardized components and manufacturing assemblies. The software industrial revolution is being compressed into a much smaller time frame, with a large impetus from the software industry. We must do our part in academia to foster the kind of thinking in students that facilitates component based software engineering in the coming years. We are pedalling as fast as we can and look forward to more rapid progress in the coming year.

9 Acknowledgments

We are appreciative of the opportunities provided and the documents produced by the Software Engineering Institute. The seemingly infinite people and written material resources provided during this year have been instrumental in the formulation of the ideas we have pursued. One of us has had the added benefit of spending a year at SEI working under the guidance of Mary Shaw. We have done our best to accurately represent the concepts presented through these resources. Any misconceptions are of course, entirely our own. As noted in this paper, all forms of documentation, from research reports to curriculum modules have been particularly useful. Mostly, however, the learning environment and patience with "new kids on the block" is appreciated.

References

1. Computer Science Technology Board. *The National Challenge in Computer Science and Technology*. National Academy Press, Washington, D.C., 1988.
2. F.P. Brooks. No silver bullet: Essence and accidents of software engineering. *IEEE Computer*, pages 10–19, April 1987.

3. B.J. Cox. Planning the software industrial revolution. *IEEE Software*, 7(6):25–33, Nov. 1990.

4. P.J. Denning, D.E. Comer, D. Gries, M.C. Mulder, A.B. Tucker, A.J. Turner, and P.R. Young. Computing as a discipline. *Communications of ACM*, 32(1):9–23, Jan. 1989.

5. ACM/IEEE-CS Joint Curriculum Task force. *Computing Curricula 91*. ACM Press and IEEE-CS Press, Feb. 1991.

6. P.A. Freeman. Separate SE program not the best solution. *Computing Research News*, Jan 1992.

7. F.L. Friedman. A separate undergraduate software engineering curriculum considered harmful. In *Proceedings of the 3rd SEI Conference on Software Engineering Education*, 1989.

8. P. Kahn. Guiding software craftsmanship. *Object magazine*, 1(2):12–14, July/Aug 1991.

9. S.M. Kaplan and R.E. Johnson. On language choice for the introductory computer science course. In *Information Processing (Proceedings of the IFIP)*, pages 563–568, 1989.

10. T.G. Lewis and P. Oman. The challenge of software development. *IEEE Software*, 7(6):9–12, Nov. 1990.

11. M.C. Linn and M.J. Clancy. The case for case studies of programming problems. *Communications of ACM*, 35(3):121–132, March 1992.

12. R.J. Reid. Object-oriented programming in C++. *ACM SIGCSE Bulletin*, 23(2):9–14, June 1991.

13. M. Shaw. Informatics for a new century: Computing education for the 1990s and beyond. Tech Report # CMU/SEI-90-TR-15, Software Engineering Institute, Carnegie-Mellon University, July 1990.

14. M. Shaw. Prospects for an engineering displine of software. *IEEE Software*, 7(6):15–24, Nov. 1990.

15. M. Shaw. We can improve the way we teach CS students. *Computing Research News*, Jan 1992.

16. S. Skublics and P. White. Teaching Smalltalk as a first programming language. *ACM SIGCSE Bulletin*, 23(1):231–234, March 1991.

17. R. Tewari. Object allocation in distributed applications. In *Workshop on Objects in Large Distributed Applications, ACM OOPSLA '91*, October 1991.

18. A.B. Tucker. Computing curricula 1991. *Communications of ACM*, 34(6):70–84, June. 1991.

19. A. Joe Turner. Introduction to the joint curriculum task force report. *Communications of ACM*, 34(6):69–70, June. 1991.

20. W.A. Wulf. SE programs won't solve our problems. *Computing Research News*, Nov 1991.

Session 9:

Product and Practice Models for the Engineering of Software

Moderator: Keith R. Pierce, University of Minnesota, Duluth

Putting the *Engineering* into Software Engineering
Software Architectures Engineering Project:
Richard S. D'Ippolito, Kenneth J. Lee, Charles P. Plinta,
Jeffrey A. Stewart, Software Engineering Institute and
Paul D. Bailor, Thomas C. Hartrum, Air Force Institute
of Technology

Educating Model-Based Software Engineers
Paul D. Bailor and Thomas C. Hartrum, Air Force
Institute of Technology

Putting the *Engineering* into Software Engineering
A Tutorial for the Sixth SEI Conference on Software Engineering Education

Software Architectures Engineering Project
Software Engineering Institute
Carnegie Mellon University
Pittsburgh, Pennsylvania 15213

Richard S. D'Ippolito, P.E., Ph.D.
Senior Member of the Technical Staff
(412) - 268 - 6752
Email: rsd@sei.cmu.edu

Kenneth J. Lee, Ph.D.
Member of the Technical Staff
(412) - 268 - 7702
Email: kl@sei.cmu.edu

Charles P. Plinta
Member of the Technical Staff
(412) - 268 - 7771
Email: cpp@sei.cmu.edu

Jeffrey A. Stewart
Member of the Technical Staff
(412) - 268 - 7743
Email: jjs@sei.cmu.edu

Air Force Institute of Technology
AFIT/ENG
WPAFB, OH 45433-6583

Major Paul D. Bailor, Ph.D.
Assistant Professor of Computer Systems
(513) - 255-3708
pbailor@blackbird.afit.af.mil

Thomas C. Hartrum, Ph.D.
Associate Professor, Department of Electrical and Computer Engineering
(513)-255-3708
hartrum@afit.ab.arpa

The Software Architectures Engineering (SAE) Project at the Software Engineering Institute (SEI) has observed that the essential element of an engineering discipline is the use of models. Models are reusable, adaptable, engineering

This work is sponsored by the U.S. Department of Defense.

assets that are patterns expressed in their most general, scalable form. The existence of proven models in a technology base provides economic and risk-avoidance incentives for engineers to constrain their design activities by expressing solutions in terms of existing models.

The traditional engineer's viewpoint, as contrasted with the prevalent software developer's viewpoint, is that the primary goal is to cast all new work as a slight variation of prior work. Driven by a culture that rewards the creation of design compositions whose qualities are predictable by formal analysis *before* they are implemented and that heavily penalizes the lack of first-time success, the engineer places primary importance on *problem setting* and not on *problem solving*. This problem setting activity is the dogged insistence of seeing the new in terms of fragments of old paradigms, and appears at first to the non-engineer to be a self-imposed restraint on artistic creativity. There *is* creativity in engineering, but it is not the sort that allows experimental structures to be tested in public buildings and machines. The creativity is in seeing new uses for old things and in synthesizing new arrangements of them to satisfy human needs. These constraints are what ensure routine designs that are less complex, more maintainable, more predictable in both cost and behavior, and more able to ensure the public safety.

Engineered products are composed from product models and practice models. Product models capture patterns from certain disciplines and become part of the delivered product. *Domain product models* capture the domain knowledge in a specific field of engineering expertise (e.g., control systems, signal processing). *Composition product models* capture patterns of control and information flow necessary to run the domain models on a computer. Thus, composition models specify the manner in which domain models are controlled and connected and provide a mechanism for implementing domain models. Practice models guide the selection and use of product models during application development.

What can we say about software? Few software engineers are educated in the disciplined approach to problem setting that other engineers are, and when attempts are made to do this education, the lack of a mature body of technology upon which to base the practice greatly hampers the effort.

In the tutorial "Putting the *Engineering* into Software Engineering," SAE project members will discuss the role of models in traditional engineering disciplines, relate that to the engineering of software, and present examples that include the following models:

- The Object-Connection-Update (OCU) model:
  - a composition product model providing a control and connection framework for composing applications from domain models.
- Domain product models from the control systems domain.
- Model-Based Software Development (MBSD):
  - a practice model guiding development using product models.

Educating Model-Based Software Engineers

Paul D. Bailor and Thomas C. Hartrum

Department of Electrical and Computer Engineering
Air Force Institute of Technology
Wright-Patterson Air Force Base, Ohio 45433
pbailor@afit.af.mil
(513) 255-3708

1 Introduction

Almost all software engineering courses are based on the notion of software system construction as an incremental model building process. However, the model building methodologies and corresponding language representations being taught and used in practice are largely informal. Therefore, success at using these models depends strongly on the creative ability of skilled individuals. This makes these methods difficult to teach, automate, and analyze intermediate results. Also, the software solutions lack the formal and rigorous engineering analysis performed as a part of traditional engineering design. The informal model building methodologies also suffer from another problem — they use a top-down approach to problem decomposition. Essentially, each software system to be built is viewed as a new problem to be solved rather than a problem that should be cast as a variation of prior work. In other words, the engineering concept of problem setting based on existing, well studied solutions is not applied. Instead, a brute force problem solving effort is applied. The top-down approaches can certainly generate effective and efficient software solutions; however, they are severely lacking from a reusability standpoint because solutions to similar systems tend to be unique. This lack of an engineering approach and foundation combined with limited levels of reusability makes for poor quality software systems that are very difficult to maintain.

Solving these deficiencies requires changes to both the model building and education processes. First, the model building process must change its focus to one that formally captures the domain knowledge in a specific field of engineering and is also able to recognize similarity between domain models — even those that appear to be dissimilar in nature. Second, the notion of decomposition must be replaced by that of composition; therefore,

Finally, the SAE project members will discuss our experiences in transitioning the OCU model and MBSD approach to organizations and the resulting implications on software engineering education curricula.[1]

For the last part of the tutorial, Dr. Paul Bailor and Dr. Thomas Hartrum with the Air Force Institute of Technology (AFIT) will present how key elements of the OCU product model and the MBSD practice model have been incorporated into their software engineering curriculum. From an educational perspective, software engineering has typically been taught (and practiced) as an incremental model building process using a top-down approach to problem decomposition. While this approach generates effective and efficient software solutions, it is severely lacking from a reusability and maintainability standpoint. Additionally, solutions to similar systems tend to be unique, and the solutions lack the formal and rigorous engineering analysis performed as a part of traditional engineering design.

Solving these deficiencies requires changes to both the model building and education process. First, the model building process must change its focus to one that formally captures the domain knowledge in a specific field of engineering and is also able to recognize similarity between domain models – even those that appear to be dissimilar in nature. Second, the notion of decomposition must be replaced by that of composition; therefore, a composition model is required that provides the means to synthesize and analyze software systems that implement domain models. Third, the "mindsets" of software engineers must be changed to emphasize routine rather than unprecedented design, i.e., problem setting not problem solving, and to emphasize composition rather than decomposition. The MBSD practice model, as defined and described by the SAE project, provides the necessary basis for changing the model building process. However, Software Engineering education must take the lead in developing new mindsets for software engineers.

At AFIT, the software engineering curriculum has recently been changed to incorporate many of the aspects required to develop this new mindset. In the accompanying paper "Educating Model-Based Software Engineers," the role of MBSD in software engineering education is described as well as how the concepts of domain and composition product models can be incorporated into courses on software analysis and design, software generation and maintenance, and formal methods. As a part of the tutorial, appropriate classroom and project examples will be presented.[2]

A brief paper by Dr. Bailor and Dr. Hartrum follows this abstract.

---

[1] The slides presented for this part of the tutorial are available from the Software Architectures Engineering Project at the SEI. Contact Ken Lee for more information.

[2] The slides presented for this part of the tutorial are available from the Department of Electrical and Computer Engineering at the AFIT. Contact Major Paul Bailor for more information.

a composition model is required that provides the means to synthesize and analyze software systems that implement domain models. Third, the "mindsets" of software engineers must be changed to emphasize routine rather than unprecedented design, i.e., problem setting *not* problem solving, and to emphasize composition rather than decomposition.

Research and development in the area commonly referred to as "formal methods" is attempting to overcome the problems associated with the model building process. Example formal methods include domain analysis, software architectures engineering, formal specification, program transformation/synthesis, and formal verification. In general, formal methods research is attempting to develop the required theoretical and engineering foundations necessary for a formal model building, model analysis, and model transformation capability. Currently, much of the formal methods work has to be considered of academic or laboratory strength; however, more and more research and industrial success stories are being published every year. Some good examples are:

- The Model-Based Software Development (MBSD) practice model, as defined and described by the Software Architectures Engineering (SAE) project at the Software Engineering Institute (SEI). MBSD provides the necessary basis for changing the model building process [1]. The domain and composition product models of MBSD have been successfully applied to several command and control and embedded software systems [1].

- The Software Refinery^{TM} environment that is commercially available and specifically targeted at the support of formal methods [2].

- The successful development of several prototype environments based on formal methods. Two recent examples are the Automatic Programming Technologies for Avionics Systems (APTAS) project [3] and the Knowledge-Based Software Assistant (KBSA) Concept Demonstration project [4, 5].

Software engineering education must take the lead in developing new mindsets for software engineers, and many schools have incorporated formal methods into their software engineering curriculum [6]. At the Air Force Institute of Technology (AFIT), we have been teaching a course entitled "Formal-Based Methods in Software Engineering" for three years, and in this course we have incorporated the use of the Software Refinery environment. Additionally, our graduate software engineering curriculum was modified in 1991 to incorporate elements of MBSD, and we have made additional refinements this year to incorporate more of MBSD. This paper and corresponding tutorial presentation discuss how the principles of MBSD have been incorporated into our software analysis and design, software generation and maintenance, and formal-based methods courses.

In the next section, we describe the role of MBSD in software engineering education from two perspectives. The first perspective involves the development of new "mindsets" for software engineers, and the second involves a "big picture" perspective of system design and engineering that corresponds with the mindset. Sections 3, 4, and 5 address how MBSD fits into the course content of our software analysis and design, software generation and maintenance, and formal-based methods courses, respectively. Section 6 is a summary of our success at incorporating MBSD into our curriculum.

2 Role of MBSD in Software Engineering Education

MBSD provides a framework in which to achieve many of the visions of software engineering as an engineering discipline. In particular, the ability to leverage off of a well engineered technology base of domain product models and corresponding composition product models realizes the vision of large scale reuse based on well engineered solutions. However, before this can happen, the mindsets of software engineers must be changed. Most importantly, software engineering students must be educated in the role of the technology base in terms of its use and development. As stated in the introduction, the traditional approach focuses more on developing a new solution rather than casting the solution in terms of existing and well engineered solutions expressed as domain product models. Thus, a software engineer must first learn to *use* the domain models contained in the technology base as a basis for composing the required solution. In the event the technology base does not contain the required domain model, a software engineer must be educated in the process of constructing and analyzing domain models.

For the use and development of technology bases to be effective, software engineering students must understand the "big picture" perspective of MBSD's role in system engineering and design. In other words, what key practices must a software engineer implement in terms of the software product engineering key process area and how does this fit into an overall software process model. At AFIT we have taken the following approach at painting this big picture. First, the student must learn to analyze a set of system requirements in such a way that the software solution is specified in the vocabulary of the problem space. One way to do this is through an object-oriented approach. Object-oriented approaches are meant to naturally model problem spaces using the commonly accepted vocabulary for that space. The vocabulary is formalized in terms of object classes consisting of attributes for maintaining state and operations for updating that state. A message passing model of computation is then used to compose a solution of interacting objects. The benefit of this approach is two fold. First, object-oriented analysis focuses on the vocabulary of the problem space. Thus, two independent software engineers now stand a reasonable chance of identifying the same set of objects and insight is given as to where to look in the technology base for the required domain models. Second, the concept of an object hierarchy in the form of ISA relationships, Is-Composed-Of (ICO) relationships, and the message passing model of computation reinforce the idea of system composition versus system decomposition.

However, an object oriented approach by itself is not the "silver bullet" some may portray it to be. While it reinforces the idea of composition, there is no explicit strategy for composition. Additionally, there is no explicit notion that the objects should become a set of well engineered building blocks, i.e., domain product models, used as a basis for system composition. While the object-oriented approach has provided a necessary step in the right direction, it is *not sufficient* for obtaining large-scale reusability through composition [1, 7]. The next paragraph examines MBSD in terms of its ability to provide the sufficient conditions.

MBSD is an object-oriented approach built upon an explicit composition model called the Object-Connection-Update (OCU) model [1, 8]. Because MBSD has the OCU model, it fills a void in terms of developing a big picture perspective for system engineering and design. Assuming an effective domain modeling effort using an object-oriented approach has been performed, the OCU model readily allows for the composition of a software system for some application area that may well cross several domains. Thus, the concepts of domain product models and composition product models directly support the software engineering vision of large-scale reusability based on existing, well engineered solutions. In other words, MBSD provides the necessary and sufficient conditions for obtaining large-scale reusability!

Unfortunately, domain modeling is not currently a well defined field, which implies the technology base needed to successfully implement MBSD is still very immature. However, domain analysis and domain modeling is receiving increased emphasis, and progress is being made as evidenced in the proceedings of Domain Analysis Workshops [9], the proceedings of the Knowledge-Based Software Engineering Conference [10], and research efforts such as DARPA's Domain-Specific Software Architectures (DSSA) project [11]. In general, formal-based methods utilizing formal specification and design languages are providing the necessary tools, languages, and environments for the proper representation of domain product models. Therefore, not only must a software engineering student learn about object-oriented approaches and composition models such as OCU, a background in formal methods is also required. Formal-based methods must be employed in the development and validation of the domain product models used as the basis for system composition; otherwise, the required engineering foundation and engineering analysis capabilities will not be present.

In the next three sections, we describe how the fundamental concepts of MBSD, domain and composition product models, are incorporated into courses on software analysis and design, software generation and maintenance, and formal-based methods[1].

3 MBSD and Software Analysis and Design

We offer two courses in software analysis and design. The first course CSCE 593, Software Analysis and Design I, concentrates on classical structured analysis methods. Even though these methods have many well known shortcomings, this course is still important. A large number of existing software systems were developed using these methods, and software systems are still being developed using these methods. Additionally, the data flow, entity-relationship, and state-transition modeling tools used by classical structured analysis are also used by many of the object-oriented approaches, just in a different order.

The second course CSCE 594, Software Analysis and Design II, concentrates on object-oriented methods, system engineering methods, and an introduction to formal-based specification and design. The first four to five weeks are spent on object-oriented analysis and design based on the book *Object-Oriented Modeling and Design* by Rumbaugh and others [12]. This is immediately followed by the concepts of domain analysis and software architectures engineering. The objective is to show the students how these

---

[1]Note that for brevity's sake, explicit classroom and project examples are not contained in this paper but will be presented at the tutorial.

concepts serve as a framework for analysis and design. In particular, the concepts clearly demonstrate the *need* to evaluate problem domains for existing engineering solutions that can be codified and used as building blocks for constructing application systems. The concepts of formal specification and design are covered last; the objective is to show students how object definitions can be formalized using formal specification languages, thereby building formal domain models. The important aspect here is that the formalization allows for formal engineering analysis. Thus, the software engineer now has tools similar to other engineering disciplines for formally analyzing what they are building at the very earliest stages of development.

4 MBSD and Software Generation and Maintenance

In CSCE 595, Software Generation and Maintenance, the generation project is based on an object-oriented system design provided to the students that is to be implemented in Ada. Initially, an object architecture as opposed to a software architecture is provided. Additionally, a small number of well defined modeling primitives are provided to the students. The students are then assembled into a representative software development group that contains elements of project management, configuration management, quality assurance, and product engineering. The objective of this course is to expose the students to software process model issues and to illustrate the role of software product engineering practices within a process model. As the students progress with this project, the MBSD concepts are reinforced, and the students begin to realize the benefits of model-based software engineering in terms of building systems based on reusable, adaptable, engineering assets. Additionally, the distinction between an object architecture and a software architecture becomes clear. The last part of the course concentrates on software product analysis and gives students the opportunity to reflect on the software product they have generated.

5 MBSD and Formal-Based Methods

Domain and composition product models are also covered in the course CSCE 793, Formal-Based Methods in Software Engineering. One of the objectives of this course is to study the field of domain analysis in more depth than in CSCE 594, and to give the students experience with developing formal specifications. As a part of this, the principles upon which the APTAS system is built are presented and discussed [3]. The APTAS system is built on a formal knowledge base containing domain models for the avionics system domain and a corresponding composition model. Course projects are than assigned to construct and prototype small domain models using the Software Refinery environment to formally specify and analyze model state space and behavior. Given that the domain models then represent well engineered and highly reusable assets, ways in which to formally develop composition models such as OCU are explored along with the ideas of program transformation systems.

6 Summary and Conclusions

We have taught the concepts of domain and composition product models inherent in the MBSD approach to one group of graduate software engineering students whose program started in July 1991. Even though our courses and projects are still evolving, the benefits of covering MBSD as defined by the SAE project have been clearly visible, especially in the area of developing new "mindsets" on how software engineering can live up to its engineering name! Most importantly, it helps to instill in students the need to strive for similarity and reuse of well-engineered solutions rather than uniqueness. Interestingly, and probably not too surprisingly, we have found that students whose undergraduate background is computer engineering rather than computer science are much more comfortable with MBSD. Because of their engineering background work, they have already developed a mindset attuned to problem setting versus problem solving.

References

[1] K. J. Lee *et al.*, "Model-Based Software Development (Draft)," Special Report CMU/SEI-92-SR-00, Software Engineering Institute, Carnegie Mellon University, Pittsburgh, Pennsylvania, December 30 1991.

[2] R. Systems, "Refine User's Guide." Reasoning Systems, Inc., 1990.

[3] P. S. Jensen and L. Ogata, "Final Report for Automatic Programming Technologies for Avionics Software (APTAS)," Technical Report

LMSC-P000001, Lockheed Software Technology Center, Palo Alto, California, July 1991.

[4] C. Green *et al.*, "Report on a Knowledge-Based Software Assistant," Technical Report RADC-TR-83-195, Rome Air Development Center, Griffis Air Force Base, New York, August 1983.

[5] A. Consulting, "Availability of KBSA Concept Demo." Electronic mail message on kbse-requestcs.rpi.edu, February 1992.

[6] S. E. C. Project, "Software Engineering Education Directory," Technical Report CMU/SEI-91-TR-9, Software Engineering Institute, Carnegie Mellon University, Pittsburgh, Pennsylvania, May 1991.

[7] D. Batory and S. O'Malley, "The Design and Implementation of Hierarchical Software Systems With Reusable Components," Technical Report TR-91-22, Department of Computer Sciences, University of Texas at Austin, Austin, Texas, January 1992.

[8] R. D'Ippolito and K. Lee, "Modeling Software Systems by Domains," in *AAAI-92 Workshop on Automating Software Design*, pp. In–Press, California: AAAI, 1992.

[9] Rubén Prieto-Díaz and Guillermo Arango, *Domain Analysis and Software Systems Modeling*. IEEE Computer Society Press, 1991.

[10] R. Laboratories, "6th Annual Knowledge-Based Software Engineering Conference," Conference Proceedings, United States Air Force Rome Laboratories, Griffis Air Force Base, New York, September 1991.

[11] DARPA, "Domain-Specific Software Architecture — Kickoff Workshop," Workshop Slides and Presentations, Software Engineering Institute, Carnegie Mellon University, Pittsburgh, Pennsylvania, July 1991.

[12] J. Rumbaugh *et al.*, *Object-Oriented Modeling and Design*. Prentice Hall, 1991.

Session 10:

Panel Discussion
Moderator: Linda Hutz Pesante, Software Engineering Institute

Continuing Education and Training for Software Process Improvement
Panel Moderator: A. Winsor Brown, McDonnell Douglas Space Systems Company

Position Papers:

Continuing Education and Training for Software Process Improvement
A. Winsor Brown, McDonnell Douglas Space Systems Company

Software Process Training: A Formal and Informal Approach at McDonnell Douglas Electronic Systems Company
Karen L. Powel, McDonnell Douglas Electronic Systems Company

Continuing Education and Training for Software Process Improvement

The Software Engineering Institute's (SEI) software engineering capability assessment method and the SEI's Capability Maturity Model call specifically for training in certain areas. Training and education are a necessary component in any software process improvement activity. Continuing education and training developed specifically to address the SEI's contractor capability assessment requirements and the software process improvements it promotes will be presented.

The panel participants will describe their organizations training program, indicating how it maps onto the current assessment questionnaire and the capability maturity model. The discussion which follows these presentations will provide an opportunity to share some of the lessons learned in the development and operation of their training programs.

Panel Participants

A. Winsor Brown
Software Engineering & Management Technology
McDonnell Douglas Space Systems Company

Rick Hefner
Software Engineering Process Group
TRW System Development Division

Jane Moon
Software Engineering Process Group
Hughes Aircraft Company, Command & Control Systems Division

Karen Powel
Software Engineering Technology
McDonnell Douglas Electronic Systems Company

Continuing Education and Training for Software Process Improvement

A. Winsor Brown
Software Engineering & Management Technology
McDonnell Douglas Space Systems Company

The Software Engineering Institute's (SEI) software engineering capability assessment method and the SEI's Capability Maturity Model call specifically for training in certain areas. Training and education are a necessary component in any software process improvement activity. Continuing education and training developed specifically to address the SEI's contractor capability assessment requirements and the software process improvements it promotes will be presented.

The panel participants will describe their organizations training program, indicating how it maps onto the current assessment questionnaire and the capability maturity model. The discussion which follows these presentations will provide an opportunity to share some of the lessons learned in the development and operation of their training programs.

1   Introduction

In 1987 the SEI introduced a structured assessment approach to augment the current USAF/DoD (Department of Defense) contractor evaluation methods. This was documented in an assessment guide "A Method for Assessing the Software Engineering Capability of Contractors", CMU/SEI-87-TR-23. The assessment methodology was based on the principal that prior experience is a good predictor of future performance. The assessment process was focussed on defining and clarifying the positive attributes of good software engineering practices. The Software Process Assessment (SPA) method is basically a set of questions based on the premises that the software engineering process is of prime importance to the quality of a software product; that the process is manageable, measurable and improvable; and that the products of interest are developed under contracts invoking a tailored DoD-STD-2167/A, Defense Systems Software Development. The questions are administered by a trained team to an entire organization.

A more recent technical report, "Capability Maturity Model for Software", CMU/SEI-91-TR-24, provides an overview of the Capability Maturity Model (CMM) and describes the process maturity framework. Coupled with a companion technical report, "Key Practices of the Capability Maturity Model", CMU/SEI-91-TR-25, which is intended to help software organizations use the CMM, they provide a more comprehensive framework for improving the maturity of software processes.

As a result of an assessment, an organization can be rated as being in one of five progressively higher Process Maturity Levels:

1. *Initial* , sometimes called *ad hoc* or *chaotic*, which is characterized as unpredictable and poorly controlled.
2. *Repeatable* , also called *intuitive*, in which previously mastered tasks can be repeated.
3. *Defined*, also called *qualitative*, in which the process is documented and reasonably well understood.
4. *Managed*, also called *Quantitative*, in which the software engineering process as a whole is measured and controlled.
5. *Optimizing*, where the focus is on process improvement.

These ratings have become part of the DoD acquisition process through a Software Capability Evaluation (SCE) based on the same set of questions but administered by a government agency. In the source selection process, organizational maturity, as reflected in the findings of an SCE, is a risk factor in expected performance of a contractor. In the case of on going programs, especially those in which periodic evaluations and activities for process improvement are part of the contract, the ratings and/or activities for improvement, including software engineering related training and continuing education, might be a factor in contract renewal/continuation, and award or fee negotiations. In either case, both the companies in the DoD software business which are only just starting to pay considerable attention to the improvement processes necessary to increase ratings, and those companies which have been using SPAs and SCEs as intended, benefit considerably from the findings and perceived weaknesses rather than focusing on the ratings.

2 SEI's Capability Maturity Model

2.1 Capability Maturity Model Structure

The Capability Maturity Model Structure's operational definition is depicted in Figure 3.1 of "Capability Maturity Model for Software", CMU/SEI-91-TR-24,. It can be represented textually in a set of entity/relationship type statements:

1. CMM contains Maturity Level(s) which
   1. Indicate Process Capability, and
   2. Contain Key Process Areas (KPA) which
      1. Achieve Goals, and
      2. Contain Key Practices which
         1. Describe Implementation or Institutionalization Activities, and
         2. Specify [things beyond the CMM]
2. Beyond the CMM, as specified above, is a
      1. Key Indicator which is a
         1. Candidate for Questions

The connection between Questions and Goals requires traveling up a chain of relationships and back down from Key Process Areas. The questions expected from the CMM have not yet been made available.

2.2   Capability Maturity Model Training KPA

The Training Program is identified as a Level 3 (Defined) Key Process Area. "Training program involves identifying the training needs of the organization, the projects, and the individuals and developing and procuring training courses to address these needs. The training program ensures that training needed to perform each of the organization's job functions is appropriate and is not circumvented inappropriately." It has three goals

1. The staff and managers have the skills and knowledge to perform their jobs.
2. The staff and managers effectively use, or are prepared to use, the capabilities and features of the existing and planned work environment.
3. The staff and managers are provided with opportunities to improve their professional skills.

There are eight activities performed under this key process area:

1. Each project develops and maintains a training plan specifying its training needs.
2. The organization's training plan is developed and revised periodically.
3. The organization's training plan is developed and revised periodically according to a documented procedure.
4. A waiver procedure for required training is established and used to independently determine whether an individual possesses the knowledge and skill covered in the training course.
5. Where appropriate, training courses are developed, maintained, and conducted at the project level.
6. Training courses at the organization level are developed and maintained according to organization standards.
7. Where appropriate, training sessions for individuals are tied to their job responsibilities so that on-the-job activities or other outside experiences will reinforce the training with a reasonable time after the course.
8. Records of training are maintained and used by management.

3   SEI Software Process Assessment (SPA)

The SPA approach is documented in "A Method for Assessing the Software Engineering Capability of Contractors", CMU/SEI-87-TR-23. It contains questions grouped under such diverse headings as "Technology Management" and "Process Metrics". Subsection 1.2 is titled "Resources, Personnel, and Training". Aside from one question concerning "private computer supported workstation/terminal", all the rest are directly related to training.

3.1   Training Related Questions from SPA Questionnaire

In the table below are the four training related questions from Subsection 1.2. The second column indicates the level at which this question must be addressed. A star next to a question number indicates that a favorable response to the question is critical to achieving that level since only one starred question at a given level can be missed.

1.2.2 Is there a required training program for all newly appointed development managers designed to familiarize them with software project management?	2
1.2.3* Is there a required software engineering training program for software developers?	3
1.2.4 Is there a required software engineering training program for first-line supervisors of software development?	3
1.2.5* Is a formal training program required for design and code *review leaders*?	3

3.2   Promoted Process Improvements

Questions 1.2.2 and 1.2.4 are obviously aimed at the software project management aspects of software engineering, either through focussing on a given audience or explicitly stating the objective of the training program.   Question 1.2.3, by focussing on 'software engineering', would seem to be addressing the processes involved.   Question 1.2.5 is interpreted by many to be hinting at formal software inspections (also known as Fagan's Inspections) since that is the only type of technical review that has always required trained leaders.   In any case, the reviews are expected to produce information, at the least 'action items', that can be used in process improvement activities.

4 The Role of Training and Education in Software Engineering Process Improvement

The "Software Engineering Process Group Guide", CMU/SEI-90-TR-24, identifies training and education as a powerful instrument of change. All improvement activities imply change. Education, referring to the process of providing information especially concepts and theory, is one of the best initiators of the *unfreezing* process for those who will participate in a change, and is a prerequisite to implementing actual change. *Unfreezing* is the first stage of the three step change process which also includes *transition* and *refreezing*. Training, referring to providing skills in the use of a technology or procedure, is the way to provide new skills to those who will use a new technology which might be part of a specific improvement activity.

Training and education are an integral part of both the SCE and the CMM. They are a part of the measurements of a DoD contractor's software engineering capability, and efforts to improve it. A Software Engineering Process Group (SEPG) is one of the recommended mechanisms to be used by an organization for improvement of its software engineering capability. One of the primary activities that an SEPG must plan and provide for is training and education. An SEPG must identify and communicate the need for training and education early in the planning process for improvements. It also should initiate training-related activities like preparing course descriptions and selecting vendors or developing course materials. The training and education itself should be scheduled by the SEPG so the people to acquire the necessary skills and information in a timely fashion.

5 Training Program Highlights

5.1 Hughes Aircraft Company, Command & Control Systems Division

The software engineering training program at the Hughes, Fullerton, facility provides a full spectrum of courses ranging from software engineering process and languages to software project management. These company-developed courses are designed to instill a software engineering "culture" in the organization, so that personnel can move from project to project carrying a common background and approach.

Courses focus on specific language and coding skills, tools, configuration management, the software development cycle and associated standards, phase-related activities such as integration and testing, software quality assurance, and management. Additional courses, oriented toward senior personnel, address design approaches, real time analysis, software cost and schedule estimation, and proposal development.

Specific courses that provide review team leader training, software project management, and all aspects of the software engineering process fully meet the criteria and intent of the SEI's Software Process Assessment questionnaire. However, the software engineering training program has been in place for many years and is periodically re-evaluated and upgraded. Under direction of the SEPG, current upgrades are focussing on adequately addressing the new SEI Capability Maturity Model, and total organizational needs.

5.2 McDonnell Douglas Electronic Systems Company (MDESC)

MDESC's software engineering process training programs, which provide instruction in their standard processes, will be presented. Programs are targetted for the software developers, managers and staff, as well as for executive, middle and program management, and project teams. The training programs are designed to meet the requirements of the SPA questinonaire.

Each course that is part of the training programs has a set of measurable objectives, re-enforcement exercises and quizzes, and a mechanism for feedback and critique from the students. Along with formal training through courses, informal training in the form of workshops is provided.

5.3 TRW System Development Division (SDD)

TRW SDD's interpretation of the CMM's training requirements will be presented along with how they are fulfilled by SDD. Also, what are seen as additional needs in the CMM's Training Key Process Area will be presented along with recommendations on how industry's continuing education and training, coupled with the university curricula, can fulfil them.

6 Panel Participants

A. Winsor Brown
Software Engineering & Management Technology
McDonnell Douglas Space Systems Company

Rick Hefner
Software Engineering Process Group
TRW System Development Division

Jane Moon
Software Engineering Process Group
Hughes Aircraft Company, Command & Control Systems Division

Karen Powel
Software Engineering Technology
McDonnell Douglas Electronic Systems Company

Software Process Training: A Formal and Informal Approach at McDonnell Douglas Electronic Systems Company

Karen L. Powel
Senior Manager
Software Engineering Technology
McDonnell Douglas Electronic Systems Company

1 Introduction

McDonnell Douglas Electronic Systems Company (MDESC) in Santa Ana, California committed to a formal program to meet the Software Engineering Institute (SEI) assessment criteria in 1989. At that time, eight employees were sent to the SEI Assessment Training, after which they conducted a self assessment on each of the MDESC locations (Virginia, Missouri, California, and Colorado). The assessment identified areas for improvement and which resulted in a formal software process improvement plan being implemented.

2 MDESC Software Process Improvement Philosophy

The MDESC executive management is committed to software process improvement. This commitment includes ALL software developed by the entire company, in all locations. Because of this commitment, a central Software Engineering Process Group (SEPG) was assembled in Santa Ana, California, where the majority of the software is being developed. In addition, a remote site SEPG at each location was established. Each remote site SEPG has the responsibility to assist in development, and review, and to comment on all process documentation. Additionally, they must ultimately infuse the processes, procedures, training, and documentation created.

The SEPG leaders have formed a Software Engineering Technology Steering Group which has defined the overall philosophy for software process improvement: Identify, develop, and establish the practices, procedures, and policies for continuous improvement of sound software engineering practices throughout MDESC. The SEI assessment criteria became a set of guidelines for software process improvement, but not the only moving force for the MDESC action plan.

3 Training Philosophy

MDESC software engineering process training was developed to instruct software engineers in the standard process used at MDESC, using the SEI training requirement as a motivator, not the primary reason. Therefore, not only was the requirement for project software management, developer, and review leader training developed and conducted, but also training for executive management, middle management, and project teams.

Each course's material is developed around a set of measurable objectives; tests or quizzes are given throughout the classes giving immediate feedback to the attendee; a measurement is recorded of the attainment of the objectives for future course improvement; and, finally, each attendee is requested to critique the course itself for relevance, content, and instructor ability.

In light of fact that the Capability Maturity Model (CMM) has not been finalized, MDESC SEPG has chosen to work with, and meet the requirements of the Assessment Questionaire, CMU/SEI-87-TR-23. The current CMM is considered to be a moving target. MDESC does not believe that the CMM, when finalized, will impact the training as developed and conducted at MDESC.

4 Training in the 'Big Picture'

Software process training at MDESC encompasses courseware targeting specific training requirements for software development engineers and upper management and process infusion designed to respond to specific needs of work groups or projects.

5 Formal Training

5.1 Software Process Training

Consistent with the SEI assessment questionaire, approaching and including level 3, MDESC has in place the necessary training for software process improvement, including (1) Software Project Management, (2) Software Engineering Process, (3) Review Leaders training, and (4) Estimation Workshop.

Software Project Management. The Software Project Management course is directed to the first-time software manager; however, since MDESC is introducing a consistent process throughout all of its sites, the course is required for every software manager. This course meets SEI question 1.2.2: "Is there a required training program for all newly appointed development managers designed to familiarize them with software project management?" The objectives of the software project management course are as follows:

- Learn to use the Software Engineering Process Manual (SEPM) as the in-house standard procedures document.
- Plan and organize a software engineering staff and make optimum use of people resources.
- Plan and replan work and obtain appropriate commitments.
- Make justifiable estimates of software size and labor-hours.
- Schedule a software project.
- Assess and manage software risk.
- Manage software subcontractors.
- Contribute appropriately to a proposal effort.
- Collect and understand process and software metrics.
- Identify corrective actions and indicate the various types of status reviews.

Software Engineering Process. The Software Engineering Process training is a required course for all software engineers, regardless of position. This class answers the SEI questions 1.2.3: "Is there a required software engineering training program for software developers?" and 1.2.4: "Is there a required software engineering training program for first-line supervisors of software development?" and has the following objectives:

- Understand how the SEI's CMM is an effective tool for change and continuous improvement.
- Understand how the SEPM addresses organizational and project management issues.
- Understand the MDESC software process model and the phase-related activities associated with it.
- Know the SEPM requirements for reviews and metrics collection.
- Know the SEPM requirements for documents and software development files.

Review Leaders. The Review Leaders course is directed toward personnel responsible for conducting a MDESC structured peer review. These structured peer reviews are patterned after a more formal Fagan's inspection. This course complies with SEI question 1.2.5: "Is there a formal training program required for design and code review leaders?" and has the following objectives:

- Understand the MDESC review process.
- Understand the review requirements in the SEPM.
- Lead an effective structured peer review.
- Train structured peer review participants.

Estimation Workshop. The Estimation Workshop, although not directly attributable to an SEI question, is an MDESC required course and supplement to the Software Project Management class. This is an actual hands-on workshop where a case study is used for both a bottom-up and a top-down (empirical) software estimate. Each attendee will use an automated modelling tool to gain experience with its operation, compare the output against the bottom-up estimates, and ultimately come up with a final justifiable software estimate. The objectives for this workshop are as follows:

- Produce justifiable estimates of labor-hours required for a software project.
- Develop a software project schedule, accommodating the overall project schedule and taking into consideration availability and optimum allocation of resources.
- Compare results of the bottom-up and top-down estimates, change assumptions as necessary, and reconcile major differences between the results of the two.
- Be able to fill in the required information in a designated set of Basis of Estimates forms.

5.2 Upper Management Training

This training focuses on the non-software person and, specifically, upper management. The MDESC Executive Management Overview encapsulates the reasons for software process improvement, the short- and long-term paybacks management should expect, and an overview of the training contents for each course. The president of MDESC has required that all vice presidents and their directly reporting staff attend this 2 hour overview.

6 Informal Training

During the process of developing and conducting training, it became evident that infusion was more difficult than anticipated. Training alone would not get the engineers to actually make use of all the materials, documentation, training, and procedures. As a result, the SEPG put together a 4-hour workshop for hands-on use by a project or group.

6.1 Injection Workshop

The process of actually making use of the new way of doing business at MDESC and introducing the engineers to the differences between what was done in the past and what is now the 'new' culture, became a challenge for the SEPG. As a result the following objectives were used for the workshop;

- Understand the SEI maturity levels and MDESC Software goals.
- Know what products, training and activities are available for software engineers.
- Be aware of the MDESC policy and its implications.
- Know what the SEPM is and how to get one.
- Know how to use the SEPM checklist and how to obtain a waiver.
- Understand which SEPM requirements are unwaiverable and why.
- How to get assistance from the local SEPG.
- Be aware of the SEI Level 3 mock assessment and how it will be used.
- Know what training is required and how to obtain it.

7 Conclusion

Training at MDESC has taken on many flavors — formal, informal, executive management, SEI compliance, and just plain 'good' software engineering practices. As the company continues to improve the software process, the SEPG will not only implement those training courses that are part of a typical software engineering curriculum, but will also look for ways to enable the end user to easily embrace the software improvement process.

Session 11:

Laboratory and Project Experiences
Moderator: Neal S. Coulter, Florida Atlantic University

Undergraduate Software Engineering Laboratory at Texas A&M University
William M. Lively and Mark Lease, Texas A&M University

Software Engineering Course Projects: Failures and Recommendations
Manmahesh Kantipudi and James S. Collofello, Arizona State University; Ken W. Collier, Northern Arizona University; and Scott Medeiros, Motorola, Inc.

Use of the Individual Exchange Project Model in an Undergraduate Software Engineering Laboratory
J. Kaye Grau and Norman Wilde, The University of West Florida

Undergraduate Software Engineering Laboratory at Texas A&M University

William M. Lively and Mark Lease

Department of Computer Science, Texas A&M University, College Station, TX 77843-3112

Abstract. The Undergraduate Software Engineering Laboratory has been funded by the National Science Foundation and is being created to provide computer science students hands-on experience with the tools and techniques used in modern software engineering. Each student receives experience in high-level system design and individual feedback about how their designs might be improved. To broaden the students' experience with computer hardware (which to this point has been dominated by personal computers), the equipment in the lab consists of state-of-the-art Unix workstations connected to a local-area network. Our presentation will overview the laboratory exercises and projects assigned to the students. The successes and failures will be discussed with insights on how to improve such a software engineering laboratory. Overall we will attempt to partially answer the question: How do you infuse structure and technology into the teaching of practical software engineering?

1 Introduction

The problem we are attacking is the education of students that allows them to be able to build better software systems and be more productive. Why is this important?

In 1968 at the NATO Conference at the Rome Air Force Base in New York, a group of software users/developers met to consider what would later be called the "software crisis". The problem addressed was that the software systems being delivered were of low quality, unreliable, not usable, not understandable, not maintainable, not modular and delivered late and overbudget. The term "failure gap" more simply describes the situation — a failure of delivered software systems to meet the user's needs. The magnitude of the problem can be appreciated when we consider that over 150 billion dollars are spent on software in the US annually.

Brooks [1] in his famous paper, called the "Silver Bullet" paper, described why software is different from many other engineered systems and consequently why the software crisis persists. Complexity, conformity, changeability and invisibility are the main culprits. Software can not be visualized like bridges and many other hardware systems. The complexity is enormous because so many states can be represented in software, and software is malleable — so easily changed. These problems exacerbate what Brooks calls the essence of software — determining the conceptual constructs for the system — the hard part. Brooks considers the implementation to be the easier part.

MCC (Microelectronics and Computer Corporation), a large consortium of companies trying to deal with major technological problems, had a Software Technology

Program (STP) attacking the software crisis. Most of the efforts were on what they called the "up-stream" problems — capturing the requirements and producing specifications (high-level design). The thrust of the work stemmed from the fact that errors discovered earlier in the development process are much easier to fix than errors found during and after the implementation phase. The work at MCC seems to support Brooks' premise.

2 Texas A&M's Approach

So the question is "how do we teach our students to be able to produce higher quality software and be more productive"? The approach the Texas A&M Department of Computer Science has taken follows somewhat the concept of addressing "up-stream" problems that MCC is attacking. The key concept here is to obtain the requirements for the user's system. Determining the requirements is a major problem because the user frequently can't tell the developer what he wants. Either he doesn't know what he wants or he can't communicate the requirements to the developer. English language communication is laddened with ambiguity and difficult in almost every context. The terminology in software engineering is not standardized, and this complicates the problem even more. The developer's lack of application domain knowledge, and the user's lack of software development domain knowledge simply exacerbate the dilemma.

So we are trying to find a way to enhance user/developer communication. Our approach has been to emphasize conceptual modeling (attacking the requirements capture and specification phases) as a means for enhancing user/developer communication. Can the developer with the right combination of graphics, structured text and natural language really communicate with the user?

The answer is no! What really must be taught (along with the use of conceptual modeling tools) is the *discovery process*. The discovery process deals with defining exactly what the problem is. We try to teach the students to become *aware* of this and a number of other significant problems. One of the major ones is the difficulty of the discovery process. We try to teach students that patience, experience, and iteration are important aspects of the discovery process. How do you mine the necessary knowledge to determine exactly what the problem is? We try to teach to students an analyst's approach with a series of questions that allow convergence to the true requirements.

3 Modeling Approaches

For fifteen years Structured Analysis (SA) has become the mode of choice for many developers to help with conceptual modeling. By SA we mean the development of dataflow diagrams, data dictionaries and data structure charts. A major problem with this approach is that the software architecture is built around functions. When maintenance occurs, typically functions are changed or added, and the software architecture begins to be disrupted. This hampers future maintenance.

The advent of a different methodology called an object oriented (OO) approach offers a possible solution to software architecture degradation. An OO approach bases the software architecture on objects instead of functions, and therefore when maintenance occurs and the functionality changes, the basic software architecture determined by the objects is not disrupted as severely as the architecture determined by a functional approach.

Therefore our approach is to attempt to teach students how to do conceptual modeling with an object-oriented flavor. The most promising methodology along these lines has been the work of Rumbaugh at General Electric [3]. The technique is called OMT (object modeling technique) and consists of building three models: an object model, a functional model (like SA) and a dynamic modeling (control and time varying properties). Basing the system on objects is very powerful. The concept of objects carries across the problem space, solution space and implementation space in a seamless fashion — the notation of objects remains constant.

4   Undergraduate Software Engineering Laboratory

At the beginning of 1991, the Department of Computer Science at Texas A&M University was awarded an Instrumentation and Laboratory Improvement (ILI) Grant from the National Science Foundation for the Development of an Undergraduate Software Engineering Laboratory. The result of this grant is a laboratory containing 20 state-of-the-art workstations running the best computer-assisted software engineering (CASE) tools available today to teach our students how to perform conceptual modeling.

The conceptual modeling effort is most effective when it can be done in a rapid prototyping mode. Rapid prototyping allows developers to rapidly build operational (computer executable) conceptual models that the users can experiment with. Such user/developer interaction greatly enhances communication between the parties. CASE tools are one way to facilitate conceptual modeling, but general operational rapid prototyping is not available yet.

The CASE tool we have initially been using is Interactive Development Environment's (IDE) STP (Software Through Pictures). The major limitation of this CASE tool is that it is based upon a SA approach. But STP is the state of the art for CASE tools today, and there is no viable object-oriented CASE tool that meets our needs.

STP does have E-R (entity-relationship) diagrams, dataflow diagrams, state diagrams, structure chart capability and data structure diagram capability. Therefore we can approach some of the concepts in an OO paradigm, but the approach is clearly not seamless. By that we mean there is not a common notation that integrates across all models and phases.

We hope that the exercises that our students will perform will begin to give them some real-world experience. Boehm [4] has stated that the most important issue in building sophisticated software systems is the experience of the developers.

5   Laboratory Experience

The goal of the Software Engineering lab is to provide students with several types of experience:

"Real world" experience. Most of the problem-solving challenges presented by college courses are oriented to demonstrating very limited principles, such as the features of a particular programming language or the properties of a specific algorithm. Therefore a major goal of the Software Engineering lab assignments is to give the students experience in solving the types of problems which might be presented to them by future employers.

Exposure to a CASE tool. To catch errors as early in the system-development process as possible, modern software engineering is placing a greater emphasis on the "up stream" of the process, the initial development of the requirements and specifications for the system. CASE is widely perceived to be a useful tool for capturing the specifications for a system. Many companies in industry are integrating CASE into their software-development environment. Having exposure to CASE tools is important to software professionals entering such an environment.

Experience working in groups. Group projects are not common during the college experience, but are very common in industry. Since working in a group requires unique talents and skills, experience in this area is also important. We hope to be able to improve the communication and interpersonal skills of our students. Again this is an introduction to the discovery process. We are trying to teach the students scenarios of questions that will allow them to capture the problem definition:

1. Who needs the solution?
2. What is it that I am doing?
3. Why am I doing it?
4. What is the scope (context)?
5. How do I do it?
6. Where do I go from here?

We want the student to learn to be in a continual mode of questioning during software development.

Exposure to state-of-the-art workstations. High-speed, graphical workstations running Unix are very popular in industry. However most of our students' experience has been with personal computers. Workstation skills will be invaluable for future software engineers.

Discussion of alternative designs and implementations. Another goal of our lab assignments is for our students to learn that the problem of software design does not usually have only a single correct solution. This is different from most problem-solving courses students are exposed to during college. We are attempting to teach the students how to prioritize non-functional software characteristics and then perform trade-off analysis for the functional requirements and thus look at a spectrum of alternatives. Trade-off issues involve cost, effort, feasibility, ethical issues and others.

6 Achieving The Goals

To achieve our goals for the course, we use both individual assignments and a group project. The individual assignments are used to make sure the students are well grounded in the principles of software design (specifically conceptual model development) so they can contribute effectively to their group project. The group project is used to demonstrate how the individual tools within STP work together. Each tool specifies some facet of the complete software system.

Individual Assignments. The first part of the semester is spent learning the individual tools within STP: the data dictionary and the major diagramming tools. Each assignment has the student use a tool to design a small, representative segment of a software system. For each tool except the entity-relationship diagram editor, the student is given a detailed set of requirements for a software system. The requirements are not complete so the student can begin to learn some aspects of the discovery process. The student is to convert the system requirements into a system specification (conceptual model) using the appropriate tool.

For the entity-relationship diagram assignment, the students are told to choose some area of interest to themselves (outside of computers). Within that area of interest, they are to imagine some system they might design. Their assignment is to decide for their hypothetical system which are the 10 most important objects. After they have selected their set of objects, they decide what the important attributes of the objects are and how the objects relate to one another. Their analysis is expressed as an entity-relationship diagram. This exercise begins to introduce students to the newer OO techniques.

In addition to the entity-relationship diagram assignment, here is a summary of the past semester's individual assignments.

1. Using dataflow diagrams, design a system for sending out the monthly billing for an electric utility company.
2. Use the data dictionary and data-structure editor to design the data structures needed to maintain a library's on-line card catalog.
3. Design the state-transition diagram for a tape recorder/player's motor controller.
4. Convert the dataflow diagram for the utility billing assignment into a structure chart.

Group Project. At the end of the semester, the class is divided into groups of 3 to 4 students for a group project. The students decide among themselves who will be in each group.

This past semester, the project was to design a library information system — including an on-line card catalog, and inventory and patron information subsystems. The description of the assignment included a fairly detailed set of requirements for the system. Each group was to design the specifications for the system and submit the data dictionary, data-structure charts, dataflow diagrams, and structure charts for the design.

The group project lasted one month. Midway through the project, each group met with the instructor for a "preliminary design review." The purpose of the design review was to make sure each group was proceeding correctly and making good progress. At the design review, each group was to have substantially completed everything but the structure charts. Such reviews are invaluable in industry to obtain multiple perspectives on software system design.

E-mail Electronic mail is used extensively to answer questions about assignments and to distribute information about the course. This then becomes an important tool of the discovery process. The email was done to supplement (rather than replace) Q&A during the lab session and the instructor's office hours.

At the beginning of the semester, a mailing list for the entire class is created. When a student has a question about the course, he/she can send a mail message to the lab instructor. Using the mailing list, the instructor will reply to the entire class when appropriate. Anything identifying the originator of the question is edited out to preserve the originator's confidentiality. Using e-mail was very successful — this past semester over 75 mail messages were distributed to the class mailing list. Through the e-mail dialog, many students became aware of problems that had not even occurred to them. This just reinforces the importance of the discovery process.

7   Empirical Insight / Problems

After conducting the course this past semester, we noticed several problems and gained some insight in the process.

Lack of Domain Knowledge. For certain, the most limiting constraint on the type of assignments which could be used in the lab was the lack of a common body of domain (or application) knowledge shared by all of the students. Our Computer Science students are free to choose their minor area of study from any college at the University — therefore every class has students with interests in business, engineering, and liberal arts. This diversity limits the applications suitable as the subject of a lab assignment to the most everyday, mundane areas: tape recorders, libraries, electric utility bills, etc. Even so there were many questions about the application in general ("Why should there be multiple 'locations' for a single book title?") and the lab assignment's system in particular ("Why does the library patron's record need to be changed when a book is returned?"). On a small scale, this lack of domain knowledge mirrors what is occurring in industry on a large scale. This again emphasizes the importance of the discovery process.

Unfamiliar Hardware/OS. Roughly half of the students start the course never having used a workstation or Unix before. These students are at a disadvantage, especially when something goes wrong and the system starts generating cryptic error messages (as Unix systems tend to do). In a distributed environment, a novice user will often not realize that the problem resides in the network or with one of the file servers, and the user will think they have done something wrong.

The sum of the learning curves for using new hardware, a new operating system, and a new windowing environment (with a lab assignment due in 2 weeks) can be quite intimidating to almost anyone. To get the students started, the instructor will hold "getting started" classes with 2 to 3 students at a time outside of the normal lab period for anyone who feels they want help. The instructor will make sure that each students' computer account is correctly setup and will demonstrate the basics of using the workstation. For the instructor, an important advantage of these "getting started" classes is that they are an opportunity to meet many of the students early.

The CASE tool we are using operates in the X window system. X allows a number of activities to be operating and visible concurrently — a new experience to most users only familiar with personal computers. Other novice users expect the highly-integrated window and application system of a Macintosh or Windows text editor. Many users have found out the hard way that X will allow you to shut down the window environment without regard to whether the files currently being edited have been saved or not.

Group Dynamics. In general students are not used to working in groups. Many groups have trouble getting organized initially, and most groups never get the work load equitably divided. There never can be too much emphasis on the importance of communication between members of the group. We are placing a greater emphasis on the students becoming aware of the importance of oral/written communication. The students can work on these skills during the project development time and then demonstrate the development of these skills in the oral and written presentations at the preliminary design review and the conclusion of the project.

Scale of the Group Project. Quite a few students were disturbed by the scale of the group project. They seemed to lack experience working with (or even thinking about) multiple programs interacting through use of common files or databases. In reality the scale we work on is still significantly smaller than many projects in industry. We want the students to be aware of the *scale-up* problem. As you try to apply the techniques and tools we teach to larger problems, they do not scale up linearly. We want students to be aware of this problem and realize efforts need to be taken to deal with increased complexity of development.

Different Solutions. During lab sessions, we compared and contrasted different solutions generated by the students. Many times there was more than one correct solution to an assignment. However quite often the differences in the solutions were due to differences in how the students perceived or weighted the design requirements. Quite often the perceptions were caused by incompleteness or ambiguity in the system's requirements. Again attempts are made to demonstrate trade-off analysis.

Importance of Documentation. We attempt to teach our students the importance of documentation. The need to capture the corporate history and artifacts that are produced during the development of software. They need to know how important the capture of design rationale is for future development and maintenance efforts. At this time they are introduced to the concept of a Life Cycle Artifact Manager (LCAM). The LCAM would be a hypertext-based system for linking the artifacts and allowing traceability forward and backwards across the phases of development.

Interest Of Potential Employers. Since the Software Engineering course is a senior elective, many of the students are interviewing for jobs as they are taking the course. Several students have commented on the real interest shown by company recruiters when they mention during an interview that they are learning about CASE tools.

Student Reaction. Our students' reaction to the Software Engineering laboratory has been very favorable (and gratifying). "This course should be required" is a common remark. Many students have said they were glad to get hands-on experience designing software. There have been 3 common complaints: the project takes too much time, the lab should be more directly object oriented, and some students would rather work on the personal computers they are familiar with. This last complaint is often heard early in the semester.

8 How to Improve?

Reflecting back on the past couple of semesters, we believe we can make a couple of changes to improve the course.

Give More Time For The Semester Project. The semester project was very pressed for time, and since it was at the end of the semester, it competed for attention with many other activities. Next semester one or two of the simpler assignments will only be given one week for completion to allow more time for the project. For our computer engineering students, they take a two semester senior design course. We see this course as providing valuable opportunities to applies the tools and techniques learned in the software engineering lab. For our computer science students, they have the opportunity to take a senior-level design project course and again apply the knowledge they have gained.

Expose The Class To A Complete Specification Earlier. One problem we noticed early was that a number of students understood the individual tools in the CASE environment but did not understand how the tools interrelated and/or did not understand how the CASE specifications fed the implementation process. To solve these problems, the lectures for the lab were changed to emphasize the role the various CASE system tools played in the specification process. Also we developed for a small system a start-to-finish set of documents — including the system requirements, specifications, and source code.

The example system, a computerized cash register implemented as an X window system client, is small enough to be wholly comprehensible to the students after a couple of hours of study — but the students are able to learn how the various specification diagrams complement each other and provide different views of the example system. The source code for the example system demonstrates how the specifications are implemented. Since the example system is an X window system client, the students are exposed to an event-driven control structure.

9 Conclusion

We feel our approach will make a viable contribution to the education of computer science and computer engineering students. The students are beginning to obtain real-world experience in conceptual modeling for software systems. They are learning to work together in groups with one another. They are beginning to see the problems that occur in developing large software systems: communications, domain knowledge, experience, reuse and others. *Awareness* of the significant issues in developing software is one of the major thrusts of our efforts.

We see this as a learning experience for us that will continue for a long time to come. We will continually be gaining insight on how to better design software systems for the foreseeable future. The building of large complex software systems is so difficult that it is likely we will never arrive at a totally satisfactory solution.

References

1. Brooks, F.P.: No Silver Bullet - Essence and Accidents of Software Engineering, IEEE Computer, April, 1987, pp 10-19
2. Boehm, B.W.: A Spiral Model of Software Development and Enhancement, IEEE Computer, May, 1988, pp 61-71
3. Rumbaugh, J., Blaha, M., Premerlani, W., Eddy, F., Lorensen, W.:Object-Oriented Modeling and Design, Prentice-Hall, 1991, Englewood Cliffs, New Jersey
4. Boehm, B.W.: Improving Software Productivity, IEEE Computer, Sept., 1987, pp 43-57

This article was processed by the author using the T_EX macro package from Springer-Verlag.

Software Engineering Course Projects:
Failures and Recommendations

Manmahesh Kantipudi[1]
kantipud@enuxha.eas.asu.edu

Ken W. Collier[2]
kwc@naucse.cse.nau.edu

James S. Collofello[3]
collofell@asuvax.eas.asu.edu

Scott Medeiros[4]

Department of Computer Science and Engineering, Arizona State University
Tempe, Arizona 85287-5406   (602) 965-3190

Abstract   In the past there has been much written about successful commercial software development projects while failures are largely ignored. Similarly, the software engineering education literature contains many references to successful course projects, while academic course project failures are rarely described. This paper provides an analysis of software engineering course project failures as well as practical recommendations for increasing the chances of successful projects. The failures are grouped into technical, personal and management categories. Our recommendations are based upon a synthesis of current approaches being adopted to various degrees in industry as well as our own personal experiences. Most of our non-technical recommendations have historically received very little attention in course offerings or even current popular software engineering texts. It is our goal in this paper to sensitize software engineering course instructors to the possible failures their project teams face as well as provide them with insight into increasing their teams chances for success.

I. Introduction

Open a computing journal and you will find approximately 80-100 pages of material describing how a particular methodology, algorithm, technique or process has succeeded in solving some of the previously existing problems in the related area. Rarely do people admit their failures and more rarely do they publish their failure(s). Failure has attached with it a negative implication. It is considered taboo and people who fail are

---

[1]Manmahesh Kantipudi has been a graduate teaching assistant of the introductory software engineering course at Arizona State University for 3 semesters.

[2]Ken W. Collier is a computer science faculty member at Northern Arizona University.

[3]James S. Collofello is a computer science faculty member at Arizona State University. Dr. Collofello has been teaching the introductory software engineering course at ASU since 1979.

[4]Scott Medeiros is a software engineer at Motorola Inc, Scottsdale, AZ. Previously, Scott worked as the graduate teaching assistant of ASU's introductory software engineering course.

marked as non-performers. Yet with the increasing demand for computing and the fact that computing is a relatively new field, failures do occur. Instead of ridiculing people who fail, we should learn from our failures and improve our development process so that these failures can be avoided in the future. In [Glass77], Bob Glass reminds us that human beings learn more from their failures than their successes. The Software Engineering Institute (SEI) and other quality conscious organizations have tried to incorporate the notion of process improvement based on previous experiences [Humphrey89]. The intent of this paper is to introduce the reader to some of the common reasons for project failure as identified in the literature and compare these reasons to our experiences with software engineering course projects. We list the reasons for failure of software engineering course projects and suggest approaches for addressing these reasons for failure. In section II we discuss the common causes for failure as addressed in the literature. In section III we describe our experience with software engineering course projects and list the common reasons for project failure. This analysis is based on the experiences of the authors in the academic environment. Section IV suggests approaches for addressing the failure conditions identified in section III. Section V is the conclusion along with a note on future plans.

II. Typical reasons for project failure.

As indicated above, there are many reasons for project failure. Projects have failed due to technical inability to do the job, due to management problems, due to poor or nonexistent cost estimation, due to bad investments in resources/tools, and also due to the market status. While all reasons for failure are not within our control (e.g., the economy is in recession), just being aware of these reasons can help us plan for the future. In this section we try to compile a list of reasons for failure. Before doing so, we need to first define what we mean by a project failure. We define a project to have failed if it does not meet the functional requirements of the specifications or it does not meet the schedule and cost requirements of the contract.

In [Glass77], Glass gives examples of failed projects. Some reasons for these failed projects are:

- Lack of proper technical training of personnel.
- Upper management is influenced by political interests.
- Incorrect cost estimates.
- Over elaborate work is done without pushing for adequate return on investment.
- Management is unaware of the latest technological advances.
- Management gets influenced to invest in fads (political interests)
- Projects are on a time constraint and hence concentrate on getting the job done rather than improving the development process.
- Poor customer relations.

- Standards are not met causing interface problems among team members. Maintaining   standards means bigger budgets.
- Projects are built from scratch, reuse is not advocated.
- Communication and Coordination problems.

In [Thayer80, Thayer82], the authors have identified 20 major issues and problems that managers feel are most important to the success of a project. These issues are classified under five categories : Planning, Organizing, Staffing, Directing, and Controlling.

Not all the issues discussed by Thayer are applicable to all projects. Small projects are vulnerable to a different set of failure conditions than large projects. The work environment also makes a difference. A project developed in an academic environment is subject to a different set of factors that lead to failure than a project developed in an industrial environment. The above list indicates typical reasons for failure of projects in an industrial setting. Our interest in this paper is to compare these reasons with the reasons for project failure in the academic environment. In the following section we present our findings.

III. Our experience with software engineering course projects

Based on the authors' experience, the following have been found to be the most common reasons for failure of software engineering course projects. This experience combines a total of 22 offerings of a software engineering course at Arizona State University (ASU), constituting over 100 projects. We have identified each of the following reasons based on our experiences, interaction with students, postmortem studies of projects that failed in the software engineering course, and some student interviews.

The project performed as a part of the one-semester undergraduate software engineering course at Arizona State University consists of students working in teams of 5-6 members per team. Team projects consist of developing some sort of software engineering tool where the instructor serves as the customer. Project sizes normally range from 7,000 to 10,000 lines of code. The usual implementation languages are Ada, Pascal or C. Projects are developed on a VAX VMS system. Teams are selected by the instructor based on student background information gathered by a student questionnaire. A balance of graduate and undergraduate students is maintained on each team. No formal project organizational structure is followed although team leaders normally surface in each team. The development methodology followed in the class is a variation of the Waterfall model with an emphasis on rapid prototyping. Typical documentation is produced at the end of each development phase. Students are evaluated on both their individual contributions to the project as well as their team's overall project grade. Peer evaluations are repeatedly performed throughout the course as well.

The major reasons for failure can be classified into the following three categories:

1. Technical Issues.
2. Personal Issues.
3. Management Issues.

1. Technical

• *Programming experience with given language/environment*: If the programmers are not familiar with the language/environment, the probability of failure is higher. This reason was not found to be a major cause for failure because students are expected to have a certain level of competence in the programming language and working environment (through prerequisites). Yet this problem was encountered occasionally because some students get into the class without the required prerequisites.

• *Last minute coding efforts*: This is a common reason for failure for students who underestimate their assigned programming tasks and hence do not give themselves enough time.

• *No programming standards followed among group members*: Similar to the previous cause, students do not strictly adhere to programming standards because they are not in the habit of doing so in the past, and later face interface problems.

• *Last minute integration efforts*: Again, the time required to integrate individual components is highly underestimated by students. It is not uncommon to see groups getting together the night before the project is due and trying to integrate the modules, only to ask the instructor for an extension of the deadline the next day.

• *Fantasy Factor*: Some team members often commit to do more than what they can actually handle. This reason was found to be a major reason for project failure. In the group project model that was followed at Arizona State University, students are required to distribute the project work among themselves. Often some students unknowingly volunteer to do a part that is tougher than the rest, and then later find out that it was too much work. This happens because of the inability of the students to anticipate the work involved. Other team members tend not to protect the volunteer because they now have less work to do and can later point fingers at the volunteer if the work is not done. "We didn't force you to choose that part." is a common refrain.

• *Having attitude of learning on project*: Students come from different backgrounds and many may be working on the particular operating system or with the particular language for the first time. Students have the attitude that they will learn as the project progresses and later find out that their inexperience proved detrimental to the group. Not having control of the pool of students who can enroll in the class leads to this sort of a failure condition.

• *No version controls or change management*: As the project gets bigger and modules start being integrated, students begin facing the problem of not having a managed process for change control. As an example, it is not uncommon that students make changes to old versions of the software.

• *No strict review/inspection process was administered*: Students do not realize the importance of the reviews/inspections imposed upon them, and often "buddy up" (You sign my module and I'll sign yours). As a result the inspection is done as a class requirement rather than a serious technical review. Later if the project fails, the reason for failure may be attributed to inefficient or unproductive inspection processes.

As seen from the above reasons, technical failures occur due to student inexperience. Students often do not appreciate the importance of change control and reviews. Students often underestimate the time required to code and integrate modules. These issues can be related to team management. If a team is assigned a leader and the leader is held responsible for the above conditions, then the leader is motivated to avoid these failures. While assigning a leader to a group may be viewed as a partiality towards the leader, a rotating group leader is a good idea. In the next section we discuss more about team building and team growth, which we feel are key issues for the success of a project. By having
procedures such as team building and leadership, many of the technical failure reasons such as the "fantasy factor", assigning less time for coding and integration, being irresponsible about change control and reviews/inspections, not following standards and learning as the project progresses can all be eliminated. The issue of language/environment experience is controllable by having strict requirement of prerequisites.

2. Personal

• *Attitude of "B is a good enough grade"*: Not all students are motivated to the same degree and hence are not interested in devoting as much time as may be required. Not all students are equally committed to the success of the project. In a team environment this attitude has a demotivational effect on other team members. This was found to be a major reason for failure.

• *Very heavy work load for some team members*: In an academic setting this would mean the student has other courses and cannot devote enough time to this project. Not being able to devote the required time to the project is a common reason for failure in the academic setting.

• *Not being able to admit having a problem till the very end, when it is too late*: This too is a common reason for failure of a project. As indicated in the introduction to the paper, people do not like to admit failure. If a member is finding it difficult to deal with a problem, instead of admitting it the member tries to solve it till the very end, when it is too late.

• *Very strong opinion of the way things are done/should be done*: In a classroom, we may have students with industrial experience advocating their style of development over the methodology taught in class. This leads to conflicts between students and hence to the break-down of the team.

3. Management issues

• *Poor Team Selection*: Team selection is a key issue. Many factors are usually considered when selecting teams in a corporate setting. In the academic environment little control exists over team selection, but students try to adjust because it is only for one semester. But even with the limited time of interaction projects fail due to incompatibility of team members.

• *Lack of Team Growth*: Once a team is built, it has to be nurtured. There are several ways of approaching this problem. In our experience, we have found that little is done in the academic setting regarding team growth (mainly because of the lack of time in a one semester class). Team members who are content are more productive, and that should be a goal of every team. We discuss this issue more in the next section.

• *Poor coordination of group meetings*: This problem typically occurs if there is no person responsible for the team. Everyone has different schedules and different preferences to meet. Inability to meet and exchange ideas is a major deterrent to team growth. If a team lacks good leadership and control, it will eventually fail. This problem was found to be common in our classroom setting, wherein groups had no leaders and hence coordination of meetings was a problem. One way to circumvent this situation is to require groups to meet and submit minutes of the meetings to the instructor.

• *Team members wanting to take control of the group*: Again, the problem of some members wanting to take over the reins of the group is a major reason for conflict, especially if there is no leadership.

• *Poor Communication*: Though it is easy to attribute failure to a lack of communication, many implicit reasons fall under this category. Cultural and language differences is one. Members should be encouraged to inculcate the habit of freely expressing their views to the group. They need to be trained in formal communication procedures and should be made to think with a broad mind, with few or preferably no prejudices. Inability to communicate, lack of communication, or insufficient communication are all strong reasons for group failure.

• *Ego*: A feeling of "I am right" causes many altercations. In a team environment where members are needed to give and take advice, the question of "whom should I listen to ?" invariably crops up. It was found to be a major cause of the breakdown of teams, further affecting the productivity of individuals.

From the above discussion, our position is that the personal and management issuesare more common reasons for failure than the technical problems. The technical issues can be overcome by implementing strategies such as training, careful team selection (in terms of technical capability), and sharing knowledge among team members. It seems more difficult to deal with the personal and management issues that were mentioned above. It may be noted that the personal and management issues lead to a breakdown of the team and even if the team is technically competent it will be unable to perform productively. We have also shown that many of the technical problems are implicitly related to the notion of team building and growth. In the following section, we address the above causes of failure, and recognizing the fact that personal and management problems are more critical, we concentrate on these issues. The intent of the above list of reasons is to make instructors aware of the common reasons for project failures in the academic setting and that even if the technical content of the course is good, it is imperative to deal with the personal and management problems that teams face. In future curriculum models, we expect that a need to address the personal and management problems will be required.

When compared to the list of project failure reasons in section II, we find that there cannot be a generic list of reasons for project failure. The reasons for failure are a function of the environment of development, the size of the team and the nature, complexity, and size of the project. One common reason for failure, however, is team management. Although there may be other approaches for avoiding failure, we feel that addressing team management issues promises a high return on investment. Inability of the team members to get along is a universal problem both in the corporate sector and in academia; both in large projects and in small projects. In the following section we discuss methods of increasing the chance of project success.

IV.   Increasing the Chance of Success

It is common in undergraduate or graduate software engineering curricula to organize classes into small software development teams. Although the small team approach to software development has been well established as an effective method, as we have seen in the previous section it is not foolproof. Many of these projects still fail. We have established factors that appear to contribute to the failure of software engineering course projects. These factors have been categorized into technical, personal and management issues. Our position is that improving team dynamics can provide a significant improvement in the likelihood that these projects will succeed. Team dynamics have been extensively studied by academic experts. Due to the difficulty of conducting valid experiments on team dynamics, effectiveness and productivity, it is difficult to make any generalizations about what works best [Shea87]. We can, however, use our own experience and intuition together with the words of experts in order to form some basic principles for increasing the effectiveness and productivity of programming teams. Here we propose a framework of team management methods which are aimed at reducing the likelihood of failure and increasing development productivity (see figure 1). Although many of the ideas presented in this framework are not revolutionary, they are well established management principles which, when combined, are likely to improve the chance for success.

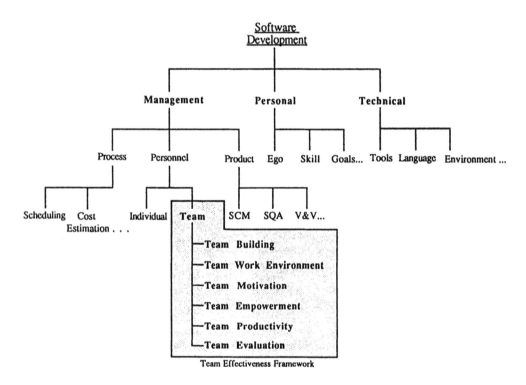

Fig. 1. A Hierarchy of Factors Affecting Software Projects

Although the focal point of this framework is primarily a team management perspective, the components address all the problems which were outlined in the previous section. It is common, when proposing management methodologies, to assume that managers have carte blanche to modify the organizational structure. Where software engineering course projects are concerned this is generally not the case. In an academic environment, there are numerous constraints placed on management flexibility (e.g., students who are in the course without having prerequisite skills). In developing this methodology we have tried to eliminate those components which are not likely to be realistic for the management of a software engineering class project.

Evaluation of the literature on this subject suggests that there are six equally important components to be considered when attempting to ensure team effectiveness. First, it is important to build a programming team carefully in order to achieve the most effective combination of personnel available. Next, a productive work environment is imperative. Third, the team as a unit must be motivated to perform as productively as possible. Fourth, teams must be empowered with responsibility and authority. Fifth, a team must be well managed. Finally, it is essential to perform constructive evaluations of both team and individual effectiveness. A synthesis of the ideas of experts together with our observations has led to the development of this framework in which these six ideas form the underlying structure. They describe what should take place in order to promote team effectiveness. Here we provide a brief look at what is involved in improving these team components.

1. Team Building

Because the team building process must take place first, it promises to be the foundation of team effectiveness. Unless a project manager possesses the techniques to build a team with potential for success, the prospect of consistently building effective teams is bleak. There are many considerations which must be made in the staffing of a software development team. Although team building in an academic environment has severe limitations (e.g., lack of knowledge of student background) we support the idea that attention to this aspect of management still has a high return on investment since it forms the foundation for success.

Before building a team it is important for the course instructor to acknowledge the attributes which are present in an effective team. In [Root84] the following characteristics are typically observed in teams which achieve significant growth and effectiveness: *clear purpose, commitment, open communication, shared leadership, appropriate membership, effective disciplines, constructive feedback, productive outcomes, good organization relationships.* These ingredients should act as the principle drivers in team building whenever possible.

In a brain trust conducted by one of the Industrial Research Institute's advanced study groups, technical managers from 11 large industrial and consumer companies discussed team building [Wolf89]. The result was that a number of principles were outlined which should increase the chances of staffing a successful and productive team. Based on these principles a course instructor should attempt to:

- Choose a proper leader.
- Establish a core of committed team members.
- Create an environment for team members to work together.

Arguably it is difficult for a course instructor to maintain total control over all of these aspects. However, in forming students into project teams it is beneficial for the course instructor to gain as much background information as possible on each student. In this way an informed analysis of potential teams can be compared with the above components in an attempt to affect the likelihood of success.

Finally, an academic semester (the typical length of project development time) is relatively short for projects of any substance. It is necessary for the course instructor to guide the team through the stages of team development as presented in [Varney89, Stokes90]: *forming (awareness), storming (conflict), norming (cooperation)* and *performing (accomplishing)*. Awareness of these stages of team development promotes team introspection and allows the course instructor to make recommendations to teams who do not seem to be developing quickly enough.

2. Provide a Productive Environment

Even the most effective team cannot be productive if its members are constantly battling an environment that is not conducive to success. There are many environmental factors which contribute to the success of a software development team. In an academic setting, it is generally the responsibility of the teams to find such an environment. However, the course instructor should provide guidance and assistance whenever possible.

• *Encourage Effective Meetings*: The team should make a concerted effort to establish a regular, convenient meeting time. Moreover, meetings should be held in an isolated comfortable room with tables for note-taking and a blackboard for idea generation. The instructor should encourage teams to make effective use of problem solving and decision making strategies (e.g., brainstorming, modelling, design alternative analysis, formal inspections) [McGarvey90, Fagan76].

• *Simplify and Formalize Team Communications*: The importance of effective communication, both internal (between team members) and external (between team and instructor), should be stressed by the instructor. The use of electronic mail and written memoranda should be encouraged for both types of communication. This formality causes communications to be carefully considered as well as eliminating some potential ambiguity. As Kistler observed, "An individual or organization can have good equipment, motivation, and a sense of direction, but if effective communications are not established, there will not be a real achievement." [Kistler89]

• *Optimize the Variables of Group Dynamics*: In [Shea87], three interrelated variables of group dynamics are discussed. These include:

  • Task Interdependence: How related are the tasks of one team member to another?

- Outcome Interdependence: The existence of consequences for task accomplishment that are shared by members of the team.
- Potency: The collective team members' perceptions about the effectiveness of the group.

It is important that a course instructor encourage a development environment with consideration given to these factors. Careful attention should be paid to the coincidence of *task interdependency* and *outcome interdependency* while always trying to enhance *potency* [Shea87].

3. Motivating Teams

Once a software development team has been built for effectiveness, it is important to motivate that team. Many of the factors outlined above in the building of a successful team also serve as motivating factors. However, a well-built team must also be a well run team in order to be effective. We can view this problem of team motivation from two perspectives. The first is the role of the project manager in promoting team motivation. The second is the more subliminal role of the manager in developing the overall attitude of the team and their perception of themselves as a team.

In a study performed by Herzberg in the late 1950's to determine motivating factors versus factors which have neutral motivational power, 200 engineers were interviewed [Lawrence84]. Based on these interviews, he described the following as motivating factors: *achievement, recognition for good work, job attractiveness, responsibility* and *advancement*. There were also several neutral factors (i.e., non-motivators): *company policy and administration, supervision, salary, interpersonal relations* and *working conditions*. An analogy between this study and the classroom can be formed by observing that, for many students, positive comments from an instructor are as motivating, if not more so, than grades.

Finally, a course instructor can encourage teams to apply Barry Boehm's win/win theories in order to resolve internal problems [Boehm89]. As was noted in our analysis of project failures it is common that members of student teams have differences of opinion and motivation which lead to a breakdown in team effectiveness. If individual members of a team can be made aware of the motives of other members, they can be better prepared to resolve conflict.

4. Team Empowerment

Related to team motivation is the notion of *team empowerment*. Teams are likely to function better when they are allowed to determine how they will function. Furthermore, teams should be given the latitude to make major decisions without an overabundance of managerial meddling. In [Owens91], the concept of *Self-Managed Work Teams* are presented. The aim of this management style is to generate motivation and to eliminate barriers to productivity. Here the team structure, itself, is the primary source of personnel motivation. Owens states, "A self-managing work team is a highly trained (and cross-trained) group, typically six to eighteen employees, given principal responsibility and authority for carrying out a well-defined function." In this strategy, management determines *what* is to be done while the team decides *how* it will be done.

Arguably, this management style is applicable to software development. In an academic environment the course instructor can allow teams to function as they see fit by allowing teams to set their own intermediate milestones and deadlines, and by giving teams the flexibility to form their own organizational structure. Clearly, Owens' ideas cannot be fully implemented in the classroom since students do not have the background and experience needed. However, if teams are carefully monitored, an instructor can simulate this quite effectively by maintaining a "hands-off until needed" attitude.

5. Project Management Should Promote Productive Teams

Clearly, the role of the course instructor is of prime importance and has a major impact on the overall morale and effectiveness of the team. In [Stokes90] some of the characteristics of an effective project manager are outlined. These can easily be adapted in an academic software development project. The course instructor together with the team leader can work towards the following goals:

- Communicate with and support each team member.
- Have the same goals as team members (win/win).
- Listen to team members' inputs and adjust strategies when appropriate.
- Act as an advocate for the team.
- Build trust by demonstrating trust.
- Reward desired behaviors.
- Do not settle for inferior performance.
- Be an effective role model.
- Focus feedback on behaviors rather than personalities.
- Concentrate on things that people can change.
- Encourage team members to find win/win solutions.

6. Team Evaluation

Of course, evaluation is a necessary part of an academic software engineering course. Minimally the instructor must provide a final evaluation of each student in the class. However, evaluations can be an good tool for improving team effectiveness if used correctly. This requires intermediate evaluations of both the team as a unit and individual evaluations of team members. These evaluations should be treated as guidelines for improvement rather than fixed and unchangeable black marks against the final evaluation. An instructor can accomplish this by beginning the evaluation session with the positive comments about team progress. This can be followed by discussing *areas for improvement*. If the team is performing well it should be acknowledged publicly, "...Not only will this boost morale but it will stimulate future teams." [Wolff89]

Part of the role of a good team is self-assessment. In addition to the evaluation of the instructor, a good team will, "...continuously monitor their process against a set of standards to guard against drifting off-target." [King88] If a team is provided with a detailed project schedule and well-defined objectives, self-evaluation should not be a difficult task. Although schedule slippage is common in software development, an effective team should perform its own spot checks and assessments to ensure that the team is not the cause of the slippage. The project manager should insist on self-evaluations, but should provide an environment where honest self assessment is likely.

V. Conclusion and Future Plans

We have identified reasons for failure of software projects in an academic environment. We have compared these failures with the existing literature on failures. Based on our experiences we have proposed a framework for increasing the effectiveness of a software development team which is aimed at eliminating the causes of software engineering course project failure identified. Furthermore, we have taken special care to develop a method which we feel, can realistically be implemented in an academic setting. We have intentionally left out specific implementation details in order that this framework can be used in conjunction with any good software engineering curriculum. Augmenting such a curriculum with the framework presented here should prove to strengthen the course and improve the success rate of the teams in the course.

In the future we hope to analyze small commercial software projects in an attempt to compare causes for failure in both academic and commercial environments. In our future analysis we intend to determine similarities and differences in these two environments. Our aim is to determine the applicability of the proposed management framework to a commercial environment. It is reasonable to believe that, with few modifications, these ideas can be applied in commercial organizations. Furthermore, we hope to continue this effort by identifying the characteristics of large scale projects which have failed and attempting to modify our scheme to fit the needs of large commercial projects.

Acknowledgements

We would like to thank Kang Zhang (Bull HN Information Systems, Phoenix) and Mike Orn (GTE Corporation, Phoenix), who were both teaching assistants for the software engineering class offered at Arizona State University. We appreciate their comments and evaluations of the problem set that we identified.

Bibliography

[Boehm84]   Boehm, B.W., M.H. Penedo, E.D. Stuckle and R.D. Williams, A Software Development Environment for Improving Productivity, *Computer*, vol. 17, June 1984, pp. 30-42.

[Boehm87]   Boehm, B.W., Improving Software Productivity, *Computer*, vol. 20, September 1987, pp. 43-57.

[Boehm89]   Boehm, B.W. and R. Ross, Theory-W Software Project Management: Principles and Examples, *IEEE Transactions on Software Engineering*, vol. 15, no. 7, July 1989, pp. 902-916.

[Brooks75]   Brooks, F.P., The Mythical Man Month: Essays on Software Engineering Addison-Wesley, 1975.

[Fagan76]   Fagan, M.E., Design and Code Inspections to Reduce Errors in Program Development, *IBM Systems Journal*, vol.15, no.3, March 1976, pp.105-211.

[Glass77]   Glass, R. L., The Universal Elixir and Other Computing Projects Which Failed, *Computing Trends*, 1977, reprinted 1981.

[Humphrey89]   Humphrey, W. , Managing the Software Process, Addison-Wesley, 1989.

[Huszczo90]   Huszczo, G.E., Training for Team Building, *Training and Development Journal*, February 1990, vol.44, pp.37-43.

[Johnson86]   Johnson, C.R., An Outline for Team Building, *Training*, January 1986, vol.23, p.48-52.

[King88]   King, D., Team Excellence, *Management Solutions*, October 1988, vol.33, pp.25-28.

[Kistler89]   Kistler, E.L., Managing Productivity More Effectively, *Proceedings of the Second International Conference on Engineering Management: Managing Technology in a Competitive International Environment*, September 10-13, 1989, pp.429-436.

[Lawrence84]   Lawrence, K. Motivating Staff, *Data Processing*, vol. 26, November 1984.

[Maccoby89]   Maccoby, M., Building Teamwork, *Research Technology Management*, November-December 1989, vol.32, pp.9-10.

[McCreight83]   McCreight, R.E., A Five Role System for Motivating Improved Performance,

Personnel Journal, January 1983, vol.62, pp.30-32.

[McGarvey90]   McGarvey, R., <u>Creative Thinking</u>,
USAIR, June 1990, pp. 34-41.

[Owens91]   Owens, T., <u>The Self-Managing Work Team</u>,
Small Business Reports, vol. 16, no. 2, February 1991.

[Raudsepp83]   Raudsepp, E. <u>How to Build an Effective Team</u>,
Machine Design, vol. 55, November 24, 1983.

[Rettig90]   Rettig, M., <u>Software Teams</u>,
Communications of the ACM, vol. 33, no. 10, October 1990, pp. 23-27.

[Root84]   Root, L.J.M., <u>IEs Should Examine Impact of Management Style on Motivation and Productivity</u>, *Industrial Engineering*, vol. 16, January 1984, pp. 94-99.

[Shea87]   Shea, G.P. and R.A. Guzzo, <u>Group Effectiveness: What Really Matters?</u>,
Sloan Management Review, Spring 1987, vol.28, pp.25-31

[Stokes90]   Stokes Jr., S.L., <u>Building Effective Project Teams</u>,
The Journal of Information Systems Management, vol. 7, no. 3, Summer 1990, pp.38-45.

[Tayntor85]   Tayntor, C.B., <u>Motivating the Maintenance Programmer</u>,
Infosystems, February 1985, vol.32, pp.97

[Thamhain87]   Thamhain, H.J. and D.L. Wilemon, <u>Building High Performing Engineering Project Teams</u>,
IEEE Transactions on Engineering Management,
vol. EM-34, no. 3, August 1987, pp. 130-137.

[Thayer80]   Thayer, R. H., Pyster A. and Wood R. C., <u>The Challenge of Software Engineering Project Management</u>, *IEEE Computer*, August 1980, pp. 51-59.

[Thayer82]   Thayer, R. H., Pyster A. and Wood R. C., <u>Validating Solutions to Major Problems in Software Engineering Project Management</u>, *IEEE Computer*, August 1982, pp. 65-77.

[Thedens84]   Thedens, M., <u>Communication is the Key</u>,
Datamation, vol. 30, May 1984, pp.147-148.

[Varney89]   Varney, G.H., <u>Building Productive Teams</u>,
San Francisco: Jossey-Bass Publishers, 1989.

[Weisbord85]   Weisbord, M.R., <u>Team Effectiveness Theory</u>,
Training and Development Journal, January 1985, vol.39, pp.26-29

[Wolff89]   Wolff, M.F., <u>Building Teams--What Works (Sometimes)</u>
Research Technology Management, November-December 1989, vol.32, pp.9-10

Use of the Individual Exchange Project Model in an Undergraduate Software Engineering Laboratory[1]

J. Kaye Grau and Norman Wilde

The University of West Florida[2]

Abstract. Organization of undergraduate project work in software engineering is always difficult because of the students' very limited computing experience. Many related concepts need to be introduced almost simultaneously: the software life cycle, the use of documentation standards, the need to use documents produced by others, the role of CASE, and the importance of configuration management. This paper describes an Individual Exchange Project Model that has been used effectively in the University of West Florida's undergraduate Software Engineering Laboratory. This model involves individuals working in small teams to develop miniature programs. Each individual carries out the entire development process exchanging intermediate documents among team members.

1 Introduction

The Computer Information Systems (CIS) option has traditionally been the largest of the computer science programs at the University of West Florida (UWF) in terms of the number of students enrolled. For some time, the Division of Computer Science has felt that students heading into the information systems area need a strong background in the principles and methods of software engineering. Even more than graduates from a traditional computer science program, they are likely to confront in their careers the difficulties of developing and maintaining large software systems in multi-person project situations.

For this reason, the CIS option at UWF has included for the last 5 years a three semester sequence of software engineering related courses: Software Engineering I, Software Engineering II, and Systems Project. We believe that the sequence has been quite successful, but the organization of the laboratory and project component has been a continuing source of difficulty.

---

[1]The Software Engineering Laboratory described in this report was partially supported by funds from NSF grant USE-9052003.

[2]Address correspondence to: Dr. J. Kaye Grau, Division of Computer Science, University of West Florida, 11000 University Parkway, Pensacola, FL 32514 or kgrau@ai.uwf.edu

An early approach was to spread laboratory work over the three semesters. In the laboratory work for the first course students would learn basic tools, such as the use of a CASE tool to draw structure charts and data flow diagrams. During the second course they would prepare a more complete specification and high-level design for a system, and then in the third course, one of these specifications would be selected for implementation. However this approach was not found to be very satisfactory. One problem was that students entering the sequence have had basic courses in programming and data structures, but have generally not been exposed to programs of more than a few hundred lines. They find it difficult to grasp the need for software engineering techniques and they often cannot see clearly the relationships between specification, design, code, and test cases.

This paper describes a new approach for teaching the first undergraduate course in software engineering. The course, given on a trial basis in Fall 1991, combined lectures on software engineering with practical experience in the Software Engineering Laboratory. Lectures on life cycles, software engineering development teams, and software engineering principles were combined with assignments which required the students to effectively use the newly acquired software development systems in the Software Engineering Laboratory. The lab-oriented assignments led each student through a complete development process on a set of very small projects. The following sections describe the acquisition and set-up of the new Software Engineering Laboratory and the first use of the new SEL in conjunction with the Software Engineering I course. Comments were solicited from students at the end of the semester and are included to provide insight into the student perceptions of the SEL and the class.

2   The Software Engineering Laboratory

The original Software Engineering Laboratory (SEL) at UWF was set up using stand-alone PCs running the Excelerator CASE tool [5]. While this tool was in many ways excellent, we found that there were distinct drawbacks in using this environment for teaching software engineering. Most student software engineering projects involve, to at least some extent, team work. Each team had to be assigned to a designated PC for the semester; the team's project data would be created on that machine and could only be worked on from that particular machine. Since there were typically four to six teams assigned to a machine, students often arrived at the lab to find that some other group was using their machine. Even if other computers were free they could not use them.

Additionally, in a PC environment only one person can use the computer at a time. Since the teams were typically three to five students, one of them would use the machine while the others watched. Soon each team developed its 'Excelerator expert' who specialized in all the machine work; other team members barely learned how to start up the tool and draw a simple diagram.

The frustrations of using the SEL often led student groups to go back to hand drawn designs or to diagrams developed using simple drawing tools instead of real CASE tools. Thus they missed the main point of CASE design, which is the use of the tool to guide stepwise refinement and identify design inconsistencies.

Upgrading the SEL began in 1990 with the aid of a grant from the National Science Foundation's Instrumentation and Laboratory Improvement Program. It was clear that multi-user access to a team's data was a key requirement so Unix networked workstations were the obvious hardware choice. Seven Sun workstations were purchased for the main University campus and an additional four workstations for our satellite campus in the Eglin AFB / Fort Walton Beach area.

> Student Comment: "The biggest problem in using the Software Engineering Lab is the number of stations available. It was difficult to get a machine when there are only 6 or 7 stations to begin with and at least 25-30 people in SE I trying to use it in addition to faculty and other classes."

The choice of a CASE tool to support teaching life cycle concepts was a more difficult decision. Fortunately from our participation in the Florida / Purdue Software Engineering Research Center we had access both to several formal CASE evaluation reports [1,2] as well as more informal advice from several of the Center's industrial affiliates who regularly evaluate the CASE state of the art. We finally chose the Software through Pictures tool [3] as the best developed system then available on our chosen platform.

> Student Comment: "I did enjoy the Sun System after working on it a few months. When it came down to finishing the project, I was amazed at what the system was capable of doing. I really liked it." "StP was a wonderful tool once I had the understanding of how the system works."

General industry experience with CASE tools [9] and our earlier experience with Excelerator both indicated that a lot of preparatory work would be needed before turning the students loose in the updated Laboratory. We started experimenting with Software through Pictures a full eight months before the Laboratory went "live"; even so, when the time came we suffered from a good many operational glitches.

> Student comment: "The problem I encountered in the SEL are as follows: paper shortage, system going down, not enough terminals, lab hours too short, and StP processes being left on machines." "The system was too vulnerable to people kicking the cable and causing the network to collapse."

Preparation focused on two issues. First, we found by experiment that Software through Pictures needed some "tailoring" for a student environment. A ToolInfo configuration file is needed to set defaults, identify the project each student is working on, tell the tool which printers to use, etc. Templates for documents needed to be provided and we found that those delivered with the system were not appropriate for student work since the output they produce was often 80% white space. A student handout, tailored to our Laboratory's environment, was written covering the use of Unix and of the CASE tool.

> Student Comment: "The students must be informed about the intricacies of the ToolInfo file. The ToolInfo might be the trickiest part of StP."

Second, we have found that students need to have some kind of example of the sort of work they are expected to produce. At the undergraduate level it is not enough to say "produce a specification" or "produce a design". Textbooks and standards provide only a partial solution since they are usually too general to provide an inexperienced student with a useful point of reference. A small example was developed of a Yourdon-Constantine design prepared using Software through Pictures to give the students a target to shoot at.

> Student Comment: "Even though we had a small handout on StP, I felt it was still too wordy. Maybe the technical writing class could develop a user friendly, one page instruction guide on how to use the software."

We decided, however, that the general philosophy of the laboratory should not be to lead students by the hand, but rather to encourage them to develop their own ability to explore an unfamiliar computing environment. Computing professionals continually face the problem of dealing with new hardware and software systems. Students need to become confident in their own ability to read manuals, use help systems, and get informal assistance from colleagues in order to become productive. Accordingly the Laboratory was furnished with sets of manuals and a "question" board on which inquiries could be posted to be answered within 24 hours. However the basic philosophy was "sink or swim".

> Student comments: "There was only one copy of the documentation available and when someone else was using, you were out to lunch." "StP documentation suffers from being too large and too complex, making it difficult to find anything. Once the controls and basic operations are understood, StP is relatively easy to use." "StP manual is so big that it is very intimidating and hard to understand." "Finding help in the lab was my hardest problem."

3 Software Engineering I Course

The Software Engineering I course offered in Fall 1991 was selected as the first course to use the newly setup SEL. In deciding what kind of project should be required, we considered several project course models, namely the Small Group Project Model and the Large Project Team Model as described by Shaw and Tomayko [8] and the Medium Sized Project Model as described by Knoke [6]. We decided to follow a different model for the introductory course which we will refer to as the Individual Exchange Project Model.

The Individual Exchange Project Model is based on the premise that each student should experience a complete software development process in the introductory course. We wanted each student to have the experience of writing a specification, designing to a specification, coding a design, and testing to a specification. Furthermore, we wanted each student to learn to effectively use the newly acquired software development systems in the SEL. We wanted students to learn to use the CASE tool to develop consistent and complete data flow diagrams, structure charts, and data dictionaries In order to accomplish these goals within a semester, we chose miniature-sized[3] projects for the students to develop.

---

[3] Scale: 1 yard = 1 mile

In our curriculum, the Individual Exchange Project Model used in the first course provides a the students with the basic skills needed to progress to a Small Project in the second and then apply their software engineering knowledge in a Medium or Large Project for a real customer in the capstone Project Course. We would not recommend using this model in curriculum where the only team-oriented project that students are exposed to is in a single semester course in software engineering.

For this first offering of the course, students were grouped into loosely coupled teams of three people. Each team was given three miniature problems to solve, namely calculation of some well-defined statistical functions. Each person in the team chose one of the problems to work on initially. Requirements were stated verbally in class with a handout from a statistics book providing the definition of the functions. Students were told that their programs were absolutely not to fail, no matter what input was provided to them. Their programs were required to accept data either interactively or from a file, to calculate accurately the required functions, and to output any intermediate calculations such as mean and the final answer. They were not required to integrate the three separate programs in any way.

> Student comment: "The most difficult thing about the project was the loose coupling between team members. This had the advantage of depending on the documentation instead of the team member. This was also a disadvantage when changes became necessary. The team experience made me realize that working on a team project is much more difficult than it appears."

The first milestone (really a yardstone) was for each student to write a complete Software Requirements Specification for their assigned problem. ANSI/IEEE Std 830-1984 [4] was used to specify the format and contents of the SRS. Students in Software Engineering I at UWF are also enrolled in a co-requisite Technical Writing class and received assistance from the Technical Writing instructor on the clarity of their specifications. The students were required to use Software through Pictures in the SEL to develop data flow diagrams and a data dictionary which were incorporated into the SRSs.

> Student Comment: "The IEEE Standard was a little overwhelming initially."

During the class period when the SRS was due, we spent a few minutes talking about holding technical reviews, what characteristics a good specification should exhibit and then the students formed into their teams and started reviewing the three specifications. As part of the review, they wrote down action items. For the next class period, the students were required to address each action item and make appropriate updates to their SRSs. Each student was asked to estimate the number of lines of code that they anticipated it would take to implement their specification. The completed SRSs were then placed under configuration control using SCCS and the students in each team exchanged specifications.

At this point, the students were given a format description for a design document and required to follow a similar process for developing a design. Each student developed a design which met a specification that was written by someone else. If any modifications were required in the specifications, the designer had to make a formal request to the specifier to change the SRS; changes were tracked using SCCS. Students used Software through Pictures to create structure charts, PDL for each module, and an elaborated data dictionary. Designs were traced back to requirements. The students were again asked to estimate anticipated lines of code. Designs were reviewed and baselined.

> Student Comment: "I think the design document with the referenced and declared objects along with the PDL made writing my code much easier." "I would have spent more time developing the SRS--changes had to be made to the SRS and design because of problems in the code."

The next step, the students prepared code for the problem that they had designed and at the same time, prepared test cases for the third problem. Applying one of the recommendations of the Cleanroom methodology [7], the students were asked not to even compile their own code. The code and test cases were reviewed and baselined. Code was compared with designs and discrepancies were corrected. A comparison of lines of code with the previous estimates were made.

> Student comments: "We followed the method rather closely except when it got down to coding. We compiled our code with the tester present but after that, we pretty much debugged our own code." "I do not like not testing my own code--I could have tested it as I went along and finished sooner."

Finally, during the test phase, each student tested another student's code, recording any errors. The error reports were passed back to the designer/coder who made the changes and then gave it back to the tester to test. Records of changes were kept using SCCS.

At the end of the semester, complete projects were handed in containing all of the products developed throughout the semester. If there had been time, an acceptance test would have been run to determine final acceptability of their software.

> Student comments: "One, I learned that software engineering is not easy! Next, I learned how a system can be built. I learned that there are different methods and techniques that can be done to get the same result--the solution to the user's problem. I will know the next time how to write a specification, how to write a design document, how to generate a proper data flow diagram and structure chart, and how to baseline all documents and changes."

> "Working with every phase of the life cycle taught me much about what goes into the development of software."

> "I have learned that code is only a small portion of a real project."

> "This project taught me how to write non-ambiguous specs, how to interpret another person's specs, and prepare a design document that follows the specs."

4 Lessons Learned

Based on our experience, we feel that the Individual Exchange Project Model is a successful model to use in our introductory class and we plan to continue using it in future offerings of this course. This opinion is based on applying this model only once with a class of about 25 students. In the following paragraphs, we summarize some of the lessons we learned in using this approach and how we plan to modify the course to improve it even further.

First, we learned that we should have started the project earlier in the semester. It would have given the students more time to meet each milestone and the end products would have been better as a result. We chose in this course to spend some time up front introducing the students to Unix, Software through Pictures, and SCCS. In the next offering, we plan to start the project at the beginning of the semester and have the students learn to use the SEL systems in the context of the project.

> Student Comments: "The only thing I would have done differently is that I would have liked to have started sooner." "We did not feel the project was done properly due to the time constraint."

Second, we have decided to add a lab course to be taken in conjunction with the Software Engineering I course. In the lab, students will get assistance in learning the SEL systems and to have more time to work together in doing reviews and in testing their software. The lab course will be a one semester hour course that will meet once a week for three hours.

> Student Comments: "Next semester, if possible, take groups from class of about 5-7 students and have them login and start StP. Tell them the basics." "We needed to have a fixed meeting time, maybe twice weekly, and talk to each other about our problems, rather than just making assumptions."

Third, while the "sink or swim" approach was the only practical one to use in the first application of the new systems in the SEL, we feel that the students should be given more guidance in using the systems than they were during this course. Now that we have some experienced users, we will have a pool of people to act as lab assistants for the next offering. However, we will not take away completely the challenge to the students to learn a new development environment on their own which is an invaluable skill for professionals.

One of the problems left to be solved in our current CIS curriculum is giving the students more experience in programming prior to taking Software Engineering I. Using a miniature-sized project in Software Engineering I does not solve this problem. We are considering the introduction of a course prior to the SE I course in which students would be given a specification and high-level design of an individually challenging project and guided through detailed design, coding, and some testing potentially in an object-oriented language. This would improve students programming abilities as well as give them more of a basis for appreciating the concepts of programming-in-the-large which are taught in the software engineering sequence.

The Individual Exchange Project Model did not take full advantage of the SEL's capability to support team projects. The other two courses in the software engineering sequence will use different Project Models and be able to make more use of this capability.

5   Conclusion

Use of the up-to-date Software Engineering Laboratory in conjunction with our Software Engineering I course has given the students a much better understanding of the kind of development environments that they can expect to find when they go to work. In the laboratory, the students learned the advantages of using the CASE tools to specify and design their software. They also learned how to use a configuration management tool to control changes to their documents and code. As a result, they are better prepared to take on the challenges of professional careers in software engineering.

Acknowledgements

We would like to thank Mr. Tom Pigoski for his assistance in setting up the SEL. Alex Vallance also deserves thanks for his initial installation and tailoring of Software through Pictures. We would also like to thank Dr. John Munson for his suggestion of using miniature problems.

References

1.   Cabral, G.; Dunsmore, H. E.; Stratton, S.; Zage, D. M.; Zage, W. M.; "An Evaluation of Excelerator," SERC-TR-15-P, Software Engineering Research Center, Purdue University, West Lafayette, IN 47907, May, 1988.

2.   Cabral, G.; Dunsmore, H. E.; Stratton, S.; Zage, D. M.; Zage, W. M.; "An Evaluation of Teamwork," SERC-TR-16-P, Software Engineering Research Center, Purdue University, West Lafayette, IN 47907, May, 1988.

3.   IDE; "Software through Pictures User Manual", Interactive Development Environments, 595 Market St., San Francisco, CA 94105, December 1990.

4.   ANSI/IEEE Std 830-1984, "IEEE Guide to Software Requirements Specification," IEEE: New York, NY, 1984.

5.   Index Technology Corporation, "Excelerator Reference Guide", Index Technology Corp., One Main Street, Cambridge, Ma. 02142, 1987.

6.   Knoke, Peter J.; "Medium Size Project Model: Variations on a Theme", *Software Engineering Education, Proceedings of the 1991 SEI Conference*, Pittsburgh, PA, October 1991.

7.   Selby, Richard; Basili, Victor; Baker, F. Terry; "Cleanroom Software Development: An Empirical Evaluation," *IEEE Transactions on Software Engineering*, Vol. SE-13, No. 9 (September 1987), pp.1027-37.

8.   Shaw, Mary;   Tomayko, James; "Models for Undergraduate Project Courses in Software Engineering", *Software Engineering Education, Proceedings of the 1991 SEI Conference*, Pittsburgh, PA, October 1991.

9.   Voelcker, John, "Automating Software: Proceed With Caution", *IEEE Spectrum*, Vol. 25, No. 7, pp. 25 - 27, July, 1988.

Session 12:

Corporate Experience
Moderator: Maribeth B. Carpenter, Software Engineering Institute

Creating a Software Engineering Training Program in a Level I Organization
Rich Pavlik and Kathy Jacobs, Honeywell Inc.

Corporate Software Engineering Education for Six Sigma: Course Development and Assessment of Success
Sandi Coker, Motorola University; Bud Glick, Motorola-SRD; Lavon Green, Purdue University; and Anneliese von Mayrhauser, Colorado State University

The IBM Cleanroom Software Engineering Technology Transfer Program
Richard C. Linger and R. Alan Spangler, IBM

Experiences with an Interactive Video Code Inspection Laboratory
Michael G. Christel, Software Engineering Institute

Creating A Software Engineering Training Program In A Level 1 Organization

By Rich Pavlik and Kathy Jacobs

Honeywell Inc.
Air Transport Systems Division
P.O. Box 21111
Phoenix, AZ 85036-1111
(602) 436-6567

Abstract. The Capability Maturity Model for Software describes a Level 1 organization as one which does not provide a stable environment for developing and maintaining software. There is a high degree of chaos in such organizations and the success of projects depends primarily on having dedicated managers and engineers. Formal training is usually nonexistent in Level 1 organizations.

Starting a software engineering training program in a Level 1 organization is a significant undertaking that requires dedication, patience, and commitment of resources that are traditionally not provided. This paper describes the process that was followed to establish a training program in such an organization.

1   Introduction

This paper documents our experience in establishing a training program for software engineers in the Air Transport Systems Division (ATSD) of Honeywell in Phoenix, Arizona. The paper begins with a brief description of the training environment as it existed when we began, identifies training problems we encountered and our solutions to them, and provides some indication of our future direction. We hope that this paper will be of benefit to other SEI Level 1 organizations that may be attempting to establish training programs for their software engineers. We also hope that this paper will provide useful information to those in the SEI and academia.

It is our belief that the situation in our division with regard to training was not unlike that of many other Level 1 organizations when we started. Our experience indicates that significant improvements in training can be accomplished through the dedication of a small number of personnel to establish the foundation for a training program. As stated by Watts Humphrey in Managing the Software Process, the key is to start by figuring out what training the people in the organization need [1]. Once these needs have been reviewed with management and funding has been agreed upon, a training plan can be developed, and the training can be provided to the personnel who need it. However, in a Level 1 organization, even if you get the courses identified, funded, and created, it is likely that one of your key problems will be to get people to attend them, simply due to the chaotic nature of a Level 1 project. As you shall see, though, there are many ways to get them to attend.

1.1   The Training Environment

In June of 1991 the authors were commissioned to "get the right training" for approximately 300 software engineers working on a large commercial avionics project in our division. This was going to be the division's first project in Ada and it was going to use new hardware, several new development methods, and many new tools. Our charter is to provide the necessary training for the software engineers on the project and then adapt that training as necessary to other projects as they are started in the future.

When we started, the division had two fully established training classes for software engineers, one in Structured Analysis/Structured Design, the other in Software Testing. Neither of the two courses had been taught in the past year. Historically, obtaining training was left up to project managers and was typically viewed as a low priority item. There was no minimum requirement for training of engineers in the division, nor was there any budget allocated to obtain training. There was no dedicated facility or computing equipment to provide the training. With regard to training, the situation in the division was similar to that of the "Herded" level of human resource management described in [2].

As of March 1992, we have identified a curriculum of approximately 35 courses for the project, and presented 12 of those courses, providing over 8,860 hours of training by using a combination of both internal and external trainers. (See Table 1 for information on the training completed.) We have also established rough procedures and numbers for estimating, a method for assessing organizational needs, a registration process, and a budgeting process for training. All of this has been accomplished primarily through the dedication of two full time software training coordinators and one part time administrative person.

Course name	Course Length (in hours)	Number of people trained	Total hours of training
Programming on the AMD 29000 Processor	8	47	376
Debugging on the AMD 29000 Processor	32	35	1120
Introduction to Ada	40	67	2680
Interleaf Training	12	114	1368
Ada - A Management Perspective	24	40	960
Software Testing Seminar	16	31	496
Introduction to Automated Configuration Management	8	26	208
Using the ATSD Documentation System	4	13	52
Object Oriented Analysis	40	23	920
Training for Inspection Moderators	8	59	472
AdaMAT	16	8	128
Change Control Process	4	20	80

Table 1 - Software Training Completed

2   Determining Customer Needs

As the first step in the process of determining customer needs, we created a training plan containing course descriptions for a series of pre-defined courses. These descriptions included the course topics and objectives, the course pre-requisites, the intended audience and the length of each the course. In addition, a rough estimate was done to determine approximate per student cost for each class. This plan was distributed to all first level managers on the project.

The managers responded with estimates of what training they felt would be needed by their people. The estimates included how many people needed which courses during which quarters of the upcoming year. We also received several suggestions for improvements to our curriculum.

We used this information to create a preliminary course schedule and a preliminary budget for our department for fiscal year 1992. The schedule defined approximately when the classes would be created and acquired, as well as how often per quarter they would be taught. The finalized list of classes and the preliminary schedule was sent to a Steering Committee (composed of management personnel from the project) for approval. The group cut some courses and allocated half the money needed for external training.

We should point out that the determination of needs on this project was somewhat chaotic. For various reasons, people simply did not know what they needed or how to plan for it. Many of the managers signed up too many people for some classes and did not consider the amount of time their people would spend in training when completing their schedules. Likewise, the trainers did not have sufficient time to review the forecasted needs with the managers.

3   Obtaining Management Commitment

As we progressed through the creation of our program, we have had a very difficult time obtaining the resources needed to support a greatly expanded training program. In general, management appears to agree that training is a necessary part of the project, but obtaining the facilities, administrative support, and internal trainers to support training is an ongoing struggle.

Until October of 1991, we lacked dedicated facilities for the software training. When we needed to schedule a class, we would need to find a conference room and arrange for any special network connections needed. As in most facilities, rooms were at a premium. Finding any room that could be used for a full week usually proved difficult. Finding a room that fit the size of the class, could be wired for network access and was usable as a classroom was virtually impossible. Finally, after many conversations with our facilities personnel, we were given a 20 person training room of our own. It has been wired for the various networks used in our classes and is not available for general use by others. We are currently attempting to acquire 2 larger training rooms (each of which will hold 30 people) and a storage room, in exchange for the smaller room we now use.

Another deficiency we discovered early on was lack of clerical and administrative support. At the start of our program, we had to take care of all administrative details for the classes. As we progressed, the Organization and Employee Development department (O&ED) took over course registration and attendance tracking. This allowed us to focus on materials tracking, course announcements, and course scheduling. We are still overloaded, even with O&ED handling registrations. Due to the economic downturn, it took us six months to get requisitions for a departmental aide and a departmental clerk to handle these and other details. Plans are for the clerk to be trained to handle all administrative and clerical duties associated with the engineering training program. The aide will be expected to support the instructors and generate program metrics. We hope this will allow the training coordinators more time to assist with the creation and evaluation of classes, as well as time to plan for the future.

A third major problem we have encountered is a lack of support, training, time, and resources for our internal trainers. For many of our internal trainers, time spent on class creation and presentation is added on top of an already overfull work week despite our numerous conversations with their managers. In general, it is very difficult for the internal trainers to get dedicated time to work on the classes. Most of the internal instructors have no formal background in training. Few of them have any background in either training or presenting. To improve the knowledge and confidence levels of our trainers, we created an informal Train the Trainer class. We are also investigating formalizing the Train the Trainer sessions. We encourage our trainers to schedule time away from their normal work areas to work on the classes. When our training room is available, the trainers are encouraged to use it for practice sessions of courses under development. We try to offer assistance in any way possible, but are not always successful. One skill most needed by our trainers is the ability to feel comfortable talking in front of a group, especially from formalized materials. We have not had much success in encouraging some of the trainers to practice their presentations, but have found that those trainers who were already experienced presenters tended to practice more.

In order to gain additional support for our future efforts, we started sending course announcements to the engineering directors. We also began monthly reports to many high level management personnel, including the Vice President of Engineering. The division has since set a policy of 40 hours of technical training per year per engineer. As our program is still in the formative stages, we are not yet meeting these goals, but at least they have been stated.

4   Providing the Training

Some of the problems we encountered during the creation and presentation of our courses have been previously discussed. These included problems defining our customers needs, problems acquiring resources and support for our internal trainers, and problems with acquiring space for presentation of the classes. We also experienced two additional problems relating to the presentation of our training: A very high no-show rate and our own lack of knowledge and experience at coordinating a large number classes. We will address these problems in this section.

During the first several months we presented classes, we found that we had an extremely high no-show rate. For some sessions of our classes, the no-show rate was almost 50%. After some informal checking, we discovered that we were offering the classes our customers wanted. However, since the customers knew that the classes would be held again and that there would be no penalty (to them, anyway) for not attending the session for which they were scheduled, our customers felt no impact for registering but not showing up. There was an impact, but our department was the only one taking the hit. No other department was noticeably inconvenienced or charged.

To increase attendance rates, we implemented a cancellation fee for short notice cancellations and no-shows. Departments are now charged a nominal fee for each student who registers for but does not attend class sessions. The new policy is clearly stated on all course announcements. It affects all students who enroll in a session, but do not attend the assigned session. Students may drop out of a session more than three business days prior to its start or send a substitute in their place without any penalty being incurred.

The nominal charge cut our no-show rate, but not enough. To reduce the number of students who did not attend because of schedule conflicts, we made two changes to the registration process. Students are now required to complete their own registration forms, rather than having management complete them. Also, when the registration form is completed, the student indicates a first choice of class date. Every effort is taken to fit students into the session of their choice. All registrations are handled on a first come first served basis. With these additional changes, we have cut our no-show rate to about 10% for most classes. There are still some classes that have a higher no-show rate, but we generally have more warning that this will be occurring.

At the start of our program, we often felt that we were an island. We were two software training coordinators, both of whom had software development backgrounds and an interest in training, surrounded by a sea of software engineers and managers. We initially lacked contact with any of the other trainers or educators in Honeywell or Phoenix. We quickly realized this needed to change.

The first contacts we made were with O&ED. These contacts gave us access to the previously mentioned automated registration system, someone to act as Registrar for our classes until we could get our own Registrar, several people to bounce ideas and process changes off, and a good sized library of training references.

The contacts we made within O&ED led to an active membership in the local chapter of American Society for Training and Development (ASTD), as well as its Technical and Skills Training subgroup. The contacts helped, but what helped even more was the magazines and information we started getting through the mail. Most of the mail either contained useful information or showed other places we could get help. We started to subscribe to two of the major training and development magazines, *Training* (published by Lakewood Publications) and *Training and Development* (published by ASTD). We also began to make contacts throughout the industry by attending training conferences such as the SEI Conference on Software Engineering Education and the College and Industry Education Consortium presented by the American Society of Engineering Education.

Another major step in the creation of our program occurred when we contacted Dr. Jim Collofello of Arizona State University. Dr. Collofello, who had created and taught our Software Testing class in the past, was able to modify it for this project and create the class "Training for Inspection Moderators". He worked with the Honeywell process teams to define these classes and currently teaches both of them.

Through our association with O&ED, we became acquainted with other trainers within the division. We collectively formed a Cross Functional Training Group to allow us all to exchange ideas and improve the quality of training at Honeywell. We meet every other Friday for two hours per meeting. We exchange practices and ideas, inform each other of new ideas implemented, share resources, and generally implement teaming for trainers. We have found that the contacts made through this group have helped us feel less isolated. There was still a missing piece in our training network, specifically, contact with the other engineering trainers outside our domain.

The next stage involves getting all of the Honeywell engineering trainers together to meet and share ideas. This group will be cross divisional, but not cross functional. Each member of the team coordinates the engineering training for his or her site. Currently, interest in this idea has been expressed by two other Honeywell divisions and ourselves. This group is still in its formative stages, with its first meeting planned for summer of 1992. We hope to be able to use this group to address such issues as standardized processes for acquiring external trainers, sharing techniques for engineering training, and sharing information on accessibility of National Technological University and other televised systems. Currently, we share some classes with another division located in Phoenix. We hope to expand this effort.

5   Future Improvements

Even though we have improved the quantity and quality of software engineering training in the organization over the past year, we believe that there are several areas which need additional improvement in the short term. Some of these include: Accurately estimating training costs, needs identification, the budgeting process, the registration process, the skill levels of our internal trainers, and the course evaluation process.

Apparently, we underestimated how much time it would take us to coordinate the creation and presentation of each class. Our original time estimates may be off by as

358

much as a factor of two or more. We are working to improve our estimating abilities for next year.

As we expand the training program from one project to projects across the organization, we will need the assistance of all the engineering managers. To aid the managers in identification of training needs, we plan to develop and circulate a list of courses that are our "best guess" at what is needed for the following year. The list created will include courses on processes, methods and tools that are anticipated to be used in the coming year. The list will be distributed to first level (section head) and second level (department) managers. They will use this information to create an internal software training budget and plan for each department. The training coordinators are made available during this planning phase to assist as needed. If the departments determine that there are courses missing, they will be able to work with the training department to determine the course topics, objectives, length, audience and costs for these courses. As new courses are added to the planning document, updates will be sent to each department. The training forecasts will require each department to determine in which quarter the department expects to need each course.

As each department details its own software training needs, the departmental training forecasts will be returned to the training department. Each department will be responsible for including time and money in its budget to cover the cost of courses presented to its technical staff. The training department will be responsible for time and money to create the courses and coordinate their presentation. The training department will develop a preliminary schedule of classes for the upcoming year.

We also plan to implement a new registration process in 1992. When registering, each student will supply a charge number from his/her department. This number will be charged to pay for the presentation costs of the course. At a preset date (noted in the course announcement), registrations for a session will be closed. At this time, a determination will be made whether there are enough students to justify holding the class session. If there are not, the class will be canceled.

Another change we plan to make in 1992 is to make students responsible for finding their own substitutes. Training coordinators currently spend much of their time finding substitutes for students who cancel at the last minute.

We are currently working with other (non-engineering) trainers in our division to develop an improved, formalized train the trainer class. Our course evaluations received to date indicate that many of our internal trainers need to improve their training skills. We also need to continuously improve our coordination skills and processes to enable us to do our jobs better.

We need to revise our evaluation forms, better analyze the data collected from existing classes and formalize our procedures for evaluating external classes and instructors. Investigation of the data gathered from the evaluation forms will help us to fix problem classes earlier.

Management has recognized the need for software engineering training, but the training is still being done in a somewhat chaotic manner. We are working to formalize our processes and contacts so that we can move upwards toward a level three training program, but realize that it will take time to get there. We have a long way to go toward defining which personnel need which training when they need it. We need to do a better job of communicating with our customers to determine their needs.

In the long term, we would like to be able to provide a "Tailored" software engineering training program that will promote the professional growth of each person in the division, enable us to track what each person needs, and integrate career development with training.[2]

References

[1]   Watts Humphrey, <u>Managing the Software Process</u>, Addison-Wesley, Reading Massachusetts, 1989.

[2]   Bill Curtis, "Managing the Real Leverage in Software Productivity and Quality;" *American Programmer*, July/August, 1990.

Corporate Software Engineering Education for Six Sigma: Course Development and Assessment of Success

Sandi Coker
Motorola University, Rolling Meadows, IL 60008

Bud Glick
Motorola - SRD, Rolling Meadows, IL 60008

Lavon Green
Purdue University, Hammond, IN 46323

Anneliese von Mayrhauser
Colorado State University, Fort Collins, CO 80523

Abstract. This paper describes the development process for a course used to help increase the level of maturity of software development at Motorola. We also describe the contents of the course and the experiences teaching it worldwide. The course is part of Motorola's comprehensive software engineering improvement program geared towards achieving Six Sigma quality levels. Course development was driven by an extensive requirements analysis. The requirements were then used to determine course topics and priorities, instructional sequence and course duration. We also report on course contents and the course's impact on the organization.

1 Introduction

Software development is a major portion of the business at Motorola. Software development is continuously increasing and faces many of the same challenges other hardware/software developers must solve. Motorola responded to these needs with a Corporate Initiative: (1) innovation, (2) improve quality, (3) reduce cycle time. Motorola performed a self-assessment and realized that its level of maturity of software development ([2]) was not high enough. The first point on the improvement agenda then indicated to raise the level of maturity of the software development process at Motorola. To achieve this required the involvement and support top-down from management and bottom-up from the developers.

These goals were highly publicized and visibly supported. Education plays a major part in achieving them. Thus the development of the central course in this improvement agenda, ENG300 Managing the software development process, became a highly visible course development project. All levels of management participated in its conception and development. All course developers knew that the community expected big results from this course. On the positive side, this meant support, on the negative side, overly big expectation could endanger the improvement program, since no single course can serve as a silver bullet.

Not surprisingly, education forms an integral part of this corporate initiative.

Motorola University (MU) is known as one of the best corporate training centers in the industry. Every Motorolan must fulfill yearly education requirements.

This paper explains Motorola University's course development process and how it was applied to the development of this course. Section 3 describes the requirements analysis for this course, section 4 the course content. Section 5 evaluates how well this process worked for this course. Section 6 reports on the results of the one year post mortem. Section 7 summarizes the experiences with ENG300 "Managing the software development process" and assesses the course as part of Motorola's comprehensive software engineering improvement program.

2 The Course Development Process at Motorola

Motorola University uses a six phase process, based on the Dick and Carey model of instructional design ([1]) to develop instructional materials for ENG300. The course development process is very similar to a phased software development process. It consists of analysis, design, development, formative evaluation, implementation and summative evaluation.

The *analysis* phase usually begins in response to a client's request for training. The analysis phase defines the problem, the target population, the current performance, the optimal performance, the impact of performance gaps to business issues, and finally, training and non-training solutions. An instructional designer and a subject matter expert (SME) conduct this analysis. Section 3 contains more detail on this phase of course development. Also consider Appendix 1. It shows partial analysis results for the target population.

Improving Motorola's level of maturity in software development clearly points to training as one of the solutions. So the analysis proceeds to high level design. The subject matter expert and instructional designer now work to identify an instructional goal and course topics and/or preliminary objectives. Observation, interviewing and surveying techniques help to prioritize and order the topics. A formal report publishes the analysis results. This report requires the approval of the Project Approval Body. This body consists of the client(s), the instructional design manager, the design director and designated members of SRD (Motorola's Corporate Software Research and Development Group).

The project then moves into the *design* phase. The instructional designer and subject matter expert construct a learning hierarchy. This design structure includes all topics and preliminary objectives from the analysis. The design structure helps to determine prerequisite knowledge, detailed objectives, essential content and sequencing.

Next, each topic is written in the form of an objective. Instructional strategies are established. Each objective is assigned a value (high, medium or low) based on analysis responses. These values influence the choice of strategy and (teaching) time allocations for the topics. The Project Approval Body then reviews this high level design. Appendix 2 shows learning hierarchies, objectives and a topic outline for module 2 of the course.

The complete development team takes over for low level design. For ENG300, the team consisted of: an instructional designer, a subject matter expert (SME), two technical writers, and a SME/master instructor. This development team generates a detailed content outline based on the learning hierarchy. The outline consists of sequenced objectives and general information about time allocations and strategies. The instructional designer creates a detailed design document from the content outline. The design document becomes the blue print for the course. For each sequenced objective, the document lists what the instructor and the participants will be doing, content information for the course materials (participant guide, instructor guide, technical reference guide and overheads), detailed instructional strategies and time estimates. The completion of the design document triggers the third review cycle by the Project Approval Body. Appendix 3 shows this detailed design for course module 2.

A review of the design document by experienced target audience members and their managers follows. This is a critical meeting, because for the first time, the target audience has an opportunity to provide input since the analysis. For ENG300, we gained very valuable insight which resulted in design changes.

After these changes, the technical writers start the *development* phase. We reduce learning curve delays by involving the writers early in the process. Each writer works from Motorola defined page layout standards on separate course modules for the participant guide, the instructor guide, and the overheads. The writers work jointly on a set of internal and external papers in a Technical Reference Guide. The Subject Matter Expert (SME) and Master Instructor (MI) provide content material to each writer for each topic in the design document. The instructional designer, the SME and the SME/master instructor review each module. Changes are made based on reviewer comments and consensus. Draft materials mark the end of the development phase.

The next phase in the process *formatively evaluates* the course. The first test, the *developmental test*, is presented to randomly selected participants representing each major business unit within Motorola. The instructional designer develops evaluation instruments which capture questions raised by the Project Approval Body and the Development Team during design and development. The participants are also asked to respond to questions dealing with the appropriateness of instructional strategies, relevancy and course effectiveness. In addition to the structured written evaluations, the master instructor "debriefs" the course, at designated points in the instruction. She discusses instructional strategies and content with participants. The entire development team attends the developmental test. While the master instructor presents the material, the writers concentrate their efforts on material problems, the SME is concerned with content and the instructional designer observes participant reactions, timing and course flow.

A post mortem follows the developmental test. The development team discusses the data collected during the developmental test and decides what changes to make. An evaluation report describes conclusions and planned actions.

The course materials are tested for a second time, the *pilot test*. Once again, the participants are randomly selected from each major business unit. The main purpose of the pilot is to refine the timings, case studies, and to test changes made following the developmental test. As with the developmental test, course delivery is evaluated with written evaluations, observation, and class discussion. All development team members attend the test and a post mortem. Final changes to the materials happen after the pilot evaluation report.

At Motorola, complete course development includes a course to Train the Trainer. The instructional designer and the SME/Master instructor design this course. The content includes the course rationale, background, Motorola audience information, strategies and content specific to the course.

The *implementation phase* for a course like ENG300 involves finalizing materials and certifying instructors. A master copy of the printed materials is approved and then baselined with the Reprographics department. This also includes documentation regarding ordering information and course scheduling requirements. We write instructor specifications and use them to recruit candidates. All instructor candidates must attend the course as a participant, attend the Motorola University Instructor Techniques course and the Train the Trainer portion for the course they wish to teach. Then the candidates must teach the course with the master instructor. Instructor candidates are evaluated for their content knowledge and their ability to clearly present the course content to the audience. The master instructor certifies the candidate after the co-teach. If however, the candidate is deficient in any area, the master instructor can recommend additional study or co-teaches.

Motorola evaluates courses on an ongoing basis. We collect written course evaluations for each course delivery. The Motorola University Evaluation Department collects and collates data from these evaluations. In addition, the course development team meet for a *six* and a *twelve month* review of the course. During these reviews, we examine evaluation data and comments by all certified instructors. We modify a course based on these reviews. ENG300 is now on an annual review cycle. However, the Evaluation Department distributes monthly reports. If any course problems arise, we hold the review earlier.

3 Requirements Analysis for Course

In developing the course, we considered not only what course to develop first, but also its content. The course should provide maximum benefit to the target audience.

For the first consideration (what course to develop first), it is important to note that prior to the development of this course, no Motorola-specific training existed in the Software Project Management area. Software is a critical factor in product success. We considered successful Project Management *the* key focus area for overall software success. Therefore, we decided to begin here. This decision also considered the large size of the Motorola software community and the need to enhance its effective management. (Motorola's total software developer population is an estimated 8000 people, including MIS staff.)

For the second consideration (what should the course material content be for a general software project management course), we had little Motorola-specific information about the required topics for course content from the target audience. We determined course content requirements as follows:

1. Determine intended course audience.
We need knowledge of the company culture and its organizational structure to assess potential course audience. This knowledge existed with the survey leaders who had broad experience working across Motorola with many software project managers in committees, working groups, and direct consulting. In addition, to optimally match course content with intended audience, we used a prior study (conducted by Motorola University, an internal company training organization). It had examined and analyzed the duties and tasks of software engineers, managers, and project managers across Motorola. This study produced *Job Models* in these three categories. We selected the categories of *Project Team Leader* and *Software Manager* as primary targets since they primarily deal with direct management of software projects (i.e., "software project management"). These two sets of people perform the bulk of the Software Project Management tasks across Motorola.

2. Obtain the training needs/ requirements of the audience.
A two-pronged approach determined the needs of the defined course audience. We first surveyed commercially-available courses and attended and evaluated a few of those which most closely and thoroughly covered the tasks defined in the Job Models study for software project management. We selected, attended, and evaluated courses aimed at "real-time" product development as well as courses for MIS.

Our second approach was to gather course requirements across the Motorola software community. The audience to be interviewed was carefully selected based on several considerations: they must provide knowledgeable opinions on what tasks they perform, what tasks they think they ought to do, and the relative priorities of training on all of these tasks. We interviewed over 80 people across 10 major business units, both in U.S. and international Motorola businesses. The interviewees fit the study profiles of the three Job Models previously mentioned. First, a group consisting of Project Team Leaders and Software Managers (i.e., the people who matched the previously mentioned profile of the tasks performed by software project managers) was selected. Next, the key senior managers and software managers of a variety of projects across the company (many of whom managed the project managers from the first group), were chosen as the second group. Finally, a third group of software engineers was selected, who were active in product development as well as MIS. A structured questionnaire was developed to investigate the specific content required for the actual course. Interviewees not only commented on topics to include in the new course, but also specified the priority for each of the topics.

The starting list of topics in the questionnaire was also initially based on the previous job models study, then refined based on additional, high priority topics supplied by the interviewees. In this way it was possible to develop a course specifically tailored to the target audience.

After attending several courses (covering product development and MIS project management), we realized that only a small (less than 25%) subset of the final list of recommended topics was covered by existing commercially-available courses. This required a relatively large amount of rework. So we decided to develop a totally new course covering Software Project Management for the Motorola practitioner. We wanted to cover as much of the functional and topical content as possible, yet roll-out the course in the near future. The course should not last longer than four days. Survey interviews determined the target duration of four days.

3. Determine Course Topics and Priorities, Instructional Sequence, and Course Duration.

An additional important aim for selected course topics was to match them to the SEI (Software Engineering Institute) maturity level topics. This was a strong influence in identifying high-priority topics, since it would match topics presented in the course and SEI organizational improvement recommendations. We also checked the topics whether they conformed to our internal Motorola Quality Policy and Quality Review. Motorola' Quality Policy for Software Development states required adherence to best practices for software development. Motorola's Quality System Review was a factor influencing the selection of Motorola as a Baldridge Award winner. One of its sections covers software quality.

Finally, after satisfying these considerations, the topics were ordered in the priority as selected by the interview questionnaires. This priority was used to determine duration and depth of coverage for each topic. When all topics were considered, more than 95% of them could be covered within four days.

Next the subject matter experts and instructional designer iteratively constructed a sequence of topics. The final, high-level sequence was selected for relevance, logical coherence, and continuity. This sequence was reviewed by a steering committee and technical writers before starting the actual course development. The next activity was to study available, existing reference material for the selected topics. For several of the topics, no suitable material could be obtained and totally new development was necessary.

4 Course Content

We designed course content to meet the requirements of Motorola as described in the previous section. The course title, "Managing the Software Development Process", emphasizes the need to manage a process in order to assure six-sigma quality of the product, in this case, a software product. The course covers all aspects of project management - project planning, project reporting, and project control. Following is a brief description of the contents of each module of the course. Refer to Appendix 4 for a relationship of each module to requirements. Included in this Appendix 4 is the time allocation for each module indicating the significance of the topic. Note the changes between this and the original plans (see earlier appendices).

Course Introduction
Module 1 - Successful Software Projects
This module emphasizes the success of a software project as it directly supports the goals of Motorola. The critical success factors of the software development project that relate to the specific corporate goals are identified as:
- six-sigma quality
- total cycle-time reduction
- product and manufacturing leadership
- profit improvement
- participative management and improvement

All of these factors contribute to raising the SEI Level of Maturity as defined by the Software Engineering Institute (SEI) of Carnegie-Mellon University.

Module 2 - Setting the Stage for Successful Software Projects
Selection of the appropriate system life cycle model forms the basis for the system development process. This module briefly discusses some of the life cycle models used within Motorola. We cover briefly the significance of tailoring the life cycle to meet the needs of the project, the role of standards and metrics, and the ongoing nature of verification, validation, and project management. We reference other Motorola courses that cover these topics in depth. The IEEE standard life cycle, as defined in the draft of Standard 1074, is the sample life cycle used throughout the course for reference.

Project Planning
Module 3 - Planning Process
This topic is the heart of the course and takes up the majority of the course time. The participants learn how to plan a software development project and how to develop the Software Project Management Plan. Throughout this module, participants practice developing sections of the plan. Near the end of the course, they have the opportunity to develop a total project plan. Because of the amount of material, we divided this topic into seven separate sub-modules.

Module 3A stresses the need to define the requirements of the ultimate user of a software product. For Motorola, this can be a retail customer, another manufacturer, an engineer or a department within the corporation. Another course within Motorola teaches the techniques for developing the requirements. This module teaches the project manager how to verify that the requirements are complete, how to prioritize the requirements, how to organize complex requirements into feature sets for multiple versions of the software product, and how to develop a master software plan based on the requirements. This product, the Software Project Management Plan, carries the name suggested in the IEEE standard life cycle.

Module 3B teaches the project manager how to use historical data to identify risks and how to develop contingency plans should an anticipated problem arise.

Participants practice techniques to identify and reduce risks such as the development of a risk reduction matrix and risk reduction dependency chart.

Module 3C covers the topic of estimating software size, effort, schedule, and cost. Models that use experiential, algorithmic, statistical, and empirical techniques are introduced. For example, the participants learn about the Rayleigh-Putnam Model, whereas they actually practice working with the COCOMO Model. We present a series of automated tools for various aspects of project estimation. This topic subsequently resulted in the development of two other courses: " Overseeing the Estimation of Software Sizing and Estimation" is a course presented to managers who have to understand the effort behind generating software estimates. "Software Sizing and Estimation" is a course for the software engineers who actually use the techniques and tools to produce the estimates.

Module 3D introduces the topic of planning for quality. Because other courses discuss how to perform quality improvement tasks, this course discusses how to incorporate the metrics, reviews, and postmortems identified elsewhere into a comprehensive Software Quality Assurance Plan. The need to build quality into the total software process is emphasized by the use of the Brettschneider Quality Model for software testing. This model was developed by a Motorolan to be used by Motorola.

The software life cycle is the basis for the discussion of scheduling techniques in Module 3E. PERT charts, Gantt charts, and probability techniques form the cadre of techniques presented to schedule specific tasks within the project. Issues that impact the software process, such as reusability, build versus buy, third party and subcontracting software, multi-site and multi-group developments, are covered in Module 3F.

Module 4 - Managing the Project: Human Factors
This module addresses the aspects of interpersonal relationships that impact the process from the perspective of the project manager and the software engineer. For the manager, leadership functions and styles are addressed. Team-building principles and communications techniques are presented to focus the project manager on the needs of the software engineer. Human factors such as culture, especially in multi-national projects, and resistance to change are additional topics.

Module 5 - Establishing Roles
This module integrates the principles of Module 3 and Module 4 to teach how to match people with tasks.

Project Reporting
Module 6 - Tracking to the Plan
In order to manage a project, the actual time spent on project tasks must be compared to the estimates. This module discusses how to collect, interpret and report on processes and products of development. This includes the actual development processes and products, as well as the verification and validation tasks, the software quality assurance tasks, the documentation tasks, and the training tasks.

Project Control
Module 7 - Updating the Plan
This module discusses how to make decisions to control the project. Alternatives available, such as scope change, end-date change, and schedule compression, all focus on the Software Project Management Plan. Throughout the course, participants perform practice exercises comprising approximately 40% of class time. The final exercise is the development and modification of a project plan.

Conclusion
The final session of the course is a discussion by each participant as to how they will put aspects of the course into practice. The participants consider the topics that are most important to them and how they will put them into practice. At this time a copy of the Management Application Guide (MAG) is distributed to the participants. They are reminded that a copy of the MAG was sent to their managers at the beginning of the course. This guide was developed one year after the course was released when participants wanted to encourage management involvement and follow-up with the course material.

5 Evaluation of Course Development Process

Course development proceeded with a very tight schedule. From May to November we were charged with course design, review, prototyping, redevelopment, course-test, further corrections and new development, training and certifying trainers, and preparation of participant and instructor materials. All team members worked on other projects as well. Because of the tight schedule, we often reworked material and developed new material in parallel. This is also one of the reasons why we had two technical writers.

While this affords a higher degree of parallelism, it also posed challenges for coordination between the writers to avoid duplicate material and gaps in topics. We successfully solved this problem by identifying formal interfaces where necessary. This happened, however, after inconsistencies surfaced while proofreading the course material. Course developers also often rushed changes and further module development to comply with lead times for word processing and material reproduction. This caused "on-the-fly" changes and some avoidable errors. Even after the acceptance test for the course we spliced in some last minute changes. The course appeared less stable than the software engineering minds among us would have liked, but our concerns about this proved incorrect. We made relatively few changes after turnover.

Course development at Motorola differs from that at other companies in another aspect: Technical writers are not necessarily subject matter experts. For extensive hard-core technical material this holds the danger of shallow treatment of topics (the technical writer does not understand the material and thus cannot write about it with substance). On the other hand, the SME makes sure the technical content is there. We credit the excellent rapport between all members of the development team and thus between the SME and the two technical writers for building a course with sophisticated technical content. For us, this division of responsibilities proved a strength: the technical writers practically ensured that the participants received clearly written materials: they had to understand the material first, otherwise they wouldn't be able to write about them.

We needed the support of many Motorolans during course development. Their enthusiastic participation and feedback in reviews and tests of course material greatly helped to develop "the right course". At various junctures we faced harsh criticism, but it was always paired with active help through project examples and experiences directing course emphasis. Support came from practitioners (first line managers, senior developers), from high level managers (who allowed their people to spend the time to attend these reviews and course tests) to corporate leadership (several came to our course tests and actively participated). We believe strongly that this support and enthusiasm at all levels helped to make this course a success. Some of our course volunteers also provided us with much helpful Motorola specific case study information and a necessary check on requirements. E. g. after feedback we selected a different set of methods for cost-effort estimation and completed our list of tool used in various parts of Motorola.

Without the enthusiastic support of Motorolans and their continued input we could well have developed a very fine course, but past Motorola's corporate culture and its needs. The guidance of the steering committee, of the future course instructors, and of the participants, ensured that this course is tailored to the Motorola culture and its needs. Without this, Motorola could have bought or licensed an existing set of courses more cheaply. In summary, the main drivers for successful course development were

*   superb requirements analysis
*   enthusiastic commitment by Motorolans and contractors throughout development time
*   a sense of importance brought about by Motorola's self assessment
*   excellent cooperation amongst contractors and between Motorolans and contractors
*   flexibility to adjust and reconsider needs for course material

6 One Year Evaluation

During the first year, 1991, the course was taught many times all over the world. In the US it has been taught in Arlington Heights, IL, Boston, MA, Phoenix, AZ, Schaumburg, IL, Boynton Beach, FL. It has also been taught in Canada, Germany, Sweden, England, Israel, Malaysia, India, and Singapore. This course is not only significant for its frequency of delivery, but, more importantly, its breadth of delivery. Throughout the corporation, from corporate headquarters in the Chicago area to Phoenix, to Europe, to the Middle East, and to Asia, the request for the course was emphatic.

We held a review meeting that included the instructors of the course approximately one year after the initial presentation of the course. Everybody agreed that all topics belonged in the course, although some resequencing of the modules would help the course flow more smoothly. The timings in Appendix 4 reflect current suggested timings that have been modified somewhat from the original. In the Communications Sector, the instructors have been following up with managers of participants of the course six months after the course was taken. They have noticed an improvement in the rigor of practicing project management techniques. Most significant is the request for advanced courses to further develop the skills developed during the original course.

There are other ways to measure the success of this course. The request for and development of the two courses on software sizing and estimation is one. The development and use of the Management Application Guide is another. The scheduling of the course in Germany, Scotland, France, Malaysia, Hong Kong, Singapore, as well as the Motorola University centers in the United States, is yet another. As a result of the review of the course, four alternative approaches to improving the materials of the "Managing the Software Development Process" course have been identified. They represent various levels of effort and are being analyzed at this time for cost/benefit. They range from making minor editorial changes to resequencing the material.

One of the goals of the course was to foster the use of automated tools in order to implement the techniques of the course. Because the course did not teach any of these tools, rather it suggests which tools are available, there is no evidence that technology transfer has occurred. However, with the introduction of the new course on software sizing and estimation, software tools are being taught in an intensive three-day course.

7 Conclusions

The impact of the course on Motorola University and the outside participants has been significant. Motorola University was able to test its course development process in a complex situation. This course development project used contractors (one subject matter expert/master instructor and two technical writers). We developed the course with a very tight schedule, Requirements came from diverse sectors of the corporation, and changing during development. The Motorola University project team developing the course realized the need for effective project management as it was developing the course. This has influenced further course development projects at Motorola University.

Only one of the two faculty members involved in the course development had been involved using an instructional design process previously. All participants, those from Motorola, those from the academic environment, and private contractors, agreed that developing this course was a worthwhile endeavor and that it was one of the most enjoyable projects in their experience. The success of this effort is an example of the possibilities for uniting the business sector and the academic sector, crossing multiple disciplines, to develop a product that is worthy of quality recognition.

Software Engineering Training as provided by MSDP represents only one of Motorola's Software Quality Initiatives. Each of the initiatives represents a thrust aimed at software improvement across the entire company. They conform with overall Motorola key initiatives for improved quality, reduced cycle time, and improved productivity. This program has been championed by the Motorola Corporate Office and, in software, consists of the following key elements:

- Software Engineering Training. Covering several areas, such as project management, testing, estimation, structured design, reviews, etc.
- Quality Policy for Software Development (QPSD). Specifying best practices for software quality.
- Quality System Review for Software (SQSR). Auditing business units for adherence to factors for software quality.
- Senior Management Forum (SMF). Covering the strategic value of software in business for business unit senior managers.
- Software Benchmarking. Both internal and external. To determine best in class software approaches.
- SEI Assessments. Software Engineering Institute-developed procedure for examining software capability of organizations.
- Software Engineering Education. Influence development of undergraduate programs in Software Engineering in Universities and Colleges.
- Software Metrics. Devise metrics to meaningfully track and improve software.

The Software Quality Initiatives have resulted in noticeable progress at Motorola. For example, recent assessments on several business units have indicated a typical improvement trend to SEI level 2 maturity levels in each business. The implications are significant in terms of improved quality, reduced cycle time, and improved productivity across Motorola. With these improvements we also expect the course to evolve and change. We will see more sophistication in the topics; we are already offering special topic courses (e. g. in cost/effort estimation, metrics) for more in depth treatment of some of the topics covered in our core course. The current version is only a snapshot in time reflecting our current needs. We are also tailoring the content to meet specialized needs of specific organizations at Motorola.

Acknowledgements

Many individuals have contributed to the success of this course. We thank them all. Special thanks go to Michael Daskalantonakis, Mary Kennedy, John Pellegrin, Bob Yaccobellis, and Bob Yusczak.

References

1. Dick, W. and Carey, L.; "The Systematic Design of Instruction" Third Edition, Scott Foresman & Co., Glenview, IL, 1990.
2. Humphrey, W.; "Managing the Software Process", Addison-Wesley, Reading, MA, 1989.

Appendix 1: Partial Analysis Results for Course Module 2

Deficiencies	Objectives	Content Outline
no software process to track insufficient understanding of the activities involved in the software development process (2a)	A. Same as above	2. Software development process a.Models of software development b.Complex model for geographically distributed, parallel development of embedded software c.Phases within complex model d.Parallel development within complex model

Appendix 2: Objectives, Topic Outline, Strategies and Learning Hierarchy for Course Module 2

Process Models		Depth of Coverage
2.0	Select appropriate process model	Medium-High
2.1	Describe simple waterfall process model for software development	Medium-High
2.2	Describe spiral process model	Medium
2.3	Describe phased development within complex model	Medium
2.4	Describe parallel development within complex model	Medium
2.5	describe distributed development within complex model	Medium
2.6.	Describe complex model of software development for geographically distributed, parallel development of embedded software	Medium
2.7.	Describe several software process models, techniques, and tools	Medium-High
2.8	Describe the impact of different process activities on the product (analysis, design, test, etc.)	Medium-High

Module 2: Strategy

Lecture/Discussion
Process model selection: waterfall, spiral, phased and parallel complex development)
(matrix on the selection of models, evolutionary versus waterfall)
Individual Exercise
Distributed development within complex model
Geographically distributed, parallel development of embedded software
Lecture
Describe several software process models, techniques, tools
Impact of process activities on product.

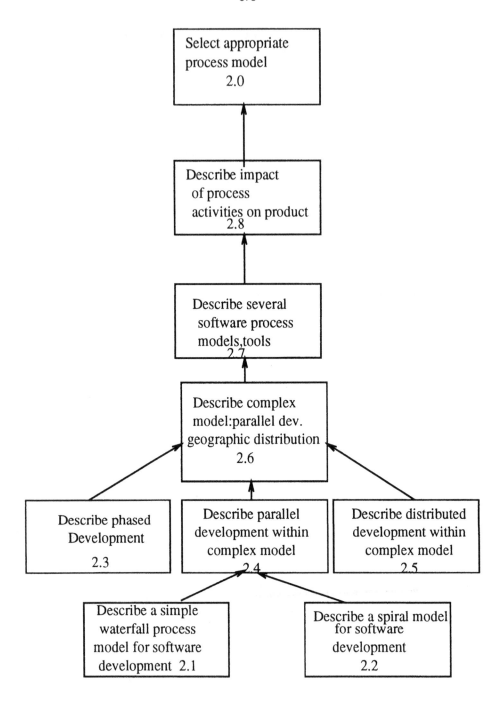

Appendix 3:Detailed Design for Course Module 2

Objectives	Instructional Strategies	Time
2.0 Select appropriate process model 2.1 Describe simple waterfall process model 2.2 Describe spiral process model 2.3. Describe phased development within complex model 2.4 Describe parallel development within complex model 2.5 Describe distributed development within complex model 2.6. Describe complex model for geographically distributed, parallel development of embedded software	**Activity**: Lecture Instructor: Presents course map and module overview, concepts on process models and model selection matrix; discusses why information is necessary - relevance to objective 1.5; Evolutionary vs. waterfall (**AVM book**); emphasize that there is no right answer. Participants: follow in PG with corresponding pages. Discussion: Instructor: asks participants if they use a similar model. Point out that this module will help them to evaluate their process so they can improve it if necessary. Participants: participate in discussion **Materials:** Overheads and PG Course map, module overview, series of charts to show complexity layers, phase overlap (reduced cycle time), communication, subcontractors. Concepts: more complexity adds more dependencies and more risk. Present along with simple Gantt chart. **Activity**: Exercise: Instructor: introduces the exercise Participants: individually complete worksheet which leads them to discover that evolutionary model works best for more complex projects (if you plan for reuse). Worksheet of 6-7 examples of projects. Participants refer to information in PG and determine appropriate process model (**AVM, GILB, Boehm -Spiral Model Paper**) **Materials:** Overhead: introduction/directions for exercise PG: worksheet with 5 columns entitled: organizational, managerial, technical, impact issues and process model. 6-7 rows contain information from example projects (**SRD-Motorola specific examples**) for first 4 columns. Examples become more complex from first to last. Answers proceed from waterfall to evolutionary. **Activity**: Debriefing Instructor: presents worksheet overhead, asks for answers. Class discussion,complete worksheet. Participants:discussion, correct worksheets. **Materials:** Overhead (worksheet), IG (correct answers)	45 m 15 m 25 m 25 m

Objectives	Instructional Strategies	Time
2.7 Describe several software process models, techniques and tools (analysis, design, test, etc.) **2.8 Describe the impact of different process activities on the product**	**Activity:** Lecture Instructor: presents matrix of available products (i. e. SPM tools and commercially available methodologies) and techniques. Points out reference sources and that no universally right answer exists. Some products/techniques are better for given models. Participant: follows in PG. Discussion: Instructor: initiates discussion around matrix and definitions from IEEE; shows examples that illustrate impact of including activities **(SRD - Senior Management Forum, 8 different scenarios)** Participant: participates in discussion. **Materials:** Overheads: Matrices of available products (one for tools, one for methodologies) and techniques. Discuss overhead on methodologies first. Include which methodologies are tied to lifecycle phases. Products overhead has matrix labelled "products" on top and "tools/techniques" on the side. **(SRD provides Motorola specific examples and IEEE standards)** PG: pages corresponding to overhead IG: paragraph descriptions of all products listed in matrix for instructor reference. Reference Guide: paragraph descriptions of all products listed in matrix.	45 m

Appendix 4: Relationship of Course Content to Requirements

Course Requirements	Course Content
Course Introduction 1 Successful Software Projects Understand the management of the systems development process Manage the software development project Raise the SEI level of maturity at Motorola Realize that project management is no "silver bullet"	1.5 hours What factors are critical to project success project
2 Setting the Stage for Successful Software Projects How to select the appropriate system life cycle model How to modify a life cycle model to reflect impact of project complexities Understand role of standards, metrics, and verification/validation in software development process	1.25 hours System life cycle models and their layers of complexity .5 hours Exercise: Selection of software life cycle Choose a life cycle model and provide a rationale for that choice

Project Planning 3A Requirements Definition How to plan a software project and develop the Software Project Management Plan Define what is needed in the Requirements Definition statement Prioritize requirements Identify feature sets Develop a master software test plan	1.25 hours How to plan a project using - a project planning checklist - a requirement definition checklist - requirement impact analysis (cost/benefit analysis) - feature sets (prioritized and modularized) - verification and validation plans - a checklist of a master software test plan 1.5 hours Exercise: Identification of feature sets Prioritize requirements and create feature sets (versions) Generate a list of questions about the requirements
3B Risk How to use historical data to identify risks and practice risk analysis and contingency planning	1 hour Advantages of risk management Types of risk How to assess risk How to use risk reduction techniques 1.5 hours Exercise: Risk reduction Conduct a risk analysis Generate a risk reduction matrix Generate a risk dependency table which highlights how a risk reduction activity can exacerbate another risk
3C Estimating Cost and Effort Identify and use alternative methods of estimating size, schedule, effort and cost Identify different tools available to assist in the estimation process Generate an estimate based on information in a Motorola case study	1.5 hours Basic software estimation techniques - Algorithmic Estimation Model (Rayleigh-Putnam) - Experiential Models (Delphi techniques) - Statistical Models (COCOMO) - Cost and effort estimation by parts: top-down and bottom-up 1.25 hours Exercise: COCOMO model practice Calculate cost of a project with basic and intermediate COCOMO models and compare the two estimates Divide project into four subprojects, running in parallel, and calculate effort estimate

3D Planning for Quality Identify the metrics, reviews and post mortems which need to be planned for the development Identify the predictive models of quality Identify and use Brettschneider Quality Model	1.25 hours How to plan for software quality - information about some software metrics - information about models of quality 2.5 hours Exercise: Development of Software Quality Assurance Plan (SQAP) Develop a quality plan consisting of a list of reviews, audits and metrics which need to be planned Calculate the amount of expected customer problems based on testing time and errors detected during testing; Determine how much more testing is needed to achieve a predetermined quality level
3E Scheduling and Task Assignment Identify and prioritize the work tasks to create the feature sets and deliverable products Develop a work breakdown structure for a multi-layered software development Assign tasks to personnel and consider resource issues Identify and plan for training needs Use critical path PERT and Gantt charts Compute probability of success of a project	1 hour How to schedule projects and assign tasks - scheduling considerations relative to the life cycle, the work breakdown structure, and architecture - checklist for tasks and resource allocation - scheduling techniques - scheduling considerations 1.25 hours Exercise: Develop a work breakdown structure Develop a WBS for the MPC project based on the requirements definition 2.5 hours Exercise: PERT/Gantt practice Determine probability of completing project on time Generate a Gantt Chart highlighting buffer times
3F Special Issues Plan for software reuse Identify trade-offs between build, buy, reuse, and subcontractors Plan for third party and subcontracting software and how to qualify vendors Identify the need for feedback time during the development life cycle Identify the issues surrounding multi-site, multi-group developments	0.5 hours How to plan for these special issues

4 Managing the Project - Human Factors	1.5 hours
Focus on process and product improvement	How to manage the human factors of a project
Awareness of business issues	
Leadership/project direction	process and product improvement
Improving interpersonal relations	the importance of business issue awareness
Developing a team	a project leadership checklist
Team communications	project leadership functions and styles
Handling project changes	aspects of interpersonal relationships
Time management and task prioritization	team development and conflict resolution
International issues	effecting change
	international issues that can impact the project
	1 hour
	Exercise: Role conflict
	Determine the type of conflict and how to turn it into an opportunity
5 Establishing Roles	
Define customer/supplier relationships and marketing	1 hour
	How to establish roles
Identify communication/team/organization paradigms	-communication networks
	-roles in software development
Describe the role of a software project manager	-various team paradigms
	-different organizational paradigms
Describe software project management responsibilities	-organizational issues
Describe software quality assurance responsibilities	1 hour
Describe software configuration management responsibilities	Exercise: Communication networks
	Generate a communication structure
Describe software testing responsibilities	
Identify problems associated with project thrashing	
Describe how to establish roles and responsibilities within multi-layered software development	

<u>Project Reporting</u> 6 Tracking to the Plan Be able to implement project tracking measurements <u>Project Control</u> 7 Updating the Plan Improve visibility and bring plan to actual	.75 hours How to track to the plan -defining project tracking -tracking projects -tracking reports by category -managing the tracking mechanism .5 hours How to update the plan 1.75 hours Exercise: Tracking and updating the plan Generate updated plans for the MPC project using metrics for the MPC project and four different scenarios which impact the schedule of the project

The IBM Cleanroom Software Engineering Technology Transfer Program

Richard C. Linger
R. Alan Spangler
IBM Cleanroom Software Technology Center
100 Lakeforest Boulevard
Gaithersburg, MD 20877

Abstract. Cleanroom software engineering is a theory-based, team-oriented process for developing zero-defect software with high probability. Cleanroom places software development under statistical quality control to permit scientific certification of product quality. Technologies applied in Cleanroom include box structure specification of user function and object architecture, function-theoretic design and correctness verification, and statistical usage testing for quality certification. Cleanroom management is based on incremental development of a pipeline of user-function increments that accumulate into the final product. The IBM Cleanroom Software Technology Center (CSTC) provides technology transfer services to IBM product laboratories and customers for initiating Cleanroom team operations. The technology transfer includes education, consultation, and tool development. Consultation support after education is a critical success factor, as are management commitment and team motivation. Experience shows Cleanroom produces remarkable quality results that more than offset the cost of technology transfer.

1 Principles of Cleanroom Software Engineering

Given the apparent inevitability of errors in software, the idea of zero defects may seem an impossible goal. Indeed, there is no theoretical way to ever know that a software product has zero defects. However, it is possible to know that a product has zero defects with high probability. The good news in software development today is that programming teams using Cleanroom technology are capable of developing software that is zero defect with high probability, and doing so with high productivity. Such performance is possible only with solid theoretical foundations and engineering discipline.

Cleanroom software engineering is a theory-based, team-oriented, incremental process that combines formal methods of software development with statistical quality certification [1,2,3]. The Cleanroom process is based on two fundamental principles:

·   The purpose of Cleanroom testing is to provide scientific certification of software quality with respect to specifications, not to debug quality in, an impossible task.

·   The purpose of Cleanroom development is to produce zero-/near-zero-defect software for quality certification by Cleanroom testing.

These principles prescribe characteristics of Cleanroom development, testing, and management, as follows:

Development: Rigorous, theory-based techniques are required for software specification, design, and correctness verification to produce zero-/near-zero-defect software for quality certification.

Testing: Statistical quality control techniques are required for software certification to permit valid inferences of product quality.

Management: Independent development and certification teams are required for accountability for quality production and measurement. Incremental development is required for continual quality feedback from certification to development teams.

The practice of Cleanroom means applying technologies that satisfy these requirements. Theoretical considerations and practical experience have shown the following technologies to be extremely effective in Cleanroom operations:

Box Structure Specification. Box structures provide a rigorous, stepwise refinement process for system specification and design [4,5,6]. The *black box*, *state box* and *clear box* of a system or system part provide three views with identical external behavior and increasing internal design [7]. The repeated refinement process from black box (external behavior in terms of history of use) to state box (introduces retained data) to clear box (introduces procedures and new black boxes) results in a hierarchy of objects derived and connected in harmonious operation at each level. Box structures scale up to large systems with no loss of precision. Box structure analysis can reveal gaps and omissions in requirements early in the life cycle.

Function-Theoretic Design and Correctness Verification. Clear boxes contain sequential logic composed of nested and sequenced control structures (sequence, ifthenelse, whiledo, etc.). Each such control structure represents a rule for a mathematical function or relation that can be recorded in design text as an *intended function*, expressed in notation ranging from natural language to mathematics. A Correctness Theorem defines a correctness relationship between intended functions and their control structure refinements in terms of from one to three *correctness conditions* to be verified for each control structure type, independent of language and subject matter [8]. Correctness conditions are verified in *mental proofs of correctness* in team reviews. Even though all but trivial programs have an essentially infinite number of paths, they contain a finite number of control structures, and their verification can be carried out in a finite number of steps. Verification is more comprehensive and powerful than unit testing and debugging, which often leads to "right in the small, wrong in the large" programs. In Cleanroom, verification takes the place of unit testing and debugging, which are unnecessary and not permitted.

Statistical Usage Testing. Cleanroom certification teams are not responsible for testing in quality, but rather for certifying the quality of software with respect to specifications. Statistical usage testing permits scientific estimates of product quality [1,10]. Cleanroom code increments undergo first-ever execution in statistical testing carried out by certification teams. In this process, test cases are randomized against various projected *usage probability distributions* and test results are used by a *software quality model* to compute expected product Mean Time To Failure (MTTF) and other statistical measures of quality. Because the software is tested the way users intend to use it, as modeled by usage distributions, errors tend to be found in failure-rate order, most virulent errors first. As a result, statistical testing is more effective at improving product quality than traditional path/coverage testing [2].

Cleanroom management is based on a life cycle of the incremental development and certification of a pipeline of user-function increments that execute in the system environment and accumulate into the final product. Cleanroom operations are carried out by small development and certification teams, with teams of teams for large projects. Experience shows that Cleanroom development teams are capable of delivering very high quality code to certification teams, who then drive development quality to zero defect with high probability through statistical usage testing.

Cleanroom is a flexible and adaptable methodology within the principles outlined above, and is being successfully applied in IBM product laboratories and other industrial and governmental organizations. The CSTC is currently supporting Cleanroom teams at numerous IBM product laboratories in the US and Europe.

2 Cleanroom Quality Results

First-time Cleanroom development teams in IBM and other organizations have produced nearly a third of a million lines of code with high productivity averaging just 2.9 errors per KLOC at delivery to certification teams, measured from first-ever execution [2,3,9,11,14]. This level of quality represents all errors ever found in testing, and compares to 30-50 errors per KLOC for traditionally developed software measured from first execution. In addition, experience shows that errors left behind by correctness verification tend to be simple mistakes easily found and fixed in statistical testing, not the deep design and interface errors often encountered in traditional development. These results include teams ranging from three to 50 members; applications including microcode, batch, distributed, multi-threaded, interactive, and real-time systems; and languages including C, C++, Jovial, PL/I, and Assembler.

3 The IBM Cleanroom Software Technology Center

The IBM Cleanroom Software Technology Center (CSTC) was established to provide technology transfer services to IBM product laboratories and customers for initiating Cleanroom team operations. The CSTC provides education, consultation, and tool development services that are packaged according to the needs of each laboratory or customer. CSTC members are experienced Cleanroom practitioners selected for their subject matter knowledge and ability to teach and consult effectively [12].

The technology transfer process progresses through four phases:

Initial Planning. The CSTC works with clients to select demonstration projects for Cleanroom introduction, review staffing and resource plans, and schedule education. Management briefings are conducted to review the Cleanroom process and discuss performance expectations and success factors. Responsibilities of both the CSTC and the client are documented in a contract.

Education. The CSTC provides intensive education through four courses. The first course is a one-day introduction to Cleanroom technology, management, and the technology transfer process. The three advanced courses deal with the technologies of Cleanroom specification and incremental development, design and verification, and statistical quality certification. Team managers and technical leaders are required to attend all courses to ensure effective planning and support for the technology transfer.

Consultation. A CSTC member is assigned to each team to provide consultation support for Cleanroom introduction in the project environment. Consultation is carried out through on-site visits, video conferences, and teleconferences. Project documentation and work products in draft to final form are transmitted to the CSTC for review and comment. A consultant may periodically call upon other CSTC members to provide support in their areas of expertise, for example, in specification strategies or statistical testing approaches.

Self-Sufficiency. Achieving self-sufficiency in Cleanroom operations is an important objective of the technology transfer process. Team cloning is an effective means for propagating Cleanroom operations. In this process, illustrated in Figure 1, members of successful teams become leaders of new teams, thereby providing knowledgeable and experienced guidance to next-generation projects. In addition, product laboratories are encouraged to establish Cleanroom Centers of Competency to provide education and consultation services to new teams. These centers can be staffed by members of initial teams, who work closely with the CSTC to keep up-to-date on new developments in Cleanroom theory and practice.

The CSTC also provides Chair Assignments to give individuals from product laboratories an opportunity to become experts in Cleanroom technology through resident participation in CSTC operations. Upon returning to their sponsoring laboratories, Chair assignees are capable of teaching and consulting in Cleanroom technologies.

4 The Cleanroom Education Curriculum

The current IBM Cleanroom education curriculum is composed of the four courses described below, totalling two intensive weeks of classroom time. Students learn the theory on which Cleanroom is based, as well as the practice of Cleanroom software specification, verification, and certification. To provide opportunities for practice and discussion, lectures are followed by laboratory sessions; mini-labs contain short exercises which reinforce basic concepts, while full laboratory exercises require students to complete substantial assignments, for example, correctness verification of 500 lines of

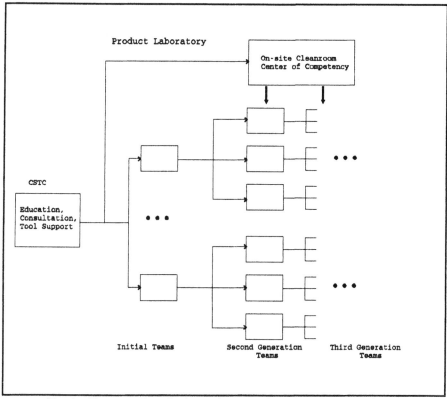

Fig. 1. Cleanroom Introduction and Propagation Through Team Cloning

design. Student feedback and Cleanroom project experience are important sources of feedback for course improvement. Figures 2-5 display the outlines of the four Cleanroom courses.

Cleanroom Software Engineering for Zero-Defect Software. This course is a one-day overview of Cleanroom technology, operations, and management. It is intended for project team management and technical personnel, plus any support organizations, such as technical publications, contracting, quality assurance, and finance, and is a prerequisite for the other Cleanroom courses.

The first lecture in this course introduces the Cleanroom Software Technology Center along with the fundamental concepts and principles of Cleanroom software engineering. Statistical software testing is emphasized as a new technology which is used to certify the quality of the software and the development process, rather than to debug the software. This motivates the need for formal methods during the specification and design phases.

The next three lectures introduce the major Cleanroom technologies: box structures for specification, correctness verification of designs, and statistical quality certification. A final lecture discusses strategies for introducing Cleanroom into an organization and

---

Cleanroom Software Engineering for Zero Defect Software
- The Cleanroom Software Technology Center
- What is Cleanroom Software Engineering?
- Cleanroom quality results
- The Cleanroom development process
- The seven essentials of Cleanroom
- A closer look at statistical testing
- Introducing Cleanroom in your organization

Cleanroom Software Specification
- System boundaries and specification strategies
- Box structures for specification
- The box structure specification process
- Scaling up to large specifications
- Specifying complex systems
- Incremental development planning

Cleanroom Software Verification
- Function-theoretic correctness verification
- Design simplification for verification
- Correctness verification in team reviews
- Software design expression
- Cleanroom design languages

Cleanroom Software Quality Certification
- Statistical quality certification
- Usage probability distributions
- Random test case generation
- Mean Time To Failure calculation
- The Cleanroom certification process

Cleanroom Operations
- Cleanroom team management
- Establishing Cleanroom operations
- Cleanroom Software Engineering Practices
- The seven essentials revisited

Fig. 2.   Cleanroom Software Engineering for Zero-Defect
Software Course Syllabus

managing a Cleanroom effort.

Cleanroom Software Specification. In this three-day course, students learn how to precisely specify system external behavior and architecture using box structures, as well as how to plan development as a series of user-function increments that accumulate into the final product. Laboratory sessions include developing a black box, state box, and clear box for the same system, as well as creating an incremental development plan.

Box structures are the vehicle for Cleanroom software specification. Box structures allow the specifier to precisely define the behavior of a system or system part at various levels of detail. Black boxes define the external, user-visible behavior solely in terms of history of use, without appealing to data or processing steps. This is a useful view of a system for discussions with customers, who are often not concerned with system internals, and for discussions with developers, who must understand required system behavior to be realized in design refinement.

State boxes re-express black box behavior by introducing state data which captures relevant information that must be retained between invocations of the system or system part. This view corresponds to a state machine or abstract data type. Finally, clear boxes add the processing steps needed to accomplish the function defined for the system and to update its state data, while often introducing new black boxes for subsequent refinement.

Box structure specifications are complete and precise; they define the behavior of a system in all possible circumstances of use. The refinement of the specification through black to state to clear boxes is a series of small steps which maintain intellectual control over the elaboration of the specification and allow verification to ensure correctness. Reading, writing, and verification of box structures are taught in this course, with special emphasis on expressive techniques for scaling up to specifications of large systems, through use of transition tables, specification functions, and formal grammars. Methods for dealing with systems which interact with their environment, as well as concurrent and interactive systems, are also discussed.

Cleanroom incremental development is taught in the specification course because increment definition influences, and is influenced by, the organization of specifications into incremental components. In the Cleanroom process, each new increment extends (reuses) previous ones, executes in the system environment to eliminate the need for test scaffolding, is small enough to retain intellectual control yet large enough to show substantial progress, and provides new function for user feedback. Students learn strategies for defining incremental development plans through a variety of examples and exercises.

Cleanroom Software Design and Verification Course. In this three-day course, students learn to develop clear box designs containing intended functions for correctness verification, and to apply function-theoretic verification in mental proofs of correctness in team reviews in place of unit testing and debugging. Students are taught to read and analyze program structures containing intended functions, and to enumerate subproofs required for verification. Examples and laboratory exercises are provided to develop skill in writing intended functions and refining them into control structure designs containing subfunctions for subsequent refinement. Expressive forms for scaling up to large designs include conditional concurrent assignments and specification functions. The correctness conditions of the Correctness Theorem are covered, and their use in team verification reviews is practiced in laboratory sessions. Cleanroom verification reviews are highly structured traversals and analyses of the correctness conditions required to verify a given design. Students verify a substantial component of the COBOL Structuring Facility [11],

Concepts and Processes
- Specification principles and processes
- Design principles and processes
- Process management

Specification Reading
- Reading a small specification

Incremental Development Planning
- Principles and practices
- Incremental development plan examples

Specification Boundary
- Boxes and box boundaries
- User views and designer views
- Boundary examples

Black Box Specification Models
- Categorizing box external interactions
- Organizing box specifications
- Model examples

Specification Elaboration: Functions
- Expressing intended functions
- Functions on stimulus histories
- Complex arguments and values
- Specification function examples

Specification Elaboration: Grammars
- Concepts and notations
- Using grammars to categorize, define groups
- Abstract interactions with common services
- Grammar examples

Validating Specifications
- Techniques and processes
- Validation examples

State Box Design
- State box definition
- Using state boxes effectively
- Evaluating state boxes
- Formal verification of state boxes
- State box examples

Clear Box Design
- Clear box definition
- State migration and common services
- Clear box examples

Project Specification Discussion

Fig. 3. Cleanroom Software Specification Course Syllabus

Program Structures
- Prime program hierarchies
- Program functions and intended functions
- The Replacement Principle
- The Algebra of Functions
- Enumerating program subproofs

Reading and Abstracting Program Structures
- Reading prime programs
- Reading by stepwise abstraction
- Analyzing intended functions

Expressing Program Functions I: Adding Precision
- Program function expression
- Conditional Concurrent Assignments
- Data structure semantics

The Correctness of Prime Programs
- Prime program verification
- Prime program correctness conditions
- Understanding prime program correctness

Loop Verification Revisited
- Loop correctness conditions

Expressing Program Functions II: Scaling Up
- Issues in scaling up to large programs
- Specification functions
- Quantifiers

Correctness Proof Tactics
- Assignment trace tables
- Conditional trace tables

Program Design for Team Verification
- Data structured design
- Intended function strategy
- Segment structured design
- Verbalizing correctness proofs

Cleanroom Verification Reviews
- Cleanroom verification reviews
- Cleanroom review operations

Cleanroom Design Languages
- Design language principles
- Specific design languages

Fig. 4.   Cleanroom Software Design and Verification Course Syllabus

the first Cleanroom-developed IBM program product, as an exercise in scaling up the verification technology.

Cleanroom Statistical Testing Motivation
- Purpose of software testing
- Statistical quality certification
- Customer usage testing
- Comparison with existing test methodology

Probability and Statistics Review
- Probability distributions
- Customer usage distributions
- Expected value, mean, and variance

Cleanroom Usage Probability Distributions
- Applying usage testing in practice
- Test case generation methods
- Test environment considerations

Cleanroom Customer Usage Simulation
- Usage specification grammars
- Test case generation
- Test Case Generator Generator overview
- Customer usage distribution development
- Markov processes for recording distributions
- Using the Test Case Generator Generator

Cleanroom Statistical Testing Foundations
- Single update level testing
- Multiple update level testing
- Cleanroom statistical model assumptions

Performing Cleanroom Statistical Testing
- Certification information model
- Cleanroom testing process
- Testing process variations
- Incremental usage distributions
- Using multiple usage distributions

Planning for Cleanroom Statistical Testing
- Certification roadmap
- Certification activities timeline
- Certification planning

Fig. 5.   Cleanroom Software Certification Course Syllabus

Techniques for simplifying designs for verification are covered, and important design language properties are discussed. Design versions of several popular implementation languages are also reviewed [13].

Cleanroom Software Certification Course. This three-day course teaches how to certify the quality of accumulating software product increments in terms of Mean Time To Failure through statistical testing against usage probability distributions. Students learn to use CSTC-developed certification tools, and laboratory sessions permit students to create usage distributions, generate and execute test cases, and analyze product quality using statistical methods and tools.

The certification course begins by discussing the effectiveness of statistical testing in manufacturing. The statistical testing ideas are extended to software testing, where the statistic of interest is the length of time the system executes until it fails (interfail time). By collecting these statistics during software testing (fixing defects as they are discovered) and using the Cleanroom Certification Model, a Mean Time To Failure can be predicted for the system. Because the test cases against which the system is tested have been randomly generated from a distribution based on expected customer usage, a Mean Time To Failure for the customer environment can be predicted, thereby certifying the quality of the system in terms of interest to the customer.

To support these statistical usage testing concepts, the course includes a review of basic probability and statistics. Methods for obtaining usage data and expressing usage distributions are discussed, with emphasis on formal grammars and Markov processes [10] for defining usage distributions. Students are taught to use the Test Case Generator Generator tool to create test cases, and the Cleanroom Certification Model to evaluate the interfail times and produce a Mean Time To Failure estimate. Planning for software certification is also discussed.

Various strategies for software certification are presented. For example, usage testing also permits independent quality certification for system functions that have low probability of use in nominal usage distributions, yet carry high consequences of failure. In such cases, additional certification can be achieved by defining *alternate distributions* that focus on such important functions. Also, since Cleanroom systems are developed in increments, a method is presented for certifying incremental subsets of function by using subsets of usage distributions.

5 The Cleanroom Consultation Process

Consultation has proven essential to successful transfer of Cleanroom technology. Students learn the methodology through the courses, but they and their management can benefit from an experienced consultant to assist in adapting Cleanroom to their project environment. A Cleanroom consultant can help a new development team make specification and design choices that may simplify the product and facilitate its verification, advise a new certification team on how to develop usage distributions and prepare for testing, and assist managers and project leaders in allocating resources, planning schedules, and assessing risks and rewards. The role of Cleanroom consultants is to provide advice on Cleanroom issues only, however, not on technical aspects of products being developed.

There are four areas in which Cleanroom consultants are the most valuable:

· Development of box structure specifications
· Team correctness verification

- Development of usage probability distributions
- Cleanroom project management

Box structures provide a great deal of power and precision for defining system specifications, but also a great deal of flexibility, with many degrees of freedom in selecting appropriate specification strategies and formats. Consultation support is important at this stage to help propose strategies, assess technical risks and rewards, and evaluate resource and schedule implications.

A principal consultation role in the design stage is to ensure that designs are prepared for correctness verification reviews, through analysis and recording of intended functions at each level of refinement. Team verification reviews are more structured and focussed than traditional inspections. The primary role of consultants in reviews is to help teams maintain concentration on the correctness conditions to be verified for each subproof. Consultants also help ensure that issues raised during verification are recorded and eventually resolved, and assist teams in verifying particularly difficult structures (or recommend that they be rewritten in simpler form for verification).

Consultants assist certification teams in developing usage probability distributions, and provide recommendations on techniques for random test case generation. They also help teams decide how to gather usage data and how to record it in formal grammars and Markov chains.

From a management viewpoint, Cleanroom differs from traditional software development processes, particularly in scheduling and resource allocation. Consultants provide recommendations on project scheduling, estimating and allocating resources, and facilitating interaction between development and quality assurance, usability, information development, and other support groups. Consultants also advise project management on appropriate measurements for this new methodology.

The CSTC assigns a primary consultant to each development team that it trains. Whenever required, other members of the CSTC who have more experience in a particular area may be called upon to assist any team with which the CSTC is consulting. This ensures effective advice for every team in all areas of Cleanroom.

To further ensure that appropriate recommendations are provided in a timely manner, consultants follow development of all work products from initial draft to final form. Good information flow must be maintained between the consultants and their teams; consultants receive copies of all versions of all work products. All available means of communication are utilized. Documents and notes are exchanged electronically, and by fax and overnight mail. Questions are posed and answered electronically or in teleconferences or videoconferences. Periodic on-site visits are arranged for more extensive discussions and reviews.

6 Cleanroom Tools

Cleanroom is not a tool-dependent process, however, the technology offers opportunities for new types of tools to automate specific operations. The two testing tools described below automate steps in the certification process, and the design languages provide a medium for recording and verifying Cleanroom designs. These tools promote acceptance of the methodology and facilitate the technology transfer.

Cleanroom Certification Tools. The Cleanroom certification process tests a product using test cases which are generated randomly based on a distribution that models expected customer usage. Given a usage probability distribution, test case generation is a mechanical process amenable to automation. One of the certification tools developed by the CSTC is the Test Case Generator Generator. It accepts a usage distribution as input and, as output, produces an executable program which generates test cases based on the input usage distribution.

In Cleanroom, software quality is measured by Mean Time To Failure (MTTF) and other statistical parameters. MTTF is computed using a statistical model and is based on the times between failures (interfail times) encountered during testing of the software. The second Cleanroom tool developed by the CSTC is a workstation-based implementation of the statistical model. Cleanroom certification engineers collect interfail time data during testing and submit the data to the Cleanroom Certification Model, which calculates MTTF estimates for the software.

Cleanroom Design Languages. Cleanroom software designs may be expressed in either non-executable or executable languages. The former can offer straightforward syntax and semantics, but require translation (often automatable) to the execution language. The latter require no translation step, but often present syntactic and semantic complexities.

The CSTC has developed design versions of several popular executable languages, such as C and C++, to permit effective use for Cleanroom design. The design versions ensure required semantics for stepwise refinement of intended functions, adequacy of proof rules for verification, and other desirable properties [13].

7 Technology Transfer Lessons

The principal lessons learned in carrying out the Cleanroom technology transfer are as follows:

The Cleanroom Process Works. As noted earlier, the CSTC-supported Cleanroom teams are producing remarkable quality results with good productivity. These results are being obtained from a variety of system and application software projects, including both new development and extensions to existing systems, as well as from a variety of team compositions and development environments. Consistent quality results from such diverse environments is encouraging.

The Technology Transfer Works. Results indicate that the CSTC has developed a successful strategy for transferring Cleanroom technology to new teams. Initial planning through management and team briefings has ensured that participants understand their roles and responsibilities as the technology transfer progresses. Cleanroom skills take study and practice to develop, and a learning curve is involved, but experience shows these start-up costs can be accommodated within project schedules and resources. The courses, consultants, and tools have been an effective combination in helping teams achieve the capability to produce Cleanroom quality code.

Additional factors have contributed to the successful technology transfer. Executive management in IBM has instituted quality initiatives that have inspired product laboratories to adopt better methods of software development. Management has demonstrated commitment and assisted the transfers through financial support. The hard work and dedication of the Cleanroom teams has also been a factor in making the transfers successful. The teams have provided invaluable suggestions for improving all aspects of the technology transfer. Furthermore, the successes achieved by the early Cleanroom teams have driven acceptance of and motivated interest in the technology.

Quality Improvements Offset Technology Transfer Costs. The investment in initial technology transfer is more than offset by quality improvements that substantially reduce the number of errors and the cost of product maintenance, as well as improve the customer perception of quality. In addition, errors are detected earlier in the development cycle, when the cost of correction is lowest. While the technology transfer requires an initial investment to train teams and traverse the learning curve, that investment leads to self-sufficiency and is ultimately leveraged across all current and future products the teams will produce.

Acknowledgements

The authors wish to thank the referees for their comments and Conni Morgan for her assistance in preparing this paper. Acknowledgment is also due to the consultants of the CSTC and the members of the CSTC-supported Cleanroom teams who, together, have developed this successful Cleanroom technology transfer program.

References

1. Mills, H.D., M. Dyer, and R.C. Linger, "Cleanroom Software Engineering," *IEEE Software*, September, 1987, pp. 19-25.

2. Cobb, R.H. and H.D. Mills, "Engineering Software Under Statistical Quality Control," *IEEE Software*, November, 1990, pp. 44-54.

3. Linger, R.C., "Cleanroom Software Engineering for Zero-Defect Software," submitted for publication, 1992.

4. Mills, H.D., R.C. Linger, and A.R. Hevner, *Principles of Information Systems Analysis and Design*, Academic Press, San Diego, CA, 1986.

5. Mills, H.D., R.C. Linger, and A.R. Hevner, "Box Structured Information Systems," *IBM Systems Journal*, Vol. 26, No. 4, 1987, pp. 393-413.

6. Deck, M.D., M.G. Pleszkoch, R.C. Linger, and H.D. Mills, "Extended Semantics for Box Structures," *Proc. 25th Hawaii International Conference on System Sciences*, IEEE Computer Society Press, January, 1992, pp. 382-393.

7. Mills, H.D., "Stepwise Refinement and Verification in Box-Structured Systems," *IEEE Computer*, June, 1988, pp. 23-36.

8. Linger, R.C., H.D. Mills, and B.I. Witt, *Structured Programming: Theory and Practice*, Addison-Wesley, Reading, MA, 1979.

9. Mills, H.D., "Certifying the Correctness of Software," *Proc. 25th Hawaii International Conference on System Sciences*, IEEE Computer Society Press, January, 1992, pp. 373-381.

10. Whittaker, J.A. and J.H. Poore, "Statistical Testing for Cleanroom Software Engineering," *Proc. 25th Hawaii International Conference on System Sciences*, IEEE Computer Society Press, January, 1992, pp. 428-436.

11. Linger, R.C. and H.D. Mills, "A Case Study in Cleanroom Software Engineering: The IBM COBOL Structuring Facility," *Proc. 12th International Computer Science and Applications Conference*, IEEE Computer Society Press, October, 1988.

12. Linger, R.C., "The Cleanroom Software Technology Center," *Creativity! (ASD-WMA Edition)*, IBM Corporation, March, 1991.

13. Rosen, S.J., "Design Languages for Cleanroom Software Engineering," *Proc. 25th Hawaii International Conference on System Sciences*, IEEE Computer Society Press, January, 1992, pp. 406-417.

14. Trammell, C.J., L.H. Binder, and C.E. Snyder, "The Automated Production Control System: A Case Study in Cleanroom Software Engineering," *ACM Transactions on Software Engineering and Methodology,*" Vol. 1, No. 1, January, 1992, pp. 81-94.

Experiences with an Interactive Video Code Inspection Laboratory

Michael G. Christel

Software Engineering Institute, Carnegie Mellon University
Pittsburgh, PA 15213

Abstract. Software engineers need practical training in addition to classroom lectures in order to obtain the knowledge and skills necessary to succeed in industry. This training is provided by laboratories in other engineering disciplines. Such laboratories have been implemented as computer-based interactive video courses in the past, with numerous advantages. Based on this success, an interactive video course was created for use as a "code inspection laboratory", in which the skills of preparing for and participating in code inspections are learned and practiced. This paper summarizes the anecdotal feedback and usage data from 120 students who used the course over the past two years. Lessons learned from these experiences are discussed, with implications for the development of future interactive video software engineering laboratories.

1 Introduction

The National Research Council's Panel on Undergraduate Engineering Education concluded in a 1985 report that it is of primary importance to emphasize the role and significance of laboratory instruction in undergraduate engineering education. Classroom instruction is not adequate for giving students practical, hands-on experience in doing things engineers do. Practicing engineers put their knowledge of science to use in an iterative cycle of analysis, design, and experiment. Laboratory experience is ideal for teaching this scientific understanding because it can condense a real-life problem into a manageable amount of time and space [12].

The laboratory provides an environment in which the students can learn how to *use* their academic learning, much as physicians learn how to apply medical knowledge through clinical training. The importance of practical training applies not only to engineers in general but to software engineers in particular [14, p. 39]:

> Many issues in software engineering, particularly in communication and configuration control, simply can not be appreciated in the absence of experience. Since most projects that fail do so because of deficiencies in those two areas, we would be doing our students an injustice by not exposing them to the problems inherent in actually working on software products.

In addition, laboratory experience is useful not only for undergraduate engineering education but for the continuing education of engineers, including software engineers, as well. Another National Research Council panel notes the importance of continuing education of engineers [10, p. 82]: "a single concentrated educational experience is not sufficient for a lifelong career."

There are many difficulties in trying to establish a traditional instructor-led laboratory experience for some software engineering issues. For example, consider the topic of software technical reviews, specifically code inspections, as defined in [5]. A traditional laboratory experience is provided by dividing a class into small groups and having each group perform an inspection. Each student in the group takes an inspector role such as the moderator or reader. The lab instructor moves from group to group to assess the students' performance in the various roles and judge the progress of the different inspections. There are at least four potential problems with such an exercise:

- The instructor cannot adequately assess an individual's performance, since his or her time must be divided in monitoring multiple groups. (Scheduling only one small group at a time is usually not feasible because of limits in the availability of the instructor, students, or both.)

- It is difficult to replicate the inspection experience so that students in all the groups can come away from the lab having acquired the same set of skills. For example, one group may have learned how to deal with an overly aggressive individual not willing to give up his opinion, but this situation may not have occurred in the other groups' inspections.

- Students have less individual control over their experience, the equivalent of having an uncooperative lab partner. Students may have to endure a bad inspection, even if they are performing their roles well, because of poor performance by others in their groups. Likewise, a student may be doing a very bad job as an inspector and still experience a good inspection because of unusually high competence by others in the group.

- Because of time constraints, this code inspection laboratory experience would typically only be performed once. The student gets experience in one of the inspector roles, but never gets to assume the responsibilities of the other roles in an inspection.

An alternative approach to delivering laboratory experience is through the use of interactive video, the use of motion video under computer control in a computer interface. Interactive video has provided instructional simulations on microcomputers since the late 1970s [6]. Many advantages of simulations made possible by interactive video are presented in [15]. From the instructor's point of view, simulations offer a unique opportunity to present consistent and replicable situations. The simulation can also present a wide variety of experiences within relatively short practice periods. The users can assume new and unfamiliar roles, and participate in those roles in safe and controlled situations. Users are actively involved with their learning environment, and are encouraged to think for themselves, thereby personalizing their learning experience. All these claims about simulations are supported with references to educational research literature in [15].

Interactive video is well suited for implementing laboratories on engineering topics, as recognized in [11, p. 57]: "New developments in educational technology, principally involving computers and television, can be of major assistance in improving the quality and versatility of engineering education." Interactive video delivery also addresses some of the major barriers to the continuing education of engineers cited in [10], including travel time and the inconvenience of obtaining needed courses. An interactive video course can be delivered on the engineer's desktop, and accessed at his or her convenience.

The focus of this paper is not to prove the utility of interactive video for delivering practical training; that information can be acquired through [6] and other sources. The arguments presented here do illustrate the potential of using interactive video to teach software engineering skills. To test this applicability, the SEI developed an interactive video course on code inspections. This paper shall briefly describe this course, and then discuss some of the lessons learned from its use during the past two years by 120 people from academia, government, and industry. These lessons are valuable in the formulation of future interactive video software engineering laboratories.

2 "A Cure for the Common Code"

"A Cure for the Common Code" is an interactive video code inspection "laboratory", with laboratory used in the sense of "a place where theories, techniques, and methods...are tested, analyzed, demonstrated, etc."[7] This course allows the student to learn about, prepare for, reference materials concerning, and participate in code inspections.

Inspections are a formal review process defined first at IBM for the purpose of finding defects in code [5]. They have been used effectively to reduce the cost of software development and improve software quality in numerous institutions, including IBM and AT&T [1]. Code inspections typically are one to three hours long, and are conducted by reviewers who have well defined roles and responsibilities. These roles include the moderator, reader, recorder, and producer.

The course creates a virtual world in the form of a software development company named Ultimex, in which the student learns about and participates in code inspections. The student takes the role of a software engineer who has just joined this company. The student can access various "rooms" in the company, as illustrated in Figure 1.

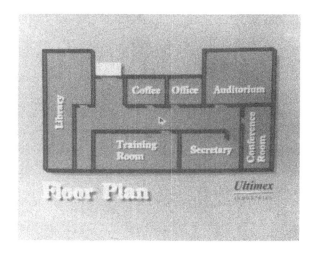

Fig. 1. Rooms in "A Cure for the Common Code"

The auditorium introduces the student to the importance of software quality and to the company environment in which the student will learn about code inspections. The training room gives background information on related topics such as the roles in an inspection and other types of software technical reviews. The library provides textual resources as well as short video segments of what to do and what to avoid during inspections. The office provides the student with tools for preparing for the inspection, such as a source level debugger and hypertext tool for examining the code. Within the conference room, the student takes part in a code inspection simulation.

The student is an active participant in the code inspection, and as such his or her comments, or lack thereof, as well as timeliness affect the course of the inspection dialogue and ultimately the success of the inspection. In addition, the role the student takes in the inspection is not predetermined but is selected by the student. The remaining roles are then assumed by and simulated by the system. An example of what the student sees during the code inspection simulation is shown in Figure 2.

A comprehensive overview of the code inspection course is provided in [17], which further describes the contents of these rooms and the instructional philosophy inherent in the course's design. The applicability of the techniques used in developing "A Cure for the Common Code" to other instructional simulations is the subject of [4].

Fig. 2. A Screen "Snapshot" from the Code Inspection Simulation

A formative evaluation of the course began in 1990, the purpose of which was to identify problems with the course and suggest improvements to its design. This differs from a summative evaluation, which is concerned with assessing the merit of a completed program for use by consumers of that program [13]. "A Cure for the Common Code" was in the formative stage during the time the student data discussed in this paper was collected. There were some limitations with the course known a priori by its developers, and others which were discovered and clarified through the formative evaluation. An examination of these deficiencies, along with the other collected usage and anecdotal data, will be presented in the next few sections.

3   Usage Data

Data was collected on the use of "A Cure for the Common Code" from August, 1990 through May, 1991, and then in January and February, 1992. During these time periods, the experiences of 120 people with the course were collected both passively through system tracking of student actions, as well as through the use of questionnaires. These 120 people were students or employees of Carnegie Mellon University, Gunter Air Force Base, Jet Propulsion Laboratory, the University of Pittsburgh, and Virginia Tech.

The usage data discussed in this report is not conducive to a formal statistical analysis for three reasons:

- The system platform on which the course runs matured during the 1990-1992 time frame. Likewise, the course itself evolved, with bug fixes and modifications suggested by this formative evaluation incorporated into the course at frequent intervals. Thus the students who took the course in 1992 had a more stable, enhanced experience than those who took it in 1990.

- The questionnaires given to the students changed from 1990 to 1992. All students did not receive the same questionnaires.

- Some of the 120 students of the course also participated simultaneously in experiments testing the use of different interfaces to the code inspection course. These experiments were intrusive and adversely affected the student's experience because they added irrelevant recall tests to the course and in some cases changed the way information was presented by the course. This point is discussed further in Section 4.

Despite these limitations, the collected data still is very useful in explaining how the course was used, documenting reactions to the course, and suggesting how this course and other interactive video laboratories can be improved in the future.

92 of the 120 students were given the explicit task to successfully finish an inspection of a short function written in Ada. Detailed timing data was gathered for these students as they used the course to achieve this goal of completing an inspection. Some students' timing data was incomplete, due to the student turning the machine off before finishing, walking away without exiting properly, or experiencing fatal errors with the system. With this incomplete data removed, there were 72 detailed timing records available for analysis.

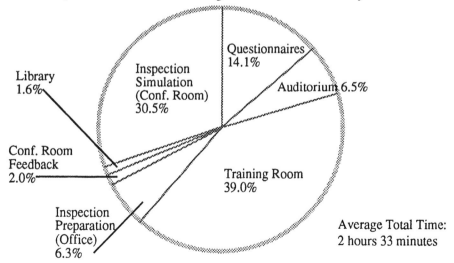

Fig. 3. Student Use of "A Cure for the Common Code"

The proportion of time the students spent with the course is illustrated in Figure 3. All the students with detailed timing data first spent a few minutes completing online questionnaires, followed by an introduction to the Ultimex environment and to the importance of software quality in the auditorium. All of these students then completed a few more questionnaires, listened to an overview of the environment's resources, and then spent time in the training room. After spending time preparing for the inspection in the office environment, the students participated in a code inspection in the conference room. They then received feedback based on their performance, and some students went on to examine more materials in the training room and library. All of these students ended their experience by completing a few more online questionnaires. The purpose of these questionnaires is explained in [3], and the adverse effects on the formative evaluation is the subject of Section 4.3.2.

The mean time spent with the course for these 72 students was 2 hours and 33 minutes. After removing the time spent answering questionnaires, the mean time spent with the code inspection laboratory was 2 hours and 11 minutes.

Based on system traces of interactions within the conference room simulation, the students did take an active role in the inspection. The one short inspection performed by the students lasted an average of 46.7 minutes, of which the student spent an average of 12.7 minutes communicating to the other three reviewers via a "talk interface." The inspection consisted of an average of 65.1 discourses, with 11.0 of those discourses coming from the student in the recorder role and the rest coming from the moderator, producer, and reader roles assumed by the system. This is an appropriate level of contribution from the recorder in a four person inspection.

4 Anecdotes and Lessons Learned

There were many insights provided by the students into the design of an interactive video software engineering laboratory. These are organized according to five basic psychological principles useful for improving the teaching-learning process [18]:

- Individualize
- Guide the student's learning
- Provide for practice
- Evaluate and give feedback
- Motivate

In addition, many students critiqued the course based on course administration concerns, and biasing effects of coincident experiments. These two points will supplement the five principles in categorizing student insights, which are supported by direct quotations taken verbatim from the written comments of the 120 students concerning "A Cure for the Common Code." The selected quotations are representative of the feedback received from these students, and identify both the strengths and weaknesses of the interactive video code inspection laboratory.

4.1 Individualized Instruction

"I think the concepts of self-paced learning, topic selection by the user, and interaction with the participants in an inspection are great."

Many students appreciated being able to control what to see, when to see it, what to examine, and what to skip. A general advantage of interactive video over traditional training delivery media is this capability to provide individualized instruction [6].

"A Cure for the Common Code" runs on an Intel Pro750™ 80386-based computer incorporating a Digital Video Interactive (DVI®) board set. This machine also has as a peripheral a standard CD-ROM drive. The course contains twenty minutes of full screen full motion video with audio, one hundred minutes of quarter and sixth screen video with audio, ten hours of AM-quality audio, two thousand still images, and five megabytes of computer data. No student was expected to view and hear all of this information, nor was all of this information pertinent to every student. Rather, the information database for the course was designed to be large, with students receiving material pertinent to their performance and needs.

For example, the training room contains over four hours of prerequisite information on such topics as other types of technical reviews, group process, communication issues, and the roles and associated responsibilities of inspectors. Most students are familiar with some of this information; a practicing software engineer taking the "A Cure..." for continuing education purposes may be familiar with a majority of it. This material therefore cannot be forced upon the student, but instead is selectable by the student to address his or her requirements.

As another example, the reviewers the student interacts with during the code inspection simulation can respond in a number of ways, based in part on how well the student is performing in the inspection. If a reviewer is not talkative and the student as moderator does not motivate that reviewer to contribute, the reviewer will tend to say nothing. If the reviewer is very aggressive and is not calmed down, the comments from that reviewer will be more emotionally charged. The discourses seen and heard by the student are combined into a complete inspection experience dynamically while the student interacts with the course. The student's experience in the code inspection simulation is individualized, with the success or failure of the inspection ultimately dependent on the student's contributions.

> *"It would be nice not to have the person reading the slides/visuals."*

While the course did present information to students based on their expressed needs and performance, it did not individualize the manner in which that material was presented. For example, in the training room there are many computer screens of text and graphics displayed with accompanying audio. As the comment above indicates, many students were annoyed with this accompanying audio and wanted to be able to turn it off and only access the visual information. This is a simple feature to add, and is indicative of the utility of formative evaluations. Student tailorability of interfaces would improve interactive video laboratories such as "A Cure for the Common Code."

4.2 Guide the Student's Learning

> *"Good coverage of tasks to be performed during a code inspection." "Thorough coverage of process."*

Students praised the all-encompassing nature of the course, which integrated pedagogical material, reference material, inspection preparation tools, and inspection simulations into a single learning environment. This led to difficulties as well.

> *"I found myself needing an agenda that I could refer to often to know where I should be and when." "I wish that there would have been some suggestions on what areas are a must to look at."*

Students were often confused as to what to do next. When they started the course they received a comprehensive overview of the learning environment, which included some advice on how to proceed. However, this advice was not repeated and was not accessible to the student for replay or elucidation. This up-front guidance should be complemented with a "road map" that students could carry around with them to let them know what has been done, what should be done next, and what are the objectives to be achieved. More ambitiously, the student could be assisted by intelligent "agents" within the system which would give advice to the student on what should be done and when based on a model of the student's background and needs.

4.3 Provide for Practice

"I wasn't able to say things in the review that I would like to have said."

The student received practice in code inspections through participation in a simulation. During this inspection simulation, the student needed to converse with the other reviewers, and did so via a "talk interface." In the talk interface, the student constructed a sentence to say back to the other reviewers by selecting phrases from text menus.

This talk interface was the most criticized component of "A Cure for the Common Code." More than 60% of the students explicitly mentioned problems with the talk interface, from it being not powerful enough to being too slow to being frustrating and difficult to learn.

A potential solution to this problem is found in "Role'm" [16]. "Role'm" is a role playing simulator developed by Apple after their exposure to "A Cure for the Common Code" through attendance at a SEI digital video design workshop based on the course. The inspection course's talk interface is based on a semantic model of code inspections originally formulated by Elliot Soloway's research group [8], and furthered by a member of his team. "Role'm" uses a talk interface based instead on goals and plans [16], which perhaps could be used to improve the inspection talk interface.

Even if the semantic model is kept, simplifications could be made to the talk interface, such as context-sensitive phrase menus rather than globally static ones. Also, students could be better directed to the help on the talk interface which exists in the training room before they actually make use of the talk interface. Many students never saw this help. System guidance issues were discussed in Section 4.2.

"An uninterrupted three-hour session which we experienced was obviously exhausting. I used up my energy before I got down to the inspection exercise. ...It's a lot better if the session can be divided into two."

The inspection simulation took a lot of student energy, in part because of the above-mentioned talk interface problems, but also because the student had to pay careful attention to what the other reviewers said as well as the tone of their comments. A majority of the students did not enter the inspection simulation until they had spent over two uninterrupted hours with the course. The students should have been encouraged to take a break before the inspection simulation, which lasted an average of 47 minutes. This point is dealt with further in Section 4.3.1.

"This was a great experience. The material is very interesting and the situations seem to be realistic."

Despite being encumbered with the talk interface, the students did learn inspection skills during the inspection simulation. This was evidenced by a log of the inspection discourse history kept by the system for each student, and the comments given by the students following completion of the course. When the inspection discourses are made more realistic by presenting them as motion video, the skills of recalling what was said, by whom, and with what tone are improved, as shown by a formal experiment using 72 of these students [3]. Thus making the practice more realistic, e.g., through the use of video if it applies to the skill being taught, does improve the laboratory experience.

4.3.1 Course Administration

The administration of educational technology is critical. Even the best instructional design can be thwarted through poor course administration. This issue was neglected during the formative evaluation of "A Cure for the Common Code", and the students paid the consequences.

"Three hours is too long for a user to sit and effectively absorb information."

For example, consider the problem of allocating system time to use the course. Most of the course administrators allocated a single three hour time slot per student. Most students were not given the opportunity to work with multiple, shorter time segments, coming back at later times to resume their work, even though this capability is implemented in the course. Thus it was not possible for students to spend an hour or so with the course, and then come back and spend an additional two hours or so. They instead spent one monolithic period with it, becoming both fatigued and frustrated as a result. Classroom lectures rarely go two hours without a break. Likewise, code inspections themselves are supposed to be limited to a few hours. Because course administrators either were not aware of multiple session possibilities or did not set up the means of achieving them, students were forced to use the course under less than ideal circumstances.

"The program is designed for someone who has never been through a review before."

This comment was given as a criticism of the course, when in fact it was a statement of truth. The course was designed for those with no prior inspection experience. The author of this comment, though, had a great deal of inspection experience and thus was bored with the course. At least ten of the other students had prior inspection experience as well. This reiterates the importance of documentation to administrators, e.g., for indicating the intended audience.

An interactive video laboratory must be seen as a tool for the educator, and as much help as possible should be given to the educator so that he or she can make effective use of the tool.

4.3.2 Biasing Effects of Coincident Experiments

> *"That $#%@$ code review machine. What horrible thing did I do that I had*
> *to endure that blasted code review 'multi-media instructional machine?'"*

92 of the 120 students were subjected to computer interface experiments while using the code inspection course. Some students received the course as designed, complete with full motion (30 images per second) video. Other students only received a slide show format (1 image every 4 seconds) of the course. Another group, which included the author of the above comment, received "stutter" video at 5 images per second. These different presentation schemes affected the students' experience with the course, especially the students receiving the 5 images per second treatment.

Of the students receiving the 5 images per second treatment, only 30% were able or willing to complete an assigned task. This contrasts with over 85% of the students receiving other interface treatments being able to complete the same task. The 5 images per second video was reported as annoying by some of its subjects, and was a significant influence behind the negative comment given by the one student above. Another contributing factor was that this student had prior inspection experience, and as mentioned before, was thus not part of the intended course audience.

> *"I found the recall tests to be useless to me as a student and more or less ir-*
> *relevant." "...difficulty in concentrating while trying to meet the demands of*
> *the interface and the 'quick-quiz' type things."*

Along with the interface treatment biasing student responses, the students who were subjects of these formal interface experiments also had to deal with extraneous questionnaires which were useful in determining interface effects but were of no importance to the code inspection course itself. Subjects in all three interface treatment groups expressed frustration over these extra questionnaires, as well as some confusion over whether the additional recall tests were actually an integral part of the course.

Using the same students for both formative evaluation and formal interface experiments allowed both efforts to be conducted in an overlapping time frame. In retrospect, the formative evaluation was adversely affected because many of the students' frustrations, such as those quoted in this section, were due to the experiments and not to the design of the code inspection course. In the future, when interactive video laboratories are evaluated, any formal studies of components of the laboratories should be conducted separately from the formative evaluation.

4.4 Evaluate and Give Feedback

Student performance was evaluated primarily during the code inspection simulation. Two types of feedback were given: a natural, immediate feedback from the other reviewers in the simulation concerning the student's actions, and a "report card" text and audio summary highlighting the good and bad points of the student's inspection performance presented after the inspection concluded.

The immediate feedback made the inspection simulation more realistic. For example, if the student as moderator aggressively attacked the producer, the student would see and hear the producer responding defensively rather than getting a text message stating that "you shouldn't be doing that as the moderator." Advantages of this type of feedback include making the experience more motivating and making the practice more realistic, both having positive effects on learning. These points are covered elsewhere in this paper.

> *"...use a checkmark on the sections already viewed* [in the training room]"

A frequent complaint early in the formative evaluation was that there was not enough feedback given back to the student pertaining to activities performed outside of the code inspection simulation. For example, the training room has nearly one hundred instructional modules organized according to a series of menus. At first there was no visual way for the student to determine which modules had been viewed already. The suggestion given above was implemented, and 1992 users saw a checkmark next to modules they had visited in the past.

An interactive video laboratory can very simply incorporate system tracking of user interactions. This information should be utilized to give the student as much feedback as possible about what has been done.

4.5 Motivation

"I had a great time. ...It was a totally new experience for me." "I thoroughly enjoyed using the system."

"A Cure for the Common Code" was designed around the principle of an intrinsically motivating fantasy. A considerable body of research has been performed looking at what makes "Nintendo" type games so captivating [9]. Important motivating design aspects include challenge (goals with uncertain attainment), curiosity (sensory and cognitive), and fantasies (especially intrinsic fantasies where the fantasy depends crucially on the task). The code inspection course incorporated these aspects. Despite the needed improvements identified by the formative evaluation, the course still produced the favorable reactions quoted here.

The system encouraged the students to learn about inspections by first providing them with news footage and a cartoon animation illustrating why software quality was important. Later, after the student had received instruction in how code inspections can be used to improve software quality, the student was able to participate in an inspection. The student immediately gained practical experience in the relevance and importance of inspection techniques, which is an advantage of the interactive video laboratory not found in the classroom [18, p. 393]:

> All too often education is based on the promise that what is learned will be useful later in life, a promise that fails to be fulfilled within a meaningful time span. Much better motivation can be achieved by making the learning process relevant to real-world activities that the student can see as valuable.

Throughout the experience the student is driven by the principal goal of finding errors in a code artifact.

Interactive video is an ideal media for improving student attitude toward both the learning activity and the subject matter, as supported by past analyses of interactive video studies [2, 6]. With the code inspection course, it was important to teach that code inspections involve a great deal of powerful group dynamics, and that the process is an active involvement of people who each have different roles and responsibilities. A formal interface experiment conducted with some of the students showed that when motion video is used and when the reality of the virtual learning environment (Ultimex) is enhanced through the use of surrogate travel navigation, then students leave the course with these improved attitudes about code inspections [3].

"Overall, I am very impressed by the capabilities of this system. I would be interested in developing other software skills using this instructional media."

5 Implications

Software engineering education can be improved through the exposure of students to real-life situations, case studies, and through simulations requiring active student participation. Such exposure can be provided through interactive video laboratories. This was demonstrated with "A Cure for the Common Code."

"A Cure for the Common Code" has been used during the past few years at a number of organizations spanning academia, government, and industry. Lessons learned from these experiences are useful for improving the next generation of interactive video software engineering laboratories. These lessons include the following:

- Emphasize individualized instruction. Interactive video, as opposed to classroom lecture, is well suited to this task; thus, take advantage of it and present students with information relevant to their needs, feedback appropriate to their actions, and evaluations specific to their performance.

- Guide the student through the material in the laboratory, especially when it is a large information space. The code inspection course utilized over 680 megabytes of data consisting of thousands of objects. Prioritize the information based on the student's needs and experience level. Such guidance should not only be in the form of an introduction to the system but should be globally accessible.

- The main purpose of the laboratory is to give the student the opportunity to practice a skill in a realistic, albeit guided, environment. In "A Cure for the Common Code", the skill was the application of group process techniques and fulfillment of inspector responsibilities. Improving the output fidelity of the laboratory can improve the learning experience. For example, use full motion video if that is appropriate to the task.

- Do not ignore the person administering the interactive video laboratory. Document clearly the intended audience, the instructional objectives, and the best ways students can learn from their interactive video experience.

- When evaluating an interactive video laboratory, limit the confounding factors introduced into your testing by avoiding the temptation to run simultaneous studies on the same students.

- Give students timely feedback on their work in the laboratory. In the context of the practice, make the feedback as natural as possible.

- Create an intrinsic fantasy to engage the student. Motivate interest in the subject by providing the opportunity to use the knowledge learned about the subject in a challenging, realistic way.

References

1. Ackerman, A. F., Buchwald, L. S., & Lewski, F. H. Software Inspections: An Effective Verification Process. *IEEE Software 6*, 3 (May 1989), 31-36.

2. Bosco, J. An Analysis of Evaluations of Interactive Video. *Educational Technology 26*, 5 (May 1986), 7-17.

3. Christel, M. *A Comparative Evaluation of Digital Video Interactive Interfaces in the Delivery of a Code Inspection Course*, Ph.D. Thesis, Georgia Institute of Technology, Atlanta, GA, 1991.

4. Christel, M. & Stevens, S. Rule Base and Digital Video Technologies Applied to Training Simulations. *SEI Technical Review '92*. Software Engineering Institute, Pittsburgh, PA, 1992.

5. Fagan, M. E. Design and Code Inspections to Reduce Errors in Program Development. *IBM Systems Journal 15*, 3 (1976), 182-211.

6. Fletcher, J. D. Effectiveness and Cost of Interactive Videodisc Instruction in Defense Training and Education. *IDA PAPER P-2372*, Institute for Defense Analyses, Alexandria, VA, July, 1990.

7. Guralnik, D.B., Editor-in-Chief. *Webster's New World Dictionary*, Second College Edition. William Collins + World Publishing Co., 1978.

8. Letovsky, S., Pinto, J., Lampert, R., & Soloway, E. A Cognitive Analysis of A Code Inspection. In *Empirical Studies of Programming*, G. Olson, S. Sheppard, & E. Soloway, Eds., Ablex Publishers, Norwood, NJ, 1988, 231-247.

9. Malone, T.W. Toward a Theory of Intrinsically Motivating Instruction. *Cognitive Science 4* (1981), 333-369.

10. National Research Council (U.S.) Panel on Continuing Education. *Engineering Education and Practice in the United States: Continuing Education of Engineers*. National Academy Press, Washington, D.C., 1985.

11. National Research Council (U.S.) Panel on Engineering Graduate Education and Research. *Engineering Education and Practice in the United States: Engineering Graduate Education and Research*. National Academy Press, Washington, D.C., 1985.

12. National Research Council (U.S.) Panel on Undergraduate Engineering Education. *Engineering Education and Practice in the United States: Engineering Undergraduate Education*. National Academy Press, Washington, D.C., 1985.

13. Popham, W.J. *Educational Evaluation*. Prentice-Hall, 1975.

14. Shaw, M. & Tomayko, J.E. Models for Undergraduate Project Courses in Software Engineering. In *Lecture Notes in Computer Science 536: Software Engineering Education SEI Conference Proceedings* (Oct 1991 in Pittsburgh, PA), Springer-Verlag, Berlin, 1991.

15. Smith, P. Low Cost Simulations. *Educational Technology 26*, 6 (June 1986), 35-39.

16. Spohrer, J.C.; James, A.; Abbott, C.A.; Czora, G.J.; Laffey, J.; & Miller, M.L. A role playing simulator for needs analysis consultants. *Expert Systems World Congress Proceedings* (Dec 1991 in Orlando, FL), Vol. 4, pp 2829 - 2839.

17. Stevens, S. M. Intelligent Interactive Video Simulation of a Code Inspection. *Communications of the ACM 32*, 7 (July 1989), 832-843.

18. Wales, C.E. *Engineering Education 66*, 5 (February 1976), 390-393.

Pro750 is a trademark of Intel Corporation.
DVI is a registered trademark of Intel Corporation.

This work is sponsored by the U.S. Department of Defense.

Session 13:

Funding, Practica, and Principles
Moderator: Gary Ford, Software Engineering Insitute

Panel: Current Funding Opportunities Through the National Science Foundation
Doris K. Lidtke and Caroline E. Wardle, National Science Foundation

The Influence of Software Engineering Paradigms on Individual and Team Project Results
William Junk and Paul Oman, University of Idaho

Engineering Principles and Software Engineering
Alfs T. Berztiss, University of Pittsburgh

Panel

Current Funding Opportunities Through NSF

Participants.

Caroline E. Wardle
Program Director
Computer & Information Science & Engineering
Institutional Infrastructure Program
National Science Foundation
e-mail: cwardle@nsf.gov

Doris K. Lidtke
Program Director
Undergraduate Science, Engineering, & Mathematics Education
Computer Science Course and Curriculum
National Science Foundation
dlidtke@nsf.gov

Abstract.

The panel will discuss current opportunities for funding through programs at the National Science Foundation, with particular emphasis on those which support undergraduate educational efforts in computer science and software engineering. Current programs address curriculum development, laboratory infrastructure, materials development, faculty enhancement and undergraduate research.

The Influence of Software Engineering Paradigms On Individual and Team Project Results

William Junk and Paul Oman

Computer Science Department, University of Idaho
Moscow, ID 83843

Abstract. For years there has been debate over which software development paradigm is best. There are many anecdotal reports extolling the advantages of prototyping over specifying approaches, but few controlled studies have been performed to quantify the differences between them. We report on some observations drawn about individual and team projects conducted in our software engineering practica and we describe a series of controlled experiments comparing spiral-prototyping to specifying in team projects. In the team developments we found that the prototyped products were completed with less effort, had lower complexity metric values, had fewer reported defects, and were rated higher on the customer's subjective evaluation of quality. We also found that management of the spiral-prototyping process is a critical element in project success or failure. Because of the experimental controls employed in our study and the realism of the programming projects performed, we believe that these results are valid equally outside the academic environment.

1   The Role of Practica in Software Engineering Education

If we take a close look at the common thread of ideas embodied in the definitions of software engineering we will find an important emphasis. That emphasis centers on the "application and use of sound engineering and management skills...." [1] to the solution of real world problems. Ultimately the foundation of software engineering is a framework for applying a problem solving methodology. Consequently, it is our contention that software engineering expertise is not a simple skill. Developing this expertise isn't accomplished by just teaching a specific development methodology, nor is it just developing familiarity with a set of tools. Rather, at a more fundamental level it requires the development of a student's abilities to recognize the need for and to adaptively apply a set of tools within a problem management and problem solving discipline. Collofello and Woodfield [4] have expressed the feeling evident in many attempts to deal with software engineering education, "to understand the basic software engineering principles completely, one must learn them not only in the classroom but also through experience."

In the early- to mid-1980s a number of articles appeared describing various approaches to teaching software engineering skills at the undergraduate level [as examples: 7, 17, 18]. A major theme of these approaches was the institution of a "projects" course with accompanying instruction in the methodologies of systematic software development.

Over the last decade the number of institutions employing software engineering practica has increased substantially [15].

The University of Idaho has required software engineering practica since 1978 when the Computer Science degree program was established. The approach evolved at first, but was solidified in its current form in 1982. Some basic software engineering concepts are addressed in lower-division courses, then culminates in a required two semester sequence of project courses during the senior year. These projects permit the actual application of a student's expertise to the solution of real problems. Project sponsors are generally members of the university community with needs for specialized computing support. The project sponsor must be willing to work directly with the student to define the project's scope. We believe that the results of a software engineering practicum should be well structured, completely functional, and thoroughly documented problem solutions.

1.1 Individual Design Project Course

The Individual Design Project course (CS 480) consists of classroom lectures coupled with the development of a moderately sized, working software product. A few representative projects recently completed in this course are:

- Inventory system for varsity athletic equipment
- Computer system administration and accounting
- Model of volcanic plumes and ash transport
- Data export program for anthropological GIS spatial information

During the initial project phase a student is given the content and format desired in the Software Requirements Specification [11] (based on IEEE Standard 830) and is advised on how to work effectively with his or her customer in identifying the requirements. During the design phase the emphasis is placed on converting the requirements into a fully documented design. Format and content of the Software Design Description [12] (based on IEEE Standard 1016) are specified. For the coding phase, programming style guidelines are provided. For the test phase, the approach to systematically validate the software is presented.

One aspect of our individual project course is relatively unique when compared with other project courses reported in the literature. Each student actually works on a different project, and one of his or her own choosing. Henry has found evidence that students perform better on a project of their own choosing [7]. Woodward and Mander, in describing their experience with the Software Hut Game, point out "If enthusiasm can somehow be generated within any group of students, by whatever means, then the most appalling difficulties can easily be surmounted ... Choose problems whose relevance can be seen" [17]. Our experience indicates that students prefer to select their own projects and we have seen evidence that they are likely to perform better because of a personal commitment and a higher level of motivation.

1.2 Group Design Project Course

Following completion of the Individual Design Project course, students perform another software development project (CS 481, Group Design Project) but this time they work in a small team (3 to 6 members) environment. Woodfield and Collofello indicated that selection of team members was one of the most difficult aspects of organizing a team-based course. In contrast to their experience, we have had very little difficulty [18]. Students will readily organize themselves into teams based on each other's perception of compatible personalities, technical abilities, or on a common interest in a problem to be solved. In some situations where we want to structure teams with nearly equal expertise, the instructor will assign students to a specific team.

As with the individual projects, the group projects are usually sponsored by members of the university community, but there are a few minor differences in the expectations held for the group projects. The size of the project attempted by the group is larger in scope than those typically attempted in the individual project course, but only larger by a factor of about two or three. While we allowed students in the Individual Design Project course to select their project, we will often assign a project to a team in the Group Design Project course. Representative of recent team project are:

- TeX to Ventura File Conversion
- Hierarchical Requirements Checklist
- Source Program Similarity Evaluator
- Maintainability Metrics Extraction Tool

Unlike the individual project course, no formal classroom instruction is given. The course "instructor" functions much like a "project manager" would in industry. A meeting is held with each team at a designated time every week. Status of the project is reviewed, problems are discussed, and individualized advice given.

Teams are permitted a reasonable latitude in determining how they will organize and function because ultimate responsibility for successful completion of the project rests with them. This meets our intent to provide an experience that is as real and representative of the professional world as can be created in an academic environment.

To date, little comparative research under controlled conditions has been conducted to evaluate the merits of specific development paradigms in either academic or industrial settings [6, 10]. The software engineering practica provide an opportunity to conduct this needed research. In the following section we present a brief summary of two software development paradigms that we have investigated.

2   Software Development Paradigms

Many different strategies, software development life cycle models, and development paradigms have been proposed. Each approach has its advocates and each is accompanied by an attendant set of advantages and disadvantages. At the center of the debate is the software development process model. The principle use of process models has been to prescribe a sequence of actions that need to be carried out during development, but ultimately a process model should aid making software development a more reliable, predictable, and productive process [8].

Early process model representations were drawn from perceived parallels in hardware or system development and manufacture. As a result they represented software development as a sequential set of independent steps. Their similarities to an "assembly line" made them simplistic and lacking in flexibility.

It seems that no single model fits all situations and it is important to recognize the circumstances that may favor a particular approach. In his analysis of software engineering methodologies, Barry Boehm [2] identified three dominant paradigms for software development: code-and-fix, specifying, and prototyping. In the following sections we will briefly review the important characteristics of latter two approaches. Code-and-fix is not discussed because it is not a development strategy we wish to promote.

2.1   The Specifying Paradigm

The specifying approach, commonly known as the *waterfall* model or as *phased refinement*, dictates that software is developed in a series of discrete, successive steps. These steps represent a systematic, sequential approach that include analyzing, designing, coding, testing, and maintaining the system [13]. Extensive and rigorous documentation requirements with consistent format and depth of detail are often associated with this approach. Although documentation is important, this seems to place the focus on artifact production rather than on their role of communicating information during system development [14]. Consequently, the waterfall model can be viewed as an artifact-driven model in which the life cycle phases exist to produce specific artifacts considered important to the development of the final software system.

The expectation that the use of specifying will ensure the development of fully elaborated work products at the conclusion of each life cycle phase is a characteristic that many software developers find unnatural and difficult to accomplish. Curtis points out that a major shortcoming of the waterfall model is its failure to treat software development as a problem solving process [5]. He also points out that a model focusing on only the end product of each major activity offers little insight into the actions and events that precede the finished artifact.

As a consequence of the approach, intermediate work products are not necessarily conceived with the product's end user in mind, but rather focus on the issues important to the developers. This may inhibit the effective participation of end users in the review process. Key misconception about what the system is supposed to do may not be uncovered until late in development or after delivery.

2.2 The Prototyping Paradigm

In contrast to the sequential nature of the waterfall paradigm, prototyping is an iterative process by which the developers capture critical features in a *model* containing selected aspects of the proposed system [16]. A prototype's purpose is to allow the user to gain experience with the proposed system in order to evaluate whether or not their expectations are being realized. Curtis states: "Managing uncertainty suggests that we reconceive the software life cycle as a learning process rather than a manufacturing process" [5]. The need for dealing with uncertainty requires that techniques, such as prototyping, be applied to identify and resolve these uncertainties. Curtis provides another warning about the use of prototyping: "Although prototyping may be useful for answering questions on a piece wise basis during development, it is certainly not the answer at the system level." By itself, prototyping is simply a useful development technique and is not a complete development process.

In his comparison of specifying to prototyping, Boehm found that both prototyping and specifying have advantages that complement each other [2]. Specifying provided the formalism and documentation necessary for long-term projects, while prototyping enabled the identification and investigation of high-risk issues and provided the flexibility to adapt to the changing perceptions of users' needs.

As a result of his work, Boehm suggested a new paradigm for software development and introduced what is now called the *spiral model* of software development [3]. The spiral model is an iterative risk-driven approach that can use both prototyping and specifying techniques. Each spiral model iteration begins with definition of objectives, alternatives, and constraints. If areas of uncertainty are found that represent significant project risk, then strategies for resolving the sources of risk are formulated. The resolution of the most significant risk drives each iteration.

3   Evaluating Life Cycle Models

Evaluating life cycle models is not easy because system development activities are complex processes with many variables and subject to significant statistical variation. In the following discussion we briefly review one often-referenced study.

3.1 Boehm's Study

In 1982 as part of a graduate software engineering course at UCLA, Barry Boehm conducted an experiment to compare the characteristics of products developed via the specification-driven approach to those developed with the prototyping approach [2]. In his experiment, seven teams developed versions of the COCOMO model for software cost estimation. This was a small-size (2K - 4K lines of code) application software product implementing the same estimation equations but allowing each team to create its own user interface to the model. Four teams used the specifying approach. Three teams used the prototyping approach.

The major milestones for the specifying teams were requirements specification, design specification, draft user's manual, acceptance test, final user's manual, and maintenance manual. The major milestones for the prototyping teams were the prototype demo, acceptance test, user's manual, and maintenance manual. The requirements and design specifications were subjected to a thorough review by the instructors. This resulted in a set of problem reports returned to the project teams and discussed in class. The prototypes were exercised by the instructors, who provided similar feedback on errors, suggested modifications, identified missing capabilities, etc.

Boehm and colleagues tested each product and rated it on a scale of 0 to 10 with respect to functionality, robustness, ease of use, and ease of learning. There was also a student subjective rating of the maintainability of the other teams' products.

In comparing specifying to prototyping products, the main results of Boehm's experiment were: (1) prototyping yielded products with roughly equivalent performance, but with about 40 percent less code and 45 percent less effort; (2) the prototyped products rated somewhat lower on functionality and robustness, but higher on ease of use and ease of learning; and (3) specifying produced more coherent designs and interface specifications which made integration of the software easier.

There were however, some uncontrolled characteristics of Boehm's experiment that may have influenced the results. These problems were team organization, team balancing, team separation, and potential experimenter bias. A summary of these problems are presented in [10].

From this study prototyping seems to offer advantages, such as facilitating early identification of high risk issues and the flexibility to adapt to changing perceptions of the user's needs. Although prototyping appears to have advantages, it is not really known if it offers the degree of process control that specifying provides. Furthermore, the characteristics of products appropriate for prototype development is not well understood. Finally Boehm saw significantly less code and effort by the prototypers in his experiment, but it is not known if this is a general characteristic to be expected from the approach or whether it might be due to differences in documentation requirements and experience levels. It is not clear what the differences are between the approaches, and which activities are responsible for those differences.

3.2 Some Initial Observations

The results that we report later in this paper are the results of a study initiated after we made some initial observations of individual and team behavior in our practica. Although customers were generally pleased with the student's effort, we noticed that in following a waterfall (specifying) development process, there was often some dissatisfaction expressed during the "final" product demonstration This was typically the first time the customer had seen the finished product. This prompted us to wonder whether or not the development paradigms and project management approach were significant factors in determining how well students satisfied their customer's requirements.

We had also notice that students' participation in their projects, as measured by the number of hours worked on the project each week, varied significantly during the semester. We were interested in investigating these work pattern to see if it was possible to early on identify those students who were having significant difficulty.

In Figure 1 we present the average hours worked per week for a section of the individual project course. The data have been divided to show separate profiles for those students successfully and not successfully completing the course. Notice that there is a significant increase in effort preceding each major deadline, where the deadlines correspond to the conclusion of a major phase in the specifying life cycle and require the submission of a development artifact. This is an area that is currently under investigation but we can report that there is a noticeable "deadline" effect evident in most individual projects. This effect is also seen in team projects, but tends to be less severe. The most severe fluctuations have been observed in projects that are not completed successfully. For these students, one frequent cause is the difficulty they have in managing their own time and their tendency to leave too much work for too late in the semester. Often they did not allow time to handle unexpected problems.

We also suspect that students have a tendency to limit the time spent on system design and head directly into detailed design, or possibly even coding. In some cases it is questionable which was done first, system design or detailed design. It is likely that this stems from an undisciplined approach emerging from their response to programming assignments in courses where the objective is perceived as requiring them only to get a program that produces the results desired by the instructor and where documentation is not required.

If a project runs short of time those activities performed at the end of the life cycle, testing and user-oriented documentation, are likely to be slighted. It has been difficult to impress upon the students the necessity of a well planned and executed testing program. To some extent this also stems from their previous approach to programming in other courses where the program was discarded once the output had been successfully produced.

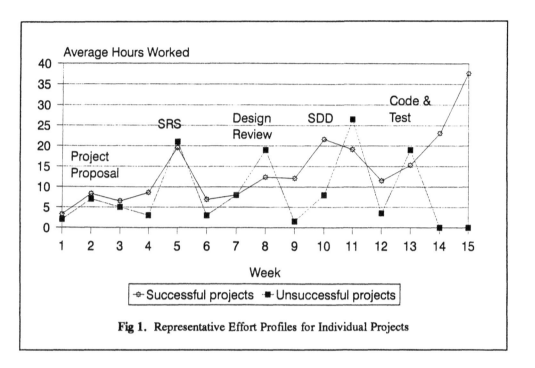

Fig 1. Representative Effort Profiles for Individual Projects

4 Our Experiments

Based on our initial observations, we decided to conduct side-by-side trials in which two development teams produced the same product but used different development strategies. The team projects were selected because the environment was more representative of the way software is developed outside academe and we felt that results would have greater external validity. We were especially interested in seeing if we could better understand the influence of development strategy on product quality and if the strategy influenced the ease with which the project and team could be managed.

4.1 Experimental Procedures

In order to study these issues in a more controlled environment than was present in [2], we conducted a series of three individual experiments which compared the traditional specifying approach to a spiral-based prototyping approach. Each experiment involved two balanced teams of experienced student programmers. The teams were given identical requirements from an independent customer. One team was selected to develop the product using a specifying approach while the other team used a spiral-prototyping approach. Team composition was controlled by the course instructors in order to provide roughly equivalent capabilities in both teams. Teams were isolated to avoid cross-fertilization of ideas.

4.2 The Specifying Life Cycle

The major features of the specifying life cycle used in our experiments are shown in Figure 2. The specifying teams produced a Software Requirements Specification (SRS), a Software Design Description (SDD), final code and test materials, and a user's manual. The teams were expected to update their documentation so that at the end of the project, it reflected all requirements and design changes implemented subsequent to initial document preparation. The teams conducted a system design review that focused on the system architecture, user interface, and major files and data structures. A final product installation and demonstration concluded the project.

4.3 The Spiral-Prototyping Life Cycle

The prototyping teams created three prototypes, then final code and test materials, a user's manual, and a maintenance document. A spiral-based prototyping model was used to support an incremental development approach. Each cycle consisted of four phases: (1)

I. Project Initiation
    1. Project Planning
        a. Schedule
        b. Team assignments

II. Requirements Definition
    1. Customer Interviews
    2. Requirement Document
        a. Usage scenario
        b. Data flow diagrams
        c. Data dictionary

III. Design
    1. System Architecture
        a. Structure chart
        b. User interface design
        c. File & data structure design
    2. System Design Review
    3. Detailed Design
        a. Module pseudo code
    4. Design Document

IV. Coding & Testing
    1. Coding
    2. Unit Testing
    3. Integration

V. Implementation
    1. User's Manual
    2. Documentation Update
    3. Installation & Demonstration

Fig 2. Specifying Life Cycle

planning/analysis phase, (2) specify/prototype phase, (3) test/review phase, and (4) analysis/replanning phase. The activities occurring during each phase may be seen in Figure 3. Each cycle was initiated by consideration of the most significant risk item facing the development and each cycle was concluded by a prototype demonstration and a review. The focus of this review was to assess the strengths and weaknesses of the prototype, how adequately it had resolved the high risk area, and to identify the content of the next prototype. A final product installation and demonstration concluded the project. The team was to document the software requirements, prepare a software maintenance manual addressing the major design concepts, and prepare a user's manual.

4.4 Team Balancing

Balanced teams were assembled to minimize the effect of variations in capabilities on the experiment's results. Balancing factors included: number of computer science courses completed, experience with mainframe and minicomputers, experience with microcomputers, number of languages known, work experience, implementation language experience, grade point average, total number of credits, and a self-determined subjective rating of their implementation language proficiency, and general programming abilities. Details are provided in [10].

4.5 Team Separation

In the first two experiments customer proxies were used to distance the real customer from the ongoing experiment and to minimize the interaction between the independent teams. The customer still provided the requirements and answered questions directly to both teams.

I. Planning/Analysis Phase
    1. Statement of the objectives
    2. Known constraints
       a. System
       b. Time
       c. Other
    3. Alternatives
       a. Feasible
       b. Other
       c. Model descriptions
    4. Potential problems
       a. Problem statements/
          possible resolutions

II. Specifications/Prototype Phase
    1. Prototype mini-specs
       a. Data flow diagrams
       b. Structure chart
       c. Module description
    2. Prototype code
       a. Prototype driver
       b. Modules & stubs

III. Testing/Review Phase
    1. Minimal test set generation
    2. Test execution
    3. Problems encountered
       a. Problem statement
       b. Actual and/or
          proposed solution(s)

IV. Analysis/Replanning Phase
    1. V&V Checklist
    2. Plan for next cycle
       a. Statement of goals
       b. Team member
          commitments

Fig 3. A Modified Spiral-Prototyping Model .

Information supplied to one team was supplied to the other team if it was a clarification of, or change in requirements. The customer was not involved in any design reviews or prototype evaluations. The customer proxies were used so that the real customer's perception of the system being developed was not altered by its ongoing development or the paradigm being used. Further, we didn't want the customer to "cross-fertilize" the two development projects by unwittingly passing design information between teams. Although from an end-product perspective it certainly would have been advantageous to have the real customer involved in the development, it was more important to keep a barrier between the teams. In the third experiment it was not feasible to isolate the customer from the project teams.

4.6 Data Collection

Effort data were collected weekly from team members during a scheduled team meeting. Team members were required to complete forms that asked them to log their time expended for each project activity they had performed. At the project's conclusion data were collected using a metric analyzer to measure code complexity through a battery of complexity metrics. These metrics were reported on a module-by-module basis and were then totaled for the entire system. The complexity data are objective measures, independent of the experimenters or customer.

4.7 Assessing Customer Satisfaction

The final product's quality was measured by customer satisfaction and reported errors. The separation between the development teams and the customer facilitated a more objective final evaluation of each product because the customer was not intimately familiar with the implementation details. After each end product was delivered, the customer was asked to test the products, complete an evaluation form, and produce an error report. Because of this procedure we believe that we have effectively eliminated experimenter bias from our experiments.

In the first two experiments the subjective customer evaluation consisted of several five-point, forced-choice positive statements, with responses ranging from 1-strongly disagree to 5-strongly agree. In each experiment the customer tested and evaluated both products. In Experiment 3 the customer was asked to evaluate each team in several areas relating to the effectiveness of their development approach.

During customer's testing, reported errors were recorded for both projects and later categorized according to errors of omission and errors of commission. Errors of omission are the results of incorrect or missing requirements. Errors of commission are errors for which requirements were correct but the implementation was flawed.

4.8   Experiment 1

The product to be developed was a visual simulator for Finite State Machines (FSM) as described by Jagielski in the *ACM SIGCSE Bulletin* [9]. The system was to allow the user to create and display a FSM state transition diagram on the computer screen, accept an input sentence from the user, and check the sentence for being in the FSM's language. As it checked the sentence, the nodes and arcs in the state transition diagram were to change color to show the path taken. Upon checking the entire sentence, a message was to be displayed as to whether the sentence was accepted by the FSM or not.

4.9   Experiment 2

The product to be developed was a system used to convert document files developed with the TeX publishing package to files matching a VENTURA format. This system was termed the TeX-to-VENTURA Bridge (TVB). Two windows were to be used to display the conversion process, with a user controllable scrolling speed. One window displayed the TeX input file, the other window showed the VENTURA file as it was being formatted. If the system found a TeX code that it could not convert, the user would be prompted to enter either a null or substitute VENTURA code.

4.10   Experiment 3

The product to be developed was a code similarity measurement tool used to evaluate suspected illicit program derivations. The program, DETECH, views a source program file as a string of words from which certain key words are extracted and counted. Similarity between two programs is determined by assessing the programs in three orthogonal dimensions that measure program structure, complexity, and style. DETECH assesses and reduces each of the three analyses to a single fixed measure of similarity which can then be compared to the similarity measure from another program.

5   Results

In the following paragraphs we present a discussion of the results observed in these experiments. The data are summarized and presented in Table 1.

5.1   Product Complexity Comparisons

For the FSM Simulators (Experiment 1), both products were of similar total size. Overall, the prototyped product contained 10% fewer lines of code. In a detailed evaluation of the code, we found that the prototyped product contained instances of

	No. of Modules	DSL	LOC	TOK	ARG	V_g	NST	N1	N2

Experiment 1: FSM Simulator

		No. of Modules	DSL	LOC	TOK	ARG	V_g	NST	N1	N2
Specifying Team	Total	34	2249	1977	14966	84	431	165	6517	4670
	Module Avg.			66.2	58.2	441.1	2.5	12.7	4.9	191.7	137.4
Prototyping Team	Total	57	2172	1686	13423	125	449	238	5479	4101
	Module Avg.			38.1	29.6	235.5	2.2	7.9	4.2	96.1	72.0

Experiment 2: TVB

		No. of Modules	DSL	LOC	TOK	ARG	V_g	NST	N1	N2
Specifying Team	Total	34	1650	1462	8790	63	338	177	4092	2399
	Module Avg.			48.5	43	259	1.85	9.94	5.21	120.4	70.6
Prototyping Team	Total	109	4771	4149	26588	225	742	282	12205	8183
	Module Avg.			43.8	38.1	244	2.06	6.8	2.6	112	75.1

	No. of Modules	*	LOC	*	*	V_g	*	N1	N2

Experiment 3: DETECH

		No. of Modules	*	LOC	*	*	V_g	*	N1	N2
Specifying Team	Total	48		4416			484		5828	3574
	Module Avg.			92.0			10.1		121.4	74.5
Prototyping Team	Total	62		3794			300		4096	2075
	Module Avg.			61.2			4.8		66.1	33.5

* Not available for "C" language implementation

DSL - Delivered Source Lines (excluding comments)
LOC - Lines of Code (executable lines)
TOK - Tokens
ARG - Arguments

V_g - McCabe's Measure
NST - Level of Nesting
N1 - Halstead's Total Operators
N2 - Halstead's Total Operands

Table 1. End-Product Complexity Comparisons

functionally redundant code that could have been implemented as utility modules. This would have further reduced the program's size.

Despite the fact that these products were of similar total size, the prototyped product contained 57 modules, while the specified product only contained 34. The average V_g (McCabe's Cyclomatic Control Flow Complexity) for the specified product was 12.7 compared to 7.9 for the prototyped product.

The TVB products (Experiment 2) were of considerably different size. The specified product contained 1650 delivered source lines as opposed to 4771 delivered source lines in the prototyped product. This large discrepancy occurred because the prototyping team used cut-and-paste editing to replicate a large amount of code with small editing changes to account for special cases. This generated a considerable amount of functionally redundant code, and can be viewed as a characteristic of their programming style. Although the metrics indicated the prototyped product contained substantially more lines of code, the per module average is slightly lower in the prototyped product. The prototyped product contained 109 modules, while the specified product only 34. Despite the fact that these products were of very different sizes, the result is that the specified product's modules were on average more complex than those of the prototyped product. The specified product had an average V_g of 9.94 compared to 6.8 for the prototyped product.

In both the FSM Simulator and the TVB products, the nesting of control structures was lower in the prototyped products, indicating that they were constructed from modules of lower average complexity. We also observed that the average Halstead metrics N1 and N2, are substantially lower in the prototyped implementations, again suggesting the existence of more compact modules. Although in these two product, the prototyped implementations contained more modules, the average number of arguments per module are about the same. The increase in modules did not seem to adversely affect the inter-module communication.

Although only a subset of the metrics were available from the C language implementations of DETECH (Experiment 3), the same patterns were observed. Again, the prototyping team showed a tendency to produce a system with more modules and a smaller average module size. The distinction between the two products was particularly evident with respect to V_g. In the specified product it averaged 10.1 compared to only 4.8 in the prototyped product.

The larger module size and V_g observed in the team specified product led us to evaluate the code itself. We found segments of unnecessarily duplicated code in multiple modules. Based on our observations we can postulate that developers using specifying may have a tendency to stick to the specified design past the point when it should have been revised. The design activity probably did not decompose the system into an adequate number of modules or failed to identify operations that could have been made into utility modules. Some of the reluctance to create additional modules during the coding phase may have been due to the mandate to modify requirements and design documents so that they accurately reflected the finished product. The reluctance to change manifested itself in modules containing additional code to implement details unforeseen at design time.

Interestingly, we observed that teams using prototyping unnecessarily duplicated code. We can postulate that they are often not looking past the immediate prototype when implementing their systems. It was more convenient to copy existing code and implement minor changes than it was to create a general purpose module. The lack of design documentation in the prototype developments may also have contributed to this tendency if team members, in the absence of detailed knowledge about other portions of the system, independently developed functionally equivalent code to support their assigned area. Unless there is intent to re-engineer the system at a later time, care should be taken to evaluate design choices in the context of how they will affect the final system. This nearsightedness can lead to systems being implemented with inefficient designs which are difficult to maintain and can lead to functionally redundant code segments.

The metric averages support the conclusion that the prototyping approach results in smaller and less complex modules when compared to the same product developed using the specifying approach. This was observed in all three experiments.

5.2 Development Effort

Effort profiles for each experiment and each team are shown in Figure 4. In Experiment 1 the specifying team logged a total of 637 hours to complete the project compared to 478 hour logged by the prototyping team. Observable in the figure is the tendency for effort to be driven by approaching deadlines. Effort peaks near the point where a deliverable, a document or prototype, is due and tends to decrease sharply after the milestone is completed.

For Experiment 2 the deadline effect is again clearly visible for the specifying team but less noticeable for the prototyping team. In this project the specifying team logged a total of 568 hours compared to a total of 455 hours for the prototyping team.

In Experiment 3 the specifying team once again required more effort to complete the project, 507 hours compared to 461 hours for the prototyping team. Deadline effects are still clearly visible for both teams. The team approach does seem to result in less severe effort fluctuations when compared to those experienced in the individual project.

While deadline effect remains a noticeable characteristic of individual projects developed under a specifying paradigm, there is clearly a reduced deadline effect in the prototyping team projects. Effort curves were smoother than those of either individual or team specified projects. Teams using prototyping not only completed their projects with less effort, but that effort also seemed to be more evenly distributed throughout the project.

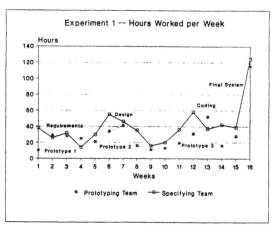

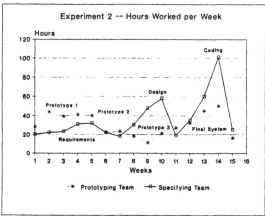

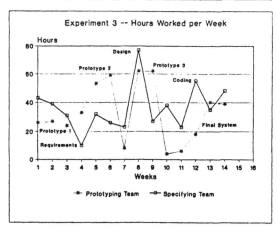

Fig 4. Weekly Effort Data for Each Experiment

5.3 Customer Evaluation

On the 20 question, 100 point subjective customer evaluation, the prototyping team's FSM Simulator was rated a score of 90 compared to a 66 for the specifying team's product. Both a pairwise t-test (T=4.7, d.f.=19, $p<0.001$) and a Wilcoxin signed-rank test ($W_+ = 4$, N=15, $p< 0.01$) indicate this difference is significant.

On a 15 question, 75 point subjective customer evaluation, the prototyping team's version of the TVB product received a score of 68 compared to the specifier's score of 54. Both a pairwise t-test (T=4.52, d.f.=14, $p<0.001$) and a Wilcoxin signed-rank test ($W_+ =0$, N=11, $p<0.005$) indicate the difference is significant.

The customer for the DETECH produced expressed a preference for the specifying team's product primarily due to several implementation errors in the counting strategy in the prototyper's product. However, he preferred the user interface of the prototyper's product. On a 5 question, 25 point subjective evaluation the customer rated both teams equally with a score of 22. The quality of the prototyper's code was rated higher, while the specifiers were rated higher on overall satisfaction of project requirements.

5.4 Reported Errors

Table 2 presents a summary of the customer reported errors found in each product. For the FSM Simulator products, significant problems were reported in the user interface of the specified product. For the TVB products, significant flaws in the specified product were related to an overly simplistic user interface and unexpected program behavior. For the DETECH product, the specifiers failed to implement some requirements, including getting the product to execute on the target computer system.

	Errors of Commission	Errors of Omission
Experiment 1: FSM		
Specifying Team	2	6
Prototyping Team	2	2
Experiment 2: TVB		
Specifying Team	3	3
Prototyping Team	3	0
Experiment 3: DETECH		
Specifying Team	3	3
Prototyping Team	5	0

Table 2. Reported Errors for Each Project

6   Conclusions and Recommendations

After more than a decade of requiring practica we remain convinced of their value in computer science and software engineering education. We have also found these courses to be a feasible environment for experimentation. Specifically, we have:

- established a mechanism for investigating software development paradigms that ensures comparability of data collected from independent software development teams,
- shown that when comparing prototyping to specifying, the prototyping process facilitated production of a larger numbers of smaller, less complex modules,
- observed that these modules took less effort to develop,
- demonstrated that spiral-prototype products contained fewer errors as a result of software reuse through the evolution of the prototypes, and
- shown that prototyped products consistently contained fewer errors of omission.

Although we have shown that the spiral-prototyping approach reduces errors of omission, we do not want to overlook the importance of project management to a successful project. If not careful, prototypers may lose sight of the original requirements as their systems evolve and may run a risk of failing to deliver a finished product. Customers and developers using prototyping in their development process must take care to:

- plan each iteration,
- examine each new requirement as to how it supports the original requirements,
- determine what implications any new requirement has on the system architecture,
- revise the system goals as necessary, and
- not let the prototyping take on a momentum of its own.

Configuration management techniques are needed to keep prototype histories and project baselines intact in order to ensure that a code-and-fix strategy does not emerge. As part of this baseline, prototypes should be accompanied by requirements specifications and design materials which document the important architectural decisions. Evolving customer requirements should also be documented as part of this baseline. Prototypes themselves do not adequately express the requirements of a system. Developers using prototyping need additional material to validate the existence of each prototype component as well as mechanisms to prevent them from simply finishing the project and then tailoring the final requirements to coincide with the final delivered system.

The spiral-prototyping   model was effective in encouraging evaluation of product constraints and alternatives.   It highlighted risk item resolution by having the development team evaluate problems and possible problem resolutions during each cycle. It helped give the process some structure that is normally lacking in a prototyping environment, with the desired result that the developers were not free to just start coding. It also gave the (proxy) customers some early experience with the system and some opportunities for affecting the direction of the ongoing development. The model template gave both the developers and the customer a good plan to follow as well as the needed confidence that they were reaching meaningful project milestones.

Although we see evidence of improved results with the spiral-prototyping process and are using it as the preferred approach in our Group Design Project course ,we believe that our students should be exposed to more than one development paradigm. We will continue to use the specifying paradigm for the Individual Design Project course. This provides a relatively controlled environment in which we can focus on developing rigor and discipline. We will then expose students to the additional dimensions of the spiral-prototyping paradigm after this foundation is established. The combination of approaches provides a solid experience base for our graduates to take with them when they enter the professional ranks.

References

1. F. L. Bauser, "Software Engineering," *Information Processing 71*, Amsterdam: North Holland Publishing Co., 1982.

2. B. W. Boehm, T. E. Gray, and T. Seewaldt, "Prototyping Versus Specifying: A Multiproject Experiment," *IEEE Transactions on Software Engineering*, Vol SE-10(3), 1984, pp. 290-302.

3. B. W. Boehm, "A Spiral Model of Software Development and Enhancement," *IEEE Computer*, May 1988, pp. 61-72.

4. James Collofello and Scott Woodfield, "A Project-Unified Software Engineering Course Sequence," *SIGCSE Bulletin*, vol. 14, pp. 13-19, Feb. 1982.

5. Bill Curtis, Herb Krasner, Vincent Shen, and Neil Iscoe, "On Building Software Process Models Under the Lamppost," *Proceedings of the 9th International Conference on Software Engineering*, March 30-April 2, 1987, pp. 96-103.

6. V. Scott Gordon and James M. Bieman, "Rapid Prototyping and Software Quality: Lessons from Industry," *Proceedings of the Pacific Northwest Software Quality Conference*, October 1991, pp. 19-29.

7. Sallie Henry, "A Project Oriented Course on Software Engineering," *SIGCSE Bulletin*, vol. 15, pp. 57-61, Feb. 1983.

8. Watts S. Humphrey, *Managing the Software Process*, Addison-Wesley, 1989.

9. R. Jagielski, "Visual Simulation of Finite State Machines," *ACM SIGCSE Bulletin*, Vol 20(4), December 1988, pp. 38-40.

10. William Junk and Paul Oman, "Comparing the Effectiveness of Software Development Paradigms: Spiral-Prototyping vs. Specifying," *Proceedings of Ninth Annual Pacific Northwest Software Quality Conference*, October 1991, pp. 2-18.

11. William Junk and Karen Van Houten, *Guidelines for Preparing the Software Requirements Specification*, University of Idaho Computer Science Department, January 1992.

12. William Junk and Karen Van Houten, *Guidelines for Preparing the Software Design Description*, University of Idaho Computer Science Department, February 1992.

13. Roger Pressman, *Software Engineering: A Practitioner's Approach Third Edition*, McGraw-Hill, 1991.

14. Winston W. Royce, "Managing the Development of Large Software Systems," *Proceedings of IEEE WESCON*, August 1970, pp. 1-9.

15. Mary Shaw and James Momoyko, *Models for Undergraduate Project Courses in Software Engineering*, CMU/SEI-TR-10, August 1991.

16. M. M. Tanik and R. Yeh, "Rapid Prototyping in Software Development," *IEEE Computer*, May 1989, pp. 9-10.

17. Martin Woodward and Keith Mander, "On Software Engineering Education: Experiences with the Software Hut Game," *IEEE Trans. Education*, vol. E-25, pp. 10-14, Feb. 1982.

18. Scott Woodfield and James Collofello, "Some Insights and Experiences in Teaching Team Project Courses," *SIGCSE Bulletin*, vol. 15, pp. 62-65, Feb. 1983.

Engineering Principles and Software Engineering

Alfs T. Berztiss

Department of Computer Science, University of Pittsburgh
Pittsburgh, PA 15260, USA (alpha@cs.pitt.edu)

and

SYSLAB, University of Stockholm, Sweden

Abstract. We identify the principal activities of engineers, formulate twelve principles of engineering in general, and establish that the problems of software engineering differ little from problems in traditional engineering. This leads to a discussion of software engineering education based on general engineering principles. Although our primary aim is to give improved structure to software engineering education, we discuss also the importance of computer science to software engineering, and show how the concepts of concurrent engineering manifest themselves in software engineering.

1 Introduction

With the December 1991 issue *IEEE Transactions on Software Engineering* had published 16,120 pages of densely laid out material. Despite this impressive body of software engineering knowledge in one journal alone, software engineering still seems to be searching for an identity. It is understood that it deals with software, but the engineering aspect lacks definition. We have had thoughtful analyses that point out that software engineering is likely to become an engineering discipline in the long run, but not quite yet [1], and that software developers would be best served by being exposed to traditional engineering training [2]. Getting at specific detail, we are being told that traditional engineering differs radically from software engineering by having a materialistic basis [3, 4], with the implication that software engineering could never become a legitimate branch of engineering.

These views are understandable if we accept a traditional definition of engineering. For example, the Engineers' Council for Professional Development (UK) defines engineering as

> "the profession in which a knowledge of the mathematical and natural sciences, guided by study, experience and practice, is applied with judgement to develop ways to utilize economically the materials and forces of nature for the benefit of mankind"

(cited in [5]). Clearly if the task of engineers is to apply the natural sciences, then software engineering is not engineering. However, by concentrating on the mathematical sciences, we could in time provide it with proper foundations in the sense of the definition. But, no matter how we try, software engineering cannot be made to relate to materials and forces of nature.

Instead of becoming constrained by definitions, it may be more profitable to look at what engineers in the traditional disciplines actually do or should be doing, and try to derive an operational prescription for software engineering from such observations. An earlier attempt at this has been the investigation of what software developers can learn from bridge designers [6]. Here we shall extend this work. Our aim is to list the activities of engineers, express the list as a set of principles, and show that the set of principles can serve as a basis for software engineering education. This will define one of two supports for software engineering, the other being computer science:

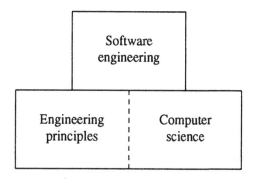

Within this framework we shall also define specific topics of computer science that are essential for a well-rounded education in software engineering. We hope that our approach to the definition of a software engineering curriculum will result in a curriculum that has cohesive structure.

2 What Engineers Do

Although the work of engineers is highly varied, ranging from research through planning and design to on-site supervision of manufacturing processes or construction projects, every engineer is required to perform at least some of the tasks listed below. Furthermore, it is hard to think of a professional engineering activity not covered by one or other of these tasks:

- Definition of requirements and making of development plans;
- Resolution of conflicts in requirements and setting of priorities;
- Use of standards;

- Anticipation of change and allowance for modifications;
- Provision for the unexpected;
- Transfer of theory into practice;
- Scaling up from models or prototypes;
- Control of quality;
- Selection of tools;
- Cooperation with other specialists;
- Management of the above;
- Engagement in technological adventure.

We shall examine each of the twelve tasks in detail, and formulate in each case a general engineering principle.

Requirements and plans. Before an object is constructed, there has to be a clear understanding by all concerned of what is to be constructed, and of the construction process to be followed. The process is defined by a plan, the object by requirements. The requirements, which may be functional or non-functional, must be verifiable, i.e., they must be stated in quantitative terms.

PRINCIPLE 1: Development of engineered objects follows a plan in accordance with quantitative requirements.

Conflicts and priorities. Requirements are often contradictory. For example, a high reliability requirement is in conflict with a low cost requirement. It is therefore essential to develop quantitative estimates of trade-offs between requirements, such as between reliability and cost, or versatility and portability, and to assign priorities to requirements. An effective approach is cost-effectiveness ranking. Reliability has a special role in this: a reliability value below 1 indicates to what extent other requirements may be relaxed. Further, when the object to be constructed is made up of distinct parts, attention to the order in which the parts are constructed can produce a useful product even when the entire project as originally planned cannot be completed. An example is a housing development: houses should be built one cluster at a time rather than all at once.

PRINCIPLE 2: Requirements are ranked according to cost-effectiveness, and the development plan, which has an incremental structure, emphasizes the higher ranked requirements.

Standards. Standards were established to allow engineered objects or their parts to be readily interchanged, thus reducing maintenance costs. Also, the initial cost of an object is reduced if the object can be constructed from standard parts. Standardization is achieved by having an enterprise or an entire industry use the same specification for the object or part, the user interface of an object, or the interfaces of a part with other parts. The notion of standardization has been extended to engineering procedures, such as the writing of requirements, but such extension may be detrimental to progress. As a rule of thumb we recommend that standardization be limited to entities that can be patented or copyrighted.

PRINCIPLE 3: Standards are used where available and applicable, with every departure from applicable standards explicitly justified.

Changes and modifications. Engineers try to anticipate changes, and allow for such changes in their designs. For example, a bridge may start out having a single deck, but with enough strength to allow a second deck to be added should traffic density grow. This is just one example of a change in the environment bringing about a modification of the engineering product. Another type of change arises from design defects – in the automobile industry such defects result in recalls. Standardization of interfaces localizes the effects of changes.

PRINCIPLE 4: Future changes are anticipated, and engineering design minimizes the cost of modifications.

The unexpected. Not all conditions can be anticipated. A sudden upsurge of pressure in a gas main can result in explosions that destroy homes. Engineers try to minimize the effects of unexpected conditions by fault-tolerant and failure-tolerant design.

PRINCIPLE 5: Fault- and failure-tolerance are built into engineering designs.

Theory into practice. The primary concern of the more mature engineering disciplines is to adapt the findings of theory to solve practical problems. For example, applied elasticity is a branch of mathematics that deals with stresses in objects; strength of materials is applied elasticity made relevant by being adapted to engineering practice; a stress calculation is a specific engineering design task.

PRINCIPLE 6: Findings of mathematics and the sciences are applied in the solution of engineering problems.

Scaling up. Engineering often starts with a *model*, i.e., a scaled-down version of the target object, e.g., a laboratory model of a chemical plant, or a *prototype*, i.e., a full-scale version of a product to be manufactured. In one case the problems to solve relate to size – results from study of flows in a system of small-bore pipes have to be adapted to a system of large-bore pipes. In the other they relate to production – the building of the prototype device may have taken one week; the device is now to be produced at a rate of 500 per hour.

PRINCIPLE 7: Efficient techniques are used to scale up size or production.

Quality control. An engineering ideal is to produce objects with zero defects, i.e., objects that fully conform to requirements, both functional and non-functional. This goal may not be cost-effective. Even the lesser goal of eliminating all defective objects before delivery to customers may not be cost-effective in the case of, say, thumbtacks. However, statistical quality control and reliability engineering can be used to impose strict control on quality levels.

PRINCIPLE 8: Quality control techniques are used to maintain quality at predetermined levels.

Use of tools. The nature of tools in engineering has changed dramatically over the past twenty years with the introduction of computer-based tools. The latter have replaced T-squares and other drafting tools, physical mock-ups of packaging, and much of other physical modeling. Electronic infrastructures have contributed to the success of concurrent engineering. However, tools can only produce representations of conceptual designs developed by engineers, and help engineers make adjustments to such representations. As yet no tool has replaced human creativity.

PRINCIPLE 9: Tools are used to improve productivity, but the use of tools is no substitute for human creativity.

Cooperation on the job. Engineering practice is not individual-oriented. Design of a large building requires the collaboration of civil, mechanical, and electrical engineers, and design engineers have to interact with architects and builders.

PRINCIPLE 10: Contributors from many disciplines participate in engineering tasks.

Management. Because of the cooperative nature of engineering, not every engineer has to become a manager, but every engineer should have an appreciation of the nature of engineering management. Cost and risk estimation, the matching up of design tasks with personnel, constant monitoring of the progress of a project, and the timely identification of problems require a good grasp of management principles and people skills, broad knowledge of the technical aspects of engineering, and much experience. Only a few engineers have these qualifications.

PRINCIPLE 11: Effective engineering management is based on a collection of skills acquired by an extensive process of learning.

Adventure. Technological adventure has a respectable tradition in engineering. The Roman Pantheon, built in early 2nd Century, has a dome 43 meters in diameter. Its builders did not know much about applied elasticity, but the building still stands after close to 1900 years. Nearer to our time, when the Wright brothers set out to initiate heavier-than-air flight they did not know much about aerodynamics, but their investigations advanced aerodynamic knowledge. When a technology for an area has not yet been developed, engineers still move ahead, and in so doing develop the technology.

PRINCIPLE 12: Technological adventure is good engineering, provided the aim is to add to engineering knowledge.

3 Problems in Software Engineering

The steep increase in the software-hardware cost ratio over the past twenty years has led to the perception of some kind of software crisis, and the fear that matters are not getting better. Actually the pattern of development of software technology is quite normal – abnormal has been the amazing decrease in the cost of raw computing power, and this has distorted our perception. Traditional engineering projects also have cost and schedule overruns, and traditional engineering problems have been the cause of numerous disasters. We recommend that Neumann's "Risks to the Public" compilations in *Software Engineering Notes* be read by all software engineers, but that they be read with a realization that risk is characteristic of *all* engineering. Although we cannot tell what the risks to the public would be if we had no software-driven control systems in place, I have a strong conviction that software systems have reduced rather than increased such risks.

But this is not an invitation to complacency. An engineering project can succeed only if proper discipline is observed in accordance with engineering principles, and this applies also to software engineering. Indeed, since software engineers often have to solve problems of great inherent complexity, they should pay particular attention to general engineering principles. We shall return to a discussion of how to accomplish this, but first we list the main problems of software engineering as seen by software developers themselves, adapted from field study reports by Thayer *et al.* [7] and Curtis *et al.* [8], with additions from [9, 10]. We have grouped the problems into three categories.

A. Planning and requirements gathering:
- System plan does not exist or is poorly formulated;
- Requirements are incomplete, ambiguous, inconsistent, unmeasurable, volatile;
- Knowledge of the application domain by software developers is sketchy;
- Communication and coordination breakdowns occur.

B. Implementation and validation:
- Programs for maintaining quality are inadequate;
- Traceability mechanisms have not been installed;
- Reliability, safety, and performance are neglected;
- Maintainability is ignored, and so is reuse potential.

C. Management:
- Management neglects its responsibilities;
- Delivery schedules and cost estimates are inaccurate;
- Risk analyses are not performed;
- Accountability is poor, particularly as regards personnel performance.

It may come as a surprise that nothing in this list is specific to software engineering. However, in expanding an entry in the list, every engineering discipline will interpret it in its own specialized way, and the method of dealing with a problem will differ from discipline to discipline. In the next section we link the software engineering interpretations of the problems to the general principles of Section 2.

4 Engineering Principles and Software Development

The principles of Section 2 are of two kinds. They relate either to the functions that make up the development process, or to attitudes to follow in the development process. We can distinguish six functions, which we again group into three categories.

A. Planning and requirements gathering:
- Planning (Principle 1);
- Requirements engineering (Principle 2).

B. Implementation and validation:
- The scaling-up process (Principle 7);
- Quality control (Principle 8).

C. Management:
- Selection of tools (Principle 9);
- Engineering management (Principle 11).

The other six principles, which relate to the manner in which these development functions are to be carried out, will be discussed as needed in an attempt to integrate Section 3 with the principles that define the development process under our three categories. For each category we shall indicate some texts that take an engineering attitude to software development – this does not always imply that we assign highest ranking to these texts compared to others that deal with the same or similar topics.

4.1 Planning and Requirements Gathering.

Under a phased software lifecycle model, requirements gathering, architectural design, detailed design, implementation, and testing are distinct sequential activities. For quite a few years it has been recognized that requirements gathering and design are necessarily intertwined [11], and concurrency of the phases becomes even more marked in a model- or prototype-based approach to software development [12]. This trend is consistent with what in traditional engineering has become known as concurrent engineering: component design, validation of the design, packaging of components, definition of the manufacturing process, and development of quality control plans proceed concurrently. The literature on concurrent engineering is still very sparse – [13] introduces some of the concepts, but may be too specialized. An instance of large-scale concurrent engineering is the development of the Boeing 777 (see, e.g., [14]).

Under concurrent engineering, a system plan, which allocates the various functions of a system to its components, still drives all other activities. But, since architectural design defines the components, it has to become part of planning, and system planning has to proceed in parallel with requirements gathering: overall system requirements suggest a partition of the system into subsystems, which is architectural design, and a statement of purpose for each subsystem suggests in turn what to look for in arriving at the detailed requirements for this subsystem. In our context an initial allocation assigns some functions to hardware, others to software. This initial partition is followed by a refinement of the software system into subsystems, these are refined further into modules, and the modules into submodules.

There is much to be said for setting up a model of the ultimate system [15], and for implementing a software system incrementally by expanding outwards from an initial model [16]. The model serves to clarify requirements with user representatives, improve the knowledge the development team has of the domain, and provide support for communication and coordination.

Requirements engineering encompasses two topics – the process of gathering requirements, and representation of requirements. A detailed coverage of representations for today's software engineering, and how to generate them can be found in [17]. The requirements gathering process is not adequately covered by any single book – Gause and Weinberg [18] deal with the process in a lively exposition that comes closest to completeness, but [19] has to be consulted for the highly effective Joint Application Development (JAD) methodology. Although performance estimation is often delayed until well after implementation has begun, a recent trend is to carry out preliminary performance estimation as part of requirements engineering – Connie Smith [20] provides an excellent introduction to this process. Early performance estimation and JAD again fit in with the practices of concurrent engineering.

Engineering practice allows modifications, but all modifications are to be made first to requirements [21, p.104], i.e., every maintenance activity is to begin with requirements. This implies that the statement of requirements should have the same modular structure as the software. Moreover, in order to satisfy Principle 4, the interfaces of modules should be designed so as to minimize the costs of maintenance. We have found it very effective to separate a software system together with its data base into data types, and processes defined in terms of operations of the data types. Under such an object-oriented approach each data type and process becomes a module.

To satisfy Principle 5, the effects of unexpected occurrences are to be minimized. This can be done by means of fault- and failure-tolerant design. The presence of a fault in a fault-tolerant system should not lead to failure; a failure-tolerant system should minimize the adverse effects of a failure. Fault tolerance is discussed in [22] (I was surprised to find no reference to this book in any of the nine general software engineering texts on my shelves); failure tolerance can be regarded as part of risk analysis, which we consider a management function.

4.2 Implementation and Validation.

Scaling up production is not an issue with software; scaling up the product size is. One solution would be to construct software systems from standard components of high reliability. However, the reuse potential of existing software is not very high, and standardization and reuse are already being practiced where feasible – we have had mathematics and statistics program libraries for many years, libraries of data structures are a more recent development (see, e.g., [23]), structured programming has standardized control structures, we use standard paradigms for the synchronization of processes, and the porting of operating systems from one computer to another has become commonplace. However, the domains in which application software operates vary greatly: the payroll program for a small manufacturing company differs from that for a university with 2- and 3-term appointments, and this in turn differs from that for a multinational corporation. Hence reuse of components in building a new application system is rather limited, but so is the reuse of bridge designs [6].

High expectations have been raised by the observation that traditional engineers use very few basic construction elements. But the basic elements that go into a wristwatch differ from those that go into a bridge, and examination of the syntax charts of programming languages will show that programs, too, are built with very few construction elements. Keep also in mind that the designers of, say, an automobile assembly plant and of a bottling plant follow the same engineering principles, but can learn little from each other as regards detailed design. Moreover, progress means innovation. This examination should curb unwarranted optimism regarding reuse: software engineers are to follow Principle 3, but be aware that domain variability and the need to be innovative make extensive reuse hard to achieve. Despite the broad range of literature on software reuse, most of it is speculative, and the proper place for the speculative aspects is in specialized seminars. However, reuse in limited and well-defined contexts, and in utilitarian ways, as exemplified by the software catalog of [23], should become more prominent in software engineering education. We emphasize again that module interfaces should be designed to facilitate module interchanges.

While American manufacturing has lost much ground to foreign competition, the software industry is still an exception. One possible reason is that established engineering may be relying too heavily on codified handbook knowledge rather than on innovation. But reinvention is not innovation, and, to prevent wasteful reinvention, we support wholeheartedly the suggestion that computer science knowledge applicable in software engineering should be assembled into a handbook [1].

The problems listed in Section 3 under Category B (Implementation and validation) all relate to quality control. To many people software quality means functional correctness, but quality control has to deal also with nonfunctional quality attributes, which include reliability, modifiability, portability, versatility, reusability, usability, understandability, and performance. These attributes are difficult to measure, except for performance and reliability. Hence software engineering education should emphasize functionality, performance, and reliability, but give attention to the other quality attributes as well. As we noted above, performance estimation should start before implementation begins. But the performance engineering process continues throughout system development. Early performance estimates are refined, and detailed design choices are made on the basis of improved estimates. Sometimes the actual performance data require readjustment of the boundary between hardware and software.

Nonfunctional requirements usually impose restrictions; only reliability relates to the *relaxation* of other requirements. Ideal software quality is achieved when the software is free of defects: zero-defect software satisfies its requirements perfectly. Unfortunately the interaction of components of a large system is often too complex for human comprehension, which means that for large systems ideal quality not only is not, but cannot be achieved. The next best position is to accept this limitation, but to make sure that deviations from the ideal are measurable and under strict control. The control is provided by reliability engineering, which has been used on hardware for a long time. Hardware reliability is improved by means of redundancy and replacement of worn parts. With software the situation is different – it is not subject to wear and tear, and redundancy is of little help. But this matters little: statistical models that give accurate reliability estimates have been developed for software as well. An excellent coverage of software reliability can be found in [24]. On software safety, which is closely related to reliability, see [25].

Reliability engineering has three aspects. First, given an acceptable overall system reliability level, which is determined by risk analysis, minimum reliability levels for individual components can be determined. Second, given the overall reliability requirement for a system, and minimum reliability limits for its components, reliability goals can be adjusted within these limits so as to reduce system development costs. Third, reliability analysis permits the current level of reliability of a system to be established from its past failure history. Software testing can stop when the required reliability level has been reached. The "cleanroom" approach to software development puts particular emphasis on reliability analysis [26, 27]. Under this approach software modules are verified by mathematical reasoning about their behavior, but are not individually tested. Only when the entire system has been assembled does testing begin, and it stops when an acceptable reliability level has been reached. Random testing has been shown to be more effective than structural testing [28, 29], and random testing is the basis of reliability analysis. This implies that in the future there should be emphasis on random testing and reliability in software engineering education.

Software development, particularly under a concurrent engineering model, is volatile – requirements change, alternative designs are elaborated in parallel and possibly discarded, performance failures necessitate redesign at the architectural level, etc. Traceability requires that, for each version of the system, requirements, design, implementation, and support literature always be consistent. The importance of traceability is well recognized in traditional engineering; it does not appear to be given adequate emphasis in software engineering education – unavailability of literature cannot be claimed as an excuse ([30] is just the latest of a number of books). Again, though, it should be noted that inconsistencies are not a problem of software engineering alone – have we not bought some appliance with instructions not quite consistent with the model we bought?

4.3 Management.

We see as the primary function of management a delicate balancing of profitability and market share, both in the short and the long term. Profitability suffers when there are cost overruns, industrial unrest, inadequate attention to new technology. Market share in our context relates to the question "Will the customer choose my company again for the next software development project?" This relates to risk analysis. Risk cannot be avoided. The objective is to weigh risks against benefits, which is a positive attitude to risk.

For purposes of risk-benefit analysis it is necessary to know costs, and the importance of cost estimation has been recognized by engineers for thousands of years – "For which of you, intending to build a tower, sitteth not down first, and counteth the cost, whether he have sufficient to finish it?" (Luke 14, 28). But risk analysis goes beyond cost estimation.

Software risks are of two kinds, those relating to the development of the software, and those relating to the effects of the software once it is put into use. Let us call them development risks and operational risks, respectively. The more important risk factors relate to strict management functions. The first in our list of management problems in Section 3 is management neglect of its responsibilities. Management assumes responsibility by giving proper attention to risk factors, and all other management problems then become tractable. Some of these problems: (1) unrealistic cost and schedule estimates, (2) inadequate screening of suppliers and subcontractors, (3) inadequate monitoring of the performance of suppliers and subcontractors, (4) inadequate monitoring of the performance of in-house personnel, (5) abdication of management control in the face of changing requirements, such as a continuous flow of demands for additional features from a client, (6) no contingency plans or insurance provisions for dealing with industrial actions, delays, or disasters, such as fires or floods.

Another management function is to ensure that there is adequate interaction between system developers and the ultimate users of a system. Poor user-developer interaction can result in prospective users refusing to have anything to do with the system, or in extensive redesign after the initial implementation. Both situations are costly – in terms of goodwill and cash.

Risk due to poor management skills or poor user-developer interaction can be controlled by improved training. Moreover, management should have adequate technical background to cope with feasibility problems, i.e., to realize when a proposed system strains or exceeds physical limits, such as when combinatorial explosion makes it impossible to meet real-time performance constraints.

Operational risks arise from poor quality control, where by quality is meant an amalgamation of various attributes. Poor control of operational risks can lead at best to prospective users not making use of the system. In a more serious category are system faults that lead to positive damage, e.g., a telephone network out of service for 12 hours, an air traffic control system that crashes without allowing for a smooth change-over to manual control, an air-defense system that shoots down friendly aircraft. If risks are too high, a project may have to be abandoned. This is a management decision.

Risk analysis is surveyed in [9]. See also [31], which is a collection of papers – it is strong on the incorporation of risk analysis in software development under the spiral model, and on the relationship between risks and costs.

Management selects tools. First, there are tools relating to the management function itself, such as Gantt charts, Pert networks, etc. Most texts on software engineering have something to say about them. Second, software developers require tools for creating representations, for management of the representations, and for communication. Tools for creating and managing representations, the so called CASE technology, are surveyed in [32]; we refer again to [30] for configuration management. Efficient communication between users and software developers, and among developers is essential – hence management must provide adequate electronic communication facilities, and personnel must be trained in their use.

5. A curriculum for software engineering

In common with Wulf [4] we oppose an undergraduate software engineering major, but we do not accept the reason that software engineering is not a mature discipline. There is enough solid engineering material in each of the three categories of Sections 3 and 4 for at least one semester of intensive study. However, the student also needs a fair amount of mathematics and computer science, and, because of the pervasive influence of computers on every aspect of human life, students in any computing field should have a broad liberal education.

A commitment to liberal education causes us to oppose Parnas' recommendation that computing education become centered on traditional engineering topics [2]. Software developers of the future can indeed be expected to become more involved with embedded control systems and communication between processors, but this does not mean that they need to learn control theory and information theory in formal courses, just as developers of information systems for banks do not have to take courses in banking law. Our Principle 10 comes into play here – software engineers, who should have professional competence in their own discipline, cooperate with professionals in other disciplines. This means, however, that a common language be spoken, and this is the language of mathematics. Much of the mathematics that Parnas would include in his curriculum [2] is needed by software engineers, but the discrete mathematics content can be reduced. I have myself stressed the importance of discrete mathematics for computer scientists [33], and still do so today, but software engineers have much greater use for continuum mathematics – a thorough familiarity with statistics is essential, and this presupposes calculus.

Now, a student with a computer science major that includes two or three software engineering courses can hardly be called a software engineer. We hope, therefore, that the number and size of graduate programs in software engineering will increase. Let us determine the computer science content that students entering such graduate programs will be expected to know or to learn as part of the program. We limit ourselves here to material that they will actually find of use in the development of software, in keeping with Principle 6. The topics are grouped under three headings.

Representation and design issues: languages, in terms of their syntax and semantics; visual representation of relationships, with emphasis on directed graphs; representations to support formal verification; concepts such as information hiding, avoidance of side effects, deadlock and livelock, mutual exclusion.

Algorithms and foundations: the design and analysis of algorithms for common computing tasks, such as sorting and searching; the use queues, trees, and other devices; searches in large state spaces; hard problems; decidability issues, particularly the non-existence of certain algorithms (to stop one looking for the impossible).

Environments: operating systems, data base management systems, interface systems, networks, as tools to be used in software development, and as environments with which the software under development is to interact; software-hardware interfaces, such as sensors.

Observe here that languages are introduced purely as representational devices – there is no mention of programming. We want to emphasize that while programming can and should be a highly skilled occupation, programming is not engineering. There are many skilled activities that have to be carried out for a traditional engineering design to be realized, such as welding, operating a bulldozer, or installing electrical circuits, but it is unusual for engineers to become proficient at these activities. Similarly, programming is the realization of a design, and this is not a task for software engineers. Their task is to design, supervise the design realization, and monitor quality maintenance, which brings us back to our categories A, B, and C.

We indicated in Section 4 what should be studied under the three category headings. Here we want to put emphasis on the packaging of the material. For each of the categories we can develop a single course or a cluster of courses. In the discussion to follow we shall draw on our experience with software engineering courses at the University of Pittsburgh: for a number of years we have offered undergraduate and graduate courses corresponding to A (Planning and requirements) and B (Implementation and validation), where the second course in each sequence touches also on management issues.

Planning and requirements gathering. The material in this category can be studied in a single course, as at the University of Pittsburgh, or it could be expanded into a number of courses for professional software engineering graduate study. The courses (or topics for a single course) can be (a) an overview of software engineering, with emphasis on engineering principles in specification and design; (b) representations of functional requirements, including both graphical and textual representations; (c) nonfunctional requirements, particularly requirements relating to performance and reliability; (d) the requirements gathering and validation process, including the use of models and prototypes in the refinement and validation of requirements; (e) planning and design of knowledge-based systems. We believe that a major group project is essential. Students have to learn to work in groups and make use of each other's expertise. They also have to understand how difficult requirements gathering really is. The group project is the first step in making students aware of Principle 10. At the University of Pittsburgh groups have had to produce formal specifications for systems to support the operation of a supermarket chain, a metropolitan transit system, a cultural institution, etc.

Implementation and validation. Again we can choose between a single course and a cluster of courses. The courses or course topics in this category are to deal with (a) verification and validation by inspections and testing; (b) reliability theory and its applications; (c) performance engineering of software systems; (d) development of safety-critical software and standard data types, including discussion of program proofs and software development by correctness-preserving transformations, as well as fault- and failure-tolerance; (e) maintenance and software configuration management. A group project is a standard part of the second University of Pittsburgh undergraduate course as well – this project requires implementation of a system from given specifications, but emphasis is on interpretation of requirements written by others and on thorough industrial-strength testing rather than on coding.

Management. We face the dilemma that cost and risk estimation and monitoring enter every phase of software development, but that these activities require much experience. We therefore recommend that, apart from a brief exposure to management issues, taking no more than a single course, serious study of software engineering management be reserved for continuing education. This is in keeping with traditional engineering education in which little, if any, attention is given to management. Although we are considering the introduction of a management course at the University of Pittsburgh, emphasis in this course would be on the selection and use of tools.

We have now discussed each of the first eleven engineering principles. Principle 12 is different – it allows deviations from strict discipline. Such deviations are excursions into the unknown, but the primary role of education is to pass on existing knowledge, i.e., Principle 12 should not be emphasized in software engineering courses.

6. Summary in the form of recommendations

(a) An engineering *attitude* is essential for the effective application of technical knowledge – a software engineering curriculum should therefore put more emphasis on engineering principles than on the latest "cures" for a non-existent malady referred to at times as software crisis. To put the cures into proper perspective, reread the silver bullet paper [16] at least once a year.

(b) As engineers become displaced from some industries, particularly defense-related industries, their engineering skills could be adapted to the needs of software engineering. Government support should be given to the development of retraining programs.

(c) A software engineering curriculum should be made to depend explicitly on computer science and mathematics. The core of computer science knowledge is now sufficiently stable to provide software engineering with a foundation; for easy access this knowledge should be codified in the form of a handbook [1]. The handbook should also contain the relevant mathematics.

(d) Extensive software engineering programs should be offered at the graduate level alone, with management courses made part of continuing professional education.

(e) Significant group projects should be a major component of software engineering education, but emphasis should be on specification, design, and quality maintenance rather than on coding.

* * * * * * *

The ideas expressed in this paper have evolved over many years, and been influenced by many colleagues and students. In particular I want to acknowledge the inspiration provided by participants at IFIP Working Group 8.1 workshops, and at courses I have offered at numerous universities and industry sites. Some of the work was done while I was enjoying the hospitality of the Department of Computer Science of the University of Stockholm – partial support was provided by STU (the Swedish National Board of Technical Development).

References

1. M. Shaw: Prospects for an engineering discipline of software. IEEE Software 7, 6, 15-24 (Nov. 1990).

2. D.L. Parnas: Education for computing professionals. Computer 23, 1, 17-22 (Jan. 1990).

3. R. Kerr: A materialistic view of the software "engineering" analogy. ACM SIG-PLAN Notices 22, 3, 123-125 (Mar. 1987).

4. W.A. Wulf: SE programs won't solve our problems. Computing Research News 3, 5, 2 (Nov. 1991).

5. B.W. Cohen, W.T. Harwood, M.I. Jackson: The Specification of Complex Systems. Wokingham, England: Addison-Wesley 1986.

6. A. Spector, D. Gifford: A computer science perspective on bridge design. Comm. ACM 29, 268-283 (1986).

7. R.H. Thayer, A.B. Pyster, R.C. Wood: Major issues in software engineering project management. IEEE Trans. Software Eng. SE-7, 333-342 (1981).

8. B. Curtis, H. Krasner, B. Iscoe: A field study of the software design process for large systems. Comm. ACM 31, 1268-1287 (1988).

9. R.N. Charette: Software Engineering Risk Analysis and Management. New York: McGraw-Hill 1989.

10. W.S. Humphrey: Managing the Software Process. Reading, MA: Addison-Wesley 1989.

11. W. Swartout, R. Balzer: On the inevitable intertwining of specification and implementation. Comm. ACM 25, 438-440 (1982).

12. R. Balzer, T.E. Cheatham, C. Green: Software technology in the 1990's: using a new paradigm. Computer 16, 11, 39-45 (Nov. 1983).

13. S.G. Shina: Concurrent Engineering and Design for Manufacture of Electronic Products. New York: Van Nostrand Reinhold 1991.

14. D.J. Yang: Boeing knocks down the wall between the dreamers and the doers. Business Week, Oct. 28, 1991, 120-121.

15. R.S. D'Ippolito, C.P. Plinta: Software development using models. Proc. 5th Workshop Software Spec. and Design, 1989, pp.140-142.

16. F.P. Brooks: No silver bullet–essence and accidents of software engineering. Proc. IFIP Congress 86, pp.1069-1076.

17. J. Rumbaugh, M. Blaha, W. Premerlani, F. Eddy, W. Lorensen: Object-Oriented Modeling and Design. Englewood Cliffs, NJ: Prentice-Hall 1991.

18. D.C. Gause, G.M. Weinberg: Exploring Requirements: Quality Before Design. New York: Dorset House 1989.

19. J.H. August: Joint Application Design. Englewood Cliffs, NJ: Yourdon Press 1991.

20. C.U. Smith: Performance Engineering of Software Systems. Reading, MA: Addison-Wesley 1990.

21. P.B. Crosby: Quality Without Tears. New York: McGraw-Hill 1984.

22. T. Anderson, P.A. Lee: Fault Tolerance: Principles and Practice. Englewood Cliffs, NJ: Prentice-Hall 1981.

23. C. Lins: The Modula-2 Software Component Library, Vols. 1-4. New York: Springer-Verlag 1989-1990.

24. J.D. Musa, A. Iannino, K. Okumoto: Software Reliability – Measurement, Prediction, Application. New York: McGraw-Hill 1987.

25. N.G. Leveson: Software safety: what, why, and how. ACM Comp. Surveys 18, 125-163 (1986).

26. R.H. Cobb, H.D. Mills: Engineering software under statistical quality control. IEEE Software 7, 6, 44-54 (Nov. 1990).

27. M. Dyer: The Cleanroom Approach to Quality Software Development. New York: Wiley 1992.

28. J.W. Duran, S.C. Ntafos: An evaluation of random testing. IEEE Trans. Software Eng. SE-10, 438-444 (1984).

29. P.A. Currit, M. Dyer, H.D. Mills: Certifying the reliability of software. IEEE Trans. Software Eng. SE-12 (1986), 3-11.

30. H.R. Berlack: Software Configuration Management. New York: Wiley 1992.

31. B.W. Boehm (ed.): Software Risk Management. Washington, DC: IEEE Computer Society Press 1989.

32. Staff of QED Information Sciences: CASE: The Potential and the Pitfalls. Wellesley, MA: QED Information Sciences 1989.

33. A. Berztiss: A mathematically focused curriculum for computer science. Comm. ACM 30, 356-365 (1987).

Lecture Notes in Computer Science

For information about Vols. 1–549
please contact your bookseller or Springer-Verlag

Vol. 592: A. Voronkov (Ed.), Logic Programming. Proceedings, 1991. IX, 514 pages. 1992. (Subseries LNAI).

Vol. 593: P. Loucopoulos (Ed.), Advanced Information Systems Engineering. Proceedings. XI, 650 pages. 1992.

Vol. 594: B. Monien, Th. Ottmann (Eds.), Data Structures and Efficient Algorithms. VIII, 389 pages. 1992.

Vol. 595: M. Levene, The Nested Universal Relation Database Model. X, 177 pages. 1992.

Vol. 596: L.-H. Eriksson, L. Hallnäs, P. Schroeder-Heister (Eds.), Extensions of Logic Programming. Proceedings, 1991. VII, 369 pages. 1992. (Subseries LNAI).

Vol. 597: H. W. Guesgen, J. Hertzberg, A Perspective of Constraint-Based Reasoning. VIII, 123 pages. 1992. (Subseries LNAI).

Vol. 598: S. Brookes, M. Main, A. Melton, M. Mislove, D. Schmidt (Eds.), Mathematical Foundations of Programming Semantics. Proceedings, 1991. VIII, 506 pages. 1992.

Vol. 599: Th. Wetter, K.-D. Althoff, J. Boose, B. R. Gaines, M. Linster, F. Schmalhofer (Eds.), Current Developments in Knowledge Acquisition - EKAW '92. Proceedings. XIII, 444 pages. 1992. (Subseries LNAI).

Vol. 600: J. W. de Bakker, C. Huizing, W. P. de Roever, G. Rozenberg (Eds.), Real-Time: Theory in Practice. Proceedings, 1991. VIII, 723 pages. 1992.

Vol. 601: D. Dolev, Z. Galil, M. Rodeh (Eds.), Theory of Computing and Systems. Proceedings, 1992. VIII, 220 pages. 1992.

Vol. 602: I. Tomek (Ed.), Computer Assisted Learning. Proceedings, 1992. X, 615 pages. 1992.

Vol. 603: J. van Katwijk (Ed.), Ada: Moving Towards 2000. Proceedings, 1992. VIII, 324 pages. 1992.

Vol. 604: F. Belli, F.-J. Radermacher (Eds.), Industrial and Engineering Applications of Artificial Intelligence and Expert Systems. Proceedings, 1992. XV, 702 pages. 1992. (Subseries LNAI).

Vol. 605: D. Etiemble, J.-C. Syre (Eds.), PARLE '92. Parallel Architectures and Languages Europe. Proceedings, 1992. XVII, 984 pages. 1992.

Vol. 606: D. E. Knuth, Axioms and Hulls. IX, 109 pages. 1992.

Vol. 607: D. Kapur (Ed.), Automated Deduction – CADE-11. Proceedings, 1992. XV, 793 pages. 1992. (Subseries LNAI).

Vol. 608: C. Frasson, G. Gauthier, G. I. McCalla (Eds.), Intelligent Tutoring Systems. Proceedings, 1992. XIV, 686 pages. 1992.

Vol. 609: G. Rozenberg (Ed.), Advances in Petri Nets 1992. VIII, 472 pages. 1992.

Vol. 610: F. von Martial, Coordinating Plans of Autonomous Agents. XII, 246 pages. 1992. (Subseries LNAI).

Vol. 611: M. P. Papazoglou, J. Zeleznikow (Eds.), The Next Generation of Information Systems: From Data to Knowledge. VIII, 310 pages. 1992. (Subseries LNAI).

Vol. 612: M. Tokoro, O. Nierstrasz, P. Wegner (Eds.), Object-Based Concurrent Computing. Proceedings, 1991. X, 265 pages. 1992.

Vol. 613: J. P. Myers, Jr., M. J. O'Donnell (Eds.), Constructivity in Computer Science. Proceedings, 1991. X, 247 pages. 1992.

Vol. 614: R. G. Herrtwich (Ed.), Network and Operating System Support for Digital Audio and Video. Proceedings, 1991. XII, 403 pages. 1992.

Vol. 615: O. Lehrmann Madsen (Ed.), ECOOP '92. European Conference on Object Oriented Programming. Proceedings. X, 426 pages. 1992.

Vol. 616: K. Jensen (Ed.), Application and Theory of Petri Nets 1992. Proceedings, 1992. VIII, 398 pages. 1992.

Vol. 617: V. Mařík, O. Štěpánková, R. Trappl (Eds.), Advanced Topics in Artificial Intelligence. Proceedings, 1992. IX, 484 pages. 1992. (Subseries LNAI).

Vol. 618: P. M. D. Gray, R. J. Lucas (Eds.), Advanced Database Systems. Proceedings, 1992. X, 260 pages. 1992.

Vol. 619: D. Pearce, H. Wansing (Eds.), Nonclassical Logics and Information Proceedings. Proceedings, 1990. VII, 171 pages. 1992. (Subseries LNAI).

Vol. 620: A. Nerode, M. Taitslin (Eds.), Logical Foundations of Computer Science – Tver '92. Proceedings. IX, 514 pages. 1992.

Vol. 621: O. Nurmi, E. Ukkonen (Eds.), Algorithm Theory – SWAT '92. Proceedings. VIII, 434 pages. 1992.

Vol. 622: F. Schmalhofer, G. Strube, Th. Wetter (Eds.), Contemporary Knowledge Engineering and Cognition. Proceedings, 1991. XII, 258 pages. 1992. (Subseries LNAI).

Vol. 623: W. Kuich (Ed.), Automata, Languages and Programming. Proceedings, 1992. XII, 721 pages. 1992.

Vol. 624: A. Voronkov (Ed.), Logic Programming and Automated Reasoning. Proceedings, 1992. XIV, 509 pages. 1992. (Subseries LNAI).

Vol. 625: W. Vogler, Modular Construction and Partial Order Semantics of Petri Nets. IX, 252 pages. 1992.

Vol. 626: E. Börger, G. Jäger, H. Kleine Büning, M. M. Richter (Eds.), Computer Science Logic. Proceedings, 1991. VIII, 428 pages. 1992.

Vol. 628: G. Vosselman, Relational Matching. IX, 190 pages. 1992.

Vol. 629: I. M. Havel, V. Koubek (Eds.), Mathematical Foundations of Computer Science 1992. Proceedings, IX, 521 pages. 1992.

Vol. 630: W. R. Cleaveland (Ed.), CONCUR '92. Proceedings. X, 580 pages. 1992.

Vol. 631: M. Bruynooghe, M. Wirsing (Eds.), Programming Language Implementation and Logic Programming. Proceedings, 1992. XI, 492 pages. 1992.

Vol. 632: H. Kirchner, G. Levi (Eds.), Algebraic and Logic Programming. Proceedings, 1992. IX, 457 pages. 1992.

Vol. 633: D. Pearce, G. Wagner (Eds.), Logics in AI. Proceedings. VIII, 410 pages. 1992. (Subseries LNAI).

Vol. 634: L. Bougé, M. Cosnard, Y. Robert, D. Trystram (Eds.), Parallel Processing: CONPAR 92 – VAPP V. Proceedings. XVII, 853 pages. 1992.

Vol. 635: J. C. Derniame (Ed.), Software Process Technology. Proceedings, 1992. VIII, 253 pages. 1992.

Vol. 636: G. Comyn, N. E. Fuchs, M. J. Ratcliffe (Eds.), Logic Programming in Action. Proceedings, 1992. X, 324 pages. 1992. (Subseries LNAI).

Vol. 637: Y. Bekkers, J. Cohen (Eds.), Memory Management. Proceedings, 1992. XI, 525 pages. 1992.

Vol. 639: A. U. Frank, I. Campari, U. Formentini (Eds.), Theories and Methods of Spatio-Temporal Reasoning in Geographic Space. Proceedings, 1992. XI, 431 pages. 1992.

Vol. 640: C. Sledge (Ed.), Software Engineering Education. Proceedings, 1992. X, 451 pages. 1992.